COASTAL SCOTLAND

Celebrating the history, heritage and wildlife of Scottish shores

STUART FISHER

**ADLARD
COLES**

LONDON · OXFORD · NEW YORK · NEW DELHI · SYDNEY

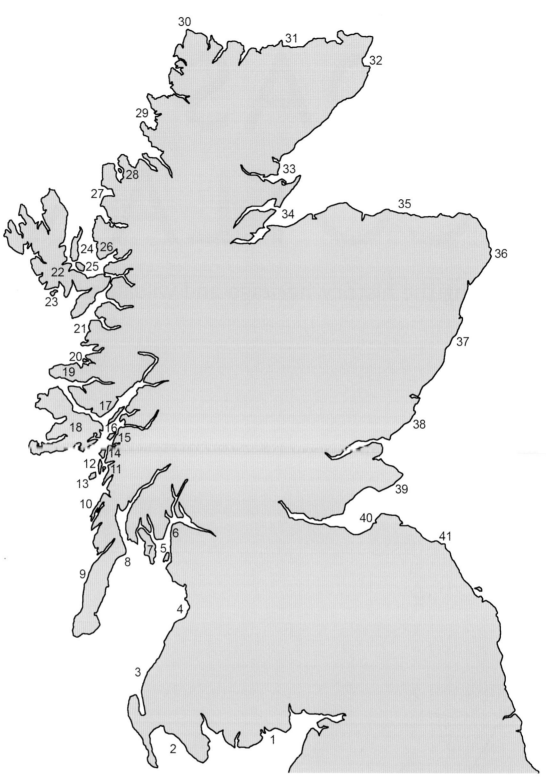

ADLARD COLES
Bloomsbury Publishing Plc
50 Bedford Square, London WC1B 3DP, UK

BLOOMSBURY, ADLARD COLES
and the Adlard Coles logo are trademarks of
Bloomsbury Publishing Plc

First published in Great Britain 2020

Some material within this book has been reproduced from
Inshore Britain (Imray Laurie Norie & Wilson Ltd, 2006)

Copyright © Stuart Fisher, 2020

A catalogue record for this book is available from the British Library.

Library of Congress Cataloguing-in-Publication data
has been applied for.

ISBN: PB: 978-1-4729-5870-9;
ePub: 978-1-4729-5876-1; ePDF: 978-1-4729-5877-8

2 4 6 8 10 9 7 5 3 1

Typeset in 9pt Bembo
Printed and bound in India by Replika Press Pvt. Ltd

To find out more about our authors and books visit
www.bloomsbury.com. and sign up for our newsletters.

MIX
Paper from
responsible sources
FSC® C016779

Contents

Introduction 5
1 Solway Firth 6
2 Southwest Galloway 10
3 Northeast North Channel 16
4 Southeast Firth of Clyde 19
5 Great Cumbrae Island 24
6 Upper Firth of Clyde 28
7 Island of Bute 32
8 East Kintyre 36
9 West Kintyre 40
10 Northeast Sound of Jura 46
11 Shuna 48
12 Luing 50
13 Scarba 52
14 Seil 56
15 Kerrera 60
16 Lynn of Lorn 65
17 Lismore 67
18 Island of Mull 70
19 Ardnamurchan 80
20 Eilean Shona 84
21 Sound of Sleat 86

22 Island of Skye 91
23 Soay 120
24 Island of Raasay 124
25 Scalpay 128
26 East Inner Sound 131
27 Southeast Minch 134
28 Isle of Ewe 137
29 Northeast Minch 140
30 Sutherland 147
31 North Highland 152
32 Caithness 156
33 Dornoch Firth 164
34 Moray 168
35 North Aberdeenshire 174
36 Northeast Aberdeenshire 178
37 Southeast Aberdeenshire 182
38 Angus 186
39 Fife 190
40 East Lothian 198
41 Borders 202
Index 205

Eilean Musdile with its lighthouse.

Broadford Bay with Scalpay and Longay in the distance.

Acknowledgements

P6 from *The Raiders* by SR Crockett.
P10 from *Clyde, the River Sailing up the Firth* by Robert Leighton.
P16 from *To Ailsa Rock* by John Keats.
P19 from *The Lord of the Isles* by Sir Walter Scott.
P24 from *The Lord of the Isles* by Sir Walter Scott.
P28 from *The Song of the Clyde* by RY Bell & Ian Gourley.
P32 from *Rothesay Bay* by Dinah Craik.
P40 from *Campbeltown Loch* by Andy Stewart.
P52 from *The Lord of the Isles* by Sir Walter Scott.
P60 from *Oban* by William Topaz McGonagall.
P70 from *The Lord of the Isles* by Sir Walter Scott.
P80 from *Farewell to Fiunary* by Norman MacLeod.
P86 from *Wha'll be King but Charlie?* by Carolina Oliphant, Lady Nairne.
P91 from *The Skye Boat Song* by Sir Harold Edwin Boulton.
P134 from *Loch Torridon* by Charles Algernon Swinburne.
P140 from *A Man in Assynt* by Norman MacCaig.
P146 from *The Lord of the Isles* by Sir Walter Scott.
P152 *The Clearances* by Iain Crichton Smith.
P156 from *The Scholars* by Rudyard Kipling.
P164 from *Tramps & Hawkers* by Bert Jansch.
P168 from *A Counting-Out Song* by Rudyard Kipling.
P174 from *Macpherson's Lament*, Anon.
P178 from *Kinnaird Head* by George Bruce from *Today Tomorrow – the Collected Poems of George Bruce 1933–2000*, published by Polygon (EUP) 2001.
P182 from *Working Away* by Alistair Russell, published by Kinmor Music.
P186 from *Montrose* by William Topaz McGonagall.
P190 from *Almae Matres* by Andrew Lang.
P198 from *Marmion* by Sir Walter Scott.
P202 from *The Beggars of Coldingham Fair*, Anon.
Every effort has been made to trace authors.
Bloomsbury are happy to correct any error or omission in future editions.

Legend for maps

Canal or river
Motorway
Other road
Railway

Open water or sea

Intertidal zone

Built up area

Woodland

Scale 1:200,000.
North is always at the top.

Introduction

An essential part of the west coast are the islands. What is an island? Obviously, any piece of land surrounded by water although that answer seems less clear the more you look at it. Sometimes it depends on the state of the tide.

Any piece of rock which pokes its head above the waves is an island and there are an infinite number of them around our coast. Thus, I have selected only the largest.

Islands seem to hold a particular attraction for us, perhaps because they usually have finite boundaries, the pace of life seems slower, people appear to be more honest and the problems of the world seem further away. On the other hand, there are fewer conveniences and life can be harder and more basic. At Kyle of Lochalsh, before the bridge was completed, I watched the Skye ferry cross. The ramp came down, a blue light went on and an ambulance drove off at speed. It may have already driven for an hour or two since collecting the patient, with a couple more to go to reach its destination.

In this book I have included islands which are close to the coast and which can be circumnavigated on saltwater. I concentrate specifically on their coastlines, both on and offshore.

Some people would discount anything with a dry land connection, including bridges, although this would eliminate more than half the islands in this book, including the largest, Skye.

Of those not accessible by bridge or causeway, some can be reached by public ferry. The rest need to be approached by boat, sometimes only after close study of the tides. I have been round them all by sea kayak although many are also approachable by larger craft and offer superb sailing or anchoring conditions. We have a fascinating variety of marine conditions around our coast. Enjoy visiting them or even looking at them from the mainland.

★ ★ ★ ★ ★

I'd checked the BBC's website weather forecast for over two months. At last their fruit machine displayed five successive daily fine weather icons, incorrectly as it turned out.

I launched my sea kayak in gentle autumn sunshine, paddling up the Sound of Mull to make Tobermory my first night's stop. Arrival in the beautiful harbour was made difficult because I was paddling directly into the setting sun. The following night I would be sleeping on a remote beach but this stop was to offer more comforts. I found a B&B run by Ian, a former Strathclyde University white water paddler, overlooking the bay which was suffused with crimson as the sun set.

Next morning was different, complete cloud cover, a leaden sky. It was still calm at this stage but the day held little promise, certainly not of being as memorable as it was about to become.

The last boat moored at the harbourmouth was the lifeboat. It was the one before it which stopped me dead as I read *Calanus*, hardly a common name. A lump immediately formed in my throat.

Could it be the same boat? The sides were higher than I remembered, I did not recall the ladders down to the working area at the stern and there were no otterboards on deck for the trawl net. The hull was of wooden construction, however, so she was probably not a recent boat. Eventually a crew member came on deck. Did she belong to the Scottish Marine Biological Association, I asked, aware that the name might have changed. No, she belonged to SAMS. He didn't know what the initials stood for but they were something to do with Scottish

marine research. That was good enough for me. How old was the boat? Thirty years, he told me. So, it was not the same boat. It was the replacement, now based in Oban for the laboratory which had moved to Dunstaffnage.

My father was a marine zoologist, making monthly visits to Scotland to go out on the former *Calanus* to collect the krill which he was studying, following the sequence of vitamin A in their eyes to the livers of whales, the biggest known source of the vitamin. When I was eight he took me with him on one of those two day trips. For me, it was the journey of a lifetime and began a love of the Scottish west coast which continues undiminished. Detailed memories from that trip far exceed those from any other aspect of that era of my life. I remember the overnight journey with Black & White Coaches from London to Glasgow and being questioned in what I thought was Gaelic by another passenger although it was actually equally incomprehensible Glaswegian.

The *Calanus* of those days was based at the research station at Millport. Most of the occupants of Mrs Simpson's B&B in Millport's end house were Glasgow University students on a course but my particular memory was being served *two* eggs for breakfast, for the first time in my life.

Our route took us up through the Kyles of Bute, a route which I was intending to visit for the third time this week with my sea kayak if the weather held. I recall watching from the bow the nearly completely circular rainbow formed by the spray. I remember having my leg pulled repeatedly by the crew. I recall the green trace of the radar scanner and the red chart of the echo sounder printout, with the difficulty in selecting the correct scale because of the irregular seabed. I remember the net containing my father's krill also holding a herring and the trawl for a net of larger fish bringing up a waterlogged section of tree trunk which required two men to heave it back over the side.

We spent the night moored at Tarbert. I have revisited the pier on sea kayak trips or, if I am honest, the hotel across the road, which had seafood second to none.

It was the best treat I ever had from my dad, who died eight years later. Sadly, I am sure there would be health and safety regulations which would prevent such a life changing experience for youngsters of today. My exit from Tobermory was a reminder of just how fortunate I had been all those years ago.

Stuart Fisher
May 2020

Thank you

I wish to pay thanks to the following:

Willie Wilson of Imray Laurie Norie & Wilson took on this project in the first place with an unpublished author and allowed me a remarkably free hand in the layout of the book.

This will be one of the first books for Elizabeth Multon of Adlard Coles after her promotion to publisher although we have worked together before.

I have worked with editor Jonathan Eyers on several books. We each have a fair idea of how far we can push the other even before we start, which results in a relaxed working relationship.

Last but not least, this book would not have happened without the practical support of my wife, Becky, who sat at many a remote spot around the coast, waiting for me to appear in the distance. Also to sons Brendan and Ross, who tested the play value of many beaches at a time when junior school teachers agreed that they were learning more on what were, effectively, geography field trips than they would have done sitting in classrooms.

1 Solway Firth

Where'er we see a bonny lass, we'll caa' as we gae by;
Where'er we meet wi' liquor guid, we'll drink an we be dry.
There's brandy at the Abbeyburn, there's rum at Heston Bay,
And we will go a-smuggling afore the break o' day.
SR Crockett

Former fish nets at Gowkesk and in use in 1992.

Herdhill Scar has the remains of a railway bridge with a corresponding embankment on the Scottish side of Bowness Wath at Seafield. The Solway Viaduct was built in 1869 to carry a direct railway route from the iron ore mines of Cumbria to the smelting furnaces of the Clyde but never carried heavy traffic as it was vulnerable to the weather. The longest bridge in Europe at 1.76km, it had 181 piers but none of the spans opened so it completed the closure of Port Carlisle by obstructing shipping that was already having difficulty with silting. James Brunlees' design suffered from water freezing in the piers in 1875, cracking them, and in 1881 ice floes damaged 45 piers and 37 spans, making two breaks in the viaduct. Trains ceased in 1921 but then began its most popular period as it was used by **Annan** men to walk to English public houses on Sundays, those in Scotland being closed on the sabbath. It was dismantled in 1935. Construction of a barrage has been considered.

It is possible to cross the estuary on foot or on horseback but the flows can be 15km/h and at times the White Steeds of Solway can be heard approaching 30km away with a bore on spring tides.

Crossing from the English county of Cumbria to the Scottish region of Dumfries & Galloway used to arrive at substantial fishing nets set in the fastest part of the flow on Gowkesk Rig but these have now been closed down, leaving more fish for anglers. Fish traps were a major issue in Sir Walter Scott's *Redgauntlet*.

Barnkirk Point, with its oil tanks among the gorse and light structure at the end, marks the mouth of the River Annan. Close by are the factories of Johnson Matthey and boilermakers NEI Cochran, both strangely isolated from Annan and their source of labour. More fishing nets stretch out between Annan Waterfoot and Newbie Mains and terns are present in quantity.

From here to Southerness Point lie vast areas of sand and mud banks at low tide so tides need to be given serious consideration. At Powfoot, established in the 18th century as a bathing resort, sand yachting is popular. Powfoot Channel is ingoing from HW Dover −0245 and outgoing from HW Dover +0115 at up to 11km/h. Running out from the caravans at the edge of the golf course are more fishing nets.

Shelducks graze on the grass banks at the high water mark behind Priestside Bank. On a sunny summer's day when the extensive flats have had a chance to get hot before the tide floods, the water at the high tide line is pleasantly warm.

Another priestly bank was that begun by local vicar Henry Duncan in 1810, the first branch of the Savings Bank (to become the TSB) which now houses the Savings Bank Museum at Ruthwell. The church houses the Ruthwell Cross, one of the most impressive stone carvings in Europe, inscribed with verses from the oldest known English poem, Caedmon's *Dream of the Rood*.

Brow Well, sited by the mouth of Lochar Water, gives mineral water contaminated with iron. It was here that Scotland's most famous poet, Robert Burns, sought a cure during his final illness.

The coast is fringed by the marshes of the Wildfowl & Wetlands Trust's Caerlaverock Wetland Centre from here to the mouth of the Nith. There is a refuge area with hides and towers at East Park Farm, used to view over 12,000 barnacle, pinkfooted and greylag geese in autumn and winter plus other winter wildfowl and, in April, the start of the return migration.

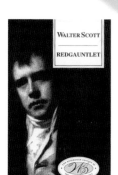

WALTER SCOTT
REDGAUNTLET

Cairnharrow ▲
Carsluith
A75
Ravenshall Pt
Fleet Bay
Islands of Fleet
Knockbrex
Kirkandrews
Wigtown Bay
Borness
Borness Pt
Kirkcudbright Bay
Little Ross
Balmae
Abbey Head
Port Mary
Balcary Pt
Rascarrel Bay
Auchencairn Bay
Urr Water

Criffel rises up on the west side of the Nith estuary, seen across the Merse.

Behind the trees is one of the finest examples of medieval architecture in Scotland, Caerlaverock Castle off the B725. Its triangular bailey with curtain and machiolated round towers and massive machiolated gatehouse in red sandstone are surrounded by a moat. Dating from 1270, it commanded a strategic landing point and was the seat of the Maxwell family, whose crest and motto appear over the gateway. Besieged by Edward I in 1330, it was taken by the Covenanters in 1638 after a 13 week siege and was ruined in 1640. It was the model for Ellangowan, the central feature of Sir Walter Scott's *Guy Mannering*, which he had visited. In *The Master of Ballantrae* Robert Louis Stevenson mentions many features which imply it is based on this part of the Solway coast.

Blackshaw Bank with its mud, sand and even quicksand, dries up to 9km out, reaching almost to the English shore on spring low waters. The sands can cover faster

haaf nets for salmon and sea trout, the men standing in the water with their nets.

Carsethorn was used by the Vikings and later served emigrant ships to the USA and Australia, including transporting convicts to the latter, which brought timber, salt and fish as return loads. There was also a Liverpool ferry service. Piles from the jetty remain. Houses in Carsethorn were built in the 19th century for the coastguard but the harbour had been there since at least 1562 when there was continental trade. It also traded with England and Ireland and there was a quarantine point. Cockles are gathered locally. Beyond them is Kirkbean's unusual former church with a dome, a sundial giving the times in Calcutta, Gibraltar and Madras (places where local men worked in Victorian days) and a font presented by the US Navy in memory of John Paul Jones. The latter is also

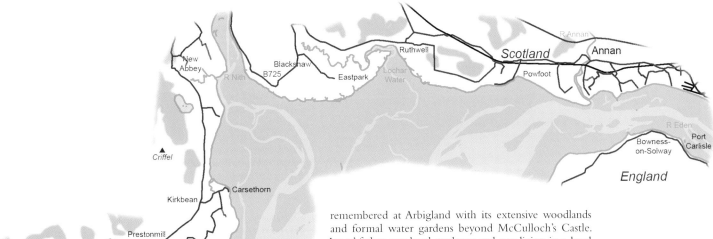

remembered at Arbigland with its extensive woodlands and formal water gardens beyond McCulloch's Castle. Jones' father was head gardener and was living in a local cottage when his son was born in 1747. Jones junior joined the merchant navy when he was 13, subsequently founded the US Navy, returned to attack Whitehaven where he had been trained and later served under Catherine the Great. *The Pilot*, by James Fenimore Cooper, was based on Jones.

A lighthouse at Southerness Point benefited schooners bound for America. Built in 1749 by Dumfries Council but not lit until 1815, it is one of the oldest in Scotland although now disused. Mussel covered rocks surround what was Salters' Ness from the 12th century salt panning industry but today it is a village of chalets, caravans, a golf course, a fish and chip shop and the Paul Jones Bar & Restaurant Flows run at up to 9km/h here.

Preston Merse is a fine saltmarsh between the A710 and Mersehead Sands which dry up to 4km out nearly to Urr Waterfoot but which the RSPB said were threatened by mechanized cockling.

Southwick Water has both the Needles Eye and Lot's Wife rocks. The golf course between Sandyhills and Portling overlooks another Needles Eye, a bad place for camels. The cliffs attract fulmars, razorbills and guillemots.

Arrival at Urr Waterfoot is marked by Castlehill Point. A series of attractive inlets follow although the RSPB said that Rough Firth, which has 590 waders in winter, was in danger of irreversible damage from cockling and

than a horse can gallop, the water can recede from shallows with frustrating speed and the channel changes position very substantially. Northgoing flows in the River Nith start when sands cover and southgoing flows start at HW Dover +0030. The estuary is discordant, possibly eroded from overlying rocks by the river flowing against the trend of the underlying rocks.

A motte stands near the shore at Ingleston and the Waterloo Monument is visible above New Abbey, but the scenery is dominated by Criffel, rising to 569m less than 3km from the coast, as seen by John Paul Jones in *The French Revolution* and mentioned several times in *Redgauntlet*. Carse Sands lie at its foot, tapering down to Southerness Point. Salmon nets are staked out in the sand and from February to September there is fishing with

The early lighthouse at Southerness.

Although bass are equally present, Balcary Fishery on the mainland catches salmon with nets staked out on the sand. Balcary House hotel was built as a headquarters for smugglers to store wine and tobacco. The Tower is just before Balcary Point with its nesting seabirds.

Towards the middle of the firth is the Robin Rigg windfarm.

The coastline is now bold and rocky to Gipsy Point. Flows from Abbey Head are ingoing from HW Dover −0530 and outgoing from HW Dover +0030.

Bigamy creeps in with a second Lot's Wife. The religious connotations continue with Adam's Chair below forts and a homestead.

Chalets and older huts grouped incongruously around roofless stone buildings back Rascarrel Bay. Thrift, bluebells, red campion and gorse enhance the attraction of the spot.

After Castle Muir Point, particularly around the caves at Dropping Craig, the cliffs are festooned with greenery and the Spouty Dennans hanging waterfall drops dramatically from the clifftop.

Port Mary is the point where Mary, Queen of Scots, was thought to have left Scottish soil for the last time as she set sail for England, but it requires calm conditions to land a kayak among the boulders, let alone a larger boat.

From here to Gipsy Point are 8km of the Abbey Head tank and artillery range danger area, reaching as far as 23km south. The army have handed over operation to civilians and it is in use 7 days a week although it closes some weekends. Boats may be escorted through in safe intervals by the range safety vessel. When the red flag is flying at Abbey Burn Foot the range is in use. Landing is not practical near the control cabin but it is possible to pass close enough to be recognized and be waved through if prior agreement has been obtained. Various military buildings are spread around Mullock Bay and gantries stand on the clifftops. Some unpleasant pieces of ordnance sometimes wash up along this coast as far as Luce Bay.

Kirkcudbright Bay is discordant and may have been eroded from a cover of newer rocks against the trend of general folding. It acts as the estuary of the River Dee. Flows start eastgoing and ingoing at HW Dover −0545 and westgoing and outgoing at HW Dover +0015 at up to 7km/h.

There are 700 waders and wildfowl in the winter, the RSPB having said the bay was in danger of permanent damage from port expansion. Little Ross was painted from below Balmae by Strachan, who took along another local murder book, Freeman Wills Croft's *Sir John Magill's Last Journey*, in Dorothy L Sayers' *The Five Red Herrings*. The island is a good place to watch bird migrations, separated from Meikle Ross by the Sound and topped by its conspicuous lighthouse of 1843. In 1960, lighthouse keeper Robert Dickson killed workmate Hugh Clark in what was described as the 'perfect murder'. The light was automated the following year.

A submarine oil pipeline runs out of Brighouse Bay to Ireland.

The coast gradually curves round into Wigtown Bay

that Auchencairn Bay, with 2,000 winter waders, was in equal danger from port expansion.

In the mouth of the latter bay is Hestan Island, the causeway of Hestan Rack leading across the sands at low tide. A Neolithic midden of oyster shells shows it was occupied from earliest times although the most significant occupant was in the now ruined manor at the north end. From 1332 it was used by the puppet King Edward Balliol, who issued decrees under the Great Seal of Scotland from Estholm. There are said to be underground caverns left by 17th and 18th century smugglers. In SR Crockett's *The Raiders* it was probably Isle Rathan. In the 19th century it was occupied by an organ builder who liked the acoustics. On top is a lighthouse while Daft Ann's Steps on the south end of the island should not offer any hope of a landing point.

Looking westwards to Hestan Island at the mouth of Auchencairn Bay.

Little Ross at the mouth of Kirkcudbright Bay has a much more prominent lighthouse than Hestan Island.

Folded strata at Ravenshall Point give interesting rock sculptures.

another cairn and a cup and ring marked rock all on the west side of the Kirkdale Burn. Sayers talks of 'the Italian loveliness of Kirkdale, with its fringe of thin and twisted trees and the blue Wigtownshire coast gleaming across the bay.'

Carsluith Castle is easily seen from the water. More a fortified family house than a castle, it dates from the 1560s and is L shaped in plan, now roofless. A much older fort site is to be found a little further up the hillside.

A limited amount of parking and a picnic bench are to be found beyond the disused quarry off the A75 at Carsluith.

where southerly winds rise with little warning and can bring heavy seas. From Borness Point with the Borness Batteries the coast is bold and rocky, topped with an assortment of forts, settlements, homesteads and duns. By Dove Cave there is a curious formation which looks as though someone has tipped a load of waste concrete down the cliff to leave a rough concrete pillar but this cannot be the case as there is an overhang to the cliff at this point. Sadly, at Meikle Pinnacle there is quite definitely a quantity of junk tipped down the cliffs.

Kirkandrews Bay has a selection of small inlets with mussel covered rocks and is surrounded by a range of artefacts including an old church, cup and ring marked rocks, motte, dun and a tower attached to what appears to be a rather unattractive church with a barrel roof, now reverted to being part of a farm.

The cliffs have already shown significant folding but they now become very complex with over 60 synclines and anticlines in the 2km to Knockbrex.

The Islands of Fleet lead up to Fleet Bay with wildfowl in winter. The Three Brethren are a group of rocks by Barlocco Isle where the grass top was once used for grazing and which is joined to the mainland by rocks at low water. Ardwall Isle or Larry's Isle was also used for grazing and is connected to land at low water by a sand ridge. It has the remains of a 9th century chapel. Early stone crosses and a Northumbrian period inscription have been found. For 50 years it was occupied by the Higgins family who opened it to smugglers and honeycombed it with hiding places. Murray's Isles are also connected to the sand at low water.

Mossyard has cup and ring marked rocks and a burial chamber. It also has two caravan sites which are prominent although *The Five Red Herrings* talks of the 'strange Japanese beauty of Mossyard Farm, set like a red jewel under its tufted trees on the blue sea's rim'. A motte and a cross are found at Low Auchenlarie.

The coast now has a shoreline of boulders but then a level strip before the land rises steeply in a tree covered hillside alongside the East Channel, eventually climbing to 456m Cairnharrow. Ravenshall Point exhibits some interesting rock features and is quickly followed by Dirk Hatteraick's Cave, a large cavern supposedly used by leading Dutch smuggler Yawkins, the name from the Dutch smuggler in *Guy Mannering*. Gauger's Loup is a precipice said to be where revenue man Kennedy was pushed to his death in the novel. Above are the border keep of Barholm, the Neolithic horned chambered cairn of Cairnholy of about 2000 BC, the Category A Kirkdale church,

Carsluith Castle dates from the 1560s on a hillside overlooking Wigtown Bay. It is roofless and lacks its intermediate floor but is otherwise in good condition with some beautiful stonework detailing.

Distance
90km from Bowness-on-Solway to Carsluith

OS 1:50,000 Sheets
83 Newton Stewart & Kirkcudbright
84 Dumfries & Castle Douglas
85 Carlisle & Solway Firth

Tidal Constants
Annan Waterfoot:
HW Dover +0110
LW Dover +0300
Southerness Point:
Dover +0040
Hesten Islet:
Dover +0040
Kircudbright Bay:
HW Dover +0030
LW Dover +0020
Garlieston:
HW Dover +0040
LW Dover +0030

Sea Area
Irish Sea

Range
Abbey Head

Connections
Solway Firth – see CBEW p331
Lochar Water – see RoB p79

2 Southwest Galloway

Avoiding Scotland's most southerly point

Along the rocky ribs of Galloway
  A margin of white foam crept to and fro;
And up the steep cliffs rose the snowy spray,
  Silent to us as snow.
Robert Leighton

Baldoon and Wigtown Sands with the tide out.

Fish caught in nets stretched out from the coast at Carsluith can be taken straight to the Galloway Smokehouse nearby for curing.

Around Kirkmabreck there are a cup and ring marked rock, standing stone, cairn and St Brioch's church from ancient times. Some rock has been levelled along the edge of the estuary as a quay. Quarrying ceased in 1990, earlier switching from granite blocks to roadstone.

The River Cree enters at the estuary's northern end with flows ingoing from HW Dover −0515 and outgoing from HW Dover +0015 at up to 9km/h. The coast of the north and west of the estuary is low and the west side is largely occupied by the Wigtown Sands and Baldoon Sands which attract 19,000 winter waterfowl including 1,800 curlews, 7,500 pinkfooted geese and numerous greylag geese. The RSPB said the area was in danger of irreversible damage from cockling, although the birds do not seem to be disturbed by jets flying low over the estuary. Fish like to sunbathe in the warm shallows.

Marsh separates the estuary from **Wigtown**, which takes its name from the Old English wic-tun, work or trading estate. On the edge of the marsh is the Martyrs'

monument to two women of 18 and 63 who were staked out on the sand for their beliefs and left to drown by the rising tide in 1685 during the Killing Times persecution of the Covenanters. They are recorded, too, in Wigtown Museum which also has a display of 1707 weights and measures. Wigtown, Drummore, Port Logan and Portpatrick were used for filming *Two Thousand Acres of Sky*.

The River Bladnoch enters between a moat and castle ruin and a disused airfield and is guided across the sands by rock breakwaters. There was a ferry across the estuary in the Middle Ages.

Nets are laid out off Innerwell Fishery which deals with salmon. It is hard to believe that terns spaced out at one per post can make such a din, sounding as if a mass fight is taking place.

After the exposed area to the north, Jultock Point is a magical spot, completely sheltered from the prevailing wind by a deciduous wood. The rocks are jagged but seaweed and thrift soften the view. The strip of woodland and the rocky shoreline continue to Eggerness Point, with vertical strata at times.

The wooded shoreline at Jultock Point.

There are sunken concrete sections near the high water line beyond the fort site at Port Whapple. During the Second World War this area was used for testing assembly of Mulberry Harbours.

Garlieston was a planned village for Lord Garlies in the 18th century and had packet steamers to Whitehaven, Liverpool and the Isle of Man. Garlieston Bay largely drains at low water and suffers from heavy swells with southeasterly winds, yet the port is active and handles fodder and fertilizers and the bay has cod, flatfish and mackerel. The colourwashed houses were built in two lines, just giving room between them for one of the narrowest bowling greens in Scotland.

A wreck and a large structure stand in the middle of Rigg or Cruggleton Bay. Between the two bays is the Category A Galloway House, dating from 1740, the former seat of the Earls of Galloway, set in walled gardens with rhododendrons and fine trees, including a handkerchief tree, and there is a heronry.

From Sliddery Point to Cairn Head the cliffs are steep, popular with guillemots, with fort sites at intervals on the top. Most notable of these is the castle on Cruggleton Point, conspicuous with its stone arch above the skyline. Behind it lies the 12th century Cruggleton Church, one of the first parish churches in the area.

From Cairn Head, where the B7063 runs along the back of Portyerrock Bay, cliffs become bold and rocky as far as Port of Counan with races off the headlands.

Vertical strata on the shoreline at Port McGean.

marked rock shows even older occupation of the location.

Burrow Head marks the turning point from Wigtown Bay to Luce Bay, the latter having anticlockwise currents up to 2km/h in the main part of the bay and being subject to southerly winds at all times of year. The head has a race yet it is home for many nesting seabirds and a good watchpoint for bird migrations. A caravan site on top is served by some conspicuous high sewerage pipes across gullies which should not be confused with the Devil's Bridge and a nearby cave. The Burrow Head Iron Age promontory fort is the most notable of the clifftop forts and homesteads which follow from here along to Port Castle Bay, where St Ninian's Cave can to be found down on the beach at the end of a well established footpath. Here the first Scottish Christian missionary had his retreat in 397. Some 8th century Christian crosses have been carved into the rock and a service is still held here annually. The cave was used in filming the burning in *The Wicker Man* and Isle of Whithorn was also used.

The whole coast from Port of Counan to Point

Isle of Whithorn at the end of the B7004 was the port for **Whithorn**. The causeway making it a peninsula rather than an island is relatively recent, a former lifeboat able to have been launched to either side to suit the conditions. Before the causeway was built, a smuggler's schooner escaped from a revenue cutter through what appeared to be a dead end. At low water the keel mark could be seen in the sand. Earlier, it was used by the Vikings.

Trading vessels carrying coal and fertilizers and steam packets to such English ports such as Whitehaven sailed from here. Heavy seas can be generated by southerly winds. The breakwater collaped in 1969. The harbour is used by fishing and pleasure craft. On the ebb the stream sets towards Screen Rocks.

On the end of the peninsula an Iron Age fort site fronts the white Cairn tower. Near the children's playground are the 13th century ruins of St Ninian's Chapel. It was an important pilgrimage site, especially in the 14th century, Robert I being one of the pilgrims. On the north side of the village a castle was built and a cup and ring

of Cairndoon is rather unusual.

There is a boulder beach, rising eventually to 146m high Fell of Carleton. Between these two extremes is a long level strip of land which slopes steeply down to the beach, covered with grass. It resembles a giant bench over which a sheet of green felt has been draped. The underlying soil looks like boulder

Wrecked Mulberry Harbour sections sunk in the shallows.

Concrete pontoon at Cairn Head, north of Isle of Whithorn.

Freugh range although only intermittently. The work is experimental, such items as laser guided bombs being dropped from considerable heights, not all of which detonate correctly. Thus, there is a lot of unexploded ordnance lying about on the seabed, some of which gets washed up onto beaches. Passage is permitted between the yellow buoys and the shoreline along each side of the bay at any time but the head of the bay and the main body of the bay should only be entered when the range is not being used.

The coast is flat from Barsalloch Point to the Mull of Sinniness although the beach continues to be boulder-strewn. Barsalloch Point itself has an Iron Age hill fort on a raised beach, the rampart and ditch dating from 300 BC.

There are bass, cod, rays and skate in the waters off the small resort of Port William, founded on this exposed coast in 1771 by Sir William Maxwell, enlarged in 1790 and again in 1848 although smugglers continued to use the beach. More significant, however, is the basking shark. Despite being quite harmless, the black triangular fins slicing through the water as the only visible signs of a large circling creature can get the adrenalin flowing very effectively. There was shipbuilding but trading vessels gave way to fishing and leisure craft after 1920.

The village had a corn mill on the Killantrae Burn. Caravans behind the beach at Port William are followed by a caravan park at Barr Point. At Chippermore Point the residents are cormorants, favourite perch rocks being whitened with guano.

The coast is only sparsely inhabited now but from earlier times is littered with homesteads, cairns and a hut circle. Corwall Port was a landing place for Irish pilgrims going to St Ninian's church in Whithorn and Chapel Finian is a small oratory there from the 10th or 11th century, St Finian having studied at Whithorn.

Gannets fly over Auchenmalg Bay where they have a choice of bass, conger, dogfish, flatfish, mullet, rays and tope while another caravan site also overlooks all.

Over the years the Mull of Sinniness, forming a prominent outcrop, has thus attracted attention. Artefacts there include a standing stone, fort, the first of many brochs around the Scottish coastline, Castle Sinniness and Sinniness Barracks, the latter built in the 1820s to house 50 revenue men trying to stamp out smuggling in the Solway. The mull ends with Stairhaven, an 18th century lobster fishing harbour which is almost deserted despite having a picnic area and toilets.

At the northeast corner of Luce Bay, behind a golf course is Castle of Park at Glenluce, a tall castellated mansion built by Thomas Hay of Park in 1590. The Wat-

clay but it is strange that it has not been eroded away in this relatively exposed position. Clifftop features include homesteads, a settlement, a cup and ring marked rock and the Laggan Camp fort.

Some sections of a substantial metal ship lie wrecked on the boulders towards the southeast end of this section. The hillside drops away after Carleton Port. At this other end there is a conspicuous metal chute into an area that resembles a silage clamp and a track down the hillside for access to the bottom of it on the beach.

Point of Lag between Back Bay and Monreith Bay has a carpark with toilets and children's wooden engine and boat. The road from it winds up across a golf course past Kirkmaiden, a sculptured rock, cup and ring marked rocks and an otter memorial to Gavin Maxwell, who was born at the Category B House of Elrig, his family having owned the Monreith estate. The A747 now follows the coast.

Virtually the whole of Luce Bay is used as the West

The truncated shoreline below Milton Fell.

The otter monument to Gavin Maxwell, overlooking Monreith Bay, a favourite spot for the author.

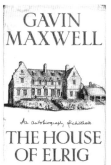

er of Luce flows past it flows and the Piltanton Burn also enters this corner of the bay. Raised beach material separates Luce Bay from Loch Ryan to the north, ending with the Torrs Warren dunes and their notable slacks, good for winter waders and wildfowl. Bareagle Forest of Sitka spruce and Corsican and Monterey pines has been planted to stabilize the shifting sands. However, the most obvious aspect of the beach material is Luce Sands which stretch right across the head of the bay, 10km long and a kilometre wide at low tide yet closed to the public. Even when the bombing range is not in use there is a rifle range which is sometimes used at weekends, putting part of Luce Sands at risk. Leading Dutch smuggler Yawkins was not inhibited from landing contraband here in his *Black Prince*.

Britain's most reported UFO sighting in 1957 was the West Freugh Incident when three radar stations separately tracked a large and four smaller objects hovering, accelerating at high speeds vertically, making impossibly tight turns and flying at up to 21km above the ground, too high for any know aircraft, the largest one having a radar footprint the size of a ship.

The danger area comes to an end with a sand pit and a caravan site or two before the B7084 joins the A716 near Sandhead. The beach in Sandhead Bay ends with a pipe which emerges vertically from the sand and curves over to dribble a liquid of unknown source into the water, not typical of other outfall pipes and an obstacle which occupies one of the obvious landing points on this coast.

Surprisingly, it is the east side of the Rhins of Galloway that is suffering erosion, the coast alternating between sandy sections and boulderstrewn areas. At Ardwell Mill there are fish nets staked out in the sea and swans also take to the salt water. Ringvinachan offers an array of domes and aerials to track the bombing movements out in the bay.

Ardwell House is beyond a caravan site. Dating from the 18th century, it has formal gardens with daffodils, rhododendrons, camellias, flowering shrubs, foliage, crazy paving and pond walks.

Another fish net is erected after Chapel Rossan in front of a prominent tower near the shore. Further tracking aerials stand on Balgowan Point. More caravans mark Drummore, a village that was once a smuggling centre. The harbour was begun in the 19th century and extended in 1889. It is sheltered and was used by vessels waiting for better conditions before rounding the null. From the 1930s to 2004 it was used by the MoD to service the bombing range.

From Cailiness Point to the Mull of Galloway there is an anticlockwise eddy on the eastgoing flow. Seals rest up on the reef to the south of Cailiness Point. One final caravan site overlooks Maryport Bay. Kirkmaiden church at Portankill is followed by St Medan's Cave.

Until the 19th century fishermen portaged from East Tarbet over the ridge to West Tarbet to avoid having to round the Mull of Galloway and this option remains open today, the mull being one of the most dangerous points on the British coastline with a heavy and violent race off the point, especially with wind against tide. It runs at 9km/h with overfalls. The visible part of the mull is extended by an underwater ridge running a long way northeast from the mull. During the eastgoing stream the race extends north northeast towards the head of Luce Bay. During the westgoing stream it extends southwest and west. The optimum approach is from the north at HW Dover −0130 when it is fairly quiet and there is only about 100m of flow to be tackled by a boat keeping close in against the rocks. This contrasts with a crossing of Luce Bay when the race must be crossed and arrival time is harder to predict. The northgoing stream begins just after Dover HW. An hour after the northerly flow reverses, an eastgoing eddy begins from Port Kemin to the mull. Tide stream directions close inshore begin much earlier than those further offshore that are documented on charts.

This most southerly point in Scotland is marked by a lighthouse operating from 1830 which was original in having a flashing light although it did not have electricity until 1971. It is used as a bird migration watchpoint and a bird sanctuary with one of the best seabird colonies in Galloway, particularly kittiwakes. Several types of flora are on the northern or southern extremities of their ranges and there is plenty of thrift and carpets of heather.

As Luce Bay gives way to the North Channel the coast becomes steep. The last two Picts were reputed to have been trapped here by Scots. Rather than reveal the secret of heather ale, which had a scent like honey, the father let them throw his son off the cliffs and then jumped to his own death. What cannot be disputed is the selection of earthworks, forts, cairns (including Kennedy's Cairn), homesteads and standing stones which cover the area.

Cormorants, gannets and seals occupy the cliff lined coast. Off Port Mona there are overfalls with more at Crammag Head and a race to 12km/h, overlooked by a tiny lighthouse, a lookout point and a dun. Guillemots, razorbills and jellyfish add to the wildlife in Clanyard Bay.

Slouchnamorroch Bay is backed by some fine folding in the cliffs with a dramatic syncline.

View from the cliffs at the Mull of Galloway.

Dunskey Castle stands on low cliffs to the south of Portpatrick.

The village of Portpatrick, an isolated haven on the Rhins of Galloway.

The first convenient landing point after the mull is at Port Logan on the B7065 where an abandoned 1820 harbour is protected by a breakwater topped by a ruined lighthouse tower with lantern and bellcote. Rennie considered this better than Portpatrick for the Irish ferry service. A sheltered sand beach and picnic tables in front of a community of whitewashed houses offers an oasis of tranquillity in a committing section of coast. On the north side of Port Nessock or Port Logan Bay a tidal fish pond was excavated in the rocks in 1800 to catch fish for Logan House, but the fish became family pets and tame cod now come to be fed when summoned by a bell. Up the hill from the pond is the Logan Botanic Garden, an outstation of Edinburgh's Royal Botanic Gardens. The mildest weather conditions in Scotland allow tree ferns, cabbage palms and exotic species from the Southern Hemisphere, such as the Patagonian fire tree, to be grown.

A prominent pillar precedes the Mull of Logan, off which there may be overfalls. At regular intervals forts and earthworks follow and Ardwell Point is topped by the broch of Doon Castle. The final set of major overfalls occur off Money Head but forts continue. The Dualdboys motte at Port of Spittal Bay has now been upstaged by Knockinaam Lodge, an exclusive hotel.

By far the most dramatic of all these fortifications is Dunskey Castle, an early 16th century ruin on top of the cliffs. A wooden bridge forms part of a public walkway along the cliffs from Portpatrick which appears suddenly, firstly as a large hotel and then as a delightful cove with all the charms of a Cornish fishing village, inns and colourwashed houses jumbling up the steep slopes. Facing across to Belfast Lough 35km away and with the Northern Ireland coastline clearly visible across the North Channel, it used to be the Irish ferry terminal for Donaghadee until 1849, the Victorian piers being damaged by waves in 1839 and the lighthouse being exported to Colombo in 1860. In 1947 the North Channel to Donaghdee was first swum. The disused 17th century church of St Patrick with its 16th century circular tower was much used for weddings by runaway Irish couples. It was also a haven for smugglers until the customs house was built. Although the harbour, with black guillemots nesting in the wall is used as a base for sailing and water-skiing, entry is still impractical in moderate southwesterly winds. The Lifeboat Week each year with raft racing and other activities is a major event, all being overlooked by an old lighthouse.

The village can be busy in season but when there is parking space the best place to land is on the small beach at the east side of the harbour.

Some visitors come here because it is the western end of the Southern Uplands Way long distance footpath.

Distance
125km from Carsluith to Portpatrick

OS 1:50,000 Sheets
82 Stranraer & Glenluce
83 Newton Stewart & Kirkcudbright

Tidal Constants
Garlieston:
HW Dover +0040
LW Dover +0030
Isle of Whithorn:
HW Dover +0040
LW Dover +0030
Port William:
HW Dover +0020
LW Dover
Drummore:
HW Dover +0050
LW Dover +0030
Portpatrick:
HW Dover +0040
LW Dover

Sea Area
Irish Sea

Ranges
Luce Bay, Luce Sands

Submarine Areas
81 Peel, 79 Beaufort

Northeast North Channel

Dodging the fast Ulster ferries

Hearken, thou craggy ocean-pyramid!
Give answer from thy voice, the sea-fowl's screams!
When were thy shoulders mantled in huge streams?
When, from the sun, was thy broad forehead hid?
How long is't since the mighty power bid
Thee heave to airy sleep from fathom dreams?
Sleep in the lap of thunder or sunbeams,
Or when grey clouds are thy cold coverlid.
Thou answer'st not; for thou art dead asleep.
Thy life is but two dead eternities –
The last in air, the former in the deep;
First with the whales, last with the eagle-skies
Drown'd wast though till an earthquake made thee steep,
Another cannot wake thy giant size.

John Keats

The northgoing flow starts at HW Dover –0130 from Portpatrick and the southgoing flow starts at HW Dover +0430. Although the cliffs tend to be less forbidding than further south, the coast becomes more remote as there is an absence of public road access until Loch Ryan.

Leaving Portpatrick, the cliffs are lined with an array of aerials surrounding a golf course. The communications theme continues at Port Kale, a cleft in the cliffs containing submarine cables from Donaghadee and Larne plus a further seven which are now disused. A double hexagonal building with pointed roofs was built in 1852 for testing the first cable.

The coastal container ship *Craigantlet* came to grief at Portamaggie on a voyage from Belfast to Liverpool in 1982. Although lots of valuable clothes were washed ashore she was also carrying chemicals which were so dangerous that the keepers of Killantringan lighthouse above on Black Head had to be evacuated for 6 weeks.

The Southern Upland Way turns eastwards and heads for Cockburnspath the peak tidal flows ease from 9km/h to 7km/h.

The coast is studded with forts, a dun, a motte and two Salt Pan Bays. In Knock Bay another disused submarine cable lands.

The coast is largely left to gannets, cormorants, terns, oystercatchers, curlews, seals and jellyfish. There is some notable folding behind Strool Bay but none more so than

Juniper Rock, a vertical slab which is roughly circular when viewed along the coast but banana shaped when looking in towards the shore. In complete contrast is Craig Laggan beacon which resembles a giant stone milk churn.

The Category A Corswall Point lighthouse was built by Robert Stevenson in 1815 on low lichen covered rocks which are characteristic of this shoreline for several kilometres. It was novel in having alternating red and white light. Much of the building is now a hotel. Up the hill from the lighthouse is St Columba's Well while a prominent aerial marks the hillside at Balscalloch.

Flows are to about 6km/h here but fall weak to Loch Ryan which provides shelter from westerly winds, the heaviest seas coming from northwesterly winds blowing against the ebb. Currents in the entrance rotate clockwise, flowing south–southwest round Finnarts Point from HW Dover –0545 and north–northeast from HW Dover +0120.

The tranquillity after Milleur Point is usually pronounced. When *The Susannah* anchors in Lady Bay in *The Five Red Herrings*, prior to switching her destination from Gourock to Larne, it was questioned whether Waters is already onboard or joins at this point. The greenery clad cliffs of Clachan Heughs provide a marked contrast to the exposed rocks on the west side of the Rhins of Galloway.

At Kirkcolm the Scar runs southeast into the widest part of Loch Ryan, an extensive area of shallow sand and stones which dries at low tide. Streams run straight in and out here and the Scar protects the Wig, a sheltered area used by seaplanes and flying boats during the two world wars. Now the Scar is used in the early summer by nesting terns and in the autumn and winter by hundreds of eiders, oystercatchers, dunlin and redshank, 2,200 wildfowl which the RSPB said were in danger of irreversible damage from port expansion, marina development, recreational pressure and pollution. Perhaps the tope are in more danger from the wildfowl. The Scar pushes the fairway across to the east side of the channel. Ferries operate from Cairnryan to Larne. Catamarans are smaller but much faster with aggressive looking forward swept outriggers. Although they drop their speed at the entrance to the loch they still move fast and so a crossing of the fairway needs to be undertaken with due respect. The pier at Cairnryan has been used for shipbreaking but they don't need assistance from wandering boaters. In the

The wreck of the Craigantlet *at Portamaggie with Killantringan Lighthouse on Black Head.*

18th century it was used as a shelter by ships operating between the Clyde and the West Indies. In the Second World War it was a main landing point for US supplies.

Behind Cairn Point, the Category A Lochryan House of 1701 is built in Dutch style. On the shoreline there is parking with toilets. A wreck in the shallows can a remind that accidents happen.

The regional boundary between Dumfries & Galloway and South Ayrshire, beyond the Taxing Stone, follows the line of the tiny Galloway Burn rather than the much more obvious route of the Water of App which enters at Finnarts Bay. The A77, which has been following the east side of the loch, does take Glen App, however, disappearing behind relatively high peaks until Ballantrae. Situated on the clifftop at Finnart Bay is an observation post with gun sites overgrown in the scrub, providing cover for the mouth of Loch Ryan.

The coast is peaceful and secluded. There is only the company of disturbed cormorants diving into the sea for cover, leaving a fishy aroma in the air.

Flows to Bennane Head start north northeast at HW Dover −0020 and south southwest at HW Dover +0545 at up to 4km/h. A cairn, enclosures and standing stones are scattered over the top of the steep Finnarts Hill. The cliffs are precipitous but there are occasional secluded landing points and the position of the house at Portandea is magnificent, all alone at the waterside with a small beach beside a tiny inlet.

Baile-an-Traigh means village on the shore, Ballantrae being located at the end of a long shingle spit which protects the mouth of the River Stinchar. A 16th century burgh, it was a fishing port and the village was known for its smuggling in the 18th century. It was central to *The Master of Ballantrae*. Its major building is Ballantrae or Ardstinchar Castle, now a column and slab ruin but formerly owned by the Bargany branch of the Kennedys. In 1566 it was visited by Mary, Queen of Scots. The church is from

the 17th century. It has the Kennedy Mausoleum and graves of those drowned at sea. Terns nest on the cliffs in a reserve run by the Scottish Wildlife Trust. Behind the village are an aerial and an old windmill.

The two conspicuous landmarks inland are Knockdolian, rising up steeply amidst what is elsewhere relatively flat land, and the aerial on top of the less

conspicuous Knockormal Hill. Between them lie Bennane Head and Bennane Lea with its cod and pollock. A race at Bennane Head is where the stream from the west divides and flows both ways along the coast, reversing on the ebb. The effect for the coastal boater is that the flow reverses at this point so that it would give most benefit to arrive at the bottom of the tide. From here it flows north northeast from HW Dover +0545 and south southwest after HW Dover −0020.

Sawny Bean's Cave at Balcreuchan Port was said to have housed a family of cannibals who had killed over 1,000 people over a 25 year period. Now there are caravan sites either side of Games Loup and a more refined eating venue in the form of a picnic area at Carleton Bay. The *Varyag* memorial records a Russian ship which sank 450m offshore in 1920 when being towed to Germany for scrapping. Carleton Castle at Little Carleton was one of the line of watchtowers along the coast belonging to the local rulers, the Kennedys, who were somewhat above the law. This one was owned by baron Sir John Cathcart, whose memory has been recorded in song for pushing seven wives over the cliff at Games Loup but being disposed of in turn by the eighth, May Culean.

Lendalfoot is at the mouth of the Water of Lendal. A memorial to the crew of a boat lost in 1711 and a group of whitewashed cottages mark the point where a couple of minor roads drop down from the higher ground to the A77 running along the shore.

Lying 14km offshore is Ailsa Craig, Gaelic for fairy rock in Gaelic or Paddy's Milestone as it lies halfway be-

Dipple

Water of Girvan

Girvan

Kennedy's Pass

Lendalfoot

A77

Bennane Head

Knockdolian

Ballantrae

R Stinchar

Glen App

Milleur Pt

Corsewall Pt

Kirkcolm

The Wig

Cairnryan

L Ryan

The Rhins

Black Head

Portpatrick

From Finnarts Point the coast is far from roads until Ballantrae.

The unmistakable silhouette of Ailsa Craig in the middle of the Firth of Clyde.

Distance
*69km from
Portpatrick to Dipple*

OS 1:50,000 Sheets
*76 Girvan
82 Stranraer
& Glenluce*

Tidal Constants
*Portpatrick:
HW Dover +0040
LW Dover
Stranraer:
Dover +0100
Ballantrae:
HW Dover +0050
LW Dover +0100
Girvan:
HW Dover +0040
LW Dover +0050*

Sea Areas
Irish Sea, Malin

Submarine Area
79 Beaufort

tween Belfast and Glasgow. Only about 1km in diameter, it rises steeply on all sides to a 338m high peak, making it a distinctive landmark for the whole of the lower Clyde. A microgranite outcrop, it is the remains of an extinct volcano, the blue granite being used for kerbstones and the finest curling stones although the quarry served by a narrow gauge railway and a forge is now closed. The lighthouse has operated since 1886 but the 6m high concrete trumpet house foghorns were replaced by newer models in 1966. Wireless communication had replaced carrier pigeons in 1935 or, when they could not be released, fire signals.

There is a ruined castle and a tower which was used by the monks of Crossraguel Abbey and once held by the Catholics for Philip II of Spain. Former tenants used to pay their rents in gannet feathers and it has been one of Scotland's largest gannetries since at least 1526, with over 30,000 pairs. A bird sanctuary, it also has guillemots, razorbills, fulmars, kittiwakes and puffins nesting, benefiting from the eradication of brown rats. Comparison is made with its seals in *Redgauntlet*. Little Ailsa on the west side has hundreds of basalt pillars and there is Swine Cave at the north end.

North of Lendalfoot the higher land crowds the coast and the A77 squeezes through Kennedy's Pass as it heads towards Ardmillan Castle, another Kennedy castle visited by Mary, Queen of Scots, during her excursion of 1563.

Formerly a temporary Roman camp, **Girvan** is on the southern bank at the mouth of the Water of Girvan, a town which has an air of gentility with its Rose Gardens, Orchard Gardens and Knockushan Gardens.

It has a memorial on the front, a golf course, putting greens, tennis courts, bowling greens, swimming pool and trampolines.

There is the Girvan Folk Festival in May and Carrick Lowland Gathering, Civic Week and Gala Parade in June. Still building traditional wooden boats, it has pleasure craft, coasting vessels and a fishing fleet which catches cod, flounders, haddock, herring, mackerel, plaice, rock cod, salmon, trout, whiting and wrasse.

The station may be where Farren and his bike join the train in *The Five Red Herrings*.

A track beside Lady Burn at Dipple gives a convenient landing point past a large population of eiders and what is unusual beach pollution, a carpet of discarded potatoes, these being a notable crop on this coast.

Assorted craft in the harbour at Girvan.

18

Southeast Firth of Clyde

Right opposite, the mainland towers
Of my own Turnberry court our powers –
– Might not my father's beadsman hoar,
Cuthbert, who dwells upon the shore,
Kindle a signal-flame, to show
The time propitious for the blow?
It shall be so – some friend shall bear
Our mandate with despatch and care;
– Edward shall find the messenger.
That fortress ours, the island fleet
May on the coast of Carrick meet. –
Sir Walter Scott

From Dipple the coast is low and sandy with rocks scattered along the shoreline and dunes behind Turnberry Bay. There may be swans, eider ducks, cormorants, terns and oystercatchers on or beside the sea away from the FMC Biopolymer alginate works and seals around Brest Rocks which run out to a prominent beacon.

Turnberry, known for its golf course, has held various championships and has the benefit of its own airstrip, one runway of which crosses the A719. There have been problems, however, the course being taken over by military command in both world wars and the Trump Turnberry Hotel used as a military hospital the second time.

Flows are weak and rotatory at Turnberry Point, the start of the Firth of Clyde. It is a notable bird migration watchpoint. Behind the 1873 lighthouse built by Stevenson is a memorial and the remains of a castle which was the home of the Countess of Carrick, mother of Robert the Bruce. This was reputed to have been his birthplace in 1274 and it may have been why he landed at Maidens in 1307 to begin his campaign.

There is a standing stone before Maidens but Maidenhead Rocks, the line of horizontal strata running across

Maidenhead Bay, are more striking. The fishing harbour wall was first built in the 1950s from rubble of wartime RAF buildings. Much earlier, Douglas Graham, smuggler and tenant of Shanter Farm to the south of Maidens, had kept his boat, *Tam o' Shanter*, here. TH White describes an incident at Maidens Castle in *The Once & Future King*.

Culzean Castle & Country Park is beyond two caravan sites. The first country park in Scotland in 1970 and still regarded as possibly the best in Britain, it is a park which looks interesting even from the sea, 50m below. The centrepiece is Culzean Castle, a mansion converted in 1777 by Robert Adam in Georgian style and thought to be his best, positioned around a 12th century Kennedy tower for David, 10th Earl of Cassillis, hence its other name of Castle Cassillis. There is an Eisenhower Presentation which explains the general's part in European history and his receipt of a top floor apartment here. It has fine paintings, furniture and plaster ceilings, round drawing room, a splendid oval staircase and an armoury with flintlock pistols and swords. There are tea rooms, restaurant, picnic sites, adventure playground and toilets. A walled garden of 1783, aviary, camellia house, orangery, viaduct, pagoda, fountain court and vinery are set in 2.3km^2 of park with its swan lake, wildfowl, red deer and red squirrels. Its the most visited property of the National Trust for Scotland. Around it are lava cliffs with agates, chalcedony and other forms of quartz, natural arches and a network of interconnected caves. The Cove of Colean, like Cassilis Downans, was noted as a haunt of fairies.

Two caravan sites surround an old well at Croy House. Above them on Croy Brae is a remarkable piece of road which seems to slope the wrong way. An optical illusion resulting from certain features of the landscape, attempts to explain it in terms of electrical effects in the past have added the alternative name of Electric Brae. Those walking up to look at it should take something round to roll 'up' the hill.

Dunure Castle has a beautiful shoreline setting among rocks, caves and arches but has a less attractive history. The

The lighthouse on Turnberry Point terminates the golf course.

Barwhin Point, part of Culzean Country Park on the north side of Maidenhead Bay.

Dunure Castle stands on the shoreline, a craggy silhouette with a disturbed past.

The Heads of Ayr rise sharply above the surrounding land.

Kennedys of Cassillis were opposed to the Reformation and in 1570 they took Allan Stewart, the Commendator of Crossraguel, to the black vault and roasted him alive twice to force him to give the abbey lands to the 4th Earl of Cassallis. Seven years earlier Mary, Queen of Scots, had stayed here with the earl, one of her staunchest supporters, after her defeat at the Battle of Langside.

Dunure has toilets and neat whitewashed houses set around a harbour improved in 1811, used for fishing boats and yachting and formerly a base for smuggling whisky from Arran. Limekilns which served the village are behind them.

Sometimes fields slope down to a shore dotted with rocks, providing sheltered pools for the heron, and sometimes there are cliffs, culminating in the vertical 79m high Heads of Ayr with low ground on each side and low ground surrounding Ayr Bay with its gannets.

The first buildings seen of Ayr are those of Craig Tara, developed by Butlin's from the 1941 HMS Scotia training camp for the Royal Navy.

The 16th century ruin of Greenan Castle has its remaining wall ready to topple down onto the beach. Mostly belonging to the Kennedys, it was in Davidson hands for a period. Thomas Kennedy of Culzean spent a night here in 1602 and was murdered at St Leonard's Road the next morning with his body being returned here.

Doonfoot has mixed flocks of foraging waders. **Ayr**, one of the biggest resorts in Scotland, runs from the River Doon to the River Ayr and beyond. Ayr and Robert Burns are inseparable. Burns Cottage is where he was born in 1759 and where he lived until 1766. There is a Robert Burns Birthplace Museum. Nearby is a Burnsiana museum and tea room. The haunted Alloway Kirk, a ruin in Burns' day, is where his father, William, is buried, inspiring the poem of Tam o' Shanter, who saw dancing witches and warlocks through its windows. The Auld Brig o' Doon, possibly 13th century, is a single arch. It is where Tam's horse, Maggie, lost her tail to the Cutty Sark witch, accompanied by a Burns monument of 1823 and gardens with statues of his characters. The Tam o' Shanter Museum is in the former brewhouse supplied with malt by Douglas Graham of Shanter Farm, alias Tam o' Shanter. The Auld Kirk in Alloway, built in 1654 with notable lofts and its original canopied pulpit, is where Burns was

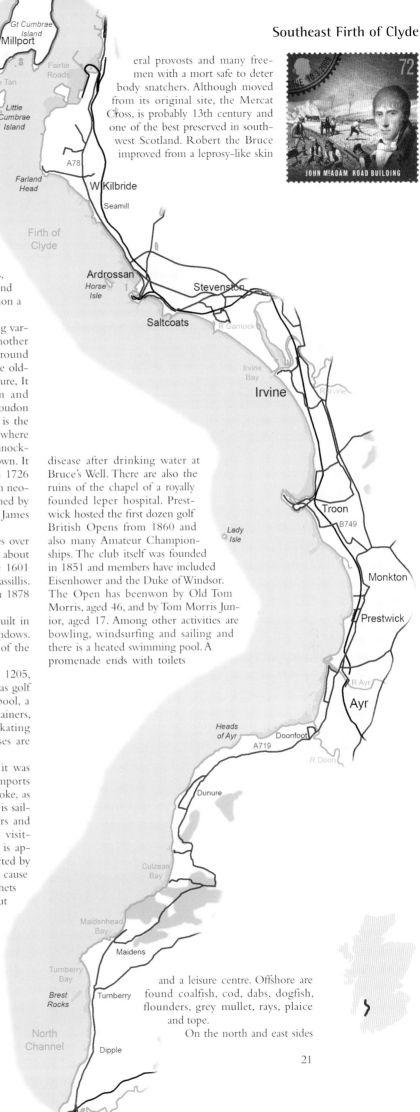

baptized and sometimes attended. There is a Burns Festival with concerts, exhibitions, competitions, ceilidhs, Holy Fair with sideshows, bands, displays and a re-enactment of Tam's ride. This is only part of the calendar. There are the Ayr County Show, Ayrshire Arts Festival with a week of plays, films and concerts, Ayr Golf Week, Ayr Bowls Week and Scotland's leading flower festival, the Ayr Flower Show.

Bellisle Park to the south of Ayr centre is a deer park with wildfowl, formal gardens, golf course and cafeteria. Rozelle is an 18th century mansion altered in the 1830s by David Bryce, the Maclaurin Art Gallery having Henry Moore and other sculpture, fine art, photographs, crafts, local military and other history, embroidery and civic relics in a converted stable block, not to mention a park with swan pond, nature trails and tea room.

Ayr Gaiety Theatre claims to be Scotland's leading variety theatre and there is also a Civic Theatre. Another notable building is Loudoun Hall dating from around 1500, a town house for a rich merchant, one of the oldest surviving examples of Scottish Burgh architecture, It belonged to the Campbells, earls of Loudoun and Moores, all prominent in this town where John Loudon McAdam was born in 1756. The St John's Tower is the remains of the Burgh Kirk of St John the Baptist where the Scottish Parliament met in April 1315 after Bannockburn to confirm the succession of the Scottish crown. It has links with John Knox and was demolished in 1726 but restored in 1914. The Wallace Tower, a 34m high neo-Gothic structure, the second on the site, was designed by Thomas Hamilton and completed in 1834 by James Thom.

Burns' *Brigs of Ayr* describes two notable bridges over the River Ayr. The 13th century Auld Brig, rebuilt about 1470 and restored in 1910, was the scene of the 1601 battle between the Kennedys of Bargany and Cassillis. The New Bridge was built in 1788 and rebuilt in 1878 after being washed away by floods.

The 38m high steeple on the Town Hall was built in 1828 with an octagonal turret and tall, narrow windows. Miller's Folly is a sentinel port built on the wall of the 1652 Cromwellian Citadel by its Victorian owner.

Ayr, formerly Inverayr and a royal burgh since 1205, is the major resort on Glasgow's seaside coast. It has golf courses, crazy golf, a boating pond, a paddling pool, a miniature railway, a children's playground, entertainers, a fairground, swimming baths, tennis, riding, skating and curling. There is an esplanade and racehorses are exercised on the beach early in the morning.

Formerly the chief port of western Scotland, it was developed on fish, wool and linen and it still imports fertilizers, minerals and fish, exporting coal and coke, as shown by the coaling plant by the harbour. There is sailing and subaqua and cod, dabs, dogfish, flounders and are caught locally. This is one of the harbours visited by the paddle steamer *Waverley*. The harbour is approached past beacons and a lighthouse and protected by a detached breakwater but westerly winds may still cause a swell in the entrance. Heavy rain may cause freshets in the river and small vessels have been carried out to sea by ice breaking up after a hard frost. There is a coastguard station but a wreck shows they are not always successful.

Prestwick, from the Old English preost wic, priest's town, is one of the oldest burghs in Scotland, from 983 James VI claimed, now contiguous to Ayr in one long sweep of housing. St Ninian's Episcopal church was built in the 12th century by Walter, High Steward of Scotland, and has the graves of knights templars, sev-

eral provosts and many freemen with a mort safe to deter body snatchers. Although moved from its original site, the Mercat Cross, is probably 13th century and one of the best preserved in southwest Scotland. Robert the Bruce improved from a leprosy-like skin

disease after drinking water at Bruce's Well. There are also the ruins of the chapel of a royally founded leper hospital. Prestwick hosted the first dozen golf British Opens from 1860 and also many Amateur Championships. The club itself was founded in 1851 and members have included Eisenhower and the Duke of Windsor. The Open has been won by Old Tom Morris, aged 46, and by Tom Morris Junior, aged 17. Among other activities are bowling, windsurfing and sailing and there is a heated swimming pool. A promenade ends with toilets

and a leisure centre. Offshore are found coalfish, cod, dabs, dogfish, flounders, grey mullet, rays, plaice and tope.

On the north and east sides

the town is bounded by Prestwick airport, the Tartan Gateway to Americans as it can take jumbo jets and is the only fog free airport in Europe, a better airport than Glasgow but not so well located for the major Scottish conurbation. It boasts being the only place in Britain to have been visited by Elvis Presley, in 1960. Now underused, it has applied to become the UK spaceport. The Pow Burn skirts the airport and emerges at the west end of the main runway.

Monkton church on the north side of the airport was dedicated to St Cuthbert in the 12th century and was where William Wallace was inspired by a dream of Caledonia urging him to fight for Scotland.

Golf courses continue with ten of them between Prestwick and Kilwinning. Royal Troon golf course, set up in 1878 with the longest British hole at 530m, has also hosted the British Open championships several times. Gailes has one of Glasgow Golf Club's two courses, this one their seaside course. Despite the sandy beaches there are significant spreads of rock close inshore, particularly Meikle Craigs and Black Rocks with a beacon on the end.

Lady Isle lies 4km off **Troon**, its name from the Gaelic an t-sron, headland, or trwyn in Old Welsh. With two towers and a light beacon, the ternery is a bird sanctuary with arctic, common and sandwich terns nesting here and roseate terns present. The surrounding waters have cod, dogfish, flounders, haddock, plaice, pollack, rays, skate, thornbacks, tope, whiting and general flatfish, together with cormorants. Docks were established in 1808, resulting in this becoming a leading British coal port. In 1816 a Stephenson Killingworth travelling engine was bought to haul wagons on the plateway to the harbour from collieries near Kilmarnock, believed to be the world's first steam hauled railway, but its pounding caused so much damage to the cast iron plates that a return had to be made to horse traction. Two drydocks, Troon Yacht Haven with berths for 400 yachts, lighthouse, gas holder and lifeboat station crowd onto the rocky promontory around the B749. Supports for a former double outfall pipeline provide an awkward obstruction off the southwest side. The Ballast Bank is from shingle dumped after being used as ballast on sailing colliers. Its current catamaran ferry service to Larne is the fastest from Scotland. The houses are often Victorian, towered and turreted in red sandstone. There is a concert hall and other activities include saunas, squash, tennis, bowling, windsurfing and subaqua.

The coast of Irvine Bay is low with sand dunes and occasional rock platforms, particularly Stinking Rocks, just before the South Ayrshire/North Ayrshire border. Offshore are the lone Mill Rock and Lappock Rock with its beacons.

Beyond Ayrshire Beach Park with its maze the Rivers

Portencross Castle guarded the turning point into Fairlie Roads.

Garnock and Irvine meet and flow into the sea at Irvine past the Irvine Bar. Between them is saltmarsh and the disused Bogside racecourse for horses. Until the Clyde was deepened during the 18th century it was Scotland's third port and is where Burns learned about flax dressing. It still imports chemicals, clay, flints, sand and timber and exports coal, bricks, fireclay goods and chemicals although it is a resort. There are toilets by the Beach Park. At the old Tide Signal Station a dozen balls on a pole would move to show the harbour water depth. It is easier to find by water than on **Irvine**'s poorly signposted roads. Irvine Harbour Festival of Light is popular and the Scottish Maritime Museum has been set up with an Irvine harbour tug, Edwardian shipyard worker's flat, wooden boat workshop and historical machinery.

There is sand yachting along Irvine Bay. For naturalists there are gannets, cormorants, eider ducks, oystercatchers, curlews and terns and for naturists there is a long expanse of sand to the north of the rivermouth. Ardeer, behind the beach, was used for Nobel Enterprises' chemicals works, employing up to 13,000 people.

Stevenston was founded in the 12th century but it wasn't a burgh until 1952, a coal town from the 17th to 19th centuries. Nearby **Saltcoats** produced salt until the 20th century and is a resort. The North Ayrshire Heritage Centre in an 18th century church has local and national exhibits and material from a former maritime museum. The harbour wall was built in 1686 but there is a heavy swell during winds from the south southwest to west. Despite this, pedaloes are still available for hire. At low water the remains of fossilized trees are visible. An indoor pool plus cafés, bars and amusements complete the attractions.

Ardrossan was built around an adjacent section of rock platform with Castle Craigs at the southern end. The 1140 Ardrossan Castle was held by the English from 1292 until Wallace lit a fire in the town and butchered them when they came to investigate, the bodies being thrown into the dungeon, known as Wallace's Larder. The harbour was planned by the 12th Earl of Eglinton from 1804 in association with Telford, Jessop and Rennie but the Glasgow, Paisley & Ardrossan Canal to serve it ran out of funds at Johnstone. It was a Burgh of Barony from 1846. Ardrossan has indoor bowling and a golf driving range. The harbour imports iron ore, limestone, oil, petrol, timber and scrap metal and exports oil, petrol, asphalt and steel. There is an ocean tanker terminal, a car ferry terminal for Brodick since 1834 and a lighthouse, all protected by a detached breakwater.

Beyond the breakwater is Horse Isle, 2ha of nature reserve topped by grass with a ternery, five species of gull and many varieties of butterfly. A 16m high x 5.8m^2 pyramidal tower was proposed by Arctic navigator John Ross in 1811 and used to hold a barrel of water for the use of shipwrecked sailors.

The coast continues sandy in front of the A78 along to Farland Head with low rocks at intervals. The railway, which has been following the coast, is very conspicuous as it runs along the hillside past motte, castle, dun and fort sites. There are caravans and a prominent bar food notice at the foot of the slope while black guillemots and jellyfish are to be found offshore.

Seamill is a village of baronial houses that have red sandstone turrets, making a glass dome greenhouse by the shore seem as out of place as the aerial on Law Hill beyond **West Kilbride**. It has a water powered mill and the 1880 Seamill Hydro Hotal was an early form of health farm.

At the end of the golf links there are submarine cables leaving for Arran before the steep Farland Head. The restored 15th century Portencross Castle stands right next to the water rather than using the higher site of the vitrified Iron Age fort and dun on the ridge on the north side of the village and was used as a departure point for

Hunterston power station.

Hunterston Terminal, Little and Great Cumbrae and Arran.

dead kings being taken to Iona for burial. This ridge runs north for 2km with a straight rock platform below it at water level.

Little Cumbrae Island has a disused lighthouse on top while there is a conspicuous ruined castle on the adjacent Castle Island.

Moving from the lower to the upper firth, neaps may have an almost continuous outward flow, especially at surface level, if there has been heavy rain or snowmelt. Northerly and easterly winds increase the outward flow and reduce the sea level, southerly and westerly winds having the opposite effect.

Piers project occasionally before Hunterston nuclear power station. Hunterston A, with two Magnox reactors, built in 1957–64 with the help of the world's largest Goliath crane, is being decommissioned. Hunterston B of 1976, also with two Magnox reactors, produces 1GW. Its intake is 700m south of Little Brigurd while its outfall pipes extend seawards on the north side of the point to a beacon where a half metre high mushroom of hot water rises from the depths of **Fairlie** Roads. The 422km 2.25GW Western Link Interconnector cable takes power to Deeside below Chester.

Hunterston House and castle are largely hidden behind the power station.

Hunterston oil platform construction yard of Ayrshire Marine Contractors was an investment to build oil rigs. Started during the heady days of the 1970s, it remained unused for its intended purpose but was employed in the construction of the Coulport Trident submarine explosives handling jetty. At 200m x 80m x 47m high, it was the world's biggest floating dock and was towed from here to Loch Long. At the time it was Europe's second most expensive civil engineering project to the Channel Tunnel, delivered two years late and £539,000,000 over budget.

The construction yard fronts the Hunterston Terminal, built to supply Ravenscraig steelworks. It can take the largest vessels afloat and might be seen unloading iron ore from Japanese bulk carriers, delivering it on a 1.6km conveyor belt to the rail terminal behind the construction yard.

Near Great Cumbrae Island is a buoyed deep water channel. Navigation regulations treat Great Cumbrae as a large traffic island and so there are fishing boats, bulk ore carriers, naval vessels and pleasure craft sailing in all directions. The Hunterston Channel is defined as a Narrow Channel under the 1972 International Regulations Preventing Collisions at Sea and in it a vessel less than 20m in length 'shall not impede the passage of a vessel which can safely navigate only within a narrow channel or fairway.'

From the southern end of the island there are views through to Arran, perhaps Ailsa Craig, and, of course, Little Cumbrae Island with the rugged drop of Craig Nabbin, separated from Great Cumbrae by the Tan at Portachur Point.

Distance
65km from Dipple to Millport

OS 1:50,000 Sheets
63 Firth of Clyde
70 Ayr, Kilmarnock
& Troon
76 Girvan

Tidal Constants
Girvan:
HW Dover +0040
LW Dover +0050
Ayr:
Dover +0050
Troon:
HW Dover +0050
LW Dover +0010
Irvine:
Dover +0010
Ardrossan:
Dover +0010
Millport:
Dover +0010

Sea Area
Malin

Submarine Areas
70 Turnberry,
63 Ayr, 47 Garroch,
46 Cumbrae

Approaching Keppel Pier on Great Cumbrae.

5 Great Cumbrae Island

In night the fairy prospects sink,
Where Cumray's isles with verdant link
Close the fair entrance of the Clyde:
Sir Walter Scott

Great Cumbrae formss part of the Bute Estate in North Ayrshire. It consists largely of an Old Red Sandstone plateau, rising to 127m at the Glaid Stone, old sea cliffs dropping to a new wavecut platform and a rocky ledge foreshore. Sheep and cattle farming predominate on the top and the road network is essentially an inner loop on the plateau, partly formed by the B899, and by an outer B896 loop at the foot of the former cliffs, this outer loop often having concrete wave defences right next to the sea. Great Cumbrae, Scotland's most densely populated island, is a place where the Sinclair C5 caught on.

Millport Field Centre is by the Keppel Pier, containing

The Lion, a distinctive igneous intrusion on Great Cumbrae.

The National Centre Cumbrae.

the Robertson Museum & Aquarium. The buildings were the headquarters of the Scottish Marine Biological Association from 1896 to 1970 when they moved to Dunstaffnage. Water surrounding the island is often clear. Sea anemones cling to the deeply pitted sandstone along the shoreline and all is quiet except for the occasional jet roaring overhead on a training flight.

The island has a number of igneous intrusions of which by far the most spectacular is the Lion, a free standing section which takes its name from its shape. Red sandstone ledges on the shoreline have been sculpted by the sea to provide extensive if less dramatic interest. Thrift adds a dash of pink to highlight the red of the rocks.

The red sandstone church towers of Largs are in sight by now.

The National Centre Cumbrae, with its purpose built chalets, was established near the north end of Great Cumbrae's east coast in 1992 and includes canoeing, sailing, windsurfing and subaqua in its repertoire. It is regularly used by national dinghy sailing squads from November to March. Concentrations of leisure boats will consequently be found between Downcraig Ferry and Holm Bay.

A Second World War flying boat wreck may be located by dive boats waiting above it. The vehicle ferry terminal contains a telephone and toilets.

Toment End is the site of the graves of Norsemen killed at the Battle of Largs in 1263. A monument stands by the water's edge and next to it is a picnic table.

Across the Firth of Clyde, Rothesay Sound divides Bute from the mainland and around is a panorama of hills. All of Glasgow's shipping passes up the Clyde between Great Cumbrae and Bute, together with naval vessels, fishing boats and yachts in profusion.

The west coast of Great Cumbrae is the rockiest and wildest section but the road does make it completely accessible to the public. At the back of Bell Bay a face has been painted on an angular section of rock, probably

The monument stands out clearly on the Toment End.

Arran rises above Bute to the west of Great Cumbrae.

first noticed as a piercing pair of eyes looking out from amongst the greenery of the cliff. Fintray Bay provides a sandy crescent, popular in the summer. It once had a lemonade factory.

From the southern end of the island there are views through to Arran, perhaps Ailsa Craig, and, of course, Little Cumbrae Island with the rugged drop of Craig Nabbin, separated from Great Cumbrae by the Tan at Portachur Point.

The southern end of the island is of Carboniferous limestone and houses most of the island's 1,200 population. Kirkton was the original settlement, identified by a caravan site, but now almost everyone lives in **Millport**, arcing around Millport Bay. Garrison House was built for the *Royal George* revenue cutter crew to oppose smuggling, later occupied by the 6th Earl of Glasgow, George Frederick Boyle. It now hosts Millport Country Music Festival.

The town became a popular play area for Glasgow

from the late 18th century with passenger steamers calling from Largs from the late 19th century. However, because of excessive fees, the steamers boycotted Millport in 1906 until a settlement was reached.

The island has always been fiercely independent. The minister for the Episcopal Cathedral of Argyll & the Isles in Millport prayed for 'the Cumbraes and the adjacent islands of Great Britain and Ireland. in the 19th century. The smallest cathedral in Europe, 12 x 6.1m but with a 37m spire, it was completed in 1851 by William Butterfield for the 6th Earl of Glasgow on his family's land. Millport

Little Cumbrae seen across the Tan from Sheriff's Port.

also has the world's narrowest house, the Wedge with a frontage of 1.19m. The town was the setting for Radio 4's *Millport* comedy series.

Millport Bay is broken up by the Inner and Outer Eileans in its centre and these help to attract wildlife, including seals. The roseate tern was first identified in the

Millport Bay is surrounded by almost all of the island's housing.

bay in 1812 and these days the curlew might be met near the bay, shelduck are seen and the whole of the island is a popular nesting site for eider ducks which try to protect their ducklings from marauding gulls. In *Rob Roy* Scott claims that the screaming of gulls on the Cumbraes is followed by foul weather.

Distance
Great Cumbrae Island is 6km long and lies 2km off Largs with ferry access

OS 1:50,000 Sheet
63 Firth of Clyde

Tidal Constant
Millport: Dover +0100

Sea Area
Malin

Submarine Area
46 Cumbrae

6 Upper Firth of Clyde

Wooded sounds forming Glasgow's playground

Imagine we've left Craigendoran behind,
And wind-happy yachts by Kilcreggan we find,
At Kirn and Dunoon and Innellan we stay,
Then Scotland's Madeira that's Rothesay they say.
Or maybe by Fairlie and Largs we will go,
Or over to Millport that thrills people so,
Maybe journey to Arran, it can't be denied,
These scenes all belong to the song of the Clyde.

RY Bell & Ian Gourley

Largs Yacht Haven, to the south of Largs on the mainland, is Scotland's largest marina.

There is a Pencil memorial in Largs to record how Hakon IV was drivn ashore on a stormy day and was defeated bloodily by Alexander III to end the Vikings' domination. A Viking longboat sculpture is sited on the seafront rocks. In September there is the burning of a replica Viking longboat, fireworks and a torchlight procession with Norwegians visiting to join in the celebrations.

Largs, from the Gaelic an leargaidh ghallda, hillside, dominated by two dark red sandstone church spires, has a promenade and is visited by the *Waverley*, the world's last seagoing paddle steamer, built on the Clyde in 1946. Smaller craft visit to take part in sailing regattas most weekends from May to September. Arrival of the railway in 1895 helped the town develop. Other touches of character range from its museum with books and photographs to its shellfish stalls. Largs Bay is between Gogo Water and Noddsdale Water. Noddle Bridge has a plaque

to Lord Kelvin of Largs, originator of the Kelvin scale which begins at absolute zero.

Sir Thomas MakDougall Brisbane, a former resident, built an observatory in Largs in 1808, cataloguing many thousands of stars, served well under Wellington and was Governor of New South Wales for four years from 1821, giving his name to the Australian city and river.

The shore is followed closely on this section of coast by the A78 up to Inverkip.

Submarine cables to Kerrycroy on Bute leave Routenburn near the golf course. Knock Castle and the restored Skelmorlie Castle are not obvious from the sea, unlike the Heywood Hotel and others which face the rocky beach at **Skelmorlie** where sea urchins may be found. Knock Hill at 217m has a vitrified Iron Age fort on top. A red building was a leading Clyde hydropathic from the 1860s to the 1930s.

A measured mile is a set of marks which allow ships to check their speeds.

From Skelmorlie to Cloch Point the flood begins at HW Dover −0500 and the ebb at HW Dover +0100 at up to 2km/h.

After North Ayrshire gives way to Inverclyde, **Wemyss Bay** is one of the main passenger ports of the Clyde with an Edwardian station and pier and a ferry service to Bute. This Caledonian Railway terminus building is one of Britain's finest stations, built in 1865 with glass on an iron framework to give a light but sheltered route to the ferries. A red stone shelter proves an interesting find on Wemyss Point. Kip Marina was the first in Scotland and is one of the largest in a village which was known in the

Largs provides the shortest crossing to Great Cumbrae.

Looking up the Clyde from Great Cumbrae.

17th century for its witchcraft and in the 18th century for its smuggling. The hamlet was developed as a marine village in the 19th century by landowning MP Robert Wallace.

Lunderston Bay has a picnic site and more submarine cables leaving it while guillemots sit out on the water. A gun emplacement has been strategically located to cover the narrow entrance to the industry and naval installations of the Clyde and surrounding lochs. Shacks are sited along the shoreline to Cloch Point where the lighthouse, built in 1797 by Robert Stevenson, had to be one of the most accessible on the British coastline, sandwiched between the water and the A770, which runs right alongside to the extent that lighthouse crews parked cars on the footway. Running the Lights was a 19th century speed trial necessity for any new steamer between Cloch and Little Cumbrae. C&DA Stevenson added a wireless device in 1930 to talk to ships in poor visibility. It is now a private house.

Gourock is below Levan Castle. A vehicle ferry service connects with Hunter's Quay. Indeed, looking across the Clyde estuary it is a rare moment when there is not at least one ferry crossing somewhere. With all the shipping interest and lochs running away in different directions it is hardly surprising that Gourock should have become a resort. Even now, it is a fascinating place just to spend time watching. At hand are public toilets.

The Gourock Waltz was something from the dance floor, not from the windswept water. The bay has notable sunsets and did provide shelter from a storm for the *Vital Spark*, despite the fact that it had grown to a shipwreck of epic proportions as Para Handy steadily expanded the tale on his train journey into Glasgow. On the other hand, Dougie, the mate, in disparaging remarks about yachting, suggested taking one's pyjamas and fruit juice to join the yacht at Gourock on a Saturday, only to find she has dragged her moorings and damaged a boat belonging to a Lloyd's surveyor. Waters leaves the *Susannah* here in *The Five Red Herrings*.

Cloch Point lighthouse with Strone Point opposite.

Iona I paddle steamer of 1862, operating in the Clyde until bought by Confederates to run blockaded southern ports during the American Civil War but sinking before departing, now a rare paddle steamer wreck.

The B833 joins the coast at **Kilcreggan** to the west of an aerial on Gallows Hill and continues around the coast, a shoreline of weathered rocks. From Baron's Point a skein of submarine cables cross Loch Long, which floods from HW Dover –0430 and ebbs from HW Dover +0130 at up to 1km/h. Because of the high mountains all around it is subject to fickle winds. It is also one of the deepest sea lochs and is used by submarines, including nuclear craft, surfaced and submerged. It is subject to Narrow Channel regulations. North of Cove it is controlled by the Clyde Dockyard Port of Gareloch and is subject to special regulations including restrictions concerning the use of whistles.

Monoliths have played an important role in local folklore. Couples used to embrace one prehistoric stone to ensure they had children and another was consulted by fishermen seeking fair winds. In 1662 a number of women were burned for trying to throw their Granny Kempock Stone into the sea to sink ships using witchcraft. As if to emphasize their failure, ferries now operate from Kempock Point across to Helensburgh, Kilcreggan and Dunoon.

The massive block of Fort Matilda was built to guard a narrow point of the Clyde estuary. Above it on Lyle Hill is a memorial taking the form of an anchor and a Cross of Lorraine to the Free French sailors who died in the Battle of the Atlantic during the Second World War. From here towards **Greenock** the coast is dominated by hammerhead Titan cranes.

Crossing the Firth of Clyde from Inverclyde to Argyll & Bute needs to be done in consultation with the charts as no less than three recommended shipping channels pass through this gap. In the centre is the wreck of the

Hunter's Quay, Holy Loch, Strone Point, Loch Long, Ardentinny and Kilcreggan, seen across the Firth of Clyde from Gourock.

The pier at Dunoon, overlooked by the castle.

Toward Point lighthouse with Bute beyond and the peaks of Arran in the distance.

Knockderry Castle guards a narrowing opposite Gairletter Point. This section of the Cowal Peninsula coast is part of the Argyll Forest Park as far as Strone Point and is followed by the A880. Despite the trees and the steep slopes, an area has been adopted as a golf course above Blairmore and Strone with its Category C St Columba's church right on Strone Point. From 1961 until 1992 Holy Loch seemed to have had a rather unsuitable name because of its hosting of US nuclear submarines. It took its name after a ship sank here while loaded with earth from the Holy Land which had been intended as a foundation for Glasgow cathedral. These days it is home for the Benmore Centre for Outdoor Education.

The Hunters Quay Hotel makes it clear that the pier receiving ferries from Gourock is, indeed, Hunter's Quay, named after the Hunter family who bought this section of coast speculatively when steamships started. Built from 1835 with Tudor styling, it is still the quickest route to Glasgow for daily use. It is not to be confused with the derelict Kirn pier by the Category C Arts & Crafts style Queen's Hotel a little further along the A815. The Clyde Model Yacht Club for smaller yachts was founded here in 1856, becoming the Royal Clyde Yacht Club in 1871 and eventually moving to the Gare Loch.

The dark red spire of the Category A St John's church is one of the early features of **Dunoon** (named from the Gaelic dun obhainn, river fort), a resort with such venues as the Argyll Hotel and Rock Café and formerly a hydropathic spa. The Esplanade Hotel's name refers to the town's 6km front. The pier receives ferries from Kempock

Loch Striven has a NATO fuel jetty.

Point and is visited by the *Waverley*. This Gateway to the Western Highlands boasts tennis, bowling greens, squash, swimming pools, sauna and solarium, not to mention 150 pipe bands taking part in the Cowal Highland Gathering at the end of August, the world's biggest Highland games. The past has been more turbulent. In 1646 hundreds of Lamonts were butchered by the Campbells, a fact recorded by the Celtic stone cross erected by the Clan Lamont Society in 1906. In 1685 Atholl invaded the Cowal peninsula and burned the royal castle of 1371. The Castle Gardens were formerly the gardens of a villa owned by the Lord Provost of Glasgow. Another memorial is the 1896 statue to Mary Campbell of Dunoon, better known as Highland Mary, the fiancée of Robert Burns, who died as they were about to emigrate to the West Indies. Para Handy was supposed to have caused darkness and the town gas supply to have been closed down on reporting a naval battle near the Cumbraes, perhaps mishearing breaking bottles on the shore at Inverkip one night.

The Gantocks are an outcrop of rocks marked by a light beacon. A Swedish ore carrier is one vessel which failed to benefit from the warning.

Flows flood up from Toward Point from HW Dover −0500 and ebb from HW Dover +0100 at up to 2km/h. Cod and angler fish are amongst those in the flow.

The Berry Burn in Morag's Fairy Glen marks the end of Dunoon. Extensive wooded slopes are broken only by a disused quarry in the side of the Tom at Bullwood.

Innellan clings to the side of another Tom but still manages a golf course and bowling green. The ruined Knockamillie Castle, which was one of the most important in the area, now overlooks an equally ruined pier, surrounded by the Osborne Inellan and local shops. Close by in the woods is the church where the blind George Mathieson wrote *O Love That Will Not Let Me Go* in 1882. Somewhere off here is where Para Handy claimed, rather excessively, that the *Vital Spark* was wrecked in a storm.

Innellan Beacon marks the Bridges shoal and is a perch for cormorants at Newton Park, a hamlet with a picnic area, overlooked by lattice tower TV masts. Another mast stands at Toward Point by the lighthouse. This low rocky area also houses a white heather farm.

The *Wallachia* sank here in 1895 with a cargo of beer and whisky. The wreck was rediscovered in 1976 and the whisky remained drinkable with much of it having been brought up by divers.

Rothesay Sound separates the Island of Bute from the mainland. Flows are weak at first.

Toward Castle was another Lamont building destroyed by the Campbells in 1646. It overlooks Toward Quay, as does Castle Toward Outdoor Education Centre, used for filming CBBC's *The Raven*.

Ardyne Burn runs in at Ardyne Point next to a series of basins which have been used as an oil platform construction area. Less obvious is that this is on the line of the Highland Boundary Fault. Submarine cables cross to Port Bannatyne on Bute.

Loch Striven is known as the Weatherglass of Rothesay as gathering clouds or mist on the shores frequently give an indication of bad weather to come. The loch was used for testing Barnes Wallis' bouncing bomb before it was used for German dam destruction in the Second World War.

Although it is now bare, Strone Point was remarkable for having been planted with trees to show the positions of the opposing armies at the Battle of Waterloo. Oaks and birches do follow the shoreline of East Kyle of Bute, but they give little shelter from the wind which manages to funnel straight down the channel even when the general wind direction is well away from the northwest. Flows increase from 2km/h to a maximum of 6km/h at the Southern Burnt Island Channel with inward flows meeting near Buttock Point, the exact position varying with the meteorological conditions.

A cairn at Colintraive precedes the shortest car ferry crossing to Bute, a route taken by the A886 and a series of submarine cables.

Here *Vital Spark* mate Dougie passed a coalfish off as a cod to a Glasgow woman. When cook Sunny Jim told the owner of the guard dog they had borrowed that he had been drowned here he complained that the collar had not been saved.

Other vessels use the kyles and Para Handy advised Dougie he should not run into the battleship *Collingwood* as it would vex the Admiralty. The ferry is hard to see when it is on the mainland side and it takes little time to cross.

Distance
63km from Downcraig Ferry via Loch Long to Colintraive

OS 1:50,000 Sheets
56 Loch Lomond & Inveraray
63 Firth of Clyde

Tidal Constants
Millport:
Dover +0010
Wemyss Bay:
Dover +0110
Helensburgh:
Dover +0120
Coulport:
Dover +0110
Rothesay Bay:
HW Dover +0100
LW Dover +0110
Tighnabruaich:
HW Dover +0110
LW Dover +0120

Sea Area
Malin

Submarine Areas
46 Cumbrae, 45 Rosneath, 43 Cove, 40 East Kyle

Connections
River Clyde – see RoB p88
Loch Long – see RoB p94

7 Island of Bute

It's a bonnie bay at morning,
And bonnier at the noon,
But it's bonniest when the sun draps
And red comes up the moon;
When the mist creeps o'er the Cumbraes,
And Arran peaks are grey,
And the great black hills, like sleepin' kings,
Sit grand roun' Rothesay Bay
Dinah Craik

This lowland isle, the junior partner in Argyll & Bute, lies off the higher Cowal peninsula. The Romans were here at their Botis Insula. The sheltered position gives it smaller waves with their limited fetch and parts of the island have the feel of somewhere much further south. It is Scotland's fifth most populous island, a festival isle with jazz and folk music and one of the oldest Highland games. Tourism, dairy cattle farming and shellfish processing are the main industries. Roe deer are present and there is a unique species of longtailed fieldmouse with shorter tail and smaller ears than its mainland cousin. To Polish detainees during the Second World War it was the Island of Snakes. To Alexander Smith in 1864 in *A Summer in Skye* it was the most melancholy of the Clyde islands but beloved by invalids.

The island is separated from the mainland by the Kyles of Bute, just 400m wide at the northern end. A ferry service, begun in 1950 with a landing craft, crosses from Colintraive, which takes its name from the Gaelic for swimming cattle across. The original slipway remains but the track leading to it must not be blocked as it is used by articulated lorries for loading catches.

The ferry plugs a gap in the A886 and a submarine water pipeline and various cables also cross East Kyle to Rhubodach.

While Beinn Bhreac is over 500m high, Windy Hill, the highest point on Bute, is a mere 278m. As the name suggests, hills affect the local weather and the kyles can be subject to squalls, even when the general wind direction is not directly along them. Bute's hills are rounded and well wooded at first. Water flows are fastest at the northern end, decreasing towards the southeast. Jellyfish float with the flow and birds include blackbacked gulls.

There is a measured distance from Ardmaleish Point to the shipyard at Undraynian Point, to which more submarine power cables cross.

Two castles have been built at the back of Kames Bay. Kames Castle, dating from the 14th century, was built for the Bannatyne family. It is an exposed location as westerly winds blow through the low gap which nearly divides Bute in two. In 1882 a horsedrawn tramway service was started from Rothesay to **Port Bannatyne**, electrified in 1902 and extended through the gap to Ettrick Bay in 1905. In use until 1936, it was the only such service on a Scottish island. Golfers on the course high above the bay must cast envious eyes over the flat land below them. Port Bannatyne was reported to have the lowest housing prices in Britain.

A submarine gas pipeline and cables cross Rothesay Sound from Ardbeg Point. The sound is used for fishing and as a submarine exercise area, surfaced submarines sometimes towing sonar equipment up to 1.5km behind.

Rothesay's 1938 Category A Pavilion is in art deco style, much used for dances during the Second World War when the town was a naval base.

Rothesay Castle's ruins at the head of Rothesay Bay include early 13th century round wall towers, a circular curtain wall of the late 12th or early 13th century, a three storey gatehouse and the early 16th century two storey chapel of St Michael, in red sandstone. It was first recorded in 1230 when besieged by the Vikings and was taken in 1263 by Haakon. It was home to Robert the Bruce and the Stewart kings, taken by Sir Colin Campbell in 1334, attacked by the Lord of the Isles in the 15th century and used by James IV and V as a base to subdue the Hebrides. Robert III considered fleeing to Bute from Perth with son James after the murder of his other son, John, in Scott's *The Fair Maid of Perth*. The ancestors of the Marquess of Bute were appointed hereditary keepers in 1498 and it was defended against the Master of Ruthven in 1527 although the town was badly damaged, as usual. The great tower was completed in 1541 but the Earl of Lennox took it three years later for the English. Much was dismantled in 1658 when Cromwell left and the Duke of Monmouth burnt and razed it. Restoration was undertaken in 1816, 1872 and 1900, the great hall being rebuilt in 1970 with a fine fireplace and the tapestry Prayer for Victory at Prestonpans. Robert III had made his son the Duke of Rothesay in 1403 when Rothesay was made a royal burgh, the title of Duke and Duchess now resting with the Prince and Princess of Wales. A museum features history, geography and natural history. The Royal Northern & Clyde Yacht Club was founded here in 1824, as was the Clyde Cruising Club in 1909. Para Handy claimed Rothesay midges could be repelled with paraffin.

The disused High Kirk has the ruins of the late medieval St Mary's chapel with its canopied tombs.

Cotton weaving was an important industry from 1779 until the early 19th century. The harbour was built in the 17th century for the fishing fleet, benefiting from the herring fishing boom. It was rebuilt and enlarged for the Clyde steamers as Rothesay with its hydropathic spa became the favourite holiday destination for Glaswegians going 'doon the watter', using such boats as the *Waverley*. The service from Wemyss Bay remains CalMac's busiest route. The largest Clyde resort, with its pier and esplanade, it features Victorian architecture. The Isle of Bute Discovery Centre in the Category A 1924 cast iron Winter Garden added to the original bandstand, a listed structure with pagoda roofs. It is one of the few remaining examples of this kind of work by Walter MacFarlane. Around it are palm trees, gardens and putting greens. Rothesay has been a Scotland in Bloom winner and the West End Café has twice been judged the UK's Best Fish & Chip Shop.

An aerial looks over the bay which was a naval anchorage from 1940 to 1957.

The Highland Boundary Fault runs through the bay, Loch Fad, Loch Quien and Scalpsie Bay, again nearly cutting the island in two. Here the hilly Dalradian schistose grit gives way to flatter Old Red Sandstone with basaltic lavas.

Bogany Point, its green pavilion topped by a cupola and ball, marks the turn into the Firth of Clyde with Skelmorlie and Largs beyond large ship anchorages. The A844 runs above the shoreline between chestnut and other deciduous trees which seem out of place, as does the Italianate church tower on Ascog Point. Ascog, approached through a striking turreted white gateway, has a Victorian fern house and gardens.

Kerrycroy Bay with its quay is the landing place for submarine cables from Largs. Razor shells and large starfish lie on the bed and black guillemots swim about. Around the back of the bay are half timbered houses which would not look out of place around a Surrey cricket green, built by the 2nd Marquis of Bute as his English wife was homesick.

Rhododendrons and the remains of a jetty mark the position within the trees of Mount Stuart house and its gardens. Built 1880–1901 by the 3rd Marquess of Bute, believed to have been the richest man in Britain, it replaced an earlier house destroyed by fire. Like a Flemish guildhall with fine stained glass windows, it is thought to be the best example of 19th century Victorian Gothic revival architecture. It was the first Scottish house with electric lighting and the world's first with an indoor pool. The site has been home to the Earls and Marquesses of Bute since the early 18th century. It has a copy of Shakespeare's first folio of 1623 and a meadery and was where Stella McCartney was married.

Hermit crabs scuttle across the bed of Kerrylamont Bay. Each side of Bruchag Point submarine power cables land from Great Cumbrae, both Great and Little Cumbrae being prominent to the southeast.

Gannets are to be found near Kerrytonlia Point and gorse is seen on the cliffs.

Across Kilchattan Bay are the quay and red sandstone houses of the hamlet of the same name at the end of the B881. A stone circle and Dabbles spinning, dyeing and weaving workshops are from different times in its history.

From Kilchattan Bay, the southern end of Bute is inaccessible to road traffic. Cormorants, eider ducks and oystercatchers have the place to themselves. Thrift appears on the rocky shoreline which rises up to 146m Torr Mòr.

A lit mark is positioned low on Rubh'an Eun at the start of Glencallum Bay with its cairn. For incoming shipping it helps to locate the pilot boarding point, between here and Little Cumbrae. From Roinn Clùmhach, on the other side of the small bay, the profile of Arran opens up with its striking peaks.

Garroch Head leads into the Sound of Bute and can have a race on its west side, especially with strong winds. Flows run to 3km/h.

Beyond St Blane's Hill is the ruin of St Blane's church, begun in 1100. It was with the monastery founded in 557 by St Catan but named after his nephew, St Blane. The cells are visible with some fine 12th century craftsmanship. Below, at Port Dornach, is the Dunagoil vitrified Iron Age fort.

Dunagoil Bay offers a sandy beach and there is another fort site at Dunstrone between Lubas Bay and Lubas Port. Stravanan Bay, backed by a golf course and airfield, has another sandy beach. Beaches on this section of coast all offer fine views of Arran, silhouetted against

The surprisingly wooded coast road at Ascog Bay.

the afternoon sunshine. Our ancestors seem to have appreciated the prospect and there is a fort site between Gallachan Bay and Scalpsie Bay, a dun site and a tumulus at the back of Scalpsie Bay and another dun site above Ardscalpsie Point. Common and grey seals also frequent the waters, as do guillemots.

The largest herring gull colony on the Clyde is on Inchmarnock, the Calf of Bute.

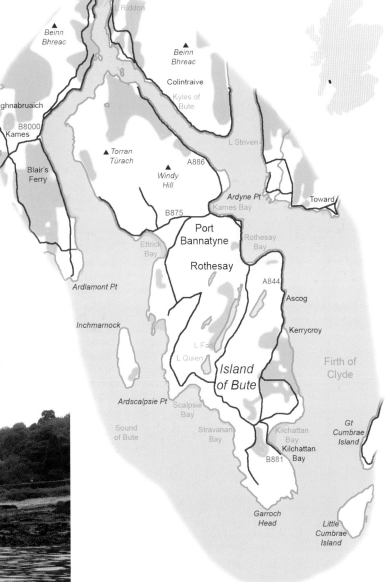

The entrance to Ascog is not easily missed.

Half-timbered houses at Kerrycroy Bay.

Diminutive light at Rubh'an Eun at the southern end of Bute.

The island rises to only 60m and supports two farms. Chapel ruins are part of the monastery founded in the 7th century by St Marnoc. A Bronze Age cairn had three burial cysts, one containing the skeleton of a young woman with an exquisite lignite collar, the Inchmarnock necklace of about 1500 BC. In more recent times the island has been a place of banishment for the inebriated and became known as the Drunkard's Isle. In 1944 it was used for commando training ahead of the D Day landings and for target practice.

St Ninian's Bay is a large inlet from Inchmarnock Sound, overlooked by the site of a castle, standing stones and, on St Ninian's Point, a chapel. Blackbacked gulls and Canada geese are the most conspicuous residents. There is another chapel ruin at Nether Androscadale while Upper Androscadale has its Watch Hill with tumulus, dun and enclosure. Lack of development has allowed these antiquities to survive.

Even the great sweep of sand in Ettrick Bay at the end of the B875 is hardly busy despite the low pass to the built

Inchmarnock Sound from Ardscalpsie Point with Inchmarnock on the left.

Looking south from Port na h-Aille to Arran.

up area of the island. It was from here that the *Vital Spark* towed the *Katherine-Anne* to Tighnabruaich in rough weather for the salvage money, only to hand her over in sympathy for the owner.

Kildavanan Point faces Ardlamont Point and is the start of the West Kyle, used by submarines, both surfaced and submerged.

Each side of Clate Point there are chambered cairns. The shoreline is wooded here and a quiet roaring may be heard, which does not seem to get any closer. This is actually the noise of successive waterfalls on streams dropping down the hillside between the trees.

Below 227m Torran Tùrach are the Glenroidean burial cairn and the remains of Kilmichael Chapel, destroyed by Norse invaders. Blair's Ferry on the mainland suggests a service that is no longer available although submarine power cables now cross the kyle. A fort site overlooks Lamb Craig.

The most westerly point on Bute is Rubha Dubh. The island coast is steep and wild. Flows are to 2km/h to Rubha Dubh but double that to Rubha Bàn. Wildlife includes blue hares, wild geese and pheasants. Instead of watching by the water, herons observe from further up the hillside, standing among the heather and outcrops of rock.

Also up the hillside are the Maids of Bute, Mery and 'Lizabeth, rocks painted as two old ladies in petticoats, allegedly by Para Handy while still crew on the *Inveraray Castle*, although the subject matter is less than clear from the water.

At Buttock Point, surrounded by bracken, West Kyle is joined by East Kyle and also by Loch Riddon or Ruel. Eilean Dubh, covered with rhododendrons, is where the 1685 insurrection of the Earl of Argyll fizzled out. A white stone beacon is accompanied by a disused miniature lighthouse by Caladh Harbour. Across the loch, Bàgh Fearnoch looks west to 454m Beinn Bhreac and east to 507m Beinn Bhreac.

The East Kyle is obstructed by the Burnt Islands, a bird haven with a fort site.

Eilean Fraoch and Eilean Mór push flows up to 6km/h, even 11km/h in the Southern Burnt Island Channel, but the direction is heavily dependent on the prevailing weather.

Balnakailly Bay is a favourite anchorage for boats awaiting the right conditions and is followed by the ferry at Rhubodnach.

Just up the hill is the Colintraive Hotel with a menu board which even says who caught which dish. It has a shop and post office in the carpark, a thriving business.

Distance
The Isle of Bute is
25km long and lies
400m off Colintraive
with ferry access

OS 1:50,000 Sheets
62 North Kintyre
& Tarbert
63 Firth of Clyde

Tidal Constants
Rubha Bodach:
HW Dover +0100,
LW Dover +0110
Rothesay Bay:
HW Dover +0100,
LW Dover +0110
Tighnabruaich:
Dover +0110

Sea Area
Malin

Submarine Areas
40 East Kyle,
46 Cumbrae,
47 Garroch,
38 West Kyle

Tighnabruaich seen up the West Kyle of Bute.

8 East Kintyre

The unintended island

Despite their small size, the Burnt Islands are a haven for birds and one of them also has a fort site. A beacon near Eilean Buidhe helps shipping through the restricted channels to Buttock Point, opposite which is Loch Ruel or Riddon which has weak flows in and out. A disused lighthouse stands to the west of Eilean Dubh and a beacon to its north. Up on the wooded hillside above there is a picnic area and a forest trail which introduces blue hares, deer, herons and wild geese.

West Kyle of Bute is more picturesque than its partner. There is a lattice radio mast below the viewpoint on Rubha Bàn, to the south of which submarine cables cross.

The B8000 runs through Kames from Tighnabruaich, the house on the hill, its wooden pier visited by the *Waverley*. It is busy with the Kyles of Bute Sailing Club, as indicated by the moorings. It has a gallery of Scottish art, is the home of Kyles Athletic, one of the top shinty teams,

and has tennis. The midges would bite through corrugated iron roofs to get at people, Para Handy claimed. Formerly there was a gunpowder factory here.

Pines stand along the shore to Carry Point where there is a collection of caravans. Oystercatchers run along the shore of Blindman's Bay and gorse adds a splash of yellow.

Ardlamont Point has long been of interest to man as a cup and ring marked rock shows. The point provides dramatic views of the peaks of the Isle of Arran and is the best place on the west coast to see harmless basking sharks.

Flow rates up into Loch Fyne are weak. Despite the relatively exposed position there are several sandy bays. Kilbride Bay or Bàgh Osde receives the Allt Osda. There are cairns at the back of Asgog Bay which is flanked by Sgat Beag and Sgat Mór, the latter with a conspicuous white lighthouse. Sandy bays each side of Eilean Aoidhe

The Burnt Islands and Colintraive on the East Kyle of Bute.

Loch Riddon leads off the heads of the Kyles of Bute.

West Kyle of Bute seen from Buttock Point.

do not quite meet up so that it is not a true island. The headland behind Rubha Stillaig has a range of antiquities, a cairn, standing stones and a chapel. This contrasts with Portavadie where an oil construction site was built in the 1970s. It never won any orders and so the wall was breached and it has been converted to a rather expensive marina. Caledonian MacBrayne's newest ferry crossing is from Portavadie to Tarbert.

Coastal, woodland and moorland habitats with nightjars and bryophytes are attributes of Glenan Forest nature reserve facing onto Glenan Bay.

Rubha Preasach was selected for a dun site while seals sun themselves on Eilean Buidhe.

Two spits almost meet at the back of Auchalick Bay, the River Auchalick keeping the centre of the bay clear as the flow enters Loch Fyne past a set of standing stones. Kilfinan Burn echoes this as it flows past a cairn and standing stone and emerges from behind a spit to enter Kilfinan Bay.

A dun on Rubha Beag is followed by forts and a motte as the coast moves up to Otter Ferry. The oitir itself projects over halfway across Loch Fyne to a beacon, resulting in deposition of sand and silt in which large otter shells are to be found. Chalets are located along a private road which follows the shore. Here, the flood starts at HW Dover −0510 and the ebb starts at HW Dover +0140 at up to 4km/h.

There is always a passage to the north of Liath Eilean, but passage to the north of Eilean Mòr and past its wreck depends on the state of the tide. The southern end of the island has an example of a pillow lava. The outside route was chosen for the submarine cable from Port Ann to Loch Gilp rather than following a more direct overland route.

Duncuan Island with its beacon guards the entrance to Loch Gilp, much of which dries at low tide. Strong southerly winds can delay low water by half an hour and reduce its effect while a strong northerly can hasten it and increase the effect, the converse resulting at high water.

The Knapdale shore brings Ardrishaig and the end of the Crinan Canal. One of the village school's leading former pupils was John Smith, past leader of the Labour Party, whose father was the headmaster.

Powerlines and the A83 follow the coast southwards.

Stronchullin Burn enters Bàgh Tigh-an-Droighinn after which the boulder strewn shoreline is steep but is uniform past the aerial topped Meall Mòr to Barmore Island. Barmore Island is not an island, being connected to the mainland, but a very distinctive feature, its rounded shape contrasting with the rugged profile of the mainland, its outline being further softened by a covering of dark fir trees. Some 20ha of shrubs from South Africa and New Zealand and rare trees including Himalayan rhododendrons over a century old surround Stonefield Castle, the baronial house built by Sir William Playfair in 1837.

The beach of scallop shells on the south side of East Loch Tarbert is a reminder that **Tarbert** catches clams, prawns and fish, was formerly the chief port of the Loch Fyne herring industry and is also used for sailing races. The fishermen were not giving up without a fight and blockaded in the contestants in the Scottish Series, Scotland's leading regatta, in 1993 in protest at limitations on the number of days on which fishing boats may put to sea. The Bielding is a platform in the centre of the harbour which formerly held a capstan used for berthing sailing boats, while Cock Island has a miniature plantation of birches. The church at the head of the harbour has a fine crown. Tarbert Castle was built in the 13th century, was strengthened in the 1320s by Robert the Bruce and has a 15th century keep. It was the last of a succession of castles that were mostly built as a defence against the Vikings. King Edgar agreed with King Magnus Barefoot in the ongoing disputes between the Vikings and the Scots, that the Scots would have the mainland and the Vikings the islands, islands being defined as anything which Magnus could sail round in his longboat. Magnus sailed round the Kintyre peninsula in 1098 and had his boat with him on board dragged 1.4km across the isthmus to complete the

West Kyle of Bute seen from Carry Point.

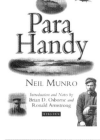

circumnavigation and claim Kintyre, something Edgar had certainly not intended, the Vikings retaining Kintyre until 1263. Tarbert features often in Para Handy stories, including Tarbert Fairs, the whole town being awakened by the *Vital Spark*'s continuous whistle and towing in a mine for safety.

Kintyre, cean tir, the head of land, is the longest peninsula in Britain. The coast is steep and remote as far as Skipness Point but offers a number of small, secluded, sandy beaches before Eilean a' Chomhraig once clear of any marine farm.

There are radar domes, probably associated with the submarine exercises, where the solitude comes to an end at Cnoc na Sgratha. The coastline levels down and thrift appears on the rocks towards Skipness Point, Norse for ship point. Skipness Point is the entrance to Kilbrannan Sound, named after Irish canoe navigator St Brendan. Tidal streams run strongly both ways round the point.

Dedicated to St Brendan of Clonfert are the remains of Kilbrannan Chapel which date from about 1300. Skipness Castle is large and roofless but under repair. It commanded Kilbrannan Sound, Loch Fyne and the Sound of Bute. Built early in the 13th century, possibly soon after 1222, it had a rectangular three storey hall and chapel which were incorporated in an advanced late 13th century quadrangular castle with crosslet arrow slits, to which a 16th century three storey tower house was added although its crenellations have been blocked in. It was owned by Dougald MacSween until 1261 and was then under MacDonald, Lord of the Isles, until given to the 2nd Earl of Argyll by the king. It held out against Colkitto and survived the 1685 firing of many of the castles

Ardlamont Point with Arran beyond across the Sound of Bute.

Looking down Loch Fyne from Loch Gilp. Ardlamont Point is on the left, Skipness Point on the right and Arran beyond.

in Argyll. It remained a Campbell stronghold until about 1700.

The post office at Skipness, overlooking the mouth of the Skipness River, acts as a general store with telephone and even serves hot drinks. It was here that Para Handy's guard dog refused to accompany him to a party and then refused to let him back aboard the *Vital Spark* afterwards so that he had to spend the night ashore.

A road now follows the coast again, as far as Claonaig where the B842 takes over. Claonaig Water enters Claonaig Bay beyond the jetty where a car ferry service leaves for Lochranza on Arran.

Powerlines return at Port Fada and run down the coast to Grogport. Clyde Port Authority jurisdiction ends before Port nan Gamhna where the Crossaig Glen water enters.

To the south of Grogport, where the road leaves, there is another dun site.

Despite the replacing of its ornate cast iron pier with a sheet piled sea wall, Carradale remains a good example of a small Scottish fishing port and is the second most important harbour on the Kintyre with herring boats present in the winter. It was a regular port of call for the *Vital Spark*, where timber was loaded, biscuit tins taken to collect wartime provisions for troops and from where she sailed for the review at Tail of the Bank. To the north, submarine power cables cross to Arran, an island crossed by the Highland Boundary Fault.

A beacon marks the harbour while palm trees show that it is sheltered not only at sea level. Despite the generally imperceptible currents, there are overfalls to the south on southgoing streams. To the south of Port Righ and the golf course there is a radio mast. Wild goats live on Carradale Point, which was used as a basking shark harpooning base by Anthony Watkins, the brother of the Arctic explorer Gino. Carradale Point Fort is one of the best examples of a vitrified fort, a 58m x 23m oval 21m above sea level.

A series of platform antiquity sites precede Torrisdale Castle, an 18th century castellated mansion which is not obvious from the sound.

A dun on Rubha nan Sgarbh and then Pluck Point Fort lead down to Saddell House, built in 1774 for Col Donald Campbell after fighting in India and becoming Commandant of Madras. The house has been restored after burning down in 1899 while its tenant, the Revd Bramwell, was out shooting.

Saddell Castle is conspicuous beside Saddell Water as it enters Saddell Bay. The castle keep was built in 1508 for the bishop of Argyll, almost surrounded by the river and sea, but this did not stop its being burned by the Earl of Sussex in 1559, when it passed to the Campbells. Inside the front door the floor can be removed to allow intruders to fall into a pit. In 1680 the roof was put back by William Ralston The Argylls made additions in 1770 but it later fell into disrepair, being restored by the Landmark Trust. Some carved stones around it come from the Cistercian Saddell Abbey, the remains of which are just up the glen. Built in 1160 by Somerled, Lord of the Isles, who is said to be buried here, it was completed by his son, Reginald, who lived outside for three years to become hardy and was said to have scattered around some blessed soil brought from Rome.

In the Middle Ages it was as important as Iona although it was later used as a quarry, including its grave stones. Tombstones from 1300 to 1560 show armed warriors, a priest with a chalice and a Cistercian monk, including Big Macdonald the Tyrant, one of whose less endearing actions was cutting off the hands of some unfortunate travellers in order to try out the blade of a new sword.

Saddell is Norse for saw dale and it is subject to heavy wind gusts down Saddell Glen although more noise is heard from low flying jets.

Ferryman's Cottage was the home of the man whose job it was to unload supplies delivered by puffer.

Ugadale Point has Bruce's Stone and a dun but Kildonan Dun is a notable example, a D shaped structure with double stairs and cell within the walls. Built in the 1st or 2nd century, it may have been occupied until the 14th century. There is a further fort on Kildonald Point where there is also a stream of rubbish down the cliff.

Jagged slabs line Carrick Point. A chambered cairn overlooks Thorn Island while Seal Rock, overlooked by a standing stone, lives up to its name as a favourite hauling out place for seals.

Glenlussa Water enters Ardnacross Bay before Peninver. Toilets, children's playground and parking accompany a caravan site while another submarine cable runs across to Blackwaterfoot on Arran.

Looking south from Carradale Point, a rocky headland frequented by wild goats.

Distance
115km from Colintraive via Loch Fyne to Peninver

OS 1:50,000 Sheets
55 Lochgilphead & Loch Awe
62 North Kintyre & Tarbert
63 Firth of Clyde
68 South Kintyre & Campbelltown
(69 Isle of Arran)

Tidal Constants
Tighnabruaich:
HW Dover +0110
LW Dover +0120
Lochgilphead:
HW Dover +0120
LW Dover +0130
East Loch Tarbert:
HW Dover +0120
LW Dover +0110
Loch Ranza:
HW Dover +0100
LW Dover +0110
Carradale:
HW Dover +0120
LW Dover +0130
Campbelltown:
HW Dover +0120
LW Dover +0130

Sea Area
Malin

Submarine Areas
40 East Kyle, 38 West Kyle, 37 Skipness, 36 Tarbert, 35 Mingard, 58 Lochranza, 59 Davaar

Connections
Loch Fyne – see RoB p98
Crinan Canal – see CoB p327

9 West Kintyre

Oh Campbeltown Loch, I wish you were whisky!
Campbeltown Loch, Och Aye!
Oh Campbeltown Loch, I wish ye were whisky!
I wid drink ye dry.
I'd buy a yacht with the money I've got
And I'd anchor it out in the bay.
If I wanted a nip I'd go in for a dip.
I'd be swimmin' by night and by day!
Andy Stewart

From Peninver the shore passes through wracks which must give Yellow Rock its name. The remains of a castle and a church lead to Campbeltown Loch, overlooked by a prominent mast. At the head of the loch is **Campbeltown** itself, formerly with a score of whisky distilleries.

close inshore before heading off towards the southern end of Arran.

There is a dun site on the Bastard, the lower levels of which reveal conglomerate rocks.

At the end of Glen Hervie an excavator has expired on the beach, accompanied by more tipped rubbish.

The Castles are a series of dramatic rock formations on Gartnagerach Point, off which seals swim.

The places to which people have managed to move caravans are astonishing but the lower land behind Polliwilline Bay is an easy target for a mass of them. The headland before Macharioch Bay is a dramatic shape which has been chosen as a burial chamber site off which there is a small race, while the bay itself has a memorial cross. A long and attractive beach running to Cove Point has not been improved by the dumping of farm implements and other scrap metal along the back. Cove

Island Davaar with Campbeltown Loch to the right and Ru Stafnish in the distance.

Caves in the southeast face of Island Davaar.

Half of the mouth of the loch is blocked by Island Davaar which is connected to the southern shore by a low tide causeway. There is a lighthouse on the north side, goats grazing on the precipitous cliffs and seven caves on the south side, one of which contains a painting of the crucifixion by Alexander MacKinnon in 1887. It was 'discovered' and repaired by him in 1934 and then maintained by a local artist. A race off the southeast corner of the island runs at 7km/h in both directions with overfalls on the ebb. Davaar House overlooks Kildalloig Bay to the south of the island, with its guillemots.

Achinhoan Head is punctured by St Kieran's and other caves. Not just punctured is a wrecked car which lies at the base of the cliffs before a cairn, cliffs now being the dominant feature to Polliwilline Bay.

Three radio masts and an aero radio beacon mark Ru Stafnish. North of here the flood begins at HW Dover at up to 6km/h while the ebb starts at HW Dover +0600 at up to 7km/h. To the south the coast is subject to the Black Tide, part of the main eastgoing tide which cuts

Sheep Island and Sanda seen across the Sound of Sanda from Ru Stafnish.

Sound
of Jura

Keillmore

B8025

L na Cille

*Island
of Danna*

L Sween

*Eilean
Mòr*

Kilmory

*Kilmory
Bay*

L Coalisport

Pt of Knap

Ormsary

Knapdale

Cretshengan

*Kilberry
Head*

B8024

L Stornoway

WL Tarbert

Ardpatrick Pt

Ronachan Pt

Balochroy

*Gigha
Island*

Ardminish

Rhunahaorine

*Sound
of Gigha*

Tayinloan

*Cara
Island*

*Clachaig
Water*

Muasdale

Glenachardoch Pt

Glenbarr

*Barr
Water*

A83

*Bellochauntuy
Bay*

Bellochauntuy

Kintyre

Westport

*Machrihanish
Bay*

Machrihanish

B843

Peninver

B842

Campbelltown

Campbelltown L

*Island
Davaar*

*Achinhoan
Head*

*Firth of
Clyde*

Earadale Pt

*Rubh' a'
Mharaiche*

North
Channel

*Corrie
Glen*

Macharioch

*Polliwilline
Bay*

Carskiey

Southend

Cove Pt

*Mull of
Kintyre*

*Brunerican
Bay*

*Sheep
Island*

*Sanda
Island*

Point, with another dun site, has sandwich terns and eider ducks.

There is a significant race through the Sound of Sanda, ebbing from HW Dover −0110 and flooding from HW Dover +0500 to 9km/h. Close inshore on the north side the activity begins 1 hour 10 minutes later and the effects are much reduced. Tum ba nach is a heavy race extending north from Sheep Island to mid sound and race activity extends west and then south of Sanda Island. The Old Red Sandstone Sanda, with a single resident, and the other islands in the group were used for sheep grazing until 1946, the same year in which the Campbeltown reserve lifeboat picked up 54 people and a dog from the *Byron Darnton* in an 18 hour rescue in terrible conditions, pulling clear with engine trouble just as the ship broke in two. There is a rusty wreck near the lighthouse on the Ship or Prince Edward's Rock which is now served by a helicopter landing pad. There have been plenty of visitors prepared to risk the waters, though, particularly the Vikings. A Norse grave is found in a burial ground. There are also ruins of the chapel of St Ninian and the Bloody Castle. A beacon is located on Paterson's Rock. Sheep and Glunimore Islands are the most important in the Clyde for puffin breeding and there are major colonies of guillemots and razorbills in the group which the RSPB said were at risk from oil exploration in the North Channel off Dumfries & Galloway. Hurricane Jack and an English gunner were claimed to have sunk a German submarine here while the crew of the *Vital Spark* took to their punt without oars, being towed in to Campbelltown to rejoin their mother ship next morning.

This area is attracting interest for renewable energy installations. Brunerican Bay has four other signs of human habitation, a framework radio mast on Rubha MacShannuich, a standing stone, a golf course and the site of Dunaverty Castle. The latter was sited on Dunaverty Rock or Blood Rock and belonged to the Macdonalds, 300 of whom were put to death in 1647 by the Covenanters under General Leslie. On the east side of the castle Conieglen Water enters Brunerican Bay while an old slipway runs down from the west side into Dunaverty Bay, behind which more caravans are sited at Southend, the southern end of the B842. There is abundant oyster-plant.

Dunaverty Bay is a surf beach with lefts off the beach-break and rights off the rocks at the west end on the upper half of the tide. Southend Reef works at low tide with long runs left and the possibility of tubes on the right. Carskey Bay, which has little stream, produces rights off the rocks at the west end and lefts and rights off the steeply shelving beach at low tide.

St Columba is said to have first landed in Scotland here in 560 and there is a Category B chapel dedicated to him with his holy well behind the churchyard. St Columba's Footsteps are two right footprints carved in the rock, perhaps 3,000 years old. They may actually be examples of Fealty Foot where a chief had to stand to promise allegiance and protection to his clan. Caves on Keil Point contain a slab which may have been an altar.

The next 25km is some of the most remote and difficult around the entire British coastline. There is no road access except to the mull lighthouse. Beaches are virtually

Dunaverty with, beyond, Borgadalemore Point, the start of the mull itself, in perfect weather conditions.

The Mull of Kintyre lighthouse with the monster silhouette below.

absent and any landing must be between large rocks with a steep hill climb of, typically, 300m and then several kilometres of walking to the nearest track or road. The mull is at the narrowest part of the North Channel, creating the fastest flows, and the west side is exposed to full Atlantic swells which funnel in, especially with northwesterly winds. Not surprisingly, there are a number of serious races.

Carskey Bay ends with Breakerie Water and there is one further sandy inlet with a wreck close by before the going gets serious. This corner of the Mull of Kintyre is high and rugged with an area of forest in the centre, with eagles and other raptors. The rugged hillsides have also provided suitable defensive positions in the past and occasional dun, enclosure and fort sites are present. At sea level the birds are cormorants and oystercatchers while the remoteness means that the rocks are frequently attractive places for seals to lie up.

From Sròn Uamha a race runs parallel to the coast as far as the mull lighthouse. There is quieter water inside although eddies may operate. East of the point it may be calm for 1¾ hours of the race but as the race ceases at HW Dover +0610 there are heavy rollers for five to ten minutes.

Rubh' a' Mharaiche is overlooked by an inconspicuous dun but Rubha Dùin Bhàin is marked by its notable horizontal strata, a useful indicator for another point facing a race.

There are several caves at Uamh Ropa, the surroundings of one being white with cormorant guano, clearly a favourite spot for them.

Halfway between here and Earadale Point is a small beach, the first since Carskey Bay and a useful bolt hole although it is still a walk of several kilometres to the nearest track. The local residents are white goats with black heads and forelegs. There is another race off Skerrinagal by Earadale Point.

Uisaed is marked by a prominent cairn. The rocks of Skerrivore and a race which usually breaks lie off it. A bird hide watches guillemots, razorbills, herons and much more. A contra eddy begins northwards at HW Dover −0300 and southwards at HW Dover at up to 1km/h. Machrihanish at the end of the B843 has toilets and a post office and usually provides a safe landing regardless of conditions elsewhere. Across Machrihanish Water lie 5km of the best surf beach in southern Scotland, best at midtide on the flood. Machrihanish Bay catches the best of the Atlantic swells. The bay is backed by an extensive

Distinctive strata on Rubha Dùin Bhàin mark it out from other headlands.

Rubha na Lice is the nearest point of Great Britain to Ulster, being only 21km from Torr Head, and is likely to be the most exposed point with the main race and whirlpools only a few hundred metres offshore and usually a large swell even in calm conditions, especially with the stream setting SE. The northgoing flow starts at HW Dover −0130 and the southgoing flow at HW Dover +0430 at up to 9km/h on springs. The view from the lookout point on top of this final extremity of the Mull of Kintyre must include some wicked conditions at times. The constriction of the North Channel pushes the wind up a force.

The mull lighthouse is over 1km north. Below it is a rounded rock with two sharp pinnacles on top which appear in murky conditions like the silhouette of some giant animal.

After another 3km of the shoreline rising steeply to the peaks of Beinn na Lice and A'Chruach, the coast reaches a remote fort site. However, the remoteness is suddenly dispelled when a modern fence is spotted marching up the mountainside from the water and disappearing over the top, a major construction in this situation.

Young seal on the rocks at Earadale Point.

Seals dotted about the rocks in Ronachan Bay. Ardpatrick Point lies on the far side of West Loch Tarbert.

dune system which is topped by golf links. These are, in turn, overlooked by a line of watchtowers down the edge of the airfield. Formerly used by NATO forces, the airfield is said to have been used by the secret American Aurora. Even the existence of the plane was denied but, were it to exist, it would be an ideal place to base it, away from roads, a long way from centres of population and with one of the longest runways in Europe at 3km. It was an emergency landing site for the Space Shuttle. Despite the runway length, the distance by road from anywhere else would seem to be a disadvantage for its suggested use as the UK's first spaceport. Standing stones mark the end of the airfield.

Westport is also a useful surfing venue as it has road access, the A83 now following the shore closely. This break has rights which are best on the upper half of the tide provided the swell is not over 2m. With larger swells the surf breaks on reefs further out.

Fort and dun sites start 6km of rocky shoreline with many sandy inlets which can be entered between the rocks in quieter conditions. Back from them is Tangy Mill, built in 1820 and restored. Another group of duns and forts are grouped around Bellochantuy where the Argyll Hotel backs onto the beach with a telephone kiosk opposite.

Before the caravan site by Bellochantuy Bay is a burial ground which gives the Graveyard surfing break its name. It works best on a rising tide and breaks onto shifting sandbars. As the coast goes north there is progressively more shelter from Islay and Jura so the swells lessen in intensity.

A prominent arched stone bridge crosses the end of Barr Water which flows down past Glenbarr with its abbey, Clan Macalister Centre, shop and teas.

There are standing stones and duns both before and after the low rocky Glenacardoch Point. There is also a cave by a small beach as the A83 returns to the shore

after a brief foray away, a point where submarine cables were previously landed. Flows start north from here at HW Dover −0100 and south from HW Dover +0500 at up to 5km/h. Tidal constants vary by up to 2 hours 40 minutes with the time of day on this stretch of coast so an almanac should be consulted if accurate times are important. There is a shoal parallel to the shoreline with a passage inside. The coast is now low, ideal for curlews to pick over the beach debris.

Clachaig Water enters at Muasdale with yet more duns dotted about. At A'Chleit a church right by a line of rocks which run out into the sea shows a small belltower like a school bell. Progressively more shelter is gained from Cara Island with its distinctive Brownie's Chair, followed by Gigha Island itself as progress is made up the Sound of Gigha. The relics of dun, chambered cairn, standing stone and church ruin continue and seem totally in character.

Largie Castle was built at Tayinloan but the village is more important today as the ferry terminal for Ardminish on Gigha, the ferry carrying only 12 cars. The terminal area has useful toilets. The submarine cable to Gigha takes the rather shorter route to Rhunahaorine Point, a low sandy elbow which sticks out into the sound with long narrow beaches to north and south, the southern beach fronting a caravan site and a wood.

An airfield was built at Ballure as a target for fighter planes from Machrihanish. Standing stones in a field at Balochroy are easily seen from the water although a cist, cairn and dun over some 3km of coast are better hidden. Wildlife includes eider ducks and rhizostoma jellyfish but the most notable locals are the grey seals which haul out in bracken fringed Ronachan Bay, a popular viewpoint as there is a parking area where the A83 takes its leave of the west coast. The name is from place of seals.

This is the mouth of West Loch Tarbert, the first of several sea lochs which make northeasterly cuts in the

The MacCormaig Isles with Dubh Sgeir, Eilean Mòr, Corr Eilean, Eilean Ghamhna, Eilean nan Leac and Eilean a' Chapuill laid out with the c

The local ladies at Keillmore with their view across the Sound of Jura to the northern end of Jura.

west coast. Down it come car ferries to Port Askaig and Port Ellen on Islay. Ardpatrick Point is the southern extremity of Knapdale. Flows start north at HW Dover −0045 and south at HW Dover −0415 at 4km/h.

The coast becomes increasingly remote. Loch Stornoway issues from between rugged hills terminated by a cliff known as the Coves. Gannets dive for fish and black backed gulls search for anything they can scavenge.

A series of rocky outcrops with intervening sandy bays and cud chewing cattle lead up to Kilberry Head. Behind Kilberry Point is Kilberry Castle and a set of crosses which are fine late medieval sculptured stones.

To the north is a waterside caravan park while at the far end of Cretshengan Bay are a ruined church and a standing stone. On the other hand, there is little to mark the site of Dun Cragach.

Somehow it seems right that knapweed should grow here but montbretia among the ragwort and brambles at Port Maluaig is a colourful intruder.

Ormsary Water discharges under the B8024 into the clear water of Loch Caolisport at Ormsary opposite the Point of Knap. Between the two are Eilean Traighe which is a beach but not an island and Liath Eilein which is a suitably grey rock island.

Point of Knap is high on the south side but drops away quickly on the north side. A beacon off the end marks Bow of Knap rocks. Flows north start at HW Dover −0040 and south at HW Dover −0545 at up to 3km/h to Rubha na Cille. The point breaks up into a series of rocky islands of various sizes from small rocks to the MacCormaig Isles for the next 7km, taking in the mouth of Loch Sween.

At the back of Kilmory Bay is Kilmory itself with a cairn, a fort and, particularly, the Kilmory Knap Chapel ruin to St Maelrubha with 30 Celtic grave slabs depicting warriors, chiefs and hunters. Outside is a 3.5m high 15th century MacMillan's Cross with medieval carving com-

parable with the best on Iona, showing Jesus Christ, St Mary, St John and sword and knotwork on the front and a hunter, dogs and stag on the back. It was constructed under the Loch Sween school of monumental architecture. Stone was supplied from a quarry here to Iona.

From Eilean na Leac the view up Loch Sween shows Castle Sween prominently. Its black bulk seen against the light can make it seem more dominating than when actually passing it on the loch.

Flows north from Eilean Ghamhna run up to 6km/h but only to 5km/h southwards. Strong streams run between all the islands, with races and overfalls. Corr Eilean has a cairn but there is greater interest in Eilean Mòr with a 6th century hermit's cell, restored 12th century chapel, cave and Celtic cross of blue slate, possibly at the west end of St Cormac's tomb. The island is associated with John Paul Jones whose sloop, *Ranger*, is said to haunt the islands. This may be the galley with black sail which is said to pay an unexpected visit to the island every year and drive witnesses mad. There was an illicit still for passing fishermen which may have contributed to the madness. These days the island is owned by the Scottish National Party.

The Island of Danna is no longer, being attached to the rest of Knapdale by a short embankment. Its calcareous rocks are the base for a rich flora.

All following the southwest–northeast trend in their orientations are Eilean nan Uan, Liath Eilean, Loch na Cille, Rubha na Cille and a number of other islets. Flows at Rubha na Cille reach 6km/h.

A possible landing point is over the rocks at Keillmore, avoiding the nonchalantly swinging horns of a herd of highland cattle to reach the parking area at the head of the B8025. It is the route chosen for a submarine power cable which runs across the Sound of Jura. Jura has been steadily closing on the mainland and is now only some 7km off, providing plenty of shelter from the west.

Distance
115km from Peninver to Keillmore

OS 1:50,000 Sheets
55 Lochgilphead & Loch Awe
62 North Kintyre & Tarbert
68 South Kintyre & Campbelltown
(69 Isle of Arran)

Tidal Constants
Campbelltown:
HW Dover +0120
LW Dover +0130
Sanda Island:
HW Dover +0040
Southend:
HW Dover +0040
LW Dover +0100
Machrihanish:
Dover +0230
Sound of Gigha:
HW Dover +0340
LW Dover +0420
Carsaig Bay:
Dover −0610

Sea Area
Malin

Submarine Areas
59 Davaar, 68 Stafnish, 67 Sanda, 66 Kintyre, 57 Earadale, 56 Gigha, 33 Jura Sound

Connections
West Loch Tarbert – see RoB p100
Loch Sween – see RoB p103

...aks of Jura in the background.

10 Northeast Sound of Jura

Keillmore has Keills chapel with a 15th century grave slab with sword and clasach, possibly for a father and son who were harpists to the MacNeills of Gigha. There are also other fine grave slabs. The chapel may have been visited by St Columba on his way to meet King Connal.

Streams start north at HW Dover –0100 and south at HW Dover +0500 at up to 7km/h but there can be eddies close inshore. South of Crinan most of the rise and fall takes place in the 3 hours 30 minutes after the turn of the tide with a stand until the next turn.

Wildlife immediately makes its presence known with seals and sea otters. Oystercatchers and curlews operate along the shoreline and cattle graze the rough pasture. The shoreline is as interesting as the peaks up to 130m Barr Thormaid would suggest and the first few metres are sloping rock up to a wavecut platform, making it difficult to get out with a boat.

The islets with their bracken and stunted bushes make a delightful trip. Inside of Leth Sgeir a northgoing eddy works on the southgoing stream. There are passages inside

Eilean nan Coinean and Eilean Fraoich. A little more care is needed inside Eilean Dubh with its herons. The passage is outside Eilean Tràighe rather than the more obvious inside passage which is a dead end.

Carsaig Bay with its clear water is popular with holidaymakers, being well sheltered with a beach off which a power cable runs under the Sound of Jura to Jura. Contra eddies run across the mouth in both directions.

Carsaig Island is not high but the vertical rock strata have fallen away to produce an interesting rock sculpture.

A dun is lost in the forest between Sàilean na h-Earba and Sàilean Mór and red deer graze openly near the edge of the water.

Flows start north at HW Dover –0130 and south at HW Dover +0450 at up to 7km/h. In the centre of the sound, where a white lighthouse stands on Ruadh Sgeir, the flows are up to 8km/h. Dolphins feed in schools, arcing over here and there as they surface for air with hydraulic hisses and disappear below the surface again.

As Jura closes in on the mainland there are two result-

Leth Sgeir, Eilean nan Coinean and Eilean Fraoich.

Jura, seen across the Sound of Jura from Knapdale.

ing effects. One is the scenery becoming steadily more stunning with Jura, Scarba, Luing, Mull and a panorama of smaller islands of breathtaking beauty. Seen with evening or morning sunlight, it is a truly memorable area. The other is that the stream flowing up the Sound of Jura is steadily accelerated until it is off Crinan where it is forced to turn left through the Dorus Mór and out between Jura and Scarba through the Gulf of Corryvreckan with its whirlpool, which can be heard roaring from Crinan when it is active.

There is a small race off Ardnoe Point to be faced by

The passage between Eilean Dubh and Eilean Tràighe is in the centre of the picture with Eilean Fraoich in the foreground on the left.

The sheltered passage between Eilean Dubh and Eilean Tràighe.

those making for the quieter waters of the Crinan Canal. Otherwise, flows at the mouth of Loch Crinan, over-looked by Ardifuir with its broch, are relatively weak. The main flow is not just making a sharp left turn but is doing so at a point where Loch Crinan, Loch Craignish and other passages are leading off from the outside of the bend and the main part of the flow is obstructed by a number of islands. The main feature is the Dorus Mór or great door between Garbh Rèisa and Craignish Point. The flow westwards begins at HW Dover −0200 and eastwards at HW Dover +0440 at up to 15km/h. There is an eddy next to Garbh Rèisa and another on the north side of the Dorus Mór, especially on the westgoing stream with heavy overfalls along the eddyline. A race up to Eil-ean nan Coinean, a race off Craignish Point and a race to the east of Rèisa Mhic Phaidean on the northgoing flow with a southgoing eddy along the mainland coast follow. During the southgoing flow there are overfalls across the north end of this channel, southwards along the mainland coast and across the entrance to the Dorus Mór. At full flow it can be a continuous area of turbulence from the south and east of the Dorus Mór to Coiresa on the westerly flow with races up to Luing and far beyond the Gulf of Corryvreckan. In 1820 it wrecked the *Comet*, the first steamship to go to sea. At slack neap tides there is barely a swirl on the surface.

Craignish Castle stands beyond the end of the B8002 at the head of the sheltered Loch Beag. Eilean Ona and its islets offer shelter to Achanarnich Bay but even on the calmest of days the Atlantic swell finds its way through and fronds of kelp are pushed out of the water by the surges like the fins of a school of sharks, watched by cormorants.

A fort, dun and cairns sit at the base of a ridge which runs along the east side of the sound, broken only by Bàgh Bàn.

Beyond Eilean Arsa in Loch Shuna a forest of masts marks Craobh Haven, a yacht harbour which has been built by linking a ring of islands together with embankments to the mainland.

Carsaig Bay, the most heavily populated point on the Knapdale coast, with hills rising to Torr Mór and Cruach Lusach beyond.

Between Jura and Scarba lies the Gulf of Corryvreckan, deceptively quiet at the turn of the tide on a still day.

Distance
31km from Keillmore to Craobh Haven

OS 1:50,000 Sheet
55 Lochgilphead & Loch Awe

Tidal Constants
Carsaig Bay:
Dover −0610
Loch Melfort:
Dover −0600

Sea Area
Malin

Submarine Areas
33 Jura Sound,
31 Mull

Connection
Crinan Canal – see CoB p325

11 Shuna

Shuna, one of the Slate Islands, is most easily reached by launching from Arduaine jetty. Eilean Creagach is a halfway stepping stone.

Currents are not strong although they are likely to be most active in Shuna Sound.

Although less than half the length of neighbouring Luing, it is almost the same height, Druim na Dubh Glaic rising to 90m, and has considerably more woodland, the northern two thirds being ringed with trees. Shuna provides excellent sheep grazing and the island's half dozen residents are crofters. The trees drop away after Poll na Gile and the coastline becomes more rugged.

Travelling westwards along the southern coast will bring the pained looks of surprised animals grazing among the rocks and stunted bushes which are the prevailing features. There are occasional fences but these appear to have been abandoned and the animals left to their own devices.

The strata dip towards the east and so this side of the island has a low sloping rockface. At intervals the onshore waves have cut through to form small bays which look out to the south. Thrift takes a foothold on the rocks and long strands of seaweed contrast with the assortment of wracks found on the west side of the island.

The islands provide an ever changing panorama. From Shuna Point the southern end of Luing is dwarfed by Scarba.

The exposure of Shuna Point to the elements is most graphically illustrated by lines of quartz which run to and fro across the rocks like trails of icing, the harder white

quartz standing proud of the softer black igneous rock. At various points on the west coast it can be seen how the cooling lava has been rolled over on itself as the molten rock flowed.

Shuna Cottage stands at the head of an inlet and the trees return at this point, windswept bushes brushed flat by the westerly wind, and yet the field to the east of the cottage can show an excellent display of buttercups in the summer. Rabbits chase around on the hillsides, a fact which does not escape the attention of a soaring golden eagle.

After the white Shuna Cottage there is a view straight up Shuna Sound, Seil Sound and perhaps even Clachan Sound, edged in turn by Shuna, Luing, Torsa, Seil and the mainland, as straight as a die for over 10km.

Because of the easterly dip of the rocks, the west coast of Shuna is higher and the broken strata stack up from the water.

Rubh'an Aoil is nearly an island, Port na Cro working back towards a corresponding inlet at the north end of Shuna. Rounding the point brings a change of view with Loch Melfort, Asknish Bay and the mountains of the mainland forming a ridge behind. Disproportionately obvious in the foreground are Scoul Eilean and Eilean Gamhna, the latter distinctively shaped like a large brimmed hat or a submarine. A float plane taking off from Loch Melfort, however, may not just be an illusion.

Passing Rubha Salach adds Eilean Creagach to the view and the following headland brings the contrasting colours of Craobh Haven into the picture.

Shuna seen from Arduaine with Eilean Creagach in front and Luing behind. The highest peak is Scarba with Jura to its left.

An otter is eating a fish on the weed in the centre of the picture.

Residents search the rocks on the southeastern side of Shuna.

Shuna Cottage beside Shuna Sound. Luing is visible beyond.

A wreck on the shore at the northern end of Shuna.

Shuna House is the most distinctive building on the island, castellated throughout and with round towers at the corners, the result of someone's flight of fancy.

A light on Sgeir Chreagag is draped in debris and takes the shape of a person standing on the rocks. Port an t-Salainn is littered with a score of rusting pontoons.

In the water the lion's mane and moon jellyfishes might be seen on the crossing back to the mainland.

Shuna House's irregular profile rises above the treeline on the northeast corner of the island.

Shuna's pier is sheltered by Sgeir Chreagag.

Distance
Shuna is 4km long and lies 1km off Craobh Haven

OS 1:50,000 Sheet
55 Lochgilphead & Loch Awe

Tidal Constants
Loch Melfort:
Dover −0600
Loch Beag:
HW Dover −0620,
LW Dover −0600

Sea Area
Malin

Submarine Area
31 Mull

Weathered rocks on the east side of the island.

12 Luing

The convenient point to launch for a circumnavigation of Luing is at Cuan Ferry, the end of the B8003 at the southern tip of Seil where there are parking and public toilets (with a notice preventing their use for changing). Although the island is well sheltered from the elements it is subject to swift currents on most sides. To make the best use of these currents it would pay to launch a couple of hours before low tide in order to get the ebb down one side and the flood back up the other. If this is not possible then it would be worth taking Shuna Sound with the current and hugging the other coast even though currents tend to be stronger in the centre of the Sound of Luing.

The fastest currents, however, are to be found in Cuan Sound. Watching the small but powerful car ferry doing high crosses of the jet of current, complete with whirlpools, which runs through the centre of the sound at times brings the point home forcefully. Residents of Luing have called for a bridge.

Water that is more placid might be encountered on moving south out of Cuan Sound. It might also bring other factors such as herds of seals, the heads of which rise and drop in the water as a boat approaches and then follow, either inquisitive or seeing it off the premises. Perhaps one of many herons takes to the air while disturbed from feeding in the narrow channel past Torsa Beag.

This channel is constricted and can produce a respectable sea rapid down into Ardinamar Bay when the tide conditions are right. Irene MacLachlan, born at Ardinamar in 1910, insisted that all passing yacht crews call in and sign her visitors' books, of which there were a total of nine volumes eventually.

Other bird life follows in a constant stream, snipes, oystercatchers, cormorants and diverse divers.

Caistal nan Con near the northern end of Torsa guards where Cuan Sound joins Seil Sound. While Seil is low

Luing seen across Cuan Sound from Cuan Ferry.

Looking south from Cuan Ferry towards Torsa.

The mountains of Mull show above Torsa.

The light on Fladda off Cullipool with Garbh Eileach and Belnahua beyond.

and largely treeless, the mainland shore of Seil Sound is steep and wooded.

The hillside on the mainland drops steadily from 273m high Dun Crutagain past Dùn fadaidh to Degnish Point.

The prevailing wind blows up Shuna Sound and this can produce a significant chop on an ebb tide. Luing has low rocks at all but the northwest corner, accessible for an emergency exit and providing some protection from westerly winds, as Torsa does to craft further north.

Not visible at Toberonochy is the ruined Kilchattan Chapel with its magnificent slate graves, including that of Alex Campbell who 'digged my grave before I died.' There is a recent church, however, and a school serving

Across the Firth of Lorn on Mull a mountain wall rises from the water with peaks behind climbing to twice that height, a majestic sight. Nearer, whitecaps mark the speed of the sheet of water sweeping down the Sound of Luing, equally to be respected.

Approaching Poll Gorm, the array of small islands becomes confusing but the lighthouse on Fladda and the white pillar on Dubh Sgeir set these two apart from the main group which offer a sheltered passage from the quartering seas. Luing's main industry, based at Cullipool, is lobster fishing, lobsters being sent to Kerrera for package and despatch. Fraoch Eilean has one of Scotland's largest lobster ponds.

Distance
Luing is 9km long
and lies 200m off Seil
with ferry access

OS 1:50,000 Sheet
55 Lochgilphead
& Loch Awe

Tidal Constants
Loch Melfort:
Dover −0600
Loch Beag:
HW Dover −0620,
LW Dover −0600

Sea Area
Malin

Submarine Area
31 Mull

the island's population of a couple of hundred. The village is formed of cottages for slate miners and had the main sorting office for Slate Islands mail.

A planted wood on Àird Luing is in such obvious contrast with the rest of the island that it forms a prominent landmark. The scenery, a vista of rugged mountains, islands and sea, reaches its best so far with ridge after ridge of mountains, each a paler grey than the one in front, reaching away down the mainland through Craignish to Knapdale Forest.

Bàgh na h-Àird gives a false indication of the southern end of Luing although there is a channel to the north of Rubh' Àird Luing at high tide, cutting the corner and avoiding the worst of the inevitable beam sea. This point is just 6km from the Corryvreckan whirlpool and a southwesterly wind and the right tidal conditions will bring its roar within hearing.

Scarba is continued northwards with Lunga, Fiola Meadhonach, Rubha Fiola, Ormsa and Belnehua.

On Luing, contorted black slate is outlined by white rock which has been twisted at the same time. A cave sits above high tide level behind Camas nan Gall and higher again may be seen the prize beef cattle for which the island is renowned.

The Atlantic Islands Centre in Cullipool has natural and cultural heritage exhibitions and a restaurant.

Until 1965 the story was different. It was then that the slate quarries were closed.

Luing is a Slate Island and 150 men were turning out 700,000 slates each year at one time, roofing structures including Iona cathedral.

Although there are some heaps of slate waste south of Cullipool, most lie to the north near the quarries, occupied now only by hooded crows. Here, Luing's cliffs are highest and the waters roughest.

The run up the final part of the west coast of Luing is dominated by the conspicuous white cottages of Easdale and Ellenabeich and by the bulk of Dùn Mór rising above them.

Whatever Cuan Sound was doing on departure, it is bound to be doing something different on return. The interesting waters surrounding Luing, like its scenery and its wildlife, can be relied upon to produce the unexpected.

Toberonochy on the east side of Luing.

13 Scarba

And Scarba's isle, whose tortured shore
Still rings to Corrievreken's roar
Sir Walter Scott

The Sound of Jura tapers in towards its northern end. As the tide floods northwards it is squeezed, at its top end finding several routes to escape to the Firth of Lorn. These routes are all fairly constricted and some dramatic water results.

In Argyll & Bute, the island forms part of the Scarba, Lunga & the Garvellachs National Scenic Area. Rugged and bleak, it covers 18km². Perhaps called the Isle of Cormorants from the Norse skarf-øy, it probably takes its name from the Norse skarpoe, rough isle. With schist at the east end and quartzite at the west, it is near the southern side of the Highland Boundary Fault.

The nearest access point without an open crossing from a mainland public road is at Traigh nam Musgan. There is some poor parking in an area which seems to be used for dumping farm waste, including slurry. The route from here passes the southern ends of Shuna and Luing and crosses Shuna Sound and the Sound of Luing. Other options include Craobh Haven or the jetty at Arduaine. An alternative shorter approach is to take the ferry to Luing and launch from Black Mill Bay.

This chapter starts from the small island towards the north end of the east side. Inside it is what serves as a jetty. There are no harbours. The east side is wooded, mostly deciduous with the occasional pine. Before the bracken and heather get going there are plenty of spring flowers, bluebells, primroses, celandines, violets and thrift. Wrack, limpets and cockles occupy the shoreline and the birdlife includes oystercatchers, blackbacked gulls, greylag geese and buzzards while peacock butterflies give the appearance of being weather worn, perhaps a true reflection of the conditions.

Rubh'a'Chùil faces Lunga across Bealach a'Choin Ghlais, the Little Corryvreckan Gulf. In the middle of the entrance is Eilean a'Bhealaich, marked by a leaning white pole. To the west of this small island run the Grey Dogs, a significant tide race with standing waves. It flows west from an hour before Dover high water on spring tides or twenty minutes before Dover high water on neaps. It is eastgoing on springs from five hours twenty minutes after Dover high water and on neaps from six hours after Dover high water although it is not unusual for these times to be up to an hour out. Spring flows run at 16km/h. When the flow is westwards there is a strong eddy on the north side and if there are westerly winds opposing the flow the race runs from the west entrance for 1.5km towards Lunga. The area just south of the island is known to be difficult. Nevertheless, herons and otters use the sound and there seem to be lobster pots around much of the island, which has clear water.

To the west of the sound a panorama of islands opens out, Guirasdeal close in, then the Garvellachs, then Mull, rising in lines of irregular peaks. This is part of a wonderful seascape which continues towards Colonsay. The highest point of Scarba, 449m Cruach Scarba, from the Gaelic for heap, is only 800m from the shoreline. The strata dip to the southeast so the northwest side of the island is steeper and higher. At intervals there are caves, not at water level but in gaps between strata beds. In calm conditions, this not being a trip to be undertaken with significant wind or swell, there are a number of cobble beaches where it is possible to land, including Port an Eag-uillt.

As well as being the Isle of Cormorants there are shags and rafts of guillemots.

The Gulf of Corryvreckan can be one of the most ferocious pieces of water in the British Isles. The tidal range at the west end is 3.4m whereas 1.6km away at the east end it is only 1.5m and high water is thirty minutes earlier. At spring tides there can be 900mm difference, the kind of fall on a white water river. The westwards flow through the gulf can be 16km/h with eddies nearly as strong as the main flow, the 32km/h differential across the eddyline helping set up the Corryvreckan whirlpool which is the world's second largest, outdone only by Norway's Maelstrom. Eastwards flows run to 11km/h.

Approaching Scarba. Jura and the Gulf of Corryvreckan are on the left and Lunga and the Grey Dogs on the right beyond Luing.

Guirasdeal with the Garvellachs just visible through the haze.

The Grey Dogs in Bealach a'Choin Ghlais with Lunga beyond.

The bottom is very uneven. The Hag or Cailleach rises quickly from over 100m to 29m deep 400m off Camas nan Bàirneach. Steeper on the east side, this rock arm sets up what is, effectively, a roostertail which can be up to 8m high and can be heard 16km away. Currents set towards the Scarba shore and are much stronger on the north side. Eddies form downstream of points and there are overfalls where eddies meet the main flow. A strong flow runs eastwards from five and a half hours after Dover high water at springs and from six hours after Dover high water at neaps. The westgoing flow runs from an hour and ten minutes before Dover high water on springs and twenty minutes before Dover high water on neaps. This westgoing flow is stronger and can have heavy overfalls for 8km at the west end as part of the Great Race which can run for 12km from ten minutes after Dover high water. When this westwards flow is running there is a huge eddy on the north side of the west end. Conditions are more exposed at the west end and it can break right across to the Jura shore with wind against tide. Ugly conditions can also be produced if there is any swell.

In calm conditions it is possible to land between the rocks below the cliffs but conditions do not stay calm for long. The island has fallow and red deer and these watch from close by, interested rather than concerned.

The gulf is named after the cauldron of Brechan, grandson of Niall of the Nine Hostages, High King of Ireland, who drowned here with his entire fleet of fifty curraghs about 1,400 years ago. Later, one of his ribs rose to greet kinsman St Columba as he sailed past, becoming caught in the whirlpool himself but stilling it by casting in some earth from the grave of his friend, St Kiaran, which he happened to have with him. How the owner of the rib was identified is not clear but stalks of kelp do passable impressions today. A Gaelic translation of the name means speckled corrie. Another explanation is that Brechan was a Norwegian prince who fell in love with an island chief's daughter and was required to prove himself by anchoring in the whirlpool for three days and nights with successive cables of hemp, wool and maidens' hair. Each failed in turn, the latter because one of the hairs' contributors was not as innocent as she should have been and her hair was under strength, and the prince drowned. His body was

The northwest coast of Scarba.

Rubha nam Faoileann towards Scarba's most westerly point.

dragged ashore by his dog and buried under a stone in Uamh Bhreacain cave. Why he did not drown on either of the previous nights is not clear.

It had also been called Morrigan's Cauldron, a morgen being a sea woman, mermaid or water spirit.

The western end of the gulf with Eilean Mòr and Jura beyond.

Caves facing onto the Gulf of Corryvreckan.

The gulf has claimed many lives and a cruiser had a near miss going through sideways during the Second World War. George Orwell's party on a camping trip in a small boat in 1947 had their outboard ripped off, the boat then capsizing. They all swam to a nearby small island and were later rescued by a fishing boat. A more recent story relates to Donald Ross, who kept sheep on Scarba in the 1950s and 60s. His dog fell in and drowned. That night Donald dreamed that the dog was on a particular rock and, in the morning, found this to be the case. It was used for the climax of the film *I Know Where I'm Going!*

On the south side of the Gulf of Corryvreckan Eilean Mòr and Eilean Beag precede Bàgh Gleann nam Muc

and 190m high An Cruachan, the most northerly peak on Jura.

At Rubha Righinn slack water is encountered two hours before low or high water and there is a south-westerly eddy into the gulf when the stream is north-wards in the Sound of Luing.

There are two houses on Scarba, one a grey bothy overlooking Bàgh Gleann a'Mhaoil, which has a rela-tively accessible boulder beach and slack conditions when a westgoing eddy runs out from the eastgoing stream.

Maol Buidhe, 103m high, stands close to the shore. Off it might be seen to be some of the island's colony

The Gulf of Corryvreckan with Eilean Mòr conspicuous. The picture was taken on a calm day, near slack water with the flow still towards the whirlpool, the breaking wave of which is just visible on the horizon immediately right of the main line of dark turbulence.

The Gulf of Corryvreckan with Jura beyond.

of common seals or even submarines exercising in the Sound of Luing. Strong tidal streams separate from the coast with calmer water inshore and a northgoing eddy on a southerly stream.

Port nan Sliseag hardly deserves the name although it has some interesting lava rolls resisting the sea. The other house is the prominent white Kilmory Lodge, usually occupied only during the deer shooting season, standing above the site of a chapel which must have had a rather limited congregation.

Back on the mainland, around Traigh nam Musgan there are limited facilities. Despite its short season and lack of licensing, the Cabin in Craobh Haven is recommended as being user friendly.

Lava rolls at Port nan Sliseag.

Kilmory Lodge, the main dwelling above the treeline on Scarba.

Distance
Scarba is 6km long and lies 4km off the Craignish peninsula. It is 2km off Luing which has ferry access

OS 1:50,000 Sheet
55 Lochgilphead & Loch Awe

Tidal Constants
*Loch Beag:
HW Dover −0620,
LW Dover −0600
Glengarrisdale Bay:
HW Dover −0530,
LW Dover −0520*

Sea Area
Malin

Submarine Areas
*31 Mull,
33 Jura Sound*

14 Seil

In order to make the best use of the tides while circumnavigating Seil it would pay to begin from Cuan Ferry at the south end of the island a couple of hours before high water, the same place at the end of the B8003 as suggested for Luing. Modest flows are met in the Sound of Insh and Clachan Sound and these should be taken into consideration. This chapter takes the clockwise direction.

Standing waves can form in the tide stream as it races through Cuan Sound. More difficult, though, are the increasing beam seas caused by the prevailing wind funelling the waves into Port a' Mhuilinn. Shelter is reached in Easdale Sound as the island of Easdale gives respite and at the same time eclipses Garbh Eileach and the seascape of other islands that have been visible this far. Easdale island was brought into prominence as the subject of Garth and Vicky Waite's *Island* wildlife study. There is enough slate left for it to have become the host to the world stone skimming championships in September.

Like Easdale, Seil is a Slate Island because of the 20th century slate industry, the dilapidated pier at Ellanabeich being a legacy. Ellenabeich was an island which became joined onto Seil by tipping slate waste. In 1881 the quarries, up to 76m deep, were breached by a storm surge. The village of Ellenabeich itself is fascinating, three rows of single storey whitewashed terraced houses, two back to back and one facing with no gardens and front doors opening straight onto the village streets, only rain butts giving protection from any passing vehicles. The village has the Highland Arts Exhibition featuring CJ Taylor, craft shops, tea rooms and such attractions to draw in the tourists during the holiday season.

Turning out into the Sound of Insh, the water becomes confused with waves reflecting off Rubha Mhic Mharcuis, not settling down until after Sloc nan Sgarbh. This coastline, the only section with cliffs which prevent easy exit, has several attempts at caves, often above present sea level.

The Colonsay car ferries pass to the north of Insh on their run in to Oban although other large ships use the Sound of Insh.

Their route up the Sound of Kerrera, together with

The Garvellachs break the horizon.

Easdale island with Mull beyond.

Kerrera and Oban can be viewed while moving up this coast.

Roe deer may possibly be seen ashore as this is one of only three British islands inhabited by this species. The quiet boater may be rewarded by an encounter with a sea otter, present in this area.

As the waves die away beyond Rubha Garbh Airde, the problem becomes one of navigation as the northern end of Clachan Sound is hard to find. At high tide it may be possible to cut between Eilean nan Freumha and Eilean nan Beathach but at other times it will be necessary to round the latter, its northern extremity marked by a red oil drum with a rock on top. After rounding it, it is important not to take the main channel which is a dead end but to look on the east side for the narrow Clachan Sound, especially at low tide when the northern end of it dries out.

It is not only the boater who has this problem. In 1873 a school of 192 pilot whales, normally rare in British waters, were stranded in the sound by the tide. It dries at low water.

Traditional cottages at Ellenabeich.

The Oyster Bar & Restaurant in Ellenabeich.

Ellenabeich and Dùn Mór.

Looking west from the foot of Beinn Mhór with Eilean nam Beathach and Seil on the left and Eilean Dùin and Mull on the right.

The Bridge over the Atlantic and Clachan Sound.

Purple-flowered fairy foxglove growing on Clachan Bridge.

Small craft moored in Seil Sound.

Islands lie dotted about in Balvicar Bay.

Clachan Sound is straight and narrow, almost like a large canal complete with swans, except for the swift currents through it and the many shells visible on the bed through the clear water. There were plans to fill in the sound but it was retained for use by fishing boats.

Constructed in 1792, Clachan Bridge is also known as the Atlantic Bridge or the Bridge over the Atlantic as it spans the Atlantic or 22m of it, carrying the B844 over a steep 8.2m high arch.

A biological rarity of the sound is the purple-flowered fairy foxglove which grows on Clachan Bridge.

The matter of being overseas was important after the 1745 uprising when the Scots could only wear kilts legally overseas. The nearby Tigh-an-Truish Hotel was used by returning men to change out of the hated trousers.

A fishing boat wreck in the early stages of decay precedes the Willowburn Hotel, another wreck resembling an early car ferry rusting away on the mainland shore opposite Balvicar Bay. Balvicar Bay is a mooring for pleasure and lobster fishing boats. Balvicar also has slate quarries, closed in 1965, and Winterton has boatyards. Research has shown that a colony of molluscs at Balvicar have marked genetic differences from a colony of the same species 150m away at Winterton. Again, there are sea otters present.

The west side of Seil Sound may have marine farms and in front of a fort site an area of the centre of the sound is laid out with closely spaced floats.

While Seil is low and treeless, the mainland shore of Seil Sound is steep and wooded. Ardmaddy Castle stands back from the head of Ardmaddy Bay but walls of extruded rock on the shoreline look like the remains of some former stronghold.

An iron pillar marks the corner north of Pòrt Mór, after which Seil's only area of woodland rises up from the shore and Torsa has also been selected for forestry.

Rounding Rubha Breac brings the accelerating currents that signal arrival back in Cuan Sound.

Distance
Seil is 7km long and lies 40m off Clachan with road access

OS 1:50,000 Sheets
*49 Oban &
East Mull
55 Lochgilphead
& Loch Awe*

Tidal Constants
*Seil Sound:
HW Dover −0540,
LW Dover −0550
Loch Melfort:
Dover −0600*

Sea Area
Malin

Submarine Area
31 Mull

15 Kerrera

A panoramic sweep of scenery

Then take a sail across to Kerrera some day,
And see Gylen Castle with its wild-strewn shore and bay,
With its gigantic walls and towers of rocks
Shivered into ghastly shapes by the big waves' thundering shocks.
William Topaz McGonagall

The north end of Clachan Sound opens out onto the Firth of Lorn and a panoramic view, perhaps seen at its best from the remains of the quarry on the east side of the sound. The west side of the sound breaks up into a group of small islands, the largest and most northerly of which is Eilean Dùin, resembling a ruined castle. Then, in

Looking across the Firth of Lorn from the northern end of Clachan Sound to Mull.

Looking up the Sound of Kerrera with Kerrera on the left and Meall Buidhe on the right.

The rugged bulk of Meall Buidhe forms the southeastern side of the Sound of Kerrera.

The Sound of Kerrera from Rubha Tolmach with Rubh' an Fheurain and the Little Horse Shoe just visible on the right.

a much broader sweep are Scarba beyond Seil and Luing, Mull, Kerrera, the Kingairloch shore and a fair bit more. It is a place to spend some minutes or more absorbing the view before moving on to change the perspective of the kaleidoscope of islands.

The quarry is at the foot of 194m high Beinn Mhór which has a fort site near its summit at an excrescence known as the Toad of Lorn. The east side remains high as it leads into the Sound of Kerrera with Meall Buidhe at 207m. Between Beinn Mhór and Beinn Buidhe is the mouth of Loch Feochan, a tortuous affair which protects the loch from the elements. Minard Point, on the north side of the loch entrance, is the location for An Dùnan while opposite it, to the east of Barrnacarry Bay, is Dùn Mhic Raonuill. Rising above all in the distance are the peaks of Cruachan.

Flows in Kerrera Sound start northeast at HW Dover −0100 and southwest at HW Dover +0500 up to 3km/h with eddies on both sides.

The Sound of Kerrera usually brings water which is more sheltered. The ivy clad cliffs support trees where they can get a grip and the location is ideal for golden eagles which might be seen perched on rocks quite close to the water. Kerrera is formed of basalts, schists and Old Red Sandstone.

Port na Tràigh-Linne and Aird na Cùile may have fish farms, one by a dun site at Gallanach, while three disused transatlantic submarine cables land at Port Lathaich.

A white navigation light tower dominates Rubh 'an Fheurain for ships using the sound, not least of which is the Colonsay car ferry.

The old slate quarrymen's cottages behind the Little Horse Shoe and below Kerrera's highest point, 189m high Carn Breugach, were used as the base for a lobster trading

Kerrera Sound with Ardentrive Bay.

business in 1910, becoming one of the largest on the west coast of Scotland, taking lobsters from Cullipool on Luing. A telephone cable from the mainland to support the business was the first on a Hebridean island. One cottage has a parrot sanctuary.

The mainland shore is now coarse conglomerate rock which can be used as a landing point at Gallanachmore to give access to the first road since Clachan Bridge.

From Gallanachmore flows start northeast at HW Dover −0100 and southwest at HW Dover +0500 at up to 5km/h with eddies on both sides.

Port nan Cuilc has a wreck which has narrowly missed a submarine power cable across to Kerrera and lies at the foot of road reconstruction at Gallanachbeg. A radio mast and fort site on Dùn Uabairtich look down on a crossing point to Kerrera which is used by a passenger ferry and two more submarine cables in Horse Shoe Bay. The passenger ferry is summoned to the mainland by turning the white warning notice so that the ferryman can see it across the sound.

The Horse Shoe itself has been the anchorage of fleets which have not been too successful in their activities. In 1249 Alexander II anchored here before attempting to win the Hebrides back from King Haakon of Norway but died suddenly of fever, the land behind the bay now being called Dalrigh, field of the king. Haakon himself anchored here in 1263 on his way to the Battle of Largs, where he was defeated. He used the anchorage on his way home but died, too, before he reached Norway.

A church dating from 1872, later a school, stands at the northeast end of the Horse Shoe. These days there is a population of 34 on the island although it was 105 in 1861.

There is a dry ski slope at Rubha Tolmach belonging to Kildowie Outdoor Centre belonging to North Lanarkshire Council.

Heather Island stands in the centre of the sound on the approach to Oban Bay, where salmon farming takes place in floating tanks.

There may be a marine farm in Ardentrive Bay, guarded by cormorants. It also contains the rusting wreck of a small boat. At one time cattle were brought across to Kerrera from Mull and were then swum from here to Oban.

Use of Oban Bay and its approaches between Kerrera Sound and Maiden Island is governed by a code of practice affecting all craft.

The northern end of Kerrera Sound with Maiden Island, Lismore and Mull and the Kingairloch beyond.

Oban with McCaig's Folly on the skyline on the left and the Caledonian MacBrayne ferry terminal on the right.

An unlikely item on the Oban skyline is McCaig's Folly of 1897–1900, built with Bonawe granite by local labour to counter unemployment. Its 9–14m high walls 600mm thick are based on the Colosseum. Local banker and gasworks owner John McCaig wanted to make it a museum to his family but he died before adding the huge lookout tower which was to have graced the centre. The next hill has another folly, the remains of what would have been a hydropathic centre where customers would have come to take the waters but the project ran out of money. An observation platform was added in 1983 and the courtyard landscaped. Floodlit at night, it is used for drama productions in the summer and the Gaelic Mod, a fortnight's festival of song, music and poetry. On each side is a transmission mast. The police just miss intercepting the *Susannah* here in *The Five Red Herrings*.

A contributory factor to the position of **Oban** (Gaelic for little bay), at the end of the A85 and A816, as one of the busiest ports in Britain, one of the best natural ports on the west coast of Scotland, and its title of the Gateway to the Isles is the island of Kerrera which acts as a substantial weatherbreak. The piers serve as bases for fishing vessels and the occasional diving support vessel but, most importantly, they include the terminal for the Caledonian MacBrayne ferries, paddle steamers having operated from here since 1851. The ferries to Mull, Coll, Tiree, Barra, South Uist, Lismore, Fort William and Morvern operate through the narrow northern entrance to Oban Bay, passing the monument to founder David Hutcheson on the northeastern end of the island. The company successfully resisted government attempts at privatization, to the widespread relief of islanders worried about their future ferry services, currently heavily subsidized.

Caves in Oban were occupied in Stone Age times. Boswell House is on the site of a 'tolerable inn' used by James Boswell and Dr Johnson. The British Society of Extending the Fisheries set up a fishing station here after the success of one in Roghadal in 1786. The Oban distillery was founded in 1794 and produces a malt whisky aged for 12 years. More recent arrivals include the railway in 1880, a vital transport link with the islands. The Roman Catholic cathedral was built as recently as 1952. Other features include Oban Glassworks, the Highland Discovery Centre with theatre, cinema and exhibition and World in Miniature with $\frac{1}{12}$th scale rooms, furniture, dioramas and holograms. There is a swimming pool. This used to be the yachting centre of the west.

The war memorial in Oban Bay is a suitable launch point with parking adjacent and a sloping ramp down to the rocky shore. Currents are not strong generally although a 5km/h current moves south past Rubha na Feundain on the ebb and an anticlockwise rotation takes place in Castle Bay on the flood tide.

Heading out past the red and white light tower at the mouth of the bay, three items of local interest are passed on the right, the diminutive lighthouse, the Dog Stone and Dunollie Castle. The Dog Stone is an isolated finger of rock where the Gaelic hero Fingal is reputed to have tethered the great dog Bran, the tether wearing the neck at the base of the pillar or perhaps it was just near the castle kennels. In fact, the neck was probably produced by wave action at the time of the forming of the many raised beaches, in the area. Dunollie Castle was the principal seat of the MacDougalls, the Lords of Lorn, who once owned a third of Scotland and have owned Kerrera since the clan was formed in the 12th century. The ivy covered ruin occupies a long used site, the Irish having burned a wooden fort on it in 698. The present structure was started in the 13th century and developed into a four storey stronghold in the 15th century. It has a barrel vaulted cellar and zigzag entrance in the north wall. Mary, wife of 19th chief Iain Ciar, held out against the

Argyll militia during the 1715 uprising until he returned. The present chief's mansion of 1746 stands below the castle.

It will not have been possible to leave Oban without getting some idea of the view beyond the lumpy bulk of Kerrera.

Maiden Island is in the middle of the exit from Kerrera Sound but Camas Bàn is well studded with rocks so larger craft all stay west of the island.

Going out beyond Maiden Island into the less sheltered waters of the Firth of Lorn brings the full majesty of the scenery into perspective. Here, in one panoramic sweep, are the Island of Mull with Duart Castle, the Sound of Mull, Eilean Musdile with its lighthouse, Lismore and the mountains of Morvern right along Loch Linnhe to Ben Nevis, Britain's highest mountain. There are few indications that man has ever been here, at least, when the yachtsmen are not out. Nature rules supreme in breathtaking surroundings.

Sgeir Dhonn consists of very coarse conglomerate. The islets to the northeast of Slatrach Bay can be confusing but the largest, Eilean nan Gamhna, is dominated by a landmark in the form of a large rectangular block at the top of its profile. Divers in the vicinity come in the form of cormorants and of people training from boats.

Like Lismore, the coast is rocky with few easy landing points on the north side but allowing emergency exit onto the rocks at most points for someone in the water.

Barr-nam-boc Bay was the ferry port for Mull, Coll and Tiree until 1860, the inn having become the farm with quay remains by the bay.

Only to the south of Port Phàdruig are there any real attempts at cliffs and here is found the sole cave. A stream runs down one of the many intrusion lines and cuts through the roof of the cave formed in the intrusion, leaving just a small arch at the front of the otherwise roofless cave.

Bach Island is a wavecut platform with three incongruous cairns in the centre.

Along most of the southwest end of the island, only a croft and Guylen Castle are visible, the latter distinguished solely by its shape on an outcrop between Port a'Chasteil and Port a'Chroinn, its colour blending in with the surrounding rocks. Guylen Castle was built on the site of a former castle in 1587 by Duncan MacDougall of Dunollie. It was besieged, burned and abandoned by General Leslie in 1647 during the Covenanting Wars. JMW Turner produced 25 sketches of the castle in 1831.

In the background, the mouth of Loch Feochan is surrounded by the mountains of Kilbride.

Distance
5km from Clachan Sound to Kerrera. Kerrera is 7km long and lies 200m off Oban with passenger ferry access

OS 1:50,000 Sheet
49 Oban & East Mull

Tidal Constants
Seil Sound: HW Dover −0540, LW Dover −0550 Oban: Dover −0520

Sea Area
Malin

Submarine Area
31 Mull, 32 Linnhe

Dunollie Castle on its rock has guarded the entrance to Oban Bay for many centuries.

Lynn of Lorn

16

Ganavan Bay is the local resort with a caravan site, bar, restaurant, shop, leisure centre, children's play area, donkey rides and watersports yet still the eider ducks are not put off. There is a submarine cable to Mull and a couple of others, now disused.

itimate son, Dugald, and to ensure the succession did not pass to Argyll he planned in 1483 to marry Dugald's mother, a MacLaren of Ardveich. In a plot involving Argyll and Sir John's brother, Walter, Allan Macdougall stabbed Sir John during the service but the priest manag-

Dunstaffnage Castle stands in the woods back from the shoreline.

A marine farm has been sited in Camas Rubha na Lia-thaig. Just across the ridge on the Dunstaffnage Bay side is the Scottish Association of Marine Science which was moved up from Millport in 1970.

Two notable buildings stand in the woods, Dunstaff-nage Castle and its chapel. The castle was built here to control entry to Loch Etive and the approach to Ard-chattan Priory. The site was close to the capital of the old Scots kingdom of Dalriada and a previous castle was home of the Stone of Destiny until 843 after it was brought from Tara. The present castle, which may have been the inspiration for Ardenvohr in Sir Walter Scott's *A Legend of Montrose*, is a 13th century quadrangle on a rock with two round towers, one of three storeys acting as a keep, with a 3m thick curtain wall, built for the Mac-Dougalls.

The chapel to St Maelrubha was built with beautiful architectural detail in wood to St Maelrubha in about 1250. It is now roofless but has been used as a burial place for many of the Captains of Dunstaffnage, the Campbell hereditary constables since the 14th century. The castle was taken by Bruce in 1300. In 1470 it passed to Colin, 1st Earl of Argyll, who married one of the three daughters of Sir John Stewart, 3rd Lord of Lorn, after the Stewarts took over the lordship. Sir John also had an illeg-

ed to complete the ceremony before Sir John died, securing the succession although Argyll did eventually receive the castle, leaving the Stewarts with Appin. In the 17th century a tower house was added over the 13th century entrance. Close by, Old Colkitto was hung from the mast of his own galley. During the uprisings the castle was garrisoned and the last notable visitor was Flora MacDonald, who, after she had assisted Prince Char-

Looking up into Loch Etive with Connel Bridge over the Falls of Lora and Ben Cruachan behind.

Rubha Garbh-àird and Rubha Fion-àird with Lismore beyond, overlooked by the Kingairloch with Glensanda superquarry.

Distance
16km from Dunollie
to Eilean Dubh

OS 1:50,000 Sheet
49 Oban &
East Mull

Tidal Constants
Oban:
Dover −0520
Dunstaffnage Bay:
Dover −0520
Port Appin:
HW Dover −0520
LW Dover −0540

Sea Area
Malin

Submarine Area
32 Linnhe

Connections
Loch Etive – see RoB
p108
Loch Linnhe – see
RoB p113

lie, was brought by Captain Fergussone in the sloop *Furnace* and held for 10 days in 1746 on her way to the Tower of London.

There is a quiet passage inside Eilean Mòr but a race runs both sides of Eilean Beag and the water is rather interesting all the way down from the Falls of Lora, crossed by the distinctive Connel bridge, built in 1898–1903 as Europe's longest cantilever bridge, spanning 71m, to take the Caledonian Railway Ballachulish branch northwards but since 1966 carrying the A828.

Flows at the entrance to Ardmucknish Bay start north-east at HW Dover −0100 and southwest at HW Dover +0500 at up to 3km/h. In addition, there may be a weak clockwise stream round the bay.

Lednaig Point forms a significant shingle spit running out from North Connel. Connel Airfield is squeezed in along the shore next to the road and is used by gliders ridge soaring around 308m high Beinn Lora. The final section of shoreline before the mountain is given over to a caravan site.

Benderloch has forest walks set out on the flanks of the mountain and has been a popular point for some time, judging by the standing stones and forts including the ruins of Beregonium vitrified fort. This was the inspiration for Angus MacColl's reel *The Road to Benderloch*. These days the attraction is the sandy beach, both for leisure and for a sand pit.

Lady Margaret's Tower rises above the trees on Garbh Ard.

The secluded but relatively weather exposed inlet of Camas Nathais is between the thrift flanked Rubha Garbh-àird and Rubha Fion-àird. Birdlife proliferates with cormorants, oystercatchers, sandpipers, blackbacked gulls and guillemots.

Flows into the Lynn of Lorn start in at HW Dover −0040 and start out again at HW Dover +0520 at up to 2km/h.

Eilean Dubh in the centre of the channel has heather on top and bootlace weed and anemones in the shallows surrounding.

The northern end of the eastern side of Lismore from the northern Eilean Dubh.

Lismore

17

The circumnavigation of Lismore offers, arguably, some of the best scenery of any sea trip in Britain that gives some shelter from the elements.

Lismore was a holy island, the seat of the diocese of Argyll from the 13th to 16th centuries, their 13th century cathedral now part of St Moluag's church. Its Gaelic name of Ieis Mor means great garden from its early Christian settlement and it was relatively fertile from the Dalradian limestone grassland on which it is based, lime being made from the underlying limestone. In the sixth century a race took place between the Pictish St Moluag and the Celtic St Mulhac, the winner claiming the island. St Moluag realized he was not going to land his boat first and so cut off his finger and threw it ashore to be the first to touch land. He founded a monastery on the island between 561 and 564. With this saintly behaviour most people might be glad to be sinners.

For the nobility rather than the peasants, *The Book of Lismore* in the 16th century was one of the first collections of poetry.

Two thirds of the island belongs to the Duke of Argyll. There are 160 residents and nearly as many more living in holiday homes, mostly towards the north of the island. Most of the trees are at this end, too, although Lismore was reputed to have been covered in oak trees 400 years ago.

The chart shows low sea cliffs around most of the island. These are very worn so that a boater could climb out at almost any point on the southeast side. At the top of the low cliffs is a wide platform and then more cliffs,

Pladda Island, Eilean Dubh, Eilean na Cloiche and Eilean nan Gamhna stand off the coast of Lismore with Mull beyond.

Bluebells and thrift on Eilean nan Gamhna.

particularly towards the southern end. The rocks are volcanic with some interesting local folding and regular intrusions of quartz and other rocks to add variety. On the northwest side the cliffs are higher and less accessible but boltholes are still to be found at frequent intervals.

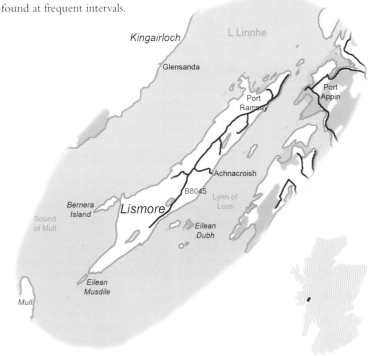

Eilean Musdile with its lighthouse.

The low northern end of Lismore, overlooked by the mountains of the Kingairloch behind.

Lismore Gaelic Heritage Centre is at Killandrist. A concrete cross at the water's edge gives notice of arrival at the village of Achnacroish. The pier is visited by the car ferry from Oban. Two large curved pillars just up the hill look quite grand until it is realized that they are, in fact, only the remains of the end of a Nissen hut.

There may be a marine farm sited at Sean Dùn. Cairns and duns dot the hillside around Dùn Mòr although they are far from conspicuous.

What appears to be a broch on Eilean na Cloiche, island of the rock, turns out to be a rock plug although there is a broch by Loch Fiart, not visible from near the island. The islets are covered with heather and Eilean nan Gamhna has a fine display of bluebells in the spring. The B8045 runs along the island above Port Kilcheran.

From here conditions become more exposed with views across to Oban, Kerrera and Mull if the weather is fine. An eddy runs southwest along the southeast shore of Lismore from here during the flood tide.

More duns follow in profusion including the broch at An Dùn and Dùn Chruban.

Appearance of the lighthouse on Eilean Musdile gives warning of the end of the island. Eilean Musdile is really two linked islands, frequented by shelducks. It is possible to pass through the gap between Rubha Fiart and the islands if the flow is appropriate as there are races through the gaps.

Slack water is needed for the crossing to Mull. This constriction where Loch Linnhe meets the Firth of Lorn has a race most of the way across, even in fine weather. This runs at up to 11km/h to Lady's Rock, then easing to 7km/h to Mull. Notwithstanding, ferries pass through here from Oban to Craignure, Lochaline, Lochboisdale on South Uist, Castlebay on Barra, Arinagour on Coll and Scarinish on Tiree.

Using the tides to help will give arrival at this point at low tide, getting the benefit of the ebb tide down the Lynn of Lorn and the flood tide up in Loch Linnhe. There is no point in arriving before low tide. The tide race between Lismore and Eilean Musdile is strong when the tide is at full ebb. At low tide this reduces to two narrow channels of still water, welcome respite on a windy day.

If the wind is from the southwest, as is usually the case, turning the corner will bring the waves onto the stern quarter which makes life a little tedious on the long run up Loch Linnhe.

The next target is the east end of Bernera Island, overlooked by Achadun Castle ruins, the seat of the bishops. Bernera is only a separate island at high tide. At low tide there is a 100m portage over the seaweed covered rocks into a bay which is pleasantly sheltered from the predominant wind. There is now a little more time to admire the mountains of Morvern and the Kingairloch on the opposite shore.

The limestone quarry at An Sailean was abandoned in the first half of the 20th century but was the only sign of modern activity on the northwest shore. Now the Glensanda superquarry faces across Loch Linnhe. The

The remains of Tirefour Castle, a broch.

ruins of the 13th century Norse Castle Coeffin stand on a headland as a dominant feature, once occupied by the MacDougalls. Apart from a single feeble attempt at a sea cave, there is nothing to break the rugged consistency of the northwest coast.

Turning the top corner of the island brings more

sheltered water among the islands around Port Ramsay. The port used to be the base for many of the lime carrying boats. Now it has white holiday houses gazing at the view up Loch Linnhe towards Ben Nevis.

Rounding the last corner brings into view the jetty at Port Appin.

If a meal is called for, the Airds Hotel & Restaurant's food in Port Appin is of high quality. Crossing the Lynn of Lorn follows the line of a passenger ferry, a small open boat which also carries cattle and other animals ('Sheep 22p each, minimum charge 83p'). Even so, the current can be 7km/h along the lynn when the tide is running and the rocks in the middle may or may not be submerged. The B8045 runs from the jetty most of the length of the island.

Moving down the Lynn of Lorn, the chunky outline of Eilean Dubh dominates at first while on Lismore the stump of Tirefour Castle, an Iron Age broch, dominates a high point. A green conical starboard buoy in the centre of the lynn warns incoming shipping away from Appin Rocks on the mainland shore where water builds up against the rocks on ebb and flood tides.

Almost from Branra Rock to the island, 40ha of artificial reef have been constructed in water to 28m deep.

An otter swims with a fish off Branra Rock with Lismore beyond.

Distance
Lismore is 15km long and lies 1km off Port Appin with passenger ferry access

OS 1:50,000 Sheet
49 Oban &
East Mull

Tidal Constants
Port Appin:
HW Dover −0520,
LW Dover −0540
Craignure:
HW Dover −0500,
LW Dover −0510

Sea Area
Malin

Submarine Area
32 Linnhe

Connection
Loch Linnhe – see
RoB p113

18 Island of Mull

Slender and steep, and battled round,
O'erlook'd, dark Mull! thy mighty Sound,
Where thwarting tides, with mingled roar,
Part thy swarth hills from Morvern's shore.
Sir Walter Scott

Mull, in Argyll & Bute, is the third largest of the Scottish islands, covering 911km² and having 480km of coastline and a population of 2,800. The name means mass of hill, most of that mass being lava, 50,000,000 year old grey tertiary volcanic rock. Mull was a centre of eruption, a lava plateau or trap with extensive Tertiary volcanic activity and dikes radiate from here over the west coast. Wildlife includes a distinct subspecies of bank vole and fallow deer, introduced in the 14th century. The *Sweet Maid of Mull* march is just one tune inspired by this island.

Crossing from Lismore to Mull passes Lady's Rock which has a light beacon. The lady in question was Lady Elizabeth, a Campbell and daughter of Archibald, 2nd Earl of Argyll. She had failed to provide an heir for her husband, Lachlan MacLean of Duart, and had twice tried to poison him so in 1523 he decided he would drown her by chaining her to a covering section of the rock. This would have left him free to marry the daughter of MacLean of Treshnish but Lady Elizabeth was rescued by Tayvallich men who were rewarded by Argyll with a mill on Loch Sween. MacLean was said to have seen her at a subsequent funeral and escaped, to be caught and murdered by her brother in law, Sir John Campbell of Calder.

Landmarks are slightly confusing as the first 9m tower like a castle is a memorial to novelist William Black and bears a sector light. It is followed on Duart Point by Duart Castle, dubh aird being a dark headland, the home of Clan Maclean since they ousted the MacDonalds as Lords of the Isles in about 1250. The keep dates from 1390, when the Macleans received their charter. Two Spanish survivors of the Armada galleon explosion were kept in the dungeons, contained in 3.7m thick walls. Some of the buildings were reconstructed in 1633 with 100 rooms by Sir Lachlan Maclean and it was acquired by the 10th Earl and 1st Duke of Argyll in 1647. It was used by troops until 1691

when it was fired by the Duke of Argyll. The Jacobite Sir Hector Maclean was imprisoned in the Tower of London during the 1745 uprising, when the castle was garrisoned, after which it fell into ruin. In 1912 it was bought back and restored by Sir Fitzroy Maclean and is still the home of the clan chief. There are exhibitions of Scottish relics, the Macleans and Scouting, Maclean of Duart having been Chief Scout in the 1960s. In the dungeon is a tableau of two Spanish officers from the Armada galleon *San Juan de Sicilia* which was blown up in 1588 while her crew were helping Maclean of Duart lay siege to Mingary Castle. Duart Castle was one of a defensive chain which could relay a message from Mingary Castle to Dunollie in half an hour. It was used for filming *I Know Where I'm Going!* and *The Tweenies*. The Millennium Wood has been planted with trees and shrubs native to Argyll.

A 150m diameter exclusion zone north of Duart Point protects the wreck of the Royalist *Swan* of 1641 but sunk four years later in the hands of Cromwell's troops. Flows north are from Dover HW +0120 and south from Dover HW −0600 to 6km/h. There can be a race but it can also be calm, especially with a southerly wind.

At the western end of Duart Bay is Camas Mòr, beside which is Torosay Castle of 1856, a sandstone Victorian baronial mansion by David Bryce. Visited by Winston Churchill, Lily Langtree, Dame Nellie Melba and the general public. It has exhibition rooms, good furniture, pictures and photographs of life at the turn of the 20th century, 5ha of Italian terraced gardens by Lorimer, a statue walk with 19 figures

The William Black memorial tower at Duart Point.

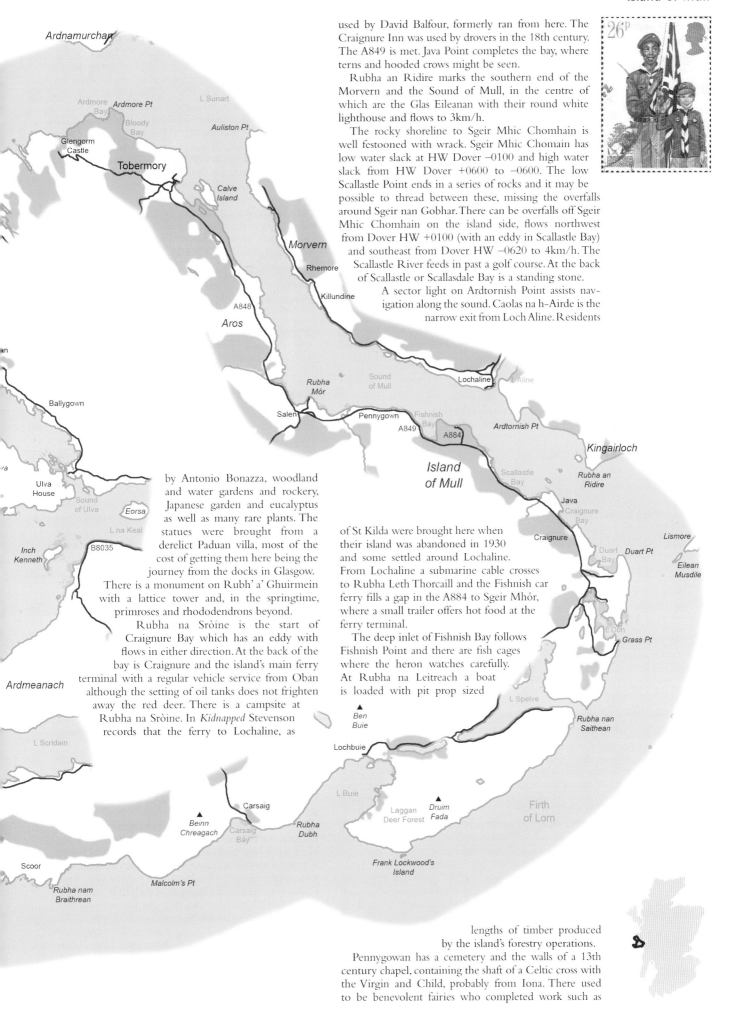

used by David Balfour, formerly ran from here. The Craignure Inn was used by drovers in the 18th century. The A849 is met. Java Point completes the bay, where terns and hooded crows might be seen.

Rubha an Ridire marks the southern end of the Morvern and the Sound of Mull, in the centre of which are the Glas Eileanan with their round white lighthouse and flows to 3km/h.

The rocky shoreline to Sgeir Mhic Chomhain is well festooned with wrack. Sgeir Mhic Chomain has low water slack at HW Dover –0100 and high water slack from HW Dover +0600 to –0600. The low Scallastle Point ends in a series of rocks and it may be possible to thread between these, missing the overfalls around Sgeir nan Gobhar. There can be overfalls off Sgeir Mhic Chomhain on the island side, flows northwest from Dover HW +0100 (with an eddy in Scallastle Bay) and southeast from Dover HW –0620 to 4km/h. The Scallastle River feeds in past a golf course. At the back of Scallastle or Scallasdale Bay is a standing stone.

A sector light on Ardtornish Point assists navigation along the sound. Caolas na h-Airde is the narrow exit from Loch Aline. Residents

by Antonio Bonazza, woodland and water gardens and rockery, Japanese garden and eucalyptus as well as many rare plants. The statues were brought from a derelict Paduan villa, most of the cost of getting them here being the journey from the docks in Glasgow.

There is a monument on Rubh' a' Ghuirmein with a lattice tower and, in the springtime, primroses and rhododendrons beyond.

Rubha na Sròine is the start of Craignure Bay which has an eddy with flows in either direction. At the back of the bay is Craignure and the island's main ferry terminal with a regular vehicle service from Oban although the setting of oil tanks does not frighten away the red deer. There is a campsite at Rubha na Sròine. In *Kidnapped* Stevenson records that the ferry to Lochaline, as

of St Kilda were brought here when their island was abandoned in 1930 and some settled around Lochaline. From Lochaline a submarine cable crosses to Rubha Leth Thorcaill and the Fishnish car ferry fills a gap in the A884 to Sgeir Mhór, where a small trailer offers hot food at the ferry terminal.

The deep inlet of Fishnish Bay follows Fishnish Point and there are fish cages where the heron watches carefully. At Rubha na Leitreach a boat is loaded with pit prop sized

lengths of timber produced by the island's forestry operations.

Pennygowan has a cemetery and the walls of a 13th century chapel, containing the shaft of a Celtic cross with the Virgin and Child, probably from Iona. There used to be benevolent fairies who completed work such as

Duart Castle, dating from the 14th century.

island chieftains to a sermon and dinner on a galley, then arrested them. After a year of cooling off they were invited to sign the Statutes of Iona, which they did, promising good behaviour and an end to riotous living. There had also been the problem that Donald Bane was the brother of Malcolm III and had a better claim than Robert the Bruce to the throne.

Beyond Port an Tobire and Port nam Buitsichean is a pier on Rubha Àrd Ealasaid.

Rubh' a' Ghlaisich is at the narrowest part of the sound opposite Dun Bàn near the Killundine River.

Mull is separated from the Morvern shore by the Sound of Mull. Caledonian MacBrayne car ferries pass through between Oban and the Hebrides at frequent intervals but it is also a submarine exercise area. Tidal flows are later and stronger at the southeast end of the sound than at the far end, with a large variation in times. Even the edges of the sound can be half an hour earlier than in the centre of the fairway. The wind funnels along the sound but with northeasterly to easterly winds in good conditions there can be a fresh breeze on the weather side of the sound but near calm conditions on the lee side. To add to the complexity, a magnetic anomaly can add up to 6° to compass readings almost to Calve Island.

The sound is narrowest between Rhemore on the Morvern shore and Rubh' a' Ghlaisich on the Aros side.

The Fishnish ferry crosses the Sound of Mull from Lochaline.

spinning or weaving left on their mound. However, when someone left a short piece of wood to be made into a ship's mast the good works ceased. In the 17th century MacIain Ghiarr found three witches in the chapel sticking pins in a clay model of MacLean of Duart. He beat them and took them to MacLean, who was wracked with pain but recovered as the pins were removed.

The River Forsa arrives around the back of the Glenforsa Airstrip, built in 54 days in 1966 by the 38th Engineers Regiment as an exercise. It is the airfield for Mull and can be very busy with light aircraft active low over the sound. Swans and fulmars are among the natural fliers here.

Also in ruins is the more westerly of the two piers at the end of the A848 at Rubha Mòr. Salen, at the back of Salen Bay, was created about 1800 by Major General Lachlan MacQuarrie. The low land between here and the head of Loch na Keal funnels wind so that a southwesterly emerges into the sound where it blows in both directions, north and east, or a northeasterly can have the opposite result. Thus, for a boat in the sound it is not unusual for the wind direction to reverse at Salen.

Salen had an important cattle market. It was from Salen that Para Handy bought a couple of herons during a chicken shortage. The eventual customer filleted them and served them to her lodgers with white sauce as ling because of the fish flavour.

The Aros River discharges past Aros Castle, built by the Lords of the Isles in the 13th or 14th century with the Tobermory galleon treasure said to be buried beneath. It was last occupied in 1608, the year in which Andrew Stewart, the 3rd Lord Ochiltree, called the

The broch of An Sean Chaisteal and a cairn precede Rubh' an t-Sean Chaisteal, a 15m high point with a wreck off it by a light buoy. There may also be overfalls off the point. Flows begin northwest at Dover HW −0030 and southeast at Dover HW +0620 to 2km/h. Beneath the surface there are conger eels, dogfish and skate. Birdlife includes curlews, cormorants, blackbacked gulls and maybe even a whitetailed sea eagle perched on the rocks. Noisier fliers are jets which conduct low level training runs up the sound and across to the west coast of the island.

Tobermory is sheltered by Calve Island, where Seumas Adam and Alistair Dunnett, later to be editor of the *Scotsman*, spent time on a farm, learning about the problems of Highland crofting, Dunnett's *Quest by Canoe* describing a 1930s paddle from Bowling to Kyleakin. The crew of the *Vital Spark* set up a brief business running people out from Tobermory to view a beached whale until ordered to dispose of its decomposing carcass. It was from Tobermory beach that captain Para Handy took home a basket of stones from the beach for his wife after Sunny Jim, his cook, managed to convince him that they made better soup than cockles.

Dòirlinn a' Chailbhe forms a southern entrance past the island with flows in from Dover HW +0120 on neap tides, later on springs when it partially dries and has the added complication of a fishing boat wreck, and out from Dover HW −0500. Cnap a' Chailbhe blocks much of the entrance and a tripod beacon stands in the gap.

The main entrance to Tobermory lies beyond Rubh' an Righ and is used by the ferries. Sadly, the BBC's *Balamory* TV series, set here, was renamed not to avoid confusion

The colourful waterfront at Tobermory as passengers are brought ashore from a cruise liner.

with the town but with the Womble named after it. The Gaelic tobar Mhoire means Mary's well. The town was visited by Johnson and Boswell in 1773 it but was not officially founded until 1788 by the British Society of Extending the Fisheries as a herring centre, together with Oban and Ullapool, after success in Roghadal, with technical advice and a church from Telford. The capital of the island, it had burgh status for a century from 1875 although it was one of the smallest burghs. A distinctive feature of the delightful harbour is that each of the houses along the front has a different colourwash, an idea since copied elsewhere. *A Summer in Skye* noted that the houses were white in 1864 and more pleasant when viewed from a distance. The Mull Museum near the lifeboat and the end of the A848 features local history. The calcium silicate hydrate mineral Tobermorite was first reported from this area in 1880 but was an essential ingredient in Roman concrete which is particulary durable in seawater. The Tobermory River had an early hydroelectric power scheme in the town. Tobermory Distillery is one of the oldest in Scotland still operational. The Isle of Mull Brewing Company had a short life, its brands now being brewed by Oban Bay Brewery. The Tobermory Chocolate factory also appeals to the palate. Cruise ships visit and a distinctive white building with cylindrical end offers modern facilities for visiting yachtsmen. Sailors visiting in 1940 were trained in anti submarine warfare by Vice Admiral Sir Gilbert Stephenson who was in his 60s but used harsh methods, described by Richard Baker in *The Terror of Tobermory*.

In 1588 the Spanish Armada galleon *Almirente de Florencia* or perhaps the carrack *San Juan de Sicilia*, reputed to be carrying 30,000,000 ducats, lent Maclean of Duart an officer, 100 men and two guns for an attack on Mingary Castle on the Ardnamurchan, in exchange for supplies and Donald Glas Maclean as a hostage. He set off the powder magazine and sank the ship in the bay. Some silver plate and silver and gold coins have been brought up but there is suspicion that much of the treasure was recovered by Governor Sacheverell of the Isle of Man a century later. It was said that Viola, the daughter of the King of Spain, dreamed she loved a man on Mull, travelled in the ship and found Maclean of Duart. His wife was not amused and ordered the ship to be blown up, perhaps by the Witch of Lochaber's fairy cats which swam out to attack the ship's crew, static electricity from the now dry fur of one setting off the powder. Captain Forrest was then sent from Spain for revenge but the wife summoned all 18 witches of Mull, disguised as seagulls, to raise a storm which sank Forrest's ship. More magic resulted when a farmer was walking with his young daughter, who offered to sink all the ships which could be seen, which she did by looking backwards between her legs at them, the only survivor being one which had some rowan onboard. She told him she had learned the trick from her mother so her father had them both burnt as witches. The galleon inspired Robert Louis Stevenson's *The Merry Men*. Entertainment these days includes Tobermory Highland

Games and the Isle of Mull Car Rally in October which closes some of the island's roads, of which there are only a limited number at the best of times.

There may be eddies on either side of Rubha nan Gall, the stranger's point, marked by a 19m white tower lighthouse, off which may be overfalls. Flows begin northwest from Dover HW −0120 and southeast from Dover HW +0610 to 4km/h.

Opposite, Auliston Point marks the end of Loch Sunart, after which the channel is significantly wider.

Bloody Bay takes its name from the 1480 sea battle where Angus Og, Lord of the Isles and descendant of Somerled, defeated his father, John, and the Scottish king's forces although his own newborn son was abducted from Islay while the battle was taking place. The oystercatcher was said to have got its red beak and legs from the blood in the bay. Jellyfish, razorbills, guillemots and kittiwakes are also seen as skerries increasingly break up the shoreline.

The Forestry Commission are the largest employer with plantations of larch and Sitka spruce as the cliffs become progressively more inaccessible, waterfalls descending in places. The peaks of the Small Isles and Skye rise above the Ardnamurchan peninsula and Coll is about to come into view, to be followed later by Tiree.

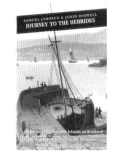

A 5m white pillar light with cubicle has a 13km range from Ardmore Point. Flows begin westwards from Dover HW −0220 and eastwards from Dover HW +0530 to 1km/h. A hide faces Ardmore Bay. More conspicuous are the masts on 264m Meall an Inbhire.

Behind Port Chill Bhraonian is Glengorm Castle of 1860, named not after its dark grey colour but after the blue smoke of the burning crofts during the Clearances perpetrated by owner James Forsyth. On making an inspection of the construction he was hit in the face by a bat, the soul of one of those evicted, and cursed with never sleeping in it, becoming ill and dying before it was completed.

Between Eilean an Fhuarain and Quinish Point are the narrow inlets of Laorin Bay and Loch Mingary

Glengorm Castle above Port Chill Bhraonain.

leading out into Cuan Mòr with Dùn Ara castle and Dùn Bàn fort guarding the two ends. Dùn Leathan guarded the east side on the approach to Poll Athach and Loch a' Chumhainn, which have weak flows in from Dover HW +0120 and out from Dover HW −0510, mackerel and saithe occupying these constricted waters. A dun by a monument on the east of Ugag faces a fort on its opposite side, defending the approach to Croig where a jetty was used for landing cattle from the outer islands on their way to the mainland. The Sgeirean Beaga provide a further line of defence out in the bay. Port na Bà has a small sandy beach tucked in on the east side of Rubha an Àird with its cairns. A submarine power cable runs out from here to Coll.

Bracken surrounds Port Langamull, above which is a standing stone and Sunipol. The local minister told his flock to beware of Sunipol at night but two of them stayed overnight, when the door opened and seaweed covered rocks pounded in. Could this have been an attempt to scare unwanted eyes away from smuggling operations?

Port na Caillich, with its puffins, ends at Caliach Point, the extremity squeezing the flow between Mull and Coll. A race can extend 3km off the point, described in *Kayak to Cape Wrath* as a 'devil of a place' and 'hell with the lid off'. Flows begin south at Dover HW −0400 and north from Dover HW +0200 to 5km/h. The Cailleach or old woman was a stack, destroyed in a storm in the 1950s. A cairn stands on top of the point. A wall is part of the system used by a breeder of Arab horses and Highland ponies to keep his stallions away from the other horses.

The cliffs have now become high and forbidding with a skirt of reefs and are to continue like this round into Loch Tuath, the haunt of the buzzard and little more. The exception is after Rubha nan Oirean where Calgary Bay leads back to the best beach on Mull, accompanied by dunes and machair and a favourite haunt of merfolk, apparently. It is a source of lobsters, one in the 1920s weighing 5.4kg. Calagharaidh is the haven by the wall, perhaps after the basalt dyke visible here. The Clearances in 1829 forced the Macneils to emigrate together but this was not the origin of Canada's city of Calgary.

The wall of mountains ahead includes 343m Carn Mòr, 288m Beinn Bhuide and 217m Cruachan Treshnish. The Treshnish Isles lie southwest of Treshnish Point, Bac Mòr or the Dutchman's Cap having a distinctive profile. These isles were the base for pirate Alan Breck, given a more friendly image in *Kidnapped*. The point was remembered in Jack Henderson's *Kayak to Cape Wrath* for surfing with a loose wartime mine. The remote Port Haunn, below a

dun and a fort, was used for filming Ken Follett's *The Eye of the Needle*.

Flow southwards from Rubh' a' Chaoil can be to 4km/h and northwards to 5km/h.

A fertile raised beach runs at the 38m level and the villages of Crackaig and Clac Gugairidh had a population of 200 until the Clearances at the end of the 19th century. An ash tree on which a villager hanged himself still grows by the stream. In Still Cave there are foundations of the illicit whisky still used until the mid 18th century. Ruined blackhouses remain and there was also a medieval chapel.

Beinn Reudle rises 232m above Lòn Reudle. Rubh' an t-Suibhein with its cave is the start of Loch Tuath with very weak flows inward from Dover HW +0140 and outward from Dover HW −0500. The south side of the loch is contained by Gometra and Ulva, both rugged.

Behind Port Burg are a range of antiquities as the cliffs become less extreme, the notable Dùn Asgain, Dùn Ban, a standing stone, a cairn and some fine natural woodland. The church at Kilninian is not named after St Ninian but after Cill Naoi Nighean or the church of the nine maidens, which has unusual benches and ornate 16th century gravestones. The beach of Tràigh na Cille lies below the church.

A cairn stands above Rubha Àrd Sgànalais, which shelters Port na Criche. Sgeir nan Ròn, the seal skerry, protects Ballygown Bay, overlooked by the notable broch of Dùn nan Gall, the stranger's fort. A memorial to car rally driver Sue Cameron, killed nearby, is placed at an excellent viewpoint over the loch. The most prominent of the waterfalls carries the notably Viking name of Eas Fors.

Sgeir Dubhail is an outlier for Eilean Garbh, a spread of islands and reefs which narrow the channel down to the proportions of a river before opening into the Sound of Ulva, still only 140m wide where the ferry crosses but subject to fierce squalls with southerly winds. The earlier crossing from Gribun was featured by Thomas Campbell

Eas Fors thunders to the shore.

Calgary Bay, the best beach on Mull.

Ben More and the other high peaks of Mull, seen from Loch Tuath.

The mouth of Loch na Keal on the left, looking south past Inch Kenneth with Ulva on the right.

in *Lord Ullin's Daughter*. This was once the departure point for tourists going to Fingal's Cave on Staffa.

Ulva was wolf's island, and has deer, Highland cattle, blackface sheep, otters, oysters, bracken which can grow to 4.6m and midges and clegs to suit. Prominent is the Boathouse tea room and Isle of Ulva Heritage Centre, covering from the Stone Age to the present. A thatched black house with turf ridge stands alongside. The island has one of Telford's churches and it had a piping college founded by a MacArthur, a McCrimmon pupil. Visitors have included Johnson, Boswell and Sir Walter Scott. Johnson and Boswell noted in their narratives of their 1773 trip to Scotland that the laird no longer spent the wedding night with the bride when a virgin was married, known as the droit de seigneur. The replacement payment of a sheep by this time took the form of five shillings in cash.

Major General Lachlan Macquarrie was born here in 1761, becoming a distinguished governor of New South Wales from 1809, earning the title the Father of Australia. Turning to another continent, the parents of explorer David Livingstone were residents. Ulva had 600 crofters and a kelp industry producing potash but between 1846 and 1851 they were victims of Francis William Clark, one of the most ruthless of the Clearance enthusiasts. On attempting to ferry his tombstone across, it proved too heavy to lift because of the weight of evil it contained. Many of his family are buried in the Clark memorial at Dùn Bhioramuill, a structure with a high wall and no gateway. The fine Ulva House, designed by Robert Adam, was burned down in 1953. There are now only around 14 residents, the most depopulated of the islands still occupied.

Loch na Keal, the loch of cliffs, joins from the east. It has low land at its head reaching over to the Sound of Mull and may have been part of a southwesterly flowing river passing to the south of Coll and Tiree. It can be subject to heavy squalls and has the island of Eorsa in the centre. On the north side it slopes up to 424m Beinn na Drise. On the other side, however, the highest peaks on Mull form a line, 561m Coire Bheinn, 966m Ben More, Beinn Fhada, Beinn nan Gabhar, Beinn Ghraig and the rest. Ben More is not only the highest point on Mull but Scotland's highest tertiary basalt peak. The Outer Hebrides and Ireland can be seen from the top or could be were it not for the usual plume of cloud from the summit.

At Rubh 'a Ghearrain flows run south from Dover HW −0520 and north from Dover HW +0100 at up to 1km/h but the wind is more likely to be the problem, violent squalls hitting Clachandhu with southeasterly winds.

Samalan Island may have a large fish farm in its vicinity. The larger Inch Kenneth has outcrops of metamorphosed chalk and conspicuous beaches. Named after a companion of St Columba, it was Iona's granary but is subject to fierce downdraughts so that slates have to be cemented to roofs. There is a cairn and the ruin of a medieval chapel, formerly a monastery. Scottish kings and chiefs were buried here when it was too rough to cross to Iona. Johnson and Boswell visited, Dr Johnson being delighted to see cart tracks, having not viewed anything as sophisticated for a long time on their journey. A four

storey house for Sir Harold Boulton was later used by the Mitford sisters. Unity was a friend of Adolf Hitler and had shot herself in the head on the day the Second World War was declared but survived and was moved here by the family out of the public gaze. She died in 1948 from meningitis caused by the bullet, which had never been removed.

Clachandhu has a conspicuous beach of sand dotted with shells next to the B8035, single track with grass along the centre in places.

The coast south from Clachandhu has 490m vertical basalt cliffs with long, green coated, scree slopes for much of their height, large boulders lying on them in places and apparently adding to the skerries which continue south from Rubha Baile na h-Airde. Larger islands visible include Little Colonsay, Erisgeir and Staffa, to which tourist boats used to depart from Gribun, where one of the large boulders at the foot of the cliffs flattened a cottage in which newlyweds were sleeping.

South of Port Uamh Beathaig is Mackinnon's Cave, the biggest cave in the Hebrides, officially 30m high and 180m long with stalactites although some have said it runs through to Tiroran on Loch Scridain or that the end has never been found. A party of a dozen men with the piper Mackinnon set out to explore it with others walking and listening above. It is said that a wicked fairy killed all the lower group except the piper, who was to be spared if he could keep playing until he reached daylight. Those above heard the notes fading away and the piper was found dying at the mouth of the cave. The Para Handy story from the beginning of the 20th century about farming pensioners by Loch Scridain in order to profit from their pensions was ahead of the thinking on old folk's homes.

Caisteal Sloc nan Ban, Caisteal Uaimh an t-Sagairt and Stac Glas Ban an Uisge draw attention to rock features. Porpoises might be seen off Rubha nan Goirteanan. An arch with light coloured boulders behind it has the strange appearance of some kind of shrine.

Bearraich at 432m is the end of the trap country, stepped layers of tertiary basalt plateau lavas, best seen from a distance, the lower levels reaching round from the Wilderness to the Burg. Aird na h-Iolaire suggests eagles but there are also hen harriers, sparrowhawks, peregrines, choughs, red deer, wild goats and the rare Scotch burnet

Bearraich and the Ross of Mull from Rubha Baile na h-Airde.

moth on this part of Ardmeanach. Iceland purslane is found on the summits, otherwise unknown in Britain except on Skye. There is a risk of falling stones from the shattered rocks with their pinnacles and gullies.

From Rubha na h-Uamha to the Ross of Mull there are some fascinating lava effects, best seen at low water. Columnar lava is conspicuous, reminiscent of Staffa. Down at water level are much smaller columns, as if someone has taken bundles of wooden stakes, stacked them together on end and then allowed them to fall apart. What appear to be stone planks are set vertically on end across an area of beach. Most notable is MacCulloch's fossil tree fern, 1.5m diameter and 12m high. This 50,000,000 year old plant was found in 1819, coated with a 50mm layer of charred wood where it was engulfed in lava. It has since been capped with cement to deter souvenir hunters. Those on foot can reach it if prepared to climb down a 6m ladder. Waterfalls drop from the mountain. On the south side of the point is Dùn Bhuirg, a 1st century galleried fort.

Loch Scridain may have been a tributary of a south-westerly flowing river passing the south coasts of Coll and Tiree. Weak flows commence inwards from Dover HW +0100 and outwards from Dover HW −0520.

The Ross of Mull is mostly low crystalline gneiss with white sand. A fort was sited between Loch na Corrbha and Bun an Leoib. Beyond Rubha Dubh is Lochan Mòr. This coastline of skerries and rocky inlets has similarities to the north coast of Mull but occasionally there are small caves and varying sizes of basaltic columns. Herring gulls wait on the rocks.

At the mouth of Loch na Làthaich, the largest inlet on this coast, are the skerries of Na Liathanaich, marked by a sector light on a square 5m white light tower, around

which streams flow to 1km/h. The cleft of Camas Tuath hides behind Carraig Ghilliondrais while Rubh' Eilean an t-Santachaidh hides Tràigh na Margaidh, a pair of beautiful dune backed sandy beaches which cannot be reached by road without a long trek across moorland.

Bàgh Inbhir h-Ailhne shelters between Rubha nan Cearc and Rubha Mhic-aoidh, where the coast turns south through a maze of steep rocky islands and sandy beaches. Kintra was used for landing cattle from the outer islands.

The narrow Bull Hole runs inside Eilean nan Ban with fast flow and leads into the Sound of Iona, where the 5km/h streams flow south from Dover HW −0540 and north from Dover HW −0020.

An underwater pipe carries water across to Iona from near a disused quarry on the 10km^2 boss of pink granite, which supplied stone for London's Albert Memorial, Holburn Viaduct, the old Blackfriars Bridge and the Skerryvore and Artach lighthouses.

Fionnphort has a sandy beach with a large split boulder at the end of the A849 and also has a visitor centre. A ceilidh in the hamlet was visited by John MacPherson, who said he would be found at Erraid the next morning and departed without leaving any footprints in the lying snow, the snow itself an unsual feature in Mull. He was found the next day exactly as described, having been drowned from a ship off Donegal's Tory Island over a fortnight earlier, and was buried in Fionnphort cemetery.

A ferry carries 250,000 passengers a year across to Iona but not visiting cars, which are banned from the island, except for those of the 180 residents. Mostly the pedestrians are visiting the rather windswept island as a place of pilgrimage. Iona takes its name from I-thona, island of waves, or I-shonna, holy island. One of Scotland's most sacred sites, it became a Christian centre for Europe. It was founded in 563 by St Columba, who landed from Ireland in a curragh with a dozen others, the nearest place from which Ireland was not visible, giving rise to the Gaelic name of Ì Chaluim Chille. A replica of the curragh

MacCulloch's fossil tree.

Basalt columns and a cave on the Ross of Mull.

The Ardmeanach peninsula across Loch Scridain, showing the trap scenery.

is on display in Derry's Harbour Museum. Possession of this sanctuary was important for the survival of the Irish in Scotland in the 7th century, when one of its products was St Aidan of Lindisfarne. The abbey buildings were sacked five times by the Vikings between 795 and 986. They were rebuilt by St Margaret in 1074, again in 1203 by Reginald MacDonald of Islay, King of the Isles and son of Somerled, being restored in 1938 and now run by the Iona Community. A former Druid temple was rebuilt as the chapel of St Oran, the brother of St Columba, by St Margaret in 1080 and restored in 1957, the oldest building on the island and maybe the mortuary chapel of Somerled, who revived Gaeldom. The 13th century Augustinian pink granite nunnery remains, the best medieval nunnery remains in Scotland, are by Reginald. The island was captured by Maclean of Duart in 1574 and retaken by Argyll in 1688. Johnson and Boswell visited and spent the night in a barn. A church is by Telford. Facilities on the island include the Argyll Hotel behind St Ronan's Bay but hotels on Iona are unlicensed.

The abbey church has cloisters, St Columba's shrine and cell and an altar of marble veined with serpentine, cut at Rubha na Carraig-gèire where a gas engine and stone saw used for this purpose until 1915 can still be seen. When the roof was to be restored in the late 1930s timber was not available but a ship inbound from Canada lost some of its deck cargo in a storm off the Clyde, timber floating 130km to wash up adjacent to the cathedral, where it was found to be cut to the required length. There are 180 medieval carved stones and crosses, the high crosses being the best of their kind. The 5.2m high 10th century St Martin's cross is especially fine. Maclean's cross is said to be the oldest Christian relic in Britain. St John's cross dates from the 8th century. Most of the other 350 crosses were destroyed in the Reformation but the 8th century *Book of Kells*, begun here, was smuggled out and survived the Reformation destruction. Highland chiefs swore their oaths on the Black Stone and the Druid Stone helped fishermen navigate the waters. The requirement to be buried as far west as possible has resulted in the abbey graveyard containing the mortal remains of 48 Scottish kings plus four Irish, four Manx, eight Norwegian and one French king, many Scottish chiefs and Labour Party leader John Smith. Eventually it was replaced by Dunfermline Abbey

as the royal graveyard. In *The Fair Maid of Perth* Eachin MacIan swore he would marry Catharine Gower before the black stones of Iona.

The low Torridonian sandstone is geologically unrelated to the rest of Mull and much older, quite unlike the pink granite across the sound. The grey green serpentine pebbles unique to Iona are said to be the solidified tears of a mermaid who was told by the saint she loved that she must give up the sea to gain the soul she wanted. These green pebbles were often taken to other Christian cells and Frank Fraser Darling, in his *Island Years*, describes digging one up from the foot of a chapel altar on North Rona. When the second flood comes Iona will be the only place to rise above the waves. In the meantime, there is machair and there are corncrakes in summer and barnacle and whitefronted geese in winter. The cuckoo may be heard on the mainland in spring. Peploe and Cadell were two of the Scottish Colourists who painted here.

Laalt Mòr and Port Mòr lead to Eilean nam Bò, which is not an island but a headland overlooking skerries which surround it, popular with waders, both avian and human. To its south is Sluggan Dubh, at the back of which is Fidden with its campsite.

Beyond Fidden and Rubha Beul à Chaolais, a cylindrical stone mark is the official guide into An Caolas but a disused observatory, painted white and cylindrical with a conical top, is much more conspicuous. It is placed high on the side of Erraid and was used as a shore station until 1967 for signalling to the Skerryvore and Dubh Artach lighthouses. The island was described by Stevenson in *Kidnapped*. He visited for three weeks while supervising engineering work for the Dubh Artach lighthouse, for which this was the construction headquarters, and may also have been the inspiration for his *Treasure Island*.

12P   The Albert Memorial

The island is now used by the religious Findhorn Foundation although it is rarely an island. South of a cairn, the sand of Erraid Sound is only covered at the highest of tides, rather less than suggested in *Kidnapped*, in which the brig *Covenant* is wrecked off Tràigh Gheal or Balfour Bay on the west side of the island. This and Eilean Dubh ensure that Bàgh a' Chnoic Mhaoileanaich is sheltered from most directions. Indeed, the archipelago around

Iona Abbey overlooks the Sound of Iona.

Slugan Dubh and An Caolas before Erraid and the observatory.

Bàgh a' Chnoic Mhaoileanaich, the extension of Erraid Sound.

the outside of Erraid provides sheltered anchorages from most wind directions and gives respite to black guillemots and eider ducks.

In turn, Eilean a' Chalmain and Eilean na Seamair protect Port nan Ròn and its seals. Where the islands and reefs decline in size and number, views to the south take in Colonsay, Islay and Jura, which lead in towards Mull as the channel gradually narrows.

Eilean Mòr provides some shelter to the sands of Tràigh Gheal and there are numerous small inlets, mostly exposed to the south and without sand.

Rubh' Ardalanish is prominent at 34m high and also marks a more subtle change as the pink rocks give way to grey. Beyond it is the sandy sweep of Ardalanish Bay, backed by a fort, a blackhouse roofed with turf and a standing stone and leading to Aird Dubh, after which is the beautiful sandy bay of Port Uisken, sheltered by reefs and backed by a dun and a cairn.

Port an t-Slaoichain and Port Bheathain are two of the narrow inlets which follow before the site of Dun a'Gheird at the back of the inlet reaching Garbh Eilean, actually a peninsula. A cave faces the sea below Scoor.

Rubha nam Bràithrean sees a reduction in the number of inlets and islets. Back from the point is the hamlet of Shiaba, a victim of the 19th century Clearances. Eas Dubh falls to Port nan Droigheann and there is another waterfall to Tràigh Cadh an Easa'.

The cliffs reach their highest, 290m, at Leac nan Leum, the green scree slopes dropping from basaltic columns up to 2m in diameter. Malcolm's Point, named after one of the followers of St Columba, is little lower at 270m and continues up to 331m Creachan Mòr. At its foot are the Carsaig Arches, still 6km from Carsaig, the nearest village. As well as a conventional cave there is a pyramid shaped structure with a hole through its base and a basalt column on its peak.

Eagles occupy this remote area. Further along, the Nuns' Pass leads to a cave where nuns from Iona sheltered from the Vikings and again after the Reformation. There are Christian carvings and graffiti from the 6th century onwards and masons' workbenches used in preparing carvings for Iona. White sandstone was quarried until 1873 to supply Iona Abbey.

In an area with high precipitous cliffs and columnar basalt, Carsaig Bay provides an unexpected break, a flatter area with a chalk outcrop and watercress and gorse growing, between 377m Beinn Chreagach and 449m Beinn Chàrsaig. The bay was used in filming *I Know Where I'm Going!* Waterfalls descend in steps from the trap hillsides. The pier at the roadhead has been damaged by the sea while the coast has been damaged by greater forces. In 20km 375 basalt dykes run northwest–southeast, some to the mainland and even as far away as Cleveland.

Eastwards from Carsaig the coast receives some shelter from Gamhnach Mhòr, outside which there is a fish trap. There is another in Loch Buie, the southwestern end of the Great Glen fault, which begins at Rubha Dubh where there are rolls of pillow lava, producing gently contoured rockpools and a magnetic anomaly. An Dùnan is an isolated stack. Birdlife around the loch includes whooper swans. There are caves at intervals along the northwest side of the loch and the mast of a wreck is visible at one point.

Lochbuie, at the head of the loch, is backed by 717m Ben Buie and 698m Creach Beinn, still in trap country. In front it is protected by Eilean Mòr and is ringed by a cairn, standing stones, a Bronze Age stone circle, the only one on Mull, and a monument to Edward VII. The 15th century Moy Castle of the MacLaines of Lochbuie was built as a tower house with a spring of clear water which never runs dry. Less attractive was a bottle dungeon where the prisoner had to sit in darkness on a rock projection surrounded by 2.5m deep water. The story is told how John Roy MacAuley was fostered here for seven years as a boy after all his brothers in Lewis had been killed in a dispute which had begun over a cow. It was used in filming *I Know Where I'm Going!* The castle was abandoned in 1752 for a new mansion close by. It was described as the Garden of Mull until the 19th century Clearances. Still present is chieftain Ewan a'Chinn Bhig, beheaded in a clan battle. His ghost gallops around the estate when the death of a descendent is imminent.

The loch ends at Rubha na Faoilinn, the cliffs running 250m high to Rubha nam Fear, on top of which are red deer in the Laggan Deer Forest.

By Lord Lovat's Bay is Lord Lovat's Cave, 46m high and 90m long.

Frank Lockwood's Island is considered the start of the Firth of Lorn. Flows from here run to 2km/h, northeast from Dover HW −0050 (with a westerly eddy to Loch Buie) and southwest from Dover HW +0520. To the south, the ridge of Jura is extended by Scarba, Lunga, the Garvellachs, Luing and Seil, getting steadily closer but lower.

Port Ohirnie gives shelter from the west for owls and midges. Below 405m Druim Fada are a magnetic anomaly and a wreck. Could they be related?

Between Rubha nan Sailthean and Rubha na Faoilinn is the mouth of Loch Spelve and another magnetic anomaly. While flows northeast from Dover HW and southwest from Dover HW +0600 run only to 2km/h, flows into the loch from Dover HW +0140 and out from Dover HW −0500 are to 7km/h and there may be overfalls off the loch entrance. Port nam Marbh, port of the dead, is named as the landing point for corpses which were then to be taken overland to Iona, surprising as neither the water conditions nor the land route seem as attractive as other locations except, perhaps, as the shortest crossing from Kerrera.

Various cairns including a chambered cairn are to be found at Port Donain, together with the Uamh na Nighinn cave.

Malcolm's Point, an uncompromising coastal feature of the Ross of Mull.

Port an t-Sasunnaich, the lowlanders' port, was a ferry terminal from Oban at the start of a pilgrims' trail to Iona, the route marked by stones and a concrete seal. At least the land part of the route seemed better established. Grass Point is at the entrance to Loch Don. Flows northwards from Dover HW +0040 and south from Dover HW −0540 are to 6km/h. Heavy overfalls run 800m offshore with races and eddies as far as Rubha an Ridire, dangerous with opposing winds. A radio tower faces down Loch Don and Eilean a' Mhadaidh provides a sheltered inshore route for small craft. Fionn Phort is a landing point for submarine cables.

Unusually, cruise liners become a significant part of the shipping, although car ferries remain the main users, passing between Lady's Rock and Eilean Musdile at the end of Lismore.

Carsaig Arches, not easily reached on land.

The pillow lava at the end of Loch Buie with Ben Buie and Creach Beinn beyond.

Rubha na Faoilinn, topped by Laggan Deer Forest.

Distance
The Isle of Mull is 49km long and lies 2km off the Kilundine River with ferry access

OS 1:50,000 Sheets
47 Tobermory & North Mull
48 Iona & West Mull
49 Oban & East Mull

Tidal Constants
Craignure:
HW Dover −0500,
LW Dover −0510
Lochaline:
Dover −0510
Salen:
HW Dover −0450,
LW Dover −0500
Tobermory:
Dover −0500
Ulva Sound:
HW Dover −0530,
LW Dover −0520
Bunessan:
HW Dover −0540,
LW Dover −0530
Iona:
HW Dover −0530,
LW Dover −0540
Carsaig Bay:
HW Dover −0530,
LW Dover −0540
Seil Sound:
HW Dover −0540,
LW Dover −0550

Sea Area
Malin

Submarine Areas
32, Linnhe, 29, Staffa, 31 Mull

Connection
Loch Linnhe − see RoB p115

19 Ardnamurchan

The wind is fair, the day is fine
And swiftly, swifly runs the time;
The boat is floating on the tide
That wafts me off from Fiunary.
Norman McLeod.

The Sound of Mull was probably a tributary of a former Firth of Lorn/North Channel/Irish Sea river. It floods and ebbs from the northwest end.

The Eileanan Glasa, the green islands, are grass covered. Dearg Sgeir has the Eileanan Glasa light beacon which replaces a lighthouse demolished in 1935 by the cargo ship *Rondo*, adrift in a storm. Low water slack here is at HW Dover +0030. Using the islands as a stepping stone to cross the Sound of Mull to the Morvern shore, avoiding the ferries, brings the boater from Argyll & Bute to the Highland region.

Possible marine farms along the northeast shore are ac-companied by many antiquities, notably the ruin of Caisteal nan Con, dog's castle, the hunting lodge of the Macleans of Duart. Around the Killundine River are a stone circle, cairns, chapel and Càrn na Caillich. The mountainside is forested with gorse on lower slopes and wracks along the rocky shore, even swans at the river-mouth. Low water slack is at HW Dover −0030. There is a local magnetic anomaly which can increase compass variation by up to 5.5°.

The B489 coast road ends beyond the burial ground at Bonnavoulin. Sea urchins may be seen perched on the rocks. There is something endearing about watching a pair of normally quarrelsome gulls sharing an urchin, tak-ing it in turns to pick daintily at the contents of their packaged meal.

Low water slack at Auliston Point is at HW Dover −0130 and there is a weak clockwise current to 2km/h in the entrance to Loch Sunart. Most of the loch is pro-tected by Oronsay which makes a sheltered haven out of

Looking south down the Sound of Mull with the Eileanan Glasa in the centre.

Looking up the Sound of Mull past Auliston Point to the mouth of Loch Sunart and the bulk of Ben Hiant.

Little now remains of Casteal nan Con at Killundine.

Loch na Droma Buidhe. The upper end of the Sound of Mull north of Tobermory is susceptible to the weather, particularly with southerly and westerly winds, and this area can be rough even when millpond conditions exist through the rest of the sound.

Beyond Rubha Aird Shlignich is Camas nan Geall, bay of the cells or churches. Either meaning could apply as there is a chambered cairn and Cladh Chiarain which was dedicated by St Columba to his friend St Ciaran who is buried here, having died in 548 after funding the monastery at Clonmacnoise on the Shannon. Contrasting with the silver sand is a red granite monolith with carvings of hunting dogs and a cross.

There is a weak eddy in Port a Chamais on the flood. At Maclean's Nose the flows start outwards at HW Dover +0130 and in at HW Dover −0415.

The scenery is of gabbro. The large protrusion on the lower flanks of Ben Hiant appears not to have been given the name Maclean's Nose by one of his friends, being flattened rather than flattering. If the nose is viewed from the front, however, and looked at as a head it takes on the striking form of a bearded face with grey eyes and well proportioned nose.

Another marine farm may be located in Camas nan Clacha' Mora.

Mingary looks right for a medieval castle, apparently cube shaped with no more than a hint of a taper and no features to break up the bottom three quarters of the plain walls. It was the seat of the MacIans of Ardnamurchan with a commanding view down the Sound of Mull. It had a 13th century high hexagonal curtain wall with sea gate and land gate, having small turrets added in the 17th century and internal barracks in the 18th century. It was besieged unsuccessfully with great loss of life by Lachlan Maclean of Duart with the help of the crew of the *San Juan de Sicilia* in 1588, thus the name Port nan Spainteach for the nearby

Maclean's Nose, a nose or a face?

the coast is steep and rocky, turning to cliffs. Sròn Bheag climbs to 342m high Beinn na Seilg. The cliff section becomes better defined after Eilean nan Secachd Seisrichean. Occasionally the cliffs are white with cormorant guano at favoured points.

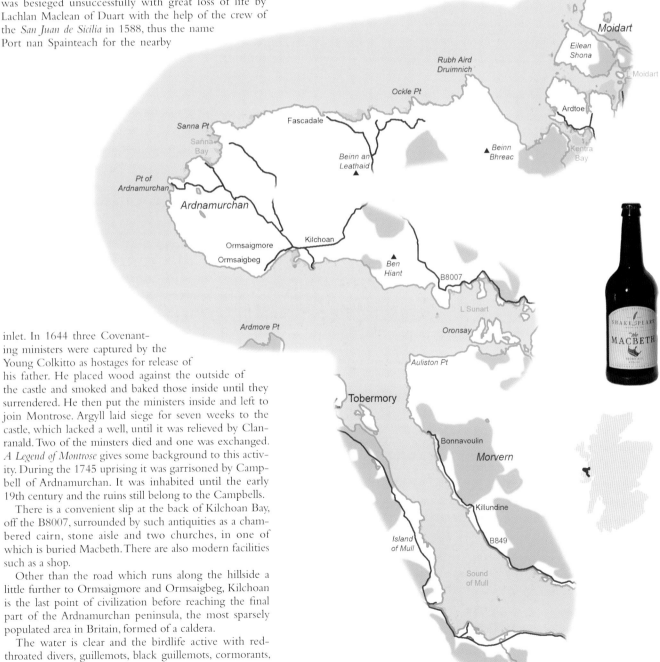

inlet. In 1644 three Covenanting ministers were captured by the Young Colkitto as hostages for release of his father. He placed wood against the outside of the castle and smoked and baked those inside until they surrendered. He then put the ministers inside and left to join Montrose. Argyll laid siege for seven weeks to the castle, which lacked a well, until it was relieved by Clanranald. Two of the minsters died and one was exchanged. *A Legend of Montrose* gives some background to this activity. During the 1745 uprising it was garrisoned by Campbell of Ardnamurchan. It was inhabited until the early 19th century and the ruins still belong to the Campbells.

There is a convenient slip at the back of Kilchoan Bay, off the B8007, surrounded by such antiquities as a chambered cairn, stone aisle and two churches, in one of which is buried Macbeth. There are also modern facilities such as a shop.

Other than the road which runs along the hillside a little further to Ormsaigmore and Ormsaigbeg, Kilchoan is the last point of civilization before reaching the final part of the Ardnamurchan peninsula, the most sparsely populated area in Britain, formed of a caldera.

The water is clear and the birdlife active with red-throated divers, guillemots, black guillemots, cormorants, blackbacked gulls and fulmars among the species present.

Streams are weak to the Point of Ardnamurchan but

Ben Hiant, seen from Kilchoan Bay.

Looking past the Ardnamurchan light towards Muck, Eigg, Rùm and Skye.

Point of Ardnamurchan, Gaelic for the point of great waves or sea nymphs, is not as dramatic as its location would suggest. It is much lower than the coast which precedes it and has bays on both sides. The first intact Viking boat burial on the UK mainland, a 5m boat from the 10th century, has been found here and there is a Neolithic chambered cairn. Although it is the most westerly point on the British mainland, it is surrounded by islands, notably Mull, Coll, Muck, Eigg, Rùm, Canna and Skye, a dramatic panorama.

The lighthouse, designed by Alan Stevenson and built by Robert Hume in 1849 of pink granite from the Ross of Mull, stands 36m high, the light 55m above the sea with a range of 32km, reached by 140 spiral steps, all of which is protected by a high white wall on this wave battered headland with its interesting display of volcanic rocks. It is said to be the world's only Egyptian styled lighthouse. On a clear day the view from the light includes Barra and South Uist. A Kingdom of Light visitor centre accompanies the lighthouse.

The wrecked ship silhouette of Rubha Carrach with some of the Moidart peaks beyond.

Streams start north and northeast at HW Dover +0130 and south and southwest at HW Dover −0430 at up to 3km/h, flows generally being weak to Rubh' Arisaig. The shoreline is rocky to Sanna Point but interspersed with those rocks are several beaches of white shell sand which now become a feature of the coast.

Eilean Carrach is the island of the uneven surface, not overstating the case. Port ne Cairidh is the port of the fish weir while the beach of Port Macneil was named after Macneil of Barra, who landed cattle here for driving along the drove roads to the Falkirk fairs.

Sanna Bay has the best beach on the Ardnamurchan peninsula, backed by dunes and spoiled only by an old water tower. There are seals, oystercatchers, sandpipers, eider ducks, mergansers, razorbills, meadow pipits, sky-

larks and even the cuckoo to be heard inland in spring. Arnamurchan is home to the belted beauty moth, of which the female is flightless.

Many tenants were moved here from Swordle, further east, about 1830. In the 1920s photographer and author Mary EM Donaldson, inspired by the local black houses,

built Sanna Bheag using local granite and heather, bracken, rushes, machair grass and straw as thatch with a garden containing birdsfoot trefoil, stonecrop, trinity and orchids, the house burning down in 1947. Alasdair MacMhaighstir Alasdair described the atmosphere in his *Song of Summer*.

Before heading off for Muck, round Scotland paddler Brian Wilson met one of our pioneering nuclear power engineers here. Brian felt the man's clothes did nothing for his image but was surprised when he removed them all a few minutes later to continue the pre season tan required by naturists if they are not to be seen as interlopers.

Beyond Sanna Point is the Dùn Bàn fort site, at the other end of the bay from which is Rubha Carrach, a 60m high black overhanging cliff etched with orange lichens like the bow of some great rusting ship. There are caves at the landward end. Every inlet seems to have an inflatable full of subaqua enthusiasts.

Further along the coast towards Meall Buidhe Mór is another cliff with the crump of waves resounding from deep inside the rocks. The 90m high cliffs have close vertical fissures but long intrusions run diagonally across them.

The cliffs come to an end at Fascadale Bay although 437m high Meall nan Con and 401m Beinn an Leathaid still push up the skyline inland. The skyline at Fascadale includes a well camouflaged hut.

Achateny Water discharges at Port Bàn, a bay with rare shells on the beach. Assorted caves, duns and a chambered cairn continue from here to Port an Eilean Mhóir from where the tenants of Swordle were displaced to Sanna.

The northeast side of Ockle Point has columnar basaltic cliffs with another dun and more caves following before Rubha Aird Druimnich.

Dunes surround much of Loch Ceann Traigh, as the name implies, together with possible fish farms, but they are overshadowed by 357m Beinn Bhreac to the south and 845m Beinn Resipol and the other peaks of Moidart, Sunart and the Morvern to the southeast, a magnificent skyline.

A channel leads in past Ardtoe to Kentra Bay. The islets at the north side of the entrance to the South Channel of Loch Moidart bring azure green water as sunlight reflects off the white sandy bottom.

The west coast of Eilean Shona is rugged grey rock with just sheep grazing on the grassy crags and low cliffs by the sea, is devoid of features. The peaks of Aonach, Cruach a' Choire, Cruach Bhuide and Sgurr an Teintein all merge into each other above Port an Sgrìodain.

Meall Buidhe Mór with its vertical basalt strata cut by diagonal intrusions.

Distance
62km from the Eileanan Glasa to Eilean Shona

OS 1:50,000 Sheets
40 Mallaig & Glenfinnan
47 Tobermory & North Mull

Tidal Constants
Salen:
HW Dover −0450,
LW Dover −0500
Tobermory:
Dover −0500
Loch Moidart:
HW Dover −0500,
LW Dover −0450

Sea Area
Malin

Submarine Areas
32 Linnhe, 29 Staffa, 25 Eigg

20 Eilean Shona

The name means island of the ford and that ford is important when planning a circumnavigation of Eilean Shona. The island reduces the mouth of Loch Moidart to two channels, of which the North Channel dries at its east end at low tide, allowing a track across to be used by the few inhabitants of this island owned by Vanessa Branson. JM Barrie used it as a family holiday retreat in the 1920s and is believed to have written a screen version of *Peter Pan* here.

Inside the islets at the north side of the entrance to the South Channel azure green water is produced as sunshine lights up the white sandy bottom. Occasional inlets contain small sandy beaches which are probably never used from one year to the next.

Passage up the South Channel is dominated by the bulks of Beinn Bhreac and Cruach nam Meann at the apparent end of the channel. Just before it, the River Shiel enters on the right and several houses are visible on the far bank of its estuary. Occasional houses have been spotted at Baileatonach, Arean and on the shore of Faodhail Dhubh but this is the first time they are found in number.

Vegetation gradually increases on Eilean Shona as conditions become more sheltered. Rhododendrons in profusion and fir trees contrast with the deciduous trees of the north shore.

Port Thairbeirt Dheas is faced by Eilean Shona House and most of the dwellings of the few families on the island. Boats, the only practical means of transport in the area, are moored in the inlet and the occasional slipways and boathouses are sheltered by Eilean Shona's bulk.

Such luxuries were not present in the eighteenth century. On the other side of the round wooded Riska Island is an islet with the mostly 15th and 17th century

Port Thairbeirt Dheas with its boathouses.

The remains of Castle Tioram.

Eilean Shona from the north.

remains of the 13th century Castle Tioram, meaning dry island. The seat of the MacDonalds of Clanranald, it was captured in 1692 by Government troops but recaptured in 1715 by Allan of Clan Ranald. It was the centre of both the 1715 and 1745 Jacobite uprisings. Earlier, Donald the Cruel had hanged his cook for taking snuff. After the 1745 uprising failed it was torched on Clanranald orders but parts remained habitable and Lady Grange spent some time here on her way to being exiled on St Kilda.

Threading between the islands with their Scots pines leads into the main part of Loch Moidart. At low tide it is necessary to follow the main channel south of Eilean an Fheidh but usually it is possible to go directly to the most practical access onto Loch Moidart, from the lay by below Cruach na Cùilidh Bige on the A861, the road used by the cycling section of the first permanent triathlon, the Ardgour & Moidart Triathlon. From Glen Dig it is noticeable that Beinn a' Bhàillidh, the peak of the island at 265m, is even higher than the rest of the rugged terrain and that the water is largely lost between the mountains. This ensures that views at water level are dramatic with spectacular mountains all around in this, the Morar, Moidart & Ardnamurchan designated National Scenic Area.

Currents in the channels can be quite swift in the lower half of the tide.

Most of Eilean Shona's woodland is on the east end and also on Shona Beag, to which it is joined by a neck of land. Shona Beag guides the user into the North Channel, which is of riverlike proportions. Both banks are wooded here with oaks, rowans and gnarled birches. Ferns, bracken

The wooded banks of the North Channel.

and heather smother the ground and mosses and lichens cling to every surface, rock, tree or bog. In the shelter of the valley all is tranquil and time seems to stand still. With the exception of the perky sandpiper, even the birds seem to soar lazily. A pair of herons flap slowly away down the side of the channel, hooded crows soar about the cliffs and a golden eagle sails on stretched wings about the peaks.

Those peaks, rugged igneous rock forming a skyline of wild and dramatic shapes, take on even more fantastic and menacing forms under a stormy sky when light and gloom are alternately playing across them. Neither is it

Smirisary Hill by the North Channel, Eigg visible beyond.

Rùm's peaks seen from the outer half of the North Channel.

just the peaks of Eilean Shona and the mainland which contribute to this breathtaking display. Directly in line at the end of the North Channel is the great saddle below An Sgurr on Eigg.

Signs of man are very few, a moored yacht, a couple of fish breeding cages and just the occasional building such as the cottage at Baramore and a derelict building at the back of the inlet beyond it.

Gradually the channel moves into an archipelago of islets and the white barnacled bottom can be seen through clear water among the floating seaweed. Both entrances to Loch Moidart are tortuous, narrow and rock studded, making passage for larger craft sailors quite risky unless well acquainted with the waters. The swell makes its presence felt beyond the bar a kilometre inside the entrance until breakers are crashing across the jagged water level rocks of Rubh' Aird an Fheidh.

Depending on conditions it may be possible to pick a line between the rocks or it may be necessary to take a safer route near the Sgeirean Dubha Fhiadhach.

From the mouth of the North Passage there is a phenomenal seascape stretching round from the Ardnamurchan peninsula through Muck, Eigg, Rùm and across the Sound of Arisaig towards Skye. Nearby, numerous islets dot the sea. The boater may be able to equal the view elsewhere but surely cannot surpass it.

For a while the scenery becomes less important than the water conditions on the open sea. The west coast of Eilean Shona, rugged grey rock with just sheep grazing on the grassy crags and low cliffs by the sea, is devoid of definite features as Sgurr an Teintein, Cruach Bhuidhe, Cruach a' Choire and Aonach all merge into each other above Port an Sgrìodain. Floats mark lobster pots by Eilean a' Choire although only shags and gulls are seen to frequent the area.

Distance
Eilean Shona is 5km long and lies 50m off Moidart with ford access

OS 1:50,000 Sheet
40 Mallaig &
Glenfinnan

Tidal Constants
Loch Moidart:
HW Dover −0500,
LW Dover −0450

Sea Area
Malin

Submarine Area
25 Eigg

Rubh' Aird an Fheidh backed by the Arnamurchan peninsula.

85

21 Sound of Sleat

There's news from Moidart cam' yestreen,
Will soon gar mony ferlie;
For ships o' war have just come in,
An' landed Royal Charlie.

Carolina Oliphant, Lady Nairne

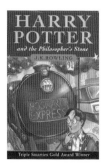

Strong flows up into Loch Moidart start at HW Dover +0110 and the ebb starts at HW Dover −0510. Rocks and islands around the entrance to the North Channel dampen out swells.

Smirisary brings a selection of holiday chalets. Rubha Ghead a' Leighe leads round into the Sound of Arisaig, the south side of which is mostly steep and rocky and catches a heavy sea with onshore winds.

Samalaman Island is 16m high and connected to the shore at low water and is an attractive spot with picnic area and the return of trees, together with yellow irises and birds from the hooded crow to the heron. Fish farms may be located in Glenuig Bay, facing onto which is the A861 and Glenuig Inn, which has rooms for divers and other watersports enthusiasts. Flows inward start at HW Dover +0110 and the ebb starts at HW Dover −0510 although flows are barely perceptible.

Eilean nan Gobhar or goat island is 40m high, the site of a vitrified fort. It stands in the mouth of Loch Ailort which winds away inland and is separated by Rubha Chaolais on the end of the Ardnish Peninsula from Loch nan Uamh. It is an area frequented by shags, blackbacked gulls, black guillemots, seals and jellyfish and surrounded by birch, larch and oak woods festooned with healthy lichens. It is overlooked by 601m high Sidhean Mór.

Below the peak, the West Highland Railway arrives across a viaduct crossing an arm at the head of the loch. Of concrete, it has two pairs of four 15m arches with a wider pier in the centre which entombs a horse and cart which fell in during construction in 1900. This is one of the most scenic railway lines in the world, as shown by the running of observation cars and the popularity of the present steam train service, boosted by its Harry Potter associations.

Very weak streams are ingoing from HW Dover +0110 and outgoing from HW Dover −0510.

Loch nan Uamh, the loch of the caves, was central to the movements of Prince Charlie. He landed in Borrodale Bay on July 25th 1745 from the *Du Teillay*. He met the chiefs in Borrodale House, later fired by Captain Fergussone of the sloop *Furnace* and the people maimed and murdered by his crew as part of the Duke of Cumberland's retribution. On 26th April 1746 at 8pm Prince Charlie sailed from here to Rossinish on Benbecula with a dozen others in an eight oared boat. Conditions were gale force and the boat lost its bowsprit as it rounded Rubh' Arisaig. A day later the privateers *Bellona* and *Mars* landed 35,000 gold Louis and six casks to help fund the cause, some of the money becoming the Loch Arkaig Treasure. The French ships had to fight a six hour battle in the loch with the 24 gun *Greyhound* and sloop *Baltimore* before making their escape. Prince Charlie made several further visits here and it was from here that he made his final departure for France in *L'Heureux* on 20th September with a reward of £30,000 on his head, the embarkation spot marked by a cairn. Prince Charlie's Cave is 30m long by 3.5m high and is where he lived for at least a week with his followers, the floor lined with heather.

Rubh' Aird Ghamhsgail has a fort site. Further up the valley of the Borrodale Burn is Arisaig House, used as the field training headquarters of the Special Operations Executive under General Sir Colin McVean Gubbins in the Second World War.

Offshore are dotted the Borrodale Islands, on Eilean an Sgùrra the 17m high block of rock resembling a castle. Further along the coast with a 10m high basaltic pillar lies Eilean an t-Snidhe. Closer inshore is Eilean a' Ghaill, 21m high, its cliffbound top looking like a ruin from the northwest although there is a real fort site on the east side. Terns and oystercatchers live on the rocks and in the sandy bays. These latter are also occupied by diverse humans, it being possible to find nude sunbathers in one bay and hikers in boots and rollneck sweaters in the next on the same day, reflecting the varied aspirations of holidaymakers.

It is possible to use routes inside islets at the mouth of Port a' Bhathaich and Eilean Port nam Murrach among drifting moon jellyfish.

A white painted mark locates Rubh' Arisaig and the start of what is arguably the most beautiful area of sea

The Borrodale shore across the Sound of Arisaig from Glenuig.

Camas an t-Salainn by Arisaig, looking to Eigg and Rùm.

in Britain. Arisaig lies at the head of Loch nan Ceall, the loch of the hermit's cell. A passenger ferry runs through the South Channel to Eigg, Muck and Rùm which all lie offshore. Inshore, however, there are 3km of skerries between which lies clear water through which the clean shell sand bottom can be seen. Largest of the islands is 17m high Luinga Mhor while numerous rocks are used by a particularly large seal colony and the smell of fish lingers on the air. Pilot whales are seen in August and September. In the shallower water waders go about their business. Streams into the North Channel begin at HW Dover +0120 and the ebb starts at HW Dover −0510, strongly in the lower half of the tide when sandbanks are uncovered. Meanwhile, streams along the coast are northgoing from HW Dover −0100 for seven and a half hours and southgoing for five hours from HW Dover −0400.

From Eilean Ighe to Mallaig the streams are northgoing from HW Dover +0115 until HW Dover −0445, weak but sometimes with eddies on a shore which is rocky but with sandy beaches as far as the River Morar.

Back of Keppoch has a selection of masts and towers plus a caravan site, more caravans and a golf course following at Portnaluchaig with an aerial and yet more caravans at Glenancross. The attraction of this coastline for the campers is not hard to see. The Polish commandos were trained from Camusdarach by the Special Operations Executive during the Second World War and Czechs trained from Garramor House.

The River Morar at low tide it reveals expanses of the whitest sand in Britain, the location used for filming Bill Forsyth's *Local Hero* in 1983. Two decades earlier the Mosquitos of *633 Squadron* had droned in over the same estuary to be filmed in action over an imaginary section of the Norwegian landscape near Loch Morar, the UK's deepest lake at 310m.

The West Highland and Marine hotels are in among the cluster of buildings which lead to the mark on Rubha na h-Acairseid. Southwards entry to **Mallaig** harbour is past the breakwater of caissons built in 1986. The northern end of the port loads 20,000 cars and 100,000 passengers yearly to Armadale with passengers ferry also to Kyle of Lochalsh. The southern end of the harbour is well used by fishing boats, this being the premier fishing port of the west coast, once Europe's largest herring port, but a decline in catches has been caused by too much fishing in the Minch. There can be over 80 boats per day handling fish, lobsters and prawns with exports to Europe, Canada and the USA. The port used by Gavin Maxwell for his basking shark fishing venture and he had a small office here. The town is at the end of the A830, the Road

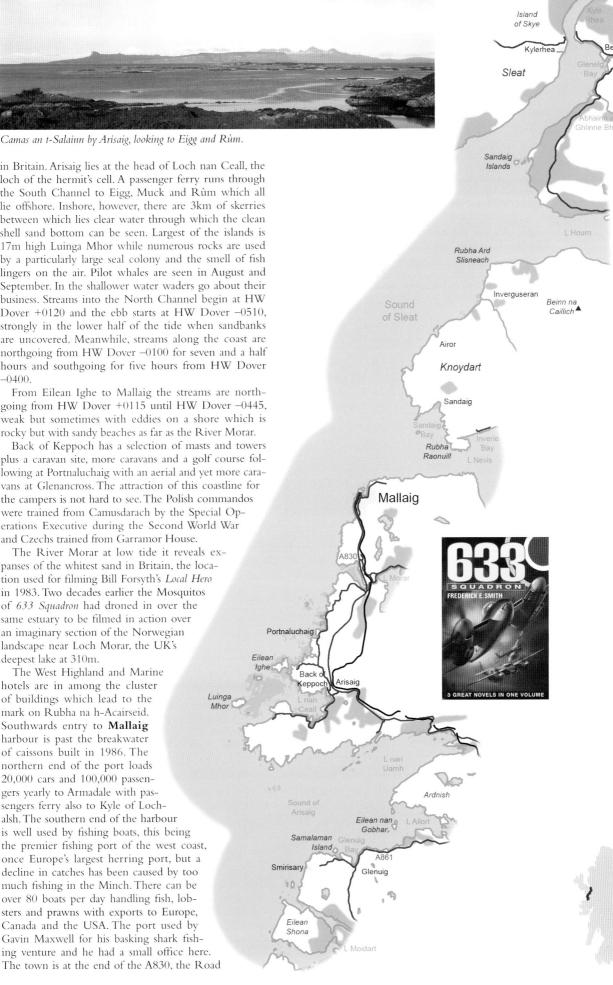

Eigg and Rùm seen over the skerries enclosing Loch nan Ceall.

to the Isles, and expanded after the arrival of the West Highland Line from Fort William in 1901. It has been the town with the second highest driving test success rate in Britain.

Off the harbour stands a 6m metal framework with a

The Jacobite arrives in Mallaig.

light. Flows are northeastwards from HW Dover +0130 and southwest from HW Dover −0430 at up to 2km/h although flows can be stronger off points.

A submarine cable crosses Loch Nevis from Mallaig-vaig to the north side, across which Prince Charlie's party outrowed Government forces before returning to Mallaig. Flows into the loch start at HW Dover −0110 and out again from HW Dover −0510. They are only up to 1km/h but winds, especially from the southwest or the southeast, can bring violent squalls of confusing direction in Loch Nevis. This is porpoise territory. The north entrance to the loch is guarded by the 104m high Rubha Raonuill with a golden statue of the Virgin Mary, Bogha Don beacon and, hidden on the east side, a cave. Norwegian commandos were trained by the loch from Glaschoille House by the SOE. The coast is rugged to Loch Hourn.

The Sleat Peninsula on Skye is also rugged and makes dramatic viewing across the Sound of Sleat as it gradually reduces in distance.

Sandaig Bay seems to collect an undue number of fish crates and floats, perhaps something to do with the fact that it is normally downwind of Mallaig. Scant wind

The busy fish pier at Mallaig with the Armadale car ferry loading beyond.

The entrance to Loch Nevis with Rubha Raonuill guarding its northern side.

Looking across the Sound of Sleat to Skye from the moorings at Airor, sheltered by Airor Island.

shelter is given to the bay by Eilean Dearg and Glas Eilean. The former is 20m high and covered with heather, Eilean nan Gàmhna being as high but covered with long grass. Sandaig itself is now little more than a couple of ruins, one being a chapel.

An Fhaochag, steep and 6m high, forms the western extremity of Knoydart. Despite its present remoteness, it has a memorial, ruins and Dun Ban to add to the interest of its caves.

Airor is a small harbour sheltered by 8m high Airor Island and a harbour wall. However, its facilities are even less comprehensive than they seem. The road goes only as far as Inverie on Loch Nevis and is not connected with the rest of the road system. For the locals this does mean that they do not have to be so fastidious with the normal driving laws. After all, they are hardly likely to be stopped by a passing police car.

Quest by Canoe says Airor offers the best view from the mainland in all the journey.

From Airor the coast continues to be inaccessible by land while beaches are of rounded tennis ball sized stones, uncomfortable to walk on. Opposite Eilean Shamadalain is a chapel ruin and a sheep shelter built from fish crates nailed together. The Sound of Sleat can be stormy.

A gravel spit has been formed by the Abhainn Inbhir Ghuiserein. Inverguseran is a sheep station, which will not have escaped the attentions of foxes and golden eagles in the vicinity.

Rubha Ard Slisneach marks the end of the southern side of Loch Hourn, a loch which always seems to be referred to with the prefix 'dark'. The surrounding high peaks block out the light and encourage precipitation. Notable on the southern side of the loch are Beinn na

Caillich, old woman's hill, at 785m and Ladhar Bheinn at 1,020m, while 974m Beinn Sgritheall presents an uncompromising slope on the north side. Loch Hourn is one of the most remote and spectacular of the western sea lochs and has one of the heaviest rainfalls in the British Isles.

At Croulin on the south shore there is an area of silt brought down from Beinn na Caillich by the Croulin Burn while a tripod on Sgeir Ulibhe, on the other side of the loch, marks another shallow area. Streams are very weak, the flood starting at HW Dover +0155 and the ebb at HW Dover −0415.

From Loch Hourn to Kyle Rhea the coast becomes increasingly high, steep and rocky.

Sandaig Island lighthouse stands on 19m high Eilean Mór, the outer of the Sandaig Islands, a 7m structure that has a white octagonal tower. Most of the Sandaig Islands are connected to each other and to the mainland at low tide, exposing banks of mussels which oystercatchers and herons pick around. This was Camusfeàrna in Gavin Maxwell's *Ring of Bright Water* and subsequent books and there are memorials near the Allt Mór Shantaig at Sandaig to Maxwell and to Edal, the last of the otters here, killed when the house burned down in 1968. Kathleen Raine returned to the site in *The Lion's Mouth*. The sighting of the ghost of a man with an otter on a lead has been claimed.

Northeastly flows in the Sound of Sleat begin at HW Dover +0130 and they start southwest at HW Dover −0430, initially at up to 4km/h although the figure increases greatly further north

Eilanreach is at the mouth of the Abhainn a' Ghlinne Bhig, up the valley of which are several broch sites. One

Loch Hourn with Beinn Sgritheall bathed in sunlight.

The Sandaig islands with Skye on the far side of the Sound of Sleat.

The old croft at Sandaig, setting for Gavin Maxwell's otter stories.

Distance
*65km from Eilean
Shona to the Kylerhea
ferry*

OS 1:50,000 Sheets
*33 Loch Alsh, Glen
Shiel & Loch Hourn
40 Mallaig &
Glenfinnan*

Tidal Constants
*Loch Moidart:
HW Dover −0500,
LW Dover −0450
Mallaig:
Dover −0450
Inverie Bay:
HW Dover −0510,
LW Dover −0450
Loch Hourn:
HW Dover −0500,
LW Dover −0500
Glenelg Bay:
HW Dover −0500,
LW Dover −0450*

Sea Areas
Malin, Hebrides

Submarine Areas
25 Eigg, 21 Sleat

of the finest Pictish brochs is Dun Telve, still 10m high despite having been used as a source of stone for the building of Bernera Barracks.

The northeastgoing flow begins to pick up. On the southwesterly stream there are northgoing eddies on both sides and there can be heavy overfalls, dangerous to small boats on the southwesterly stream if southwesterly winds are blowing across Bàgh Dùnan Ruadh.

The Sound of Sleat seems to end promptly at Glenelg Bay but Kyle Rhea leaves in the north corner between steep mountainsides.

Below 739m Sgurr na Coinnich is Coalas an Lamh-achaidh with the shortest vehicle ferry crossing to Skye, the only one until the railway came to Kyle of Lochalsh, the starting point for Johnson and Boswell's 1773 tour of the Hebrides. It is Britain's last manually operated turntable ferry and runs only in the summer. Until 1906 cattle were swum across here at slack water, up to 8,000 per year in strings of six to eight tied behind boats. A less conspicuous crossing came later, submarine cables from Glenelg to Bàgh Dùnan Ruadh, where the Kylerhea River enters.

Looking up the Sound of Sleat. Kyle Rhea cuts through the cleft in the centre.

Island of Skye

Speed, bonnie boat, like a bird on the wing;
'Onward!' the sailors cry;
Carry the lad that's born to be king
Over the sea to Skye.
Sir Harold Edwin Boulton

To Ptolemy it was Scitis Insular. To the Norse it was Skuyo, the isle of clouds, because of its cloud cap. To the Celts it was the winged isle, An t-Eilean Sgitheanach. In Gaelic it is also Eilean a' Cheò, the isle of mist. At 77km long and covering 1,740km², it has over 1,600km of coastline yet nowhere is more than 8km from the sea. It is the largest of the Inner Hebrides, inhabited for at least 4,000 years and under Viking control until 1263. In the mid 19th century, before the Clearances, the population was triple its present 10,000. It was opened up by the Victorians when they brought the railway to Kyle of Lochalsh but nearly half still speak Gaelic and the Sabbath is widely kept, including by most of the few petrol stations. It is mentioned in more songs and poems than any other place, including in Somhairle MacGill-Eain's *The Island*. Dog enthusiasts know it for the Skye terrier.

The oldest rock on Skye is the gneiss of Sleat, Norse for level land, into which are intruded the dyke swarms which run northwest–southeast across the island. Sleat is known as the Garden of Skye because of its luxuriant coastal vegetation. The Moine Thrust runs down the west side of Kyle Rhea and then down the Sleat peninsula.

Going southwards, on the Skye shore there are woods below 610m Ben Aslak, the shoreline with stunted oaks and violets, bluebells and red campion in the spring and the most westerly ash wood in the UK, also the ruin of the hamlet of Leitir Fura, abandoned in 1782.

The sound widens beyond the Sandaig Islands with their lighthouse. To the south of Loch na Dal, the mouth of the Abhainn Ceann-locha, is the island of Ornsay which has a mark at the northeast corner and the remains of a church at the south end, off which is Eilean Sionnach with its 19m white lighthouse of 1857 by the Stevensons and Eilean an Eòin. These shelter the Harbour at Isleornsay, formerly with a herring fishing fleet, especially at low water when they mostly connect to Ard Ghunel. Many emigrants departed from the pier here. Salmon nets will be out at times. Gavin Maxwell owned these keeper's cottages. Amenities around Eilean Iarmain include the Gallery an Talla Dearg.

A Summer in Skye reports how a missing sailor was found here by dragging with line and hooks. For the previous three months there had been loud cries on calm nights from the place where the corpse was landed, the hooks had jangled on their line and they had appeared to have water droplets on them. Author Alexander Smith also reported having a meal here of trout which had been left in a field by a stream in spate although it had taken the owner's crop of potatoes instead.

South of Isleornsay the Sleat peninsula consists of Old Red Sandstone with gneiss.

The remains of Dùn Bàn stand between Camus Croise and Ob Snaosaig and there is a further inlet at Camas Barabhaig. Small sawtooth ridges of strata at 45° run down to the sea, the channels between them being filled with fist sized stones which are very unstable underfoot.

Many of the stones from Knock Castle, at the back of Knock Bay, were used to build Knock House but the castle remains are an ivy clad block which was defended in the 15th century by the MacDonalds against attack by the MacLeods. Beyond is the Torabhaig whisky distillery. After Teangue are a radio mast, memorial, church remains and maybe a fish farm. The height of the Sleat peninsula is easing down to the southwest with Maol Buidhe a peak at 233m.

Kilbeg's notable building is the cylinder of Sabhal Mòr Ostaig, the Gaelic college, which has courses in Gaelic and piping as well as hosting the Skye Festival of food and music and the Skye Sea Kayak Symposium. Gaelic is making a recovery.

Dun Ela was built at the back of Bàgh a' Mhuilinn. The adjacent 69km² estate contains the castellated ruin of Armadale Castle of 1790 for the 1st Lord Macdonald, extended in 1815–19 by Gillespie Graham, suffering a

Ben Aslak stands above Kylerhea and the ferry slipway.

Primroses beat the trees into spring growth near Port Aslaig.

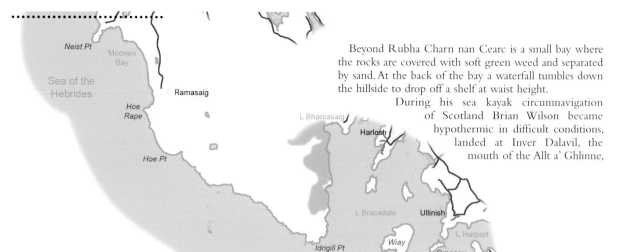

Sea of the
Hebrides

Beyond Rubha Charn nan Cearc is a small bay where the rocks are covered with soft green weed and separated by sand. At the back of the bay a waterfall tumbles down the hillside to drop off a shelf at waist height.

During his sea kayak circumnavigation of Scotland Brian Wilson became hypothermic in difficult conditions, landed at Inver Dalavil, the mouth of the Allt a' Ghlinne,

major fire in 1855. Armadale House had been burned by the king's fleet in 1690. Gardens covering 16ha include North American hardwoods, conifers, Australasian and European trees and silver firs from 1795. Earlier, Dr Johnson had been impressed earlier by the ashes. There are nature trails, Clan Donald Skye & Museum of the Isles, material on the Clearances and the Bay Pottery.

Armadale Bay receives swells with winds from the north to the southeast. Down from a cairn is the pier at the end of the A851, serving the vehicle ferry to Mallaig in the summer and offering the Pasta Shed for refreshment.

Irises, thrift and midges are the mixed delights. A hide on Rubha Phòil looks over an archipelago which largely disappears at high water. Ardvasar offers the last sheltered beach with road access on the east side of Sleat.

The sheltered bay at Ardvasar is near enough to the pier at Armadale to hear the piper welcoming visitors and for Alexander Smith's party in *A Summer in Skye* to watch blasting in a rock quarry while waiting for the *Clansman* paddle steamer, the hamlet also being home to Angus-with-the-dogs. There are red deer on the hills and oystercatchers, cormorants, blackbacked and herring gulls and guillemots on the water. Flows in the Sound of Sleat run south from HW Dover −0440 and north from HW Dover +0120 to 2km/h. Views across the sound are to Loch Nevis and Mallaig, the first of many fine views.

Above Tormore the flanks of 280m Sgurr nan Caorach are covered with Calligarry Forest. Between Port a' Chùil and Port na Long is Ard Thurnish, at the back of which is the crofting village of Aird of Sleat with the watercolour gallery of Peter McDermott at the end of the road although a gated track does continue west beyond the remains of a chapel. It may be remote enough for a school of dolphins to be met hunting yet jets shatter the silence as they practice low level mountain runs.

Camas Daraich is tucked in between Leir Mhaodail and Point of Sleat with its 7m high square white light tower structure. In calm conditions, such as inside Eilean Sgorach, the water is clear. The rocks are often folded and contorted.

From the Point the Cuillin hills come into view, first the Black Cuillin to the west and then the Red Cuillin as well to their east. With the sun on them or a changing pattern of sun and clouds there is no better view in Britain. Moving north brings them ever closer. The Black Cuillin with their jagged frost 990m shattered crown of peaks consist of 50,000,000 year old gabbro with plutonic intrusions, elsewhere only found in northern Norway. The Red Cuillin are more rounded granite with acid plutonic intrusions, often looking more white than red. The name is thought to come from the Norse kjölen, high rocks or kjöllen, keels. This is the incomparable backdrop to this route. Also visible are various combinations of the Small Isles to the west.

and slept in a cave with vivid dreams for twelve hours until he recovered.

Dalavil was cleared in the 1870s as it was cheaper to evict the crofters than to provide a school, as the new Education Acts required. Mackerel, ling and shellfish provided an important part of the residents' diet.

249m Sgurr Breac separates this from the next inlet, Tarskavaig Bay, where a heron may fish among the wrack. Islets litter the coast from Tarskavaig Point. At the back of Camas Daraich are the remains of a wooden boat which came to grief on them.

Flows in Loch Eishort are ingoing from HW Dover +0120 and outgoing from HW Dover −0440 but flows are weak.

Overlooking Ob Guascavaig is Dunscaith, the castle of gloom, ruined but well preserved with a drawbridge. This is one of the longest fortified headlands in the Hebrides, built by the MacAskills in the 14th century, the home of the MacDonalds from the 15th century until 1570, when they moved to Duntulm. The site had been home to the legendary Queen of Skye, Scathach, who taught warfare to the 3rd century Irish hero Cuchulainn and who had ramparts protected by an iron palisade with severed heads, then a pit of poisonous snakes and then a collection of beaked toads. He beat them all then married Bragela, the lonely sunbeam of Dunscaith, and the large Clach Luath stone is where he tied his dog after hunting.

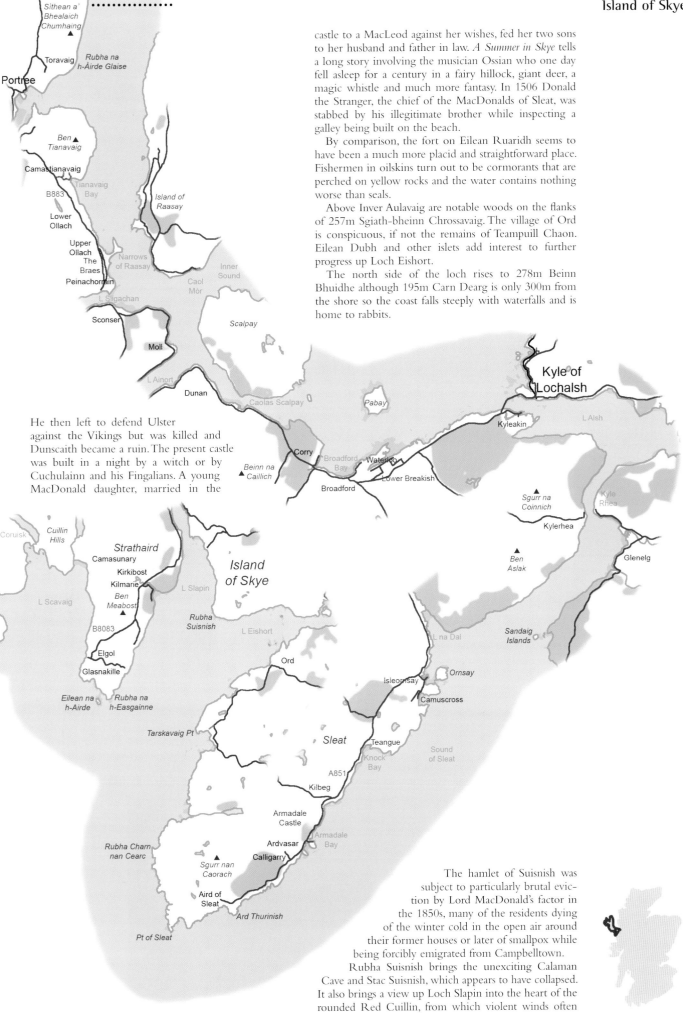

castle to a MacLeod against her wishes, fed her two sons to her husband and father in law. *A Summer in Skye* tells a long story involving the musician Ossian who one day fell asleep for a century in a fairy hillock, giant deer, a magic whistle and much more fantasy. In 1506 Donald the Stranger, the chief of the MacDonalds of Sleat, was stabbed by his illegitimate brother while inspecting a galley being built on the beach.

By comparison, the fort on Eilean Ruaridh seems to have been a much more placid and straightforward place. Fishermen in oilskins turn out to be cormorants that are perched on yellow rocks and the water contains nothing worse than seals.

Above Inver Aulavaig are notable woods on the flanks of 257m Sgiath-bheinn Chrossavaig. The village of Ord is conspicuous, if not the remains of Teampuill Chaon. Eilean Dubh and other islets add interest to further progress up Loch Eishort.

The north side of the loch rises to 278m Beinn Bhuidhe although 195m Carn Dearg is only 300m from the shore so the coast falls steeply with waterfalls and is home to rabbits.

He then left to defend Ulster against the Vikings but was killed and Dunscaith became a ruin. The present castle was built in a night by a witch or by Cuchulainn and his Fingalians. A young MacDonald daughter, married in the

The hamlet of Suisnish was subject to particularly brutal eviction by Lord MacDonald's factor in the 1850s, many of the residents dying of the winter cold in the open air around their former houses or later of smallpox while being forcibly emigrated from Campbelltown.

Rubha Suisnish brings the unexciting Calaman Cave and Stac Suisnish, which appears to have collapsed. It also brings a view up Loch Slapin into the heart of the rounded Red Cuillin, from which violent winds often

The Sandaig Islands, seen across the Sound of Sleat.

Loch Hourn on an unusually light day.

gust fiercely. Gannets are used to the conditions and dive for fish, regardless.

On the Strathaird peninsula, owned by the John Muir Trust, Nead an Fhir-eion rises to 334m and Ben Meabost to 345m. Dùn Ringill stands by the shore, backed by woods which front Kirkibost and Kilmarie, which was home to the Mackinnon chiefs, Abhainn Cille Mhaire discharging through a sheltered estuary. A graveyard, cemetery, fine 4,000 year old chambered cairn and the remains of a dun are located around the woods. Wild raspberries, small but full of flavour, grow along the shoreline. Castle Keep produces hand forged swords, knives and dirks and Duncan House is where Garth Duncan produces traditional knives and Celtic jewellery in gold, silver and platinum.

There is another tomb near the remains of Dùn Liath and, before Dùn Grugaig, the Spar Cave which has many stalactites although some have been removed as souvenirs. It was where Scott had Allan killed in *The Lord of the Isles*. In the 9th century, after an attack by the king of Ulster, the capture of the young Colonsay, a reprisal raid, shipwreck in Loch Slapin, rescue by Princess Dounhuila's men and a subsequent child to the pair, it was used for the upbringing of the child, with final reconciliation between its warring grandparents. Colonsay's dog was also rescued and kept guard on the cave, where singing mermaids drove men to madness, it was claimed. The narrow band of marble and limestone here stretches to the north coast of Scotland at Smoo Cave.

Beyond Rubha na h-Easgainne and Eilean na

The Ornsay lighthouse on Eilean Sionnach.

An Ceannaich

L Pooltiel

Oisgill Bay

Lower Millovaig

Neist Pt

The sheltered inlet at Ardvasar.

The view across the Sound of Sleat into Loch Nevis.

h-Airde is Port an Luig Mhòir with Prince Charles's Cave, where the Pretender hid on 5th July 1746 before leaving for Mallaig, his final departure from the island with which he is so closely associated.

In the past, Suidhe Biorach, the pointed seat, was used by infertile couples who came to drink the water of a nearby well and invoke the well's guardian spirit to make them fertile. Rounding the point brings into view the spread of the Black Cuillin, their peaks separated by corries and cliffs. They are best seen by the general public from Elgol at the end of the single track B8083. Lillian Comber moved here during the Second World War and, as Lillian Beckwith, wrote *The Hills is Lonely* and other light semi autobiographical

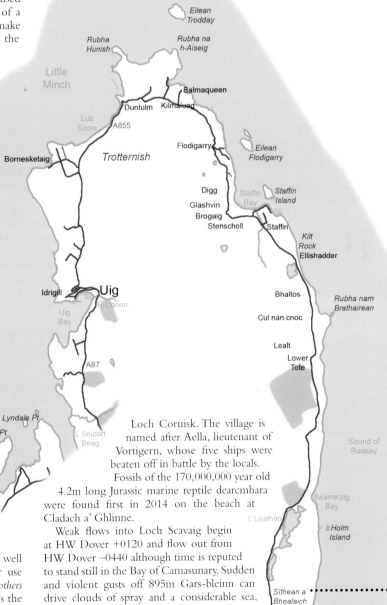

books. Maxwell was paid well when he hired his boats for use during the filming of *The Brothers* here. Operating from the jetty is the *Bella Jane*, offering what is claimed to be Scotland's only 5 star boat trip, to Loch Coruisk. The village is named after Aella, lieutenant of Vortigern, whose five ships were beaten off in battle by the locals.

Fossils of the 170,000,000 year old 4.2m long Jurassic marine reptile dearcmhara were found first in 2014 on the beach at Cladach a' Ghlinne.

Weak flows into Loch Scavaig begin at HW Dover +0120 and flow out from HW Dover −0440 although time is reputed to stand still in the Bay of Camasunary. Sudden and violent gusts off 895m Gars-bleinn can drive clouds of spray and a considerable sea, especially near the head of the loch, but are quickly past, leaving calm conditions. The

95

Eigg and Rùm seen from Aird of Sleat.

A school of dolphins hunting in the Sound of Sleat.

The Point of Sleat light tower.

compass is also unreliable in this area but it should not be hard to identify Camas Fhionnairigh with the Abhainn Camas Fhionnairigh flowing into it, Loch nan Leacd and Loch na Cuilce, meaning recess, with the Scavaig River flowing into it from glaciated Loch Coruisk, perhaps the most evocative place in Europe. Fortunately, the plan to moor a high class floating hotel complete with a brass band at the head of Loch Scavaig, mentioned in *A Summer in Skye*, came to nothing. The climb from Loch Coruisk to the top of 965m Sgurr a Ghreadaidh is one of the longest in Britain but the views from the top reach to St Kilda. Sgurr Alasdair, the highest peak in the Cuillin, is named as it was first climbed in 1873 by Alexander Nicholson with local shepherd Angus Macrae. Botanists will find this the only British location of alpine rock cress.

Porpoises may be found in Loch Scavaig. In the early 20th century young Sandy Campbell and two men were fishing for the teeming herring near the head of the loch with many other small boats on a calm autumn evening. About 50m from them a tapering column like a waving tail rose steadily to a height of at least 6m, attached to a large dark mass in the water. It submerged equally smoothly and then produced an effect like a passing steamer wake as the terrified fishmen rowed for the shore as fast as they could. An incident in 1917 involving two lobster fishermen and a 9m tail produced a similar response.

Soay Sound to the north of Soay has continuous westerly flow. With clear conditions it is possible to see perhaps 10m down onto sea urchins among the variety of bootlace and other seaweeds and much less to the striking varieties of jellyfish floating through.

Beyond the Cuillin the western half of the island is a very large basic lava plateau. The peaks drop away dramatically with Cnoc Leathan at 171m and Ceann na Beinne at 225m although the shoreline is still steep. Allt

na Meacnaish drops down a long waterfall into a small pool deep enough for swimming, a refreshing way of removing the salt on a hot day. There are also caves nearby. A cave near Rubh' an Dùnain was used in Stone Age and Iron Age times.

Atlantic grey seals collect at Sgeir Mhòr, Skye having 40% of the world's population, and the remains of crabs suggest it is a feeding area for other wildlife. Rubh' an Dùnain, where a beluga was seen in 1951, has long proved of interest with a fine 4,000 year old horned chambered cairn underground dwelling which has produced Neolithic and Beaker pottery and six skeletons There was also other cairn and cave activity. A galleried dun was used by the MacAskills, the Lieutenants of the Coast, to watch out for storms and for attacks by Clan Ranald from the Small Isles on behalf of the MacLeods, who stationed galleys on the landlocked Loch na h-Airde in order to have them quickly available. The Small Isles are visible from the Point of Sleat onwards but the view from here is as good as from anywhere. The MacAskills are supposed to have been Irish but asketill is Norse for a sacrifical container for the gods. The last MacAskill here died in 1864. The area was subject to the Clearances in the 19th century.

Camas a' Mhùrain is the start of Loch Brittle, where the intruders from the Small Isles these days are white tailed sea eagles, larger than the local golden eagles, which tend to perform their aerobatics when there is enough wind. Foxes are also present. Another long tailed sea monster with similar appearance and behaviour to the Loch Scavaig sighting, except taller, was seen at a distance of kilometres, off the mouth of Loch Brittle on a fine summer's day, its speed about 9km/h.

The view up the loch is to the Cuillin again. These offer some of Britain's best climbing and Glen Brittle is the main climbing centre on Skye. It is surprising how many different superlative views there are of the Cuillin from the water.

Magnificent 150m cliffs, some of the best basaltic coast cliffs there are, follow to Loch Bracadale with lava flows and sills so that they look like stratified rocks, although they are crumbling. Southerly or southwesterly winds can produce a lot of swell. Flows are northwestwards from HW Dover +0120 and southeastwards from HW Dover −0440 to 2km/h. The highest point on this peninsula is 435m An Cruachan. Rubha Theama Sgurr is the noticeable projection from the cliffs, perhaps as the result of rockfalls, but the unique feature is Stac an Tuill, shaped like a handbell but with a hole through the middle.

Loch Eynort suffers from swells from the west and has fierce squalls as a result of northerly winds. Most of Glen Brittle Forest grows along its eastern shore. It was used by a large force of MacDonalds in 1395 when avoiding the MacAskills in attacking the MacLeods but the MacLeods drove them back, by which time the MacAskills had moored their boats offshore and they were apparently all killed.

The next section of cliff to 280m is topped by 445m Beinn Bhreac and 347m Prashel Beg, mostly cliff nearly vertical but with some unusual green pyramid shapes at one point. There are also some dramatic waterfalls. Added to an afternoon cold power shower is the image of a complete circular rainbow.

The squat Stac a' Mheadais looks like a Martello tower or a dun. Just before it are two caves. The first is low with just the crumps of a striking waves. The other is long and high, however, with waves breaking on a rock beach at the far end. About a third of the way back it is wide enough to turn a sea kayak. In the afternoon the sunlight shines in and the lighter colour at the top of the cave takes on an eerie green appearance, as if lit from some source further back in the cave.

Further up the coast are more caves, both the submerged kind which produce internal gurglings from deep inside and the kind which can be explored by small craft. One has two entrances.

Talisker Bay, backed by 416m Stockval ending in the prominent Preshal More, has a steep boulder beach and a notice banning vehicles from the last kilometre of track. This suits naturists who appreciate the privacy but not surfers with kit to carry. Boswell thought it not as bad as the rest of Skye when visiting in 1773 and climbed Preshal More, his route still carrying his name, but Johnson was less enthusiastic. Cuchulainn, the hero of Ulster, landed here in two strides from Northern Ireland, ready to study warfare in Scathach's school for heroes.

The Talisker distillery, the only one on Skye, was begun by Kenneth MacAskill of Talisker House but it was later moved to Fiskavaig and then, in 1830, to Carbost.

The 90m waterfall on the north side of the bay is one of the best coastal falls in Scotland and is to be followed by more of the same. Lava flows 2–12m thick give a stratified appearance.

Around Rubha Cruinn there is a channel inside all the reefs, so uniform in shape that it could almost have been cut. Below 253m Beinn nan Dubh-lochan the cliffs are only about 6m high but then they soar back to full height from the overhanging Rubha nan Clach.

Caves might be expected to face the open sea but one of the ones before Gob na h-Oa faces northwest with the appearance of a mineshaft entrance.

Fiskavaig Bay offers a fairly reliable sandy landing beach, facing north northwest with the open sea to the southwest and, if necessary, the mouth of the Fiskavaig Burn on the west side of the bay providing an even more sheltered landing, albeit with a more difficult walk out.

Herons, oystercatchers, cormorants, jellyfish, porpoises, dolphins and whales frequent the clear waters from Fiskavaig Bay. Dùn Ardtrek is less conspicuous than the small white tower lighthouse on Ardtrek Point, sheltering the entrance to Loch Harport which has flows ingoing from HW Dover +0120 and outgoing from HW Dover –0440 1km/h.

Loch Bracadale is dotted with islands which each have dark cliffs at their seaward ends, those on the tilted wedge of Oronsay rising to a 72m peak. Between the island and Ullinish Point there is a drying reef although it is only a short portage across the causeway when the tide is low. However, there are breakers over the reef to its south in most conditions. The grass is used for sheep grazing and there are twites, larks and fulmars. A fort site occupies a headland on the west side north of Ullinish Point.

The larger island of Wiay rises to 60m with a 56m high overhanging cliff on its south side, yellow lichen contrasting with the dark rock. There are a couple of caves, an arch in the northeast corner being accessible with the tide in. The island is used for summer grazing.

Loch Bracadale has weak tidal streams, making it a suitable place for Hakon to shelter his fleet in the 13th century after the Battle of Largs although swells from the southwest make their way between Tarner and Harlosh Islands into Loch Caroy and also into Loch Vatten, Loch na Faolinn and Loch Bharcasaig.

Fishing at Orbost was just one track inspired locally for the Peatbog Faeries, with a recording studio in the village.

The view northwest is dominated by Healabhals Mhòr and Bheag, Macleod's Tables North and South respectively, both of flat topped basalt lavas, the former at 489m, apparently truncated by a giant to provide a table and bed for St Columba. The story is told of how 9th MacLeod chief Alasdair Crotach was being entertained in Edinburgh with waiters serving food onto fine furniture lit by chandeliers, his host baiting him by suggesting he could not match the opulence at home. MacLeod duly brought his host to Skye and had a meal served by his clansmen on top of one of his Tables, lit by the stars of the firmament, the city man conceding he had been upstaged.

The southeast end of the Duirinish peninsula has been

A stream tumbles onto the beach by Rubha Charn nan Cearc.

In weed and skerries off Tarskavaig Point.

Looking from Camas Daraich into Loch Eishort.

Clouds cap the peaks of the Red Cuillin as the wind blasts out of Loch Slapin.

Rock pillar at Cadha nan Ingrean.

Cliff formations on the Glasnakille coast.

Cliffs beyond Suidhe Biorach with a the cow on the brink.

planted with fir trees, now being replaced with broad leaved varieties, including Rebel's Wood in memory of Joe Strummer of the Clash. Caves and arches are found between Brandarsaig Bay and Camas na h Uamha where there are remains of cultivation lazy beds at the former village of Idrigill while Idrigill Point has a pillar which resembles the bust of a man in naval uniform with epaulettes. He gazes out at a seascape which includes Rùm, Canna and, across the Sea of the Hebrides, the peaks of Barra and South Uist. Commercial ships pass through the sea at intervals.

The cliffs run 60–180m high with fantastic forms and potential powerful downdraughts. The section to Moonen Bay is claimed to be the best cliffscape in the Hebrides but this is surely an understatement. The scale

Suidhe Biorach with Sgurr Aladair rising behind.

The best view in Britain. The Black Cuillin rise in a sweep above Loch Scavaig with Sgurr na Stri in the centre.

Camas Fhionnairigh with Blà Bheinn, the blue mountain, behind.

is such that every hole in the cliffs turns out to be a cave far exceeding its promise. It is also a prolific source of fish floats, buoys and fenders.

Flows run northwest from HW Dover +0120 and southeast from HW Dover −0440.

First and most conspicuous are Macleod's Maidens, three basaltic stacks to 65m which can be seen from a considerable distance. They are named after the wife and daughters of the 4th MacLeod chief who drowned near

here after crossing from Harris. The skerries around the feet are a favourite place to find barnacles, mermaids and evil spirits and the venue was used by Campbell of Ensay for shipwrecking with lights. There are waterfalls into Inbhir a' Gharraidh.

At the end of Glen Lorgasdal there are stacks on the cliffs and in the water. Between them is an arch, behind which is a powerful waterfall and near which is a cave with a curtain of water across its entrance, a feature of

Loch na Cuilce and Loch nan Leachd lead in to the Scavaig River which runs down from Loch Coruisk.

Soay Sound with Soay on the left and Ulfhart Point to the right.

The Allt na Meacnaish falls down into a deep pool.

Rock sculptures along the north side of Soay Sound.

a number of caves along this coast. It lacks only a sandy beach, the boulders being slippery except under the waterfall where there is dense weed like moss on the rocks, so a cold power shower can be taken standing or seated on a hot day. In the middle of the day the sun lights up the fall through the arch and there is not just a full circle of rainbow but much of a second ring. This has to be the most magical spot on the entire British coastline. Seals live amongst the rocks, blackbacked and other gulls plus hooded crows live on the cliffs and golden eagles soar at their tops.

There are various skerries which cover up to 2km offshore although the slab of An Dubh Sgeir stays clear of the water at all times, the most distant of the rocks.

Along past the foot of 244m Ben Connan there are arches, caves and waterfalls in profusion. There is scope for spending hours exploring all the caves in calm conditions.

Lorgill Bay takes its name from the glen of the deer's cry. In 1830 all ten families were evicted with the choice of emigration to Nova Scotia or prison, those over 70 also having the option of the poorhouse.

Hoe Point starts the Hoe, 233m high and only 300m from the cliffs, the cliffs reaching 200m high at Gob na Hoe, home for such birds as shags and herring gulls. At Hoe Rape the black cliffs have horizontal red veins at 6m intervals.

Beyond Ramasaig Bay and a significant waterfall is 309m Ben Vratabreck. More conspicuous behind Moonen Bay, the bay of fairies, is the angular Waterstein Head of lavas and sills, 296m high and falling almost vertically from its peak to the sea and An Stac. Also beyond its foot is Camas nan Sidhean, at the back of which are lower but substantial waterfalls onto the beach. It has also been noted for basking sharks.

A jetty with a derrick crane serves the lighthouse on low Neist Point, a 19m white light tower. The point has vertical basaltic columns related to those forming the Giant's Causeway and can be reached by the public on foot. Purple sandpipers and Manx and sooty shearwaters on migration join kittiwakes, common gulls, common and Arctic terns, razorbills, black guillemots, skuas, eiders, long tailed ducks, great northern divers, wheatears, rock and meadow pipits, buzzards and many other species.

There can be a race off the point. Flows northwards run from HW Dover +0420 until HW Dover −0440, the flow then dividing to add an eddy in the bay until HW Dover −0200 when flows begin south around the point until HW Dover +0120, the flows strong inshore, up to 3km/h northwards to Dunvegan Head, a rip tide running northwest from this point for 3km on northgoing springs. To add interest there may be a magnetic anomaly increasing compass readings by 10–20° to An Ceannaich.

There are more caves at intervals and basaltic columns. The Merchant is a detached basaltic column. There is also an arch beyond An Ceannaich to the north of Oisgill Bay.

Sheltered landing can usually be found behind Meanish Pier at Lower Milovaig where the B884 ends at Loch Pooltiel.

Heading north across Loch Pooltiel at the mouth of the

The strange landlocked Loch na h-Airde by Rubh' an Dùnain.

Eigg, Rùm and Canna seen across Sgeir Mhòr from the dun on Rubh' an Dùnain.

Looking north from Rubh' an Dùnain across the end of Loch Brittle.

Looking up Loch Brittle past Creag Mhòr towards the Black Cuillin.

Hamara River brings more cliffs and more high waterfalls down them. There are blackbacked and herring gulls while gannets fish a little further out. The view across the Little Minch is to the hills of North Uist with the rest of the Outer Hebrides reaching away to the north and south, just a line of peaks as the lower land is hidden over the horizon.

The peninsula has a TV mast on Scoval, the land rising through 202m Ben Ettow and 307m Ben Skriaig to Biod an Athair where the 313m summit is only 250m from the coast and there is an overhang where rabbits have burrowed away the soil. Dunvegan Head itself is 300m high with at least 25 lava sheets on top of each other. Golden eagles soar around the cliffs. Offshore there may

be pilot whales or exercising submarines. Ahead is the Waternish peninsula.

A little way into Loch Dunvegan is the Am Famhair arch. There is also a dry cave used by pigeons, the mess and smell being rather less pleasant than even for a typical sea washed cave occupied by cormorants.

Galtrigill was the birthplace of Donald MacLeod, who knew the local waters and acted as pilot for Prince Charlie. A monument on Gob na Hoe, however, is to record that there was a piping college for the MacCrimmons, hereditary pipers to the MacLeod chiefs from 1500 to 1800. The MacCrimmons were the first composers, players and teachers of the pibroch. The first young MacCrimmon piper flung down his pipes in tears

Stac an Tuill with Stac a' Mheadais just visible beyond.

A cave by Stac a' Mheadais, one of many on this coast.

The Cuillin again, this time above Loch Eynort.

Stac a' Mheadais beyond Loch Eynort.

but a fairy offered him the choice of being a celebrated piper or of being unknown but great. He chose the latter and she gave him a silver chanter. He became MacLeod's piper, the head of the college and the father of a fine player. MacLeod opposed the 1745 uprising, taking him on the campaign. Convinced he would not return, he composed *MacCrimmon's Lament*. The payoff was that he was to go when the fairy called, as she did. He gave his pipes to his son, took the chanter and followed her to the great cave at Harlosh on Loch Vatten where he disappeared. The same tale is told about Mac Coitir's

Striking cliffscape below Ben Scaalan.

Surprisingly powerful waterfall near Sgurr nam Fiadh.

More speleology before Talisker Bay.

Cave 20km away beyond Portree on the other side of the island, it being claimed that the two caves connect.

Dùn Borreraig is a broch before Uig. Beyond Totaig are the Dùn Colbost broch and a monument to the Glendale Land Leaguers, 600 crofters who challenged government forces and won, now owning the Glendale Estate. In the cliffs beyond Leinish Bay is the Piper's Cave. Below Beinn na Crèiche is Colbost with a black house preserved as a Colbost Croft Museum since 1965, behind it a replica illicit whisky still. The Raven Press Gallery sells wood engravings prepared using an Albion handpress of the 1840s. The head of the loch is dotted with islands used for sheep grazing.

Beyond the islands is the cube of Dunvegan Castle, a MacLeod seat for nearly eight centuries, its most revered artefact being the Fairy Flag, given to Iain, the 4th MacLeod chief, by the fairy to whom he was married. Another possibility is that it had belonged to Harald Hardrada of Norway, beaten by Harold of England in 1066. The fact that it was woven in the 7th century in Rhodes using yellow silk from the Near East supports the suggestion that it was brought back from the Crusades by a MacLeod chief. If waved when the MacLeods are in danger it will save them. It can be used three times in this way. So far it has been used twice.

Beyond the head of the loch the magnificent view is through to the Cuillin.

The headland which completes Camalaig Bay is protected by Dùn Fiadhairt, a 2,000 year old Iron Age broch with 3.7m thick walls, a 9.4m diameter space inside and guardrooms in the walls each side of the entrance.

Beinn Bhreac ridge separates Loch Bay from the main part of Loch Dunvegan.

Although beaches are almost all storm beaches of boulders, around Lampay and through An Dorneil there are striking white beaches of coral sand, formed by Lithothamniun seaweed. The water can be very clear with local birds including snipes and herons and there are also seals, otters and midges.

The 1.6km long Isay, named after the porpoises which might be seen around it, belonged to Roderick MacLeod

Approaching Talisker Point with Rubha Cruinn beyond.

Preshal More towers above Talisker Bay.

Fiskavaig Bay offers a sheltered landing. Beyond is Oronsay.

Tables on Oronsay mimic the Healabhals on Duirnish.

had been buried in Duirinish, as another had been buried in Edinburgh at the time of her initial disappearance.

The graveyard also contains the Trial Stone, in which someone accused would be blindfolded and have to throw a stone into a very small hole to prove innocence.

At Roghead, just up from Ardmore Point, there is a wall of natural arches. From Ard Beag the streams are continuously south to Ardmore Point and north to Waternish Point to 2km/h, from where the stream becomes continuous westwards. Despite the 30m dark cliffs at Ard Beag, submarine power cables run out just north of the point across the Little Minch towards Harris and South Uist.

The cliffs up the Waternish peninsula are about 80m high but the land drops away from 284m Ben Geary to be low at the point. Successive large cairns mark the deaths

in the 16th century. He wished it to pass to his grandson but this meant having to murder the two people next in line, done after treating them to a meal as a preliminary to discussing the inheritance. It was offered as a gift to Dr Johnson on condition that he built a house on it and lived there at least one month per year. He declined. Boswell was particularly keen to visit it but weather prevented this. More recently it was bought by singer Donovan. Cottage remains include black houses.

In the intervening period, 1860 to be precise, the neighbouring islands of Mingay and Clett with their basalt cliffs were cleared of their residents.

Earth cliffs stand behind Ardmore Bay.

At Trumpan are the ruins of a church. The MacLeods were at prayer in 1578 when they were discovered by MacDonalds from Uist, who fired the church and killed the escapers in revenge for the Eigg massacre. One woman did get away and raised the alarm in Dunvegan. It was one of the two occasions when the Fairy Flag was used. The MacDonalds ran for their eight boats at Ardmore Bay but the tide was out and they were outnumbered. They were all killed and buried in a dyke by felling a wall on top of them, the battle being known as the Spoiling of the Dyke. A more recent grave is that of Lady Grange, thought by her husband, James Erskine, to be a Government spy against his part in the 1715 Jacobite Rising. She was exiled to St Kilda for 8 years by her husband, to die 3 years after being discovered and brought back in 1742, initially to a cave near Idrigill Point. She eventually went insane. She was buried here secretly after a coffin of earth

of John MacLeod and his son, Roderick, in the 1530 2nd Battle of Waternish. Dùn Borrafiach, with notably large stones, and Dùn Gearymore are brochs along the western side of the summit ridge. A waterfall down the cliffs has eroded itself a dead end mini canyon into the rocks at its foot, crossed by several low arches, an interesting route at the right state of the tide. Urchins may be seen on the seabed.

There are overfalls 2km off Waternish or Vaternish Point, flows running northeast from HW Dover +0420 and southwest from HW Dover –0120 at up to 5km/h. The point is marked by a 7m white light tower.

It was the first attempted landfall on Skye for Prince Charlie on 29th June 1746, the island with which he is so closely associated although he spent two months in the Outer Hebrides and only a week on Skye, of which two days were actually on Raasay. He was disguised as maid Betty Burke but this did not fool anyone and the party had to move on after being fired upon.

East of the point are more caves at the start of Loch Snizort, a loch with less spectacular views at its head, this time, the seascape being more impressive the other way to Harris and the rest of the Outer Hebrides stretching away in both directions.

Caisteal an Fhithich is at the foot of cliffs where golden eagles soar. Off it are Eilean Iosal, Eilean Creagach, Eilean Garave, South Ascrib, Sgeir a' Chapuill and Sgeir a' Chuainn, collectively the Ascrib Islands 3km offshore, used for grazing sheep and cattle and with seals and seabirds including a large puffin colony. The islands provided the stone for Caisteal Uisdein.

Stack Aros is below Gillen. At Loch Losait the coast swings out to Oans Point and there is extensive forest planted along the side of 298m Beinn Sgùmain. Cliffs run 50–140m high with caves, an arch and a 33m waterfall on the Allt Achaidh Bhig.

At the head of the loch are several small lochs, Loch Diubaig, Loch Greshornish and Loch Shnizort Beag. Hidden on the back of Greshornish Point is Dun na h'Airde and the site where Ellen MacArthur had a house built, already having sailed her yacht here. Loch Greshornish and Loch Snizort Beag each have weak flows in from HW Dover +0140 and out from HW Dover –0440, the two lochs separated by Lyndale Point.

Trotternish is the last of the three great peninsulas at the northwest end of Skye. Dùn Maraig hides in Poll na h-Ealaidh behind Ard nan Eireachd but Caisteal Uisdein is a prominent cube on the shore to the southeast. The latter was built about 1580 by Hugh MacDonald, who plotted against his cousin, Donald Gorm, eighth chief of

The military stack at Idrigill Point.

104

Macleod's Maidens are visible from a considerable distance over a wide arc.

Waterfall at the back of Inbhir a' Gharraidh.

The fall at the end of Glen Lorgasdal, arguably the most magical spot on the British coastline.

the MacDonalds of Sleat, for his pains meeting his end in 1586 in a cell in Duntulm Castle with a piece of salt beef and an empty water jug.

In one clash MacDonalds executed MacLeads and rolled their heads down the hill into the loch. As they rolled, the heads called out that they had almost won. The name Almost Hill is still used. These days rusting machinery, including the odd car, has been pushed into a lochside gully instead.

A particularly long narrow cave cuts into Cnoc Fadail. Herring gulls and oystercatchers frequent the area.

At the back of Uig Bay is **Uig**, which means bay. The A87 ends at the jetty serving ferries to East Loch Tarbert and Loch Maddy. At South Cuil is a round tower folly built by Captain Fraser. Of more interest these days, Uig is home of the Isle of Skye Brewing Company, set up in 1995 by two Portree schoolteachers and producing such beers as Young Pretender, Red and Black Cuillin and Avalanche in the winter, using no artificial ingredients. Above the River Conon, Balnaknock resembles a

Caves and arches proliferate, many with Gothic cathedral proportions.

An arch at Gob na Hoe as the cliffs lead away to Hoe Rape.

miniature Quirang. Inland, for over 20km a line of cliffs runs north–south down the centre of the Trotternish peninsula, its details not obvious from the water and such peaks as 611m Beinn Edra and 466m Bioda Buidhe being less conspicuous than 174m Creag Liath with a mast on its shoulder and a stratified cliff above a grassy scree slope down to Ru Idrigill. Dùn Skudiburgh fort site on its northwest flank stands above Stack of Skudiburgh.

In 1732 the MacDonalds of Sleat built a fine house at Monkstadt on a monastery site. It was in the ownership of Sir Alexander MacDonald when 24 year old Flora MacDonald, a Uist born local woman educated in Edinburgh, brought the defeated Prince Charlie from Loch Maddy, landing at what is now Prince Charles's Point. However, the king's men were guarding the house

Ramasaig Cliff rises to Waterstein Head then drops to the Neist lighthouse.

A golden eagle soars above the cliffs.

and they had to flee. The house was used until 1795, when a move was made to Armadale on the far corner of Skye and it is now a ruin. The occasional jet thunders over.

The Càrn Liath chambered cairn was built on a ridge overlooking the Cashel beehive dwellings on Eilean Chaluim Chille, the name remaining despite the draining of Loch Chaluim Chille in 1824.

The ruins of Dùn Liath are sited above Cairidh nan Òb, the start of a striking stretch of coast with columnar basalt columns rather than horizontal strata. Beyond Rubh'a'Chàirn Lèith is Camas Mor with the Sgeir Lang slipway at the back, serving Bornesketaig. Local Donald MacDonald is reputed to have raced another clan for a small piece of land. Seeing that he was going to lose, he chopped off his left hand with his sword and threw it ashore in order to touch first. It is similar to the Lismore story except that on that occasion the prize was larger and for a more noble cause and a smaller piece of anatomy, making it more plausible. The crofting township includes Beaton's Croft House, a thatched 18th century house.

The bay ends at Ru Bornesketaig with a broch site on top and caves at its foot. Flows begin northeast from HW Dover +0420 and southwest from HW Dover

–0200, reaching up to 5km/h off Ru Bornesketaig and Rubha Hunish. Eddies in the bays, of which the largest is Lub Score, run northeast from HW Dover –0030 and southwest from HW Dover +0600. The sand along the shore has a green tint from the erosion of olivine from the cliffs.

Flora MacDonald was buried here and there is a new Celtic cross monument to her, replacing the one taken away in pieces by tourists. Prince Charlie and Flora MacDonald relics are amongst the exhibits in the Skye Museum of Island Life situated in seven 19th century thatched black houses, including a weaver's house and a smithy. A young woman always puts an attractive gloss on any campaign. Grace Darling is still the RNLI's best seller and Leila Khaled and Bernadette Devlin are just two more recent campaigners who have attracted media which might otherwise have shown less interest in their

Uncompromising cliffs of An Ceannich.

The cliffs rise to a peak at Biod an Athair then drop to Dunvegan Head.

causes. Flora MacDonald was the toast of London for a while after her release.

The A855 runs along the shore briefly to Duntulm. Below a transmission mast is Ru Meanish. The site was used for the MacDonalds' Duntulm Castle, built with three sides falling sharply and a deep ditch on the landward side, an Iron Age broch, a Pictish Dun Dhaibidh fort and a Viking stronghold. It was used by MacLeods then MacDonalds from 1539, visited by James V in 1540 with a large fleet in a show of strength and modernized by chief Donald Gorm in the early 17th century but abandoned in favour of Monkstadt House, either because of visits of the ghost of Donald Gorm or because a child fell out of a window when dropped by his nurse, who was then cast adrift in a leaking boat or hidden while a dummy was set adrift. It is now a ruin with a cairn to the MacArthurs, their pipers.

Tulm Island offers more protection to Tulm Bay than to Port Duntulm. It is less of an island than a ridge of strata up on edge like a giant fish. *A Summer in Skye* considers Duntulm more impressive than the Drachenfels.

Rubha Voreven begins Loch Hunish, where the former Meall Tuath coastguard lookout has become a bothy. Rubha Hunish is the most northerly point on Skye, from where Cape Wrath may be seen. Strong southwesterly flows come close to the point, as do young basking sharks, and there are heavy overfalls with a fresh wind against the tide, this being reputedly the roughest place in the Minch. Runrig cultivation strips are visible below the pinnacle near Port Lag a'Bhleodhain. Rorquals, minke, killer and other whales might be seen further out.

Standing off Lewis are the Shiant Islands. Much closer is Fladda-Chùain with a chapel dedicated to St Columba, its blue stone altar said to bring fair winds to becalmed fishermen, probably not often a problem here. Sir Donald MacDonald is supposed to have hidden his title deeds here before joining the 1745 uprising. Perhaps this is why large black rabbits dig here. Closer inshore is Gaelivore Island, the Cleats, Gerran Island and Lord Macdonald's Table, all basalt columns with flat tops, Gearran with a cave running west to east through it at the right tide level.

There is a wreck and probably an eddy in Lùb a' Sgiathain, which extends towards Rubha na h-Aiseig. Off this latter point is Eilean Trodday, troll's island, which once

More waterfalls north of Loch Pooltiel.

Flying buttress in Loch Dunvegan.

The wall of arches at Roghead.

caves, the latter including a series of linked caves and caves in the front of what looks like a bulging kilt. It is a section of coast which requires time to explore in detail, as falcons and climbers do.

Sheltering Poldorais from the east are Sgeir na Eireann and Eilean Flodigarry. The latter rises to 56m on its east side but this has not stopped its use for agriculture. It once had its corn reaped in two nights by 150 fairies who then asked for more work so the owner set them to empty the sea. They failed. This area of sea is often filled with common seals.

A prominent building in Flodigarry is the turreted Flodigarry Hotel, the much extended cottage of Flora MacDonald after the uprising, where she met Johnson and Boswell in 1773.

The cliffs which run down the spine of the Trotternish peninsula now begin. Sgurr Mòr at 492m and 543m Meall na Suiramach are two of the higher peaks but the Quirang is one of the most amazing rock formations in Britain. Meaning pillared stronghold, it was used to hide cattle during raids. It has the Table, a flat topped rectangle

Isay, Mingay and Clett with the mountains of Harris on the horizon.

Samuel Johnson 1709–1784
Lexicographer, critic and poet

supported a herd of cattle and still has sheep and a 5m white round tower lighthouse. Flows begin eastwards from HW Dover +0440 and west from HW Dover −0140 at up to 5km/h. The scenery changes but is no less dramatic as the peaks of Wester Ross appear across Inner Sound. The area around the Aird was known as the Granary of Skye because of the fertile basaltic soil. Behind, there are fantastic shapes, horizontal slabs, rounded summits and rugged peaks bursting upwards like bolting lettuces, the Quirang in the centre. The eastern fringe of the northern half of Skye consists of Mesozoic rocks.

There are the remains of a church at the head of Port Gobhlaig, the sheltered inner part of Kilmaluag Bay.

All along Bàgh nan Gunnaichan are stacks, rocks and

with a quartzite summit plus pillars, gullies and teeth, including the Needle and the Prison. Towards the shore are Dùn Vàllerain, Dùn Mòr and Dùn Beag. Digg has crofting land in strips. With strong westerly winds, fierce gusts sweep down over Glashvin, Brogaig and Stenscholl where the Stenscholl River empties into Staffin Bay. The bay is protected to the east by Staffin Island, used for grazing and for nesting by curlews, oystercatchers and gulls and with a fishermen's bothy, off which are moorings. It was, presumably, a rougher day when a Spanish Armada galleon was reputedly wrecked near here. Some Spanish coins have been found and there are locals who claim Spanish descent. Ship activity now includes submarines exercising offshore.

The bay and An Corran have sandy beaches, in short supply in this area, the latter with adjacent parking.

The Ascribs from the mouth of the Abhainn a' Ghlinne.

Lealt Falls, cut through lava to Mesozoic rocks, one of the most powerful falls on Skye. The valley has other signs of former industry, including a now dismantled railway which brought quarry material down from Loch Cuithir.

Beyond the Dùn Grainan fort site is the church shaped Eaglais Bhreagach where Clan MacQueen raised the Devil using the ancient Taghairm ceremony which

A cave picture which could belong in an anatomy textbook.

Another fine fall, this one off the Waternish peninsula.

It was from Staffin in 1935 that James Adam undertook the first known solo kayak crossing of the Minch to Scalpay.

By a smooth rock platform at Ob nan Ròn is the Staffin Community Slipway, a popular launching point with a parking area for trailed boats. For some wave directions it gives more shelter than the beach at An Corran. In 2000 there were millennium schemes to be launched all over the country but the Princess Royal made time to come here to open this village project at the far end of the back of beyond.

The shoreline rises steeply again, hiding Garafad and its chambered cairns and even 466m Bioda Buidhe. The malevolent ghost of Colann gun Cheann murdered people by throwing his head at them. He was banished to Arisaig until a young man caught the head on the end of his sword and made the ghost promise to return to Skye where, presumably, he remains a danger.

The 60m high Kilt Rock with columnar black basalt at the top, turning horizontal at the bottom, is noted for its shape. In fact, its lines fall well short of the one at Bàgh nan Gunnaichean but this time there is a viewpoint for coach parties by the Mealt Falls draining Loch Mealt. A black house by the loch at Ellishadder is now Staffin Museum, including dinosaurs, and Dùn Grianan broch stands by the loch. Dùn Raisaburgh broch and Dùn Dearg fort are also close by.

Sandstone strata at Bhaltos have spherical rocks of various sizes embedded at the same level, suggesting they might be volcanic bombs which rained down in considerable numbers.

611m Beinn Edra stands inland as part of the long basalt escarpment which runs parallel to the coast. In 1945 it was hit in the mist by a Flying Fortress. These days there are jets carrying out training flights in the area. There is also birdlife which includes guillemots, black guillemots, puffins, razorbills, cormorants, common, blackbacked and herring gulls and fulmars.

The cliffs rise again, hiding Cul nan Cnoc and Lonfern with a memorial by the A885, Dùn Connavern and the remains of beehive dwellings from the early Christian era. There is also a settlement site on the neck of Rubha nam Brathairean which stretches out towards Rona.

The remains of industrial buildings used for drying diatomite on the shore at Inver Tote draw attention to the mouth of the Lealt River although salmon find their own way in. Almost hidden between two hillsides are the

Stac a' Bhothain in Loch Snizort.

A cave has been eroded by the wind blowing this substantial fall against the cliff.

Looking across Loch Snizort from Greshornish Point towards the Waternish peninsula.

Loch Greshornish and Loch Snizort Beag separate Eilean Mòr and Eilean Beag from the Trotternish peninsula.

An unexpectedly long cave at Cnoc Fadail.

involved roasting live cats. A cairn helps to locate it from the road, together with a couple of kilometres of coast with caves and arches, not Skye's most spectacular.

Unmarked on the OS 1:50,000 map is what must be the most enjoyable water feature in Britain, theme parks included. The Rigg Burn delivers a powerful jet of water almost vertically down a slot in the cliff onto a horizontal sandstone ledge. This has resulted in scouring out a saucer which is over 2m deep below the jet but the depth reduces to nothing as the water trickles over the edges all round. The current flows strongly in all directions from the jet, making it a challenge to reach, even with the help of a stunted tree overhanging one side of the pool, like a powerful, inverted, cold water jaccuzi. It is a white water swimming spot second to none. Finally, the water leaves the sandstone ledge by various routes including a significant fall in the centre. Reaching the top of the ledge is easy as it is possible to walk up the adjacent shingle beach. Primroses and celandines complete the setting.

Ru Idrigill guards Uig Bay and Uig while Stack of Skudiburgh is conspicuous to its left.

Overlooking one of the largest landslips in Britain, 30km long, is the Storr, meaning great, at 719m, fiacaill storàch meaning buck tooth. In fact, it is the 50m high Old Man of Storr which is of greater interest. He and his wife went hunting a lost cow but looked back while running away from some magical giants. His wife has fallen over but he remains as a leaning black obelisk, 49m high with a pointed top and just 12m in diameter. The remains of a volcanic plug, the first successful ascent of it was made in 1955 by Don Whillans' team and this is still a popular challenge for climbers.

Striking cliffs with vertical strata at the top lead into Bearreraig Bay where the waterfall down from Loch Leathan is less obvious than the pipes down the hillside to the 1952 Storr Lochs power station on the shore, reached by a pulley operated railway. Small ammonites abound on the shore. A more notable find in 1891 was of 28 silver objects such as jewellery and ingots, 92 10th century Anglo Saxon coins and 18 silver coins from Samarkand, thought to have belonged to a Norse sailor.

Holm Island is a landmark on the Skye shore and was considered to be Tir-nan-h'Oig, the Celtic land of perpetual youth. Across the Sound of Raasay, Rona, Fladday and Raasay are gradually closing on the mainland. Weak flows in the sound begin south from an hour after Dover high water and north from five hours before Dover high water, later in the south. There is submarine and fishing activity in the sound, including by dolphins and common seals.

Beyond 349m high Fiurnean is Prince Charles's Cave where he landed on 3rd July 1746 after two days on Raasay. It is not at all obvious, perhaps an important feature. The cliffs rise to 392m Sithean a' Bhealaich Chumhaing before easing to 310m Bealach Cumhang from where a steep grass slope drops almost continuously to Rubha na h-Àirde Glaise.

The first of the sea lochs on the east side of Skye is Loch Portree. Like the others, it suffers violent squalls out of the harbour with strong easterly or southwesterly winds.

Facing the entrance is Toravaig with the remains of a chapel, Dùn Torvaig and, near a raised beach, Mac Coitir's Cave, said to run right under the island to Bracadale.

Portree sits deeper in the loch. Kiltragleann was renamed Port Righ, king's port, after James V came in 1540 with a dozen ships to claim the allegiance of the chieftains of Skye, who tended to be a law to themselves.

The south side of the loch entrance is dominated by 413m Ben Tianavaig. The lochside at Udairn has Scarf Caves and Tom Cave while other caves, pinnacles and overhanging rocks continue to Tianavaig Bay where there are fish traps, overlooked by Camastianavaig.

A submarine cable crosses to Raasay and Dùn Vlarveg fort stands on the shoreline between Lower Ollach and Upper Ollach. Sgeir Dhubh occupies the approach to the bight of Camas a' Mhòr-bheòil. Topped by Dunan an Aisilidh, a finger of land projects to form the Narrows of Raasay, flows to 6km/h running southeast from HW Dover +0200 and northwest from HW Dover −0340. Caves in the cliffs are used by nesting cormorants.

Behind Balmeanach Bay are the Braes where troops suppressed crofter demonstrations in 1882. There was a battle between fifty Glasgow police and crofters who were being denied grazing rights, claimed to have been the last battle on British soil. Gunboats were sent with marines to Uig. Gladstone set up a Royal Commission to look into the conditions for crofters in the Highlands and islands, its first hearing being in Ollach church. In 1886 the Crofters' Holdings (Scotland) Act was established to protect their rights and give security of tenure at a fair

Ru Bornsketaig with a cliff of columnar basalt columns.

Rubha Hunish seen across Lub Score. Tulm Island is just visible as a pale ridge.

Looking into Port Duntulm with Tulm Island on the left and Duntulm Castle on the right. Cnoc Roll rises behind Duntulm.

A young basking shark feeding just off Rubha Hunish.

Balmacqueen backed by Sgurr Mòr, Meall na Suiramach and the Quirang while Eilean Flodigarry stands off to the southeast.

A seal swims off Galta Mòr.

Looking northwest from Creag na h-Eiginn towards Eilean Trodday and the Outer Hebrides.

rent. The community has a mixture of black houses and modern bungalows.

The bank up to the road at Gedintailor is high and steep while Balmeanach has fenced sheep fields which make road access difficult.

Submarine power cables run from Balmeanach Bay to Raasay while a fish farm may be stretched out across the bay. A practical landing point is to round the spit at Rubh' an Torra Mhòir into Loch Sligachan and past another Sgeir Dhubh to reach the end of the B883 at Peinachorrain where it is possible to get a vehicle down a steep track to the water. Loch Sligachan has flows in from HW Dover +0140 and out from HW Dover −0440. It can suffer from very heavy squalls, likely to be imminent if cloud caps are blowing off the peaks. Ben Lee provides a 444m backdrop on the north side of the loch.

Opposite Peinachorrian is Sconser, terminal for the Raasay car ferry at the foot of 775m Glamaig, a sentinel for the Cuillin although *A Summer in Skye* describes it as 'supremely ugly'. Also beside the loch is the Portree to

Sgeir na Eireann and Eilean Flodigarry offer shelter to Poldorais. Beyond are some of the peaks of Wester Ross.

Staffin Bay with Staffin Island, seen from Creag na h-Eiginn, a headland riddled with linked caves.

Flora MacDonald's cottage, now the turreted Flodigarry Hotel, stands below the Quirang.

The sweep of Staffin Bay with Brogaig, Glashvin and Digg backed by Bioda Buidhe, Dùn Mòr, Meall na Suiramach, Sròn Vourlinn round to F

The Storr and the Old Man of Storr.

Staffin Island, seen from the Staffin Community Slipway.

The official Kilt Rock.

The fall below Loch Mealt.

Aiesig with Eilean Flodigarry off to the east and Lewis beyond.

Kyleakin road, built in 1812 by Telford, and a conspicuous quarry provides stone for other construction projects.

There are heather, gorse and primroses along the shore and wrack is found in the increasingly sheltered channels. Seals bob about in the water and birdlife includes cormorants, mergansers, puffins, oystercatchers, curlews and, heard in the spring, cuckoos.

Caol Mòr provides a channel to Inner Sound and separates Raasay from Scalpay. Rounding Meall Buidhe and Meall a' Mhaol, a fish farm may be located at the mouth of the Moll River before Loch Ainort, which can blast out fierce squalls from 736m Marisco at its head past Leathad Chrithiun, Glas Bheinn Mhòr, big green mountain, and Am Meall.

Loch na Cairidh separates Scalpay from Skye, the main road running along the shore through Dunan and Strollamus, visited by those attending a fertility well which is particularly potent and produces twins if invoked correctly.

The hefty final fall on the Lealt River at Inver Tote.

The loch narrows through Caolas Scalpay and passes Ob Apoldoire, now below 732m Beinn na Caillich, hill of the old woman. She may have been the 10th century Norwegian princess Saucy Mary, said to be buried below a cairn and above a pot of gold, on the top of the summit with the first recorded ascent on Skye in 1772. The other Beinn na Caillich, with the same claim, would have been closer to her Caisteal Maol so the 18th century climbing record may stand here.

From Camas na Sgianadin the basalt shoreline is intensively forested although the wind has scattered the firs in places, leaving groups lying at all angles. Fish farms may also be located at intervals along this wooded section of shore.

The woods finish before Rubh' an Eireannaich, the start of Broadford Bay, which can have a short sea with wind and clapotis off Corry with its pier at the end of the former railway from the marble works. The crofting village of Broadford has become the main centre for the southern end of Skye. The Broadford Hotel on the bank of the Broadford River was the first place to brew Drambuie to a secret recipe given to the landlord by Prince Charlie, dram buidheach being the satisfying drink. In the late 1700s the village added a cattle market. *A Summer in Skye* tells how a crew sailing from Harris to the mainland saw an apparition of two men dangling from their shrouds. On reaching Broadford, their boat was used to hang two criminals who had just been sentenced by a court. More recently, it was a rare place to which Paul Theroux wished to return in *A Kingdom by the Sea*.

An interesting coastal rock formation near Eaglais Bhreagach.

A chambered cairn stands to one side of the rivermouth while there is a small harbour to the other. The *Family's Pride II*, a glass bottomed tourist boat, operates from the village, helped by the clear water often found in the vicinity. Village attractions include Sandbank Studio with Duncan Currie watercolours, Rupert Copping Gallery with Skye landscapes and abstracts, Three Herons Studio with photographs, paintings and weaving, the World of Wood, Skye Environmental Centre and the International

Ammonite imprint in a rock on the shore.

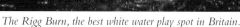

The Rigg Burn, the best white water play spot in Britain.

it has a jetty and the remains of a chapel and is of blue limestone with fossils.

Ardnish, leading to Rubha Ardnish, has trap dyke outcrops which resemble jetties. Inside is Ob Breakish, the name from a'bhreac or smallpox which ravaged the island in the 17th and 18th centuries. The old schoolhouse was the 1972 office of the controversial campaigning

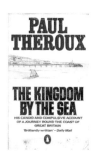

Otter Survival Fund. Skye Serpentarium Reptile World, with snakes, frogs, lizards, tortoises, a breeding centre and a refuge for illegally imported reptiles, burnt down in 2006 but has been rebuilt.

There is another chambered cairn at Waterloo, a name which results from the 1,500 Skye men who took part in the 1815 battle, many of whom settled here.

Flows run northeast in Caolas Pabay from HW Dover + 0120 and southwest from HW Dover −0440. A green metal framework mark is located on Sgeir Gobhlach while Pabay rises beyond to 28m. Meaning priest or monk isle,

Rubha na h-Airde Glaise with Ben Tianavaig on the far side of Loch Portree.

Tan Cave at the mouth of Loch Portree.

Camas a' Mhòr-bheòil with the Cuillin rising behind.

newspaper, the *West Highland Free Press*, which also attempted to cover as wide an area as possible. Skye was one of the first places to support the Yes campaign in the 2014 independence referendum. *A Summer in Skye* reports that Captain John Macdonald claimed that by the age of 15, in about 1740, he could quote between 100 and 200 Gaelic poems of various lengths which he had learned off an 80 year old man.

At Lower Breakish, beyond the Tobar Ashik site, is a graveyard which includes those of 1942 from HMS *Curaçao* which was cut in half by the *Queen Mary* while acting as her escort. Adjacent is Broadford Airfield with

Raasay ferry leaves Sconser on Loch Sligachan below Glamaig.

Broadford Bay with Scalpay and Longay in the distance.

its geodesic hangar. It was near here that Ireland's St Maolrubha preached, hanging his bell from a tree. August 25th was celebrated for Maolrubha as patron saint. St Columba also visited in 585.

Beyond Sgeir Dubh are the Ob Lusa and Ob Allt an Daraich inlets and sand and gravel pits along the shoreline, served by a substantial pier.

The Skye Bridge of 1996, built to carry the A87 over Kyle Akin, was designed as a pair of balanced cantilevers resembling seagulls in flight. However, the fact that it had the highest toll in Europe until made free in 2004 resulted in widespread ill feeling towards the structure and its owners. The 21m Kyle Akin lighthouse of 1857 by the Stevensons is disused and is partly obscured by the bridge. Both use Eilean Bàn. The island is the ongoing inspiration for Adam Melfort in John Buchan's *A Prince*

of the Captivity. There is a museum to Gavin Maxwell, who lived in the keeper's cottage. He bought the island in 1963 to turn it into a zoo for West Highland birds and mammals and moved here in 1968. After his early death the following year his partner, John Lister-Kaye, wrote a book about the island and the project. Teko, the last otter, is buried here.

The village of Kyleakin has lost its former importance for four centuries as Skye's ferry point for Kyle of Lochalsh, now bypassed by the bridge. The Sunday ferry service did not start until 1965 and even then it was in spite of strong protest from the kirk locally. It still has a memorial which acts as a viewpoint and the Bright Water Visitor Centre featuring otters and wildlife. A local craft is the *Seaprobe Atlantis*, Britain's only glass bottomed semi submersible. Kyle House has 1.2ha of gardens planted in

the 1960s by Colin Mackenzie with a notable kitchen garden and tender plants attaining large size because of the warmth of the Gulf Stream. An t-Ob almost puts the village on an island.

Caisteal Maol, roofless castle, or Dun Akin, is a 29m high square tower used as a lookout post and defence against Norse raids, the stronghold of the MacKinnons of Strath from the 12th to 15th centuries. Its original owner, possibly in the 8th or 10th century, had been a Norwegian princess with the unlikely name of Saucy Mary who ran a chain across the loch to sink any ship not paying a toll. A meeting of clan chiefs in 1513 proclaimed Sir Donald MacDonald of Lochalsh Lord of the Isles. The worst of the structural damage was done by a storm in 1948.

Times of tidal flows in the kyle vary considerably not only with the wind, heavy rain and snowmelt but also with the day of the tidal cycle. Several islands stand in the centre of the kyle, especially the Eileanan Dubha, 15m high and heather covered. A 5m high white metal framework lightbeacon is located on an islet at the east end.

Rubha Ard Treisnis stands 13m high in the middle of Loch Alsh, dividing Loch na Béiste, loch of the beast, from Kyle Akin. The latter took its name from King Hakon of Norway who took his fleet through in 1263 prior to his defeat at the Battle or Largs.

Flows are weak in Loch Alsh, up to 2km/h but affected by wind, heavy rain and snowmelt.

Black guillemots and gulls fly over the water and moon jellyfish drift in the currents. A noisy fish farm may be located near where the wreck of HMS *Port Napier* lies submerged by Sròn an Tairbh.

Sgeir na Caillich lightbeacon is a 2m concrete pillar below 753m Beinn na Caillich, the old woman referred to possibly having been Saucy Mary. Alternatively, it may have referred to Grainnhe, wife of Fionn, chief of the Fiennes family of giants, a pot of gold and jewels being buried beneath her grave at the summit. In *Kayak to Cape Wrath* Jack Henderson tells how he camped at Rubha na Caillich in the middle of the 20th century and met an old sea dog who told him he had seen enough sharks in Kyle Rhea to be able to walk across. However, Mac an Raeidhinn, after whom the kyle is named, failed to jump the gap while racing back from Glenelg to defend the stronghold of the Fiennes from attack.

The southgoing stream begins at HW Dover −0420 at up to 15km/h while the northgoing stream begins at HW Dover +0140 at up to 13km/h although it has been measured at 22km/h. The former is increased in strength and duration by strong and long lasting northeasterly winds, snowmelt and rainfall while converse factors increase the northerly flow. Powered craft being washed through out of control are not unusual. There may be eddies along the edges.

Kylerhea forest nature reserve has ancient birch, ash and oakwood with golden eagles, dolphins, porpoises, guillemots, herons and hooded crows. Otters are observed

The Skye Bridge.

Kyleakin with the island's main ferry slipway, now retired.

from a hide near the Kyle Rhea lightbeacon on the west side and so this area should be avoided so that the watchers are not disturbed.

Powerlines pass high over the kyle. Kyle Rhea, straight of the king, was named after Hakon. It can have overfalls during a southwesterly flow with southerly or southwesterly winds, standing waves and boils in less extreme conditions and violent squalls with northwesterly winds.

As the channel opens into the Sound of Sleat, flows ease to 3km/h, southgoing from HW Dover −0440 and northgoing from HW Dover +0120.

Caisteal Maol, also expensive to pass in its day.

Loch Alsh with Kyle Rhea leading off to the right.

Quite large ships use Kyle Rhea.

Kyle Rhea during a summer evening slack, looking northwards towards Loch Alsh.

Distance
The Island of Skye is 77km long and lies 400m off Glenelg with road access

OS 1:50,000 Sheets
23 North Skye
24 Raasay
& Applecross
32 South Skye
& Cuillin Hills
33 Loch Alsh, Glen Shiel & Loch Hourn
(39 Rùm,
Eigg & Muck)

Tidal Constants
Glenelg Bay:
HW Dover −0500,
LW Dover −0450
Loch Hourn:
HW Dover −0420,
LW Dover −0500
Camas nan Gall:
HW Dover −0450,
LW Dover −0440
Loch Harport:
HW Dover −0500,
LW Dover −0450
Loch Snizort
(Uig Bay):
HW Dover −0440,
LW Dover −0420
Loch a'Bhraige:
Dover −0420
Portree:
Dover −0440
Broadford Bay:
Dover −0440
Kyle of Lochalsh:
HW Dover −0440,
LW Dover −0420

Sea Area:
Hebrides

Submarine Areas
21 Sleat, 25 Eigg, 20 Rhum, 19 Canna, 16 Bracadale, 15 Neist, 11 Dunvegan, 7 Trodday, 12 Portree

119

23 Soay

Soay being Norse for island of sheep, not necessarily Soay sheep, it is to be expected that there should be more than one island with the name. This is not the St Kilda or the Iona ones but the one off the south coast of Skye, on the edge of the Sea of the Hebrides. In fact, it is very nearly two islands, only a low 400m wide isthmus joining them at the centre.

The nearest practical place to launch is the lobster pot littered jetty at Elgol, 24km along the single track B8083.

Soay is of Torridonian sandstone, an infertile heather

Soay across Loch Scavaig from Elgol. Sgurr a Choire Bhig is to the right.

The headland at An Dubh-liamhrig.

An Dubh-liamhrig's natural arch.

Looking across Camas nan Gall to the isthmus with Skye beyond, the Cuillin rising steeply on the right.

Cave at Rubha Dubh.

moor plateau almost completely surrounded by cliffs somewhat over 10m high which make it difficult to land anywhere except in the calmest of conditions.

The highest point, Beinn Bhreac near the northeast end, is only 141m high, in stark contrast with the Cuillin backdrop.

A stone beach at Clachan Uaine is one of the points where it would be easiest to land. Brown sheep graze behind a shoreline where terns, herring and blackbacked gulls and oystercatchers are active.

At An Dubh-liamhrig a block of rock has been punched out to leave an arch with a cill above water level. On the following corner is the first cave, occupied by cormorants, hence the strong fish smell and the white guano marks below favourite perches.

Skerries are at their most extensive around An Dubh-sgeire at the entrance to Camas nan Gall, the island's largest inlet, which has two gravel beaches with a heavy sea during southerly and southeasterly gales. Along the west side is Mol-chlach, site of the school and where the

Cave at Rubh' Aonghais.

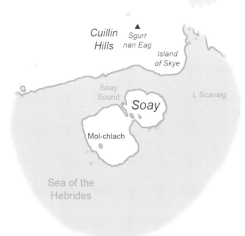

Cuillin Hills

▲ Sgurr nan Eag

Island of Skye

Soay Sound

Soay

L Scavaig

Mol-chlach

Sea of the Hebrides

Rùm, seen from Rubh' Aonghais.

single resident lives. In recent years there have been nearer a dozen, some artists but mostly lobster fishermen and prawn fishermen supplying Europe.

Until 1823 there was only one family on the island but the Clearances had the opposite effect from that in most of Scotland, where crofters were driven off the land. There was a movement here from Skye and by 1861 the population had risen to 129. Soay had the world's first solar powered telephone exchange but there seems little need for it now.

The island was bought in 1945 by author Gavin Maxwell, who built a jetty and a factory for a basking shark fishing industry, steam provided by a GWR engine boiler, described in his *Harpoon at a Venture*. However,

Intrusions doing some interesting things to the strata on the west end of Soay.

Another of Soay's rectangular caves, this one on the west end.

Soay Sound, backed by Sgurr nan Eag and Sgurr a Choire Bhig. An eagle is soaring above the shoulder in the centre of the picture.

the business folded three years later. The wreck of a shark boat remains. His harpoonist, Tex Geddes, whose own autobiography was called *Hebridean Sharker*, stayed on the island and was met by Brian Wilson during his Scottish circumnavigation. Geddes was of the opinion that whistling in a boat would bring strong wind. Brian whistled frequently in his sea kayak but Tex did not consider that to be a boat. In 1953 there was a high profile general evacuation of the residents to Mull. Geddes bought the island, became the Laird of Soay and lived here until his death in 1998.

A recent resident to write a book on the island was Lawrence Reed of tailors Austin Reed, although some existing residents dismissed his farming as gardening. Among the plants growing are fuchsias, honeysuckle, rhododendrons, rowans, silver birches and ramsons. A noted local resident has been MacNamara, a prize brown Shetland ram with a leather collar. The old salts in *The Merry Men* discuss encountering a sea devil off Soay. Provisions come on a monthly boat from Arisaig.

On the far side of Camas nan Gall the cliffs continue from Rubha Dubh to the corner at Rubh' Aonghais where the largest of the caves is situated. The view ahead has been building but now the arc of the Small Isles is complete with Eigg, Muck, Rùm, Sanday and Canna all visible, some distinctive peaks among them.

The coast turns northwest past offlying reefs and the strata do interesting things, including intrusions like a tuning fork which sweep through the existing rock beds. A paving stone quarry on the cliffs provided high quality paving slabs for a number of Liverpool streets. Another Rubha Dubh is passed and a wall of strangely pitted sandstone stands beside a cave entrance.

At Leac nam Faoileann the coast turns northeast into Soay Sound, now a bit more sheltered but with a continuous westwards flow and occupied by seals and guillemots. It was also popular with basking sharks. The sound runs towards the mighty wall provided by Sgurr nan Eag, 992m Sgurr Alasdair, Sgurr Dearg and other such peaks.

Soay Harbour is a much narrower cleft than Camas nan Gall. There is a bar inside the entrance which it is suggested should only be crossed at half tide on the flood. At the southern end is drying mud while the broken down pier on the east side has not been repaired in case boats moor and bring rats.

Rubha Bàgh Clann Nèill looks over a rather larger inlet which could easily be mistaken for the harbour.

An Dubh chamas, black bay, may have a fish farm and another stone beach on which it would be possible to land in reasonable conditions, the last such beach until return to Clachan Uaine.

The inconspicuous small mouth of Soay Harbour.

An Dubh chamas with its fish farm, a possible landing place.

Distance
Soay is 5km long and lies 1km off the Island of Skye

OS 1:50,000 Sheet
32 South Skye
& Cuillin Hills

Tidal Constants
Camas nan Gall:
HW Dover −0450,
LW Dover −0440

Sea Area
Hebrides

Submarine Area
20 Rhum

24 Island of Raasay

Norse for roe deer island, Raasay has red deer, otters, blue hares that have been introduced, water shrews and a subspecies of bank vole with a larger skull than usual. The woods and parkland of Liassic origin encourage rare wildlife and a rich variety of small birds. The fertile soils and mild climate, protected by Skye, grow alpines, saxifrages, orchids, ferns, mosses, sea aster and bog asphodel and it is the only British location for Balearic sandwort. The notable absence is of children of secondary school age, who have to board in Portree.

The island was owned by the MacLeods between the 16th and 19th centuries. They sent a hundred men from Peinchorran on Loch Sligachan, rounding the spit of Rubh' an Torra Mhòir and crossing Balmeannach Bay to reach the Narrows of Raasay. Here the flow in the Sound of Raasay is forced through a kilometre wide gap where currents can reach 6km/h and breaking waves form in some conditions, not least after cloud caps blowing off the Skye peaks, indicating violent squalls to follow. Flows are northwards from HW Dover −0500 and southwards from HW Dover +0100. Buoyage is set for boats travelling northwards. The Sound of Raasay is a submarine exercise area.

Raasay has high cliffs on the east side, falling across

Oskaig hamlet stands inland from Oskaig Point.

Holoman Island close to Raasay's west coast.

Raasay and Rona to support the Jacobite cause in 1745, as a result of which the Royal Navy ship *Furnace* burned every house, killed every domestic animal and destroyed all the boats. A century later, an attempt under private landlords to improve the island failed and many hundreds of residents were forcibly evicted under the Clearances to make way for sheep and game, being sent to the northern end of the island, the rock platform of Rona or the other side of the world.

Poet Somhairle MacGill-Eain was born here, just part of the island's strong tradition of poetry, music and dancing. In 1893 a very strict sect of the Free Church had been set up on the island, banning such frivolities. Today there are about 160 residents, mostly Gaelic speaking crofters, strict Protestants who keep the Sabbath.

A suitable launching place is the end of the B883 at

What serves as a beach at Manish.

The keyhole shaped arch at Manish.

124

Loch Arnish with low Eilean Fladday below Beinn na h-Iolaire.

the island to much lower cliffs on the west. The southern part is of red Torridonian sandstone with some granite and Torridonian shales which contain the oldest known plant remains. In *A Journey to the Western Islands of Scotland* Johnson noted that cattle often perished on Raasay by falling off precipices. He also noted that stone arrowheads were found frequently, the locals calling them elf bolts because they thought fairies fired them at the cattle.

The Narrows of Raasay are constricted by Eilean Aird nan Gobhar, connected to Raasay by a drying reef. Birds on the sea include puffins, guillemots, razorbills, blackbacked, common and herring gulls, eider ducks and cormorants.

Beyond Oskaig, above Oskaig Point, there is little in the way of habitation although there are a few houses at the far end of Holoman Bay, overlooking Holoman Island, a heather and grass covered block attached to Raasay by another drying reef.

Rubha an Inbhire hides Eilean an Inbhir, Inver having royal associations and being appreciated by the Queen, who landed from the Royal Yacht. Another royal visitor was Prince Charlie, who spent two days at Glame from the night after the burnings in 1746 to wait for a French ship which never came, as a result of which he returned to Skye.

Glame has loam at 60–90m, suggesting it was not glaciated and accounting for rare flora present.

The northern end of the island is of lower Archaen gneiss. Perhaps a falcon might be seen hunting along the coast.

There are shielings at Manish Mòr and Manish Beg. Caves include one with a keyhole at the back, leading to a rocky beach beyond, and there is a more conventional shape of arch. Manish Island, again connected to the shore by a drying reef, hides Manish Point at the entrance to Loch Arnish.

Fladday Harbour is surprisingly hard to find, considering Eilean Fladday rises to only 39m while Beinn na h-Iolaire stands at 254m on the adjacent section of Raasay. Ard an Torrain and the island off it are both conspicuous but the pair of islands further west are low and not easy to see. The former schoolhouse at Torran was used by the 1883 Royal Commission into conditions for crofters to take evidence from residents, who were numerous at the poor northern end of Raasay at the time.

The route through Caol Fladda is obstructed by a rough stone causeway across. Small fishing dinghies lie about in the kelp and golden eagles hunt above. In the 1920s and 1930s the five families on Fladda asked for a dry causeway or a bridge as their children were often cut off by the tide when travelling to and from school in

Torran, a request rejected on the grounds of cost. They responded by withdrawing their children from school, followed by a rate strike. The education department built a school on the island and employed a teacher, nearly as expensive as a bridge but funded by a different department's budget. A new footpath along the coast was built from Torran to the island in the winters from 1949 to 1952 by Calum and Charles MacLeod, funded by the council, but the crossing is still on the tidal causeway.

It is worth sighting from the causeway past Rubha Breacaichte to locate the drying channel between the northern tip of Raasay and Eilean Tigh, which can be very hard to find from the Loch a' Sguirr end although obvious from Caol Rona.

Caol Rona flows southeast from HW Dover +0040 and northwest from HW Dover −0520 at up to 4km/h. Eilean an Fhraoich stands in the centre of the caol with No 4 beacon while the full extent of Rona, seen end on, is not obvious although the peaks rise quite high.

Shielings stand on the hillside at intervals. Caol Rona ends at Rubha Ard Ghlaisen which bears the 9m high pole of No 5 beacon as Inner Sound is joined. The steep cliffs on the east side of Raasay hint at Inner Sound's being the deepest place on the continental shelf, down to 324m. It is a submarine exercise area and home of the British Underwater Test & Evaluation Centre. Flows southwards are from HW Dover +0100 and northwards from HW Dover −0500, the times later to the south and

Caol Fladda with the causeway at low water.

Caol Rona with Eilean an Fhraoich in the centre and Sgeir nan Eun to the left.

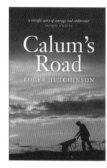

reaching 2km/h off salient points. Gannets hunt overhead. On the far side of the sound are the soaring peaks of Applecross Forest in Wester Ross.

Beyond Sithean Mòr Rainy's Wall crosses the narrowest part of the island. Supposedly a deer fence, the 1.8m high stone wall was not so much to check the movement of deer as to keep the crofters to the unfertile northern end of the island, where they were forbidden to take action against the game ravaging what crops they were able to grow.

There is a small and steep beach below the ruins of Brochel Castle on a volcanic plug, probably built in the

15th century by Calum, the first Raasay chief of the MacLeods of Lewis as a base to raid shipping in Inner Sound, in the process attracting other criminals to the clan. Used until about 1671, the castle ruins appear as dark shapes flanking a whitewashed house beyond, approached by road.

The first 3km of road north from here were built by hand by Arnish crofter Calum MacLeod, recalled in *Calum's Road* and a strathspey of the same name by Capercaillie. He spent his free fortnights on it when not working as Rona lighthouse's assistant keeper in order to try to stop the decline of the northern part of the island

The remains of Brochel Castle.

The peak of Dùn Caan shows above buoy D.

because of the lack of transport. He began by buying a book on roadbuilding and then spent a decade wearing out tools before the council finally adopted it, widened it and surfaced it. A cairn by the castle marks his work although there has been a call for it to be made a World Heritage Site.

Around Brochel Castle primroses cover the hillside in spring before a section of Raasay Forest flanks Brochel Bay. Cliffs from here run at 120–280m high. Between North and South Screapadal is a township site, less conspicuous than the cormorants, gannets, black guillemots, guillemots and razorbills which live below the cliffs.

Yellow pillar buoy D marks the southern end of the submarine Outer Sea Area. Kelp forms in some places.

The cliffs of Druim an Aonaich run for several kilometres at the top of the steep drop to Inner Sound. Above them is the 443m volcanic plug of Dùn Caan, looking like a fort as the name suggests and only 900m from the sea. Boswell and Johnson paid a visit in 1773 and a jig of joy was danced on the summit. Boswell records in *The Journal of a Tour to the Hebrides* how a kelpie in Loch na Mna had eaten a man's daughter, to which he responded by roasting a sow to attract it with the smell and then killed it with a red hot spit.

Another tale relates how the island blacksmith lost a daughter to a kelpie. He and his son made large hooks to trap it on land. This it was not able to stand for long and was found as a strange heap of jelly.

A conspicuous waterfall drops from the former settlement of Hallaig before Rubha na' Leac, at the northeast end of 319m Beinn na' Leac, the island's southeastern buttress. Hallaig was remembered in verse by Somhairle MacGill-Eain, himself remembered by a cairn beyond Rubha na' Leac.

North and South Fearns are the start of flatter coastline. At South Fearns crofters from Rona set up camp in 1921, cleared sheep from what previously had been their land and were prepared to pay fair rents. The Government did not offer the crofts they had promised before the First World War and the Rona Raiders became a national cause. Police were brought over but unable to find the five named ringleaders. They gave themselves up to the second detachment of police to arrive on the island and were taken to Portree, where there was considerable popular support for them. There was public outcry when they were tried and jailed in Inverness. Following their release they were piped home with support right from the jail. The Board of Agriculture set up a number of new holdings for crofters at the more fertile southern end of the island and the population of the northern end drifted south.

A 5m white metal framework lighthouse stands on Eyre Point, which looks onto Caol Mòr. Unexpectedly, conditions are often calm even when there are strong winds elsewhere in the vicinity. Flows are westwards from HW Dover −0420 and eastwards from HW Dover +0120 at up to 4km/h. On the other side of the caol is Scalpay with Loch na Cairidh leading off to the south and Loch Sligachan to the west, often a source of strong winds.

Above Rubha na Cloiche is 141m high Suisnish Hill. Boxes of gravel inside the old ferry pier gave mass

Artist Tom Newton's studio on the shore at Suisnish.

which helped to resist the impact forces of berthing ferries. A railway formerly ran up the hill to the iron ore mines, worked during the First World War with German prisoner of war labour.

Submarine cables run across from Skye to Suisnish with its memorial. Inverarish has a school and a post office and store which were built for the mine workers.

Henderson's Bridge is reputed to emit the sounds of human voices and dogs barking. It has been claimed that the high iron ore content in the stones used for the bridge traps sounds and later releasess them, which seems hardly more believable.

In the main part of Raasay Forest, developed in the 1950s, is the Dùn Borodale broch with parts of walls and galleries remaining.

A northerly eddy forms in Churchton Bay during the southerly flow. Clachan has the island's car ferry terminal pier for Sconser, a service only begun in 1976 after a long campaign in favour. CalMac's 2012 MV *Hallaig* was the world's first diesel electric hybrid Ro-Ro ferry.

A conspicuous building is Raasay House, inspiration for a pipe tune, built on the site of a tower of 1549. Johnson and Boswell stayed in 1773, Boswell spending the night in the company of their host's many unmarried daughters. The 250 year old mansion has a 200 year old Regency frontage and a battery of 1807 with cannon and two mermaids. The house was derelict from the 1960s to the 1980s but, following a fire in 2009, has been restored as an outdoor centre featuring watersports.

There is a nearby hotel and the 13th century chapel of St Molnag ruins. Another building may be 11th century and a stone with Pictish symbols may date from the 7th century. Despite many attempts to repair it, a clock on a clocktower still shows the time at which 36 men of the island assembled to leave for the First World War. Only 14 returned. Boswell recorded that 100 men had gone to fight in the 1745 uprising, again only 14 returning.

Distance
The Island of Raasay is 20km long and lies 1km off Gedintailor with ferry access

OS 1:50,000 Sheets
24 Raasay
& Applecross
(32 South Skye
& Cuillin Hills)

Tidal Constants
Loch a'Bhraige:
Dover −0420
Portree:
Dover −0440

Sea Area
Hebrides

Submarine Areas
12 Portree,
14 Raasay

Raasay House stands by Churchton Bay.

25 Scalpay

Not to be confused with the more distant but much better populated island of the same name off Harris, the Scalpay by Skye has just a few houses at its southeast end to account for nearly all of its building. It rises to 396m with Mullach na Càrn in its southern half, on the northeast flanks of which sit three large lochans, Loch an Leòid, Loch Duth and Loch a' Mhuilinn. Some areas are forested lower down around the southern side and connected by a track but it is mostly an island of rough heather and rock, used for deer and sheep grazing.

A vehicle or two can be parked behind Ob Apoldoire, where a couple of tracks lead off the A87, providing access is not blocked. At high water it is possible to portage over the crash barrier and a couple of sheep fences straight onto Ob Apoldoire, otherwise it is a longer portage over broken stone and wrack. Alternative parking might be found in Strollamus or in Dunan although it will probably be a longer walk to the water.

Crossing Caolas Scalpay takes the boater to Rubha Aosail Sligneach where a submarine cable also crosses from Skye despite the rocks littering the point. Caolas Scalpay is subject to frequent squalls of irregular direction. This not just because of Creag Strollamus, Glas Bheinn Bheag and Am Meall which rise on the southwest side to make a valley but also, behind them, the Cuillin Hills. They tower high above, Beinn na Caillich, Beinn na Crò, Glas Bheinn Mhòr and, higher still, Garbh-bheinn and Bla Bheinn to 928m, not just the height but the fantastic shapes. Such is the dramatic backdrop to Loch na Cairidh, the Red Cuillin, those east of Glen Sligachan.

Features on Scalpay are much less extreme but the white cottage at Corran a' Chinn Uachdaraich, used for

Mullach na Càrn on Scalpay, seen across Caolas Scalpay from Ob Apoldoire. Note the A87 sheep fences.

Looking south from Rubha Aosail Sligneach with Creag Strollamus on the left and Beinn na Caillich in the centre.

Loch na Cairidh from Ob Apoldoire at low water with Meall a' Mhaoil on the left. Beyond Corran a' Chinn Uachdaraich on Scalpay is Suisnish Hill on Raasay. The Narrows of Raasay are in the centre distance.

Looking up Loch Ainort with Marsco in the centre and other Cuillin, leading round to Glamaig on the right.

Caol Mòr from Rubh' a' Chonnaidh with Eyre Point on Raasay to the left and the mainland by Applecross across Inner Sound.

Camas na Geadaig starts the more remote side of Scalpay.

holiday letting, stands out distinctly against the brown of the heather and grass.

The A87 turns away at Rubh' an Aird Dhuirche to follow Loch Ainort. On the far side of this loch, Leathad Chrithian forms a ridge close to its summit level for nearly 2km while Marsco stands at the head of the loch with Beinn Dearg Mhor round to Glamaig plus a smattering of peaks which are lesser only in comparison. These funnel many winds down into Loch Ainort so that fierce squalls are blasted out against the Scalpay shore. Beinn Chàirn at 228m and 225m Beinn Reireag Bheag on Scalpay give the winds a final lift on their way.

The woods now come to an end. The island was developed in the 19th century by Sir Donald Currie who planted the trees and built the tracks. Part of the northwest end of the island is now fenced for intensive deer farming for export to Europe.

Between Meall a' Mhaoil and Meall Buidhe and the Isle of Raasay the Sound of Raasay leads off through the Narrows of Raasay while Loch Sligachan enters from the west past Ben Lee, again with very heavy squalls. This

Empty sea urchin cases.

would seem to suggest that Caol Mòr between the end of Scalpay and the cliffs on the southern end of Raasay might be a very turbulent place but this is not so, the channel often having less wind than elsewhere in the vicinity. Caol Mòr flows east from HW Dover +0140 and west from HW Dover –0420.

Visible above the cliffs on Raasay is the stumpy peak of Dùn Caan. After Rubh' a' Chonnaidh, Scalpay has its longest inlet, Camas na Geadaig, at the head of which is a ruined croft, facing out to Eyre Point on Raasay with its 5m white metal lighthouse.

From Rubh' a' Chinn Mhóir the coast becomes more sheltered from the prevailing wind despite facing out to Inner Sound. Fringing reefs edge the northeastern half of the island and kelp runs out to the Sgeirean Tarsuinn. From the grassy islet of Eilean Leac na Gainimh the reef is at its most irregular until Rubh' an Lochain where there are not only barnacles, limpets, mussels and whelks on the rocks but also large red sea urchins which have been hollowed out by gulls. Seals can also be heard singing at times and there are otters about. Cormorants whiten the rock peaks and guillemots rove between the reefs.

Off Rubha Doire na Boceinein a mark locates the low Sgeir Thraid, the first of the Sgeirean Tarsuinn, past which flows run to 2km/h.

South of Sgeir Dhearg a green conical light buoy marks Gulnare Rock which is just awash. Across the sound are the Crowlin Islands off the mouth of Loch Carron and the Applecross shore.

The last of the Sgeirean Tarsuinn is Longay, by far the largest. To its right can be seen, in the distance, the Skye bridge.

Below 291m Beinn Loch a' Mhuilinn are Scalpay's highest cliffs. Between these and Longay flows run south from HW Dover +0140 and north from HW Dover –0420 at up to 4km/h.

Pabay is a much larger and lower island, rising to only 28m. To its southwest can be seen the houses on the Skye shore at Broadford.

Orange buoys in Camas na Fisteodh mark underwater cages used in shellfish research but there may also be fish farms as far as Caolas Scalpay. A heron indicates this is the sheltered end of the island. The two bays between Rubh' an Tòrn Mhòir, Rubh' an Tòrr Bhig and Rubh' an Trusaidh front the cultivated area, Scalpay House, the burial ground and the Celtic cell remains at Teampuill fraing. The tiny population was once larger, including Browny, a robust fairy, according to Dr Johnson, who did a lot of work in return for food and kindness. Opposite 24m high Guillamon Island a mark stands in the mouth of the second bay where the pier is a ruin. The water can be so clear that gazing down onto the dark weed and white sand in calm conditions can be enough to induce a feeling of vertigo.

On the Skye shore a forest rises above Rubha na Sgianadin. On Scalpay, gorse below 274m Beinn nan Caorach gives way to a stand of Scots pines. Oystercatchers and herring and blackbacked gulls are seen as Caolas Scalpay narrows and return is made to Rubha Aosail Sligneach.

Cliffs below Beinn Loch a' Mhuilinn at the east end of Scalpay.

Mark between Rubh' an Tòrr Bhig and Rubh' an Trusaidh.

The built up flat section of Scalpay. Beyond is Creag Strollamus, overlooked by Beinn na Caillich and the Cuillin towards Glamaig.

Distance
Scalpay is 7km long and lies 500m off Strollamus

OS 1:50,000 Sheets
(24 Raasay & Applecross)
32 South Skye & Cuillin Hills

Tidal Constant
Broadford Bay:
Dover –0440

Sea Area
Hebrides

Sgeir Dhearg, the central island of the Sgeirean Tarsuinn.

Longay lies to the northeast of Scalpay.

Kyle of Lochalsh is at the end of the railway line from Dingwall. Submarine cables cross the kyle here.

In 1893 Dr Matheson at Kyle of Lochalsh gave the first of many reports of a sea monster with a tapered waving tail which rose steadily many metres in the air and submerged equally steadily, on a large body which moved fast under the water, a description not fitting any early submarine. A local resident was Alexander MacRae who emigrated to Australia and founded Speedo.

Kyle House has 1.2ha of gardens planted in the 1960s by Colin Mackenzie with a notable kitchen garden and tender plants attaining large size because of the warmth of the Gulf Stream.

Eilean Bàn, the white island, has the 21m white tower of Kyle Akin lighthouse, built in 1857 by the Stevensons but disused as it is partly obscured by the bridge. This is Dan Boothby's *Island of Dreams* and is the ongoing inspiration for Adam Melfort in *A Prince of the Captivity*. Another author here, to whom there is a museum, was Gavin Maxwell who bought the island in 1963 to turn it into a zoo for west Highland birds and mammals. He moved there in 1968. After his early death the following year his partner, John Lister-Kaye, wrote a book about the island and the project. Boothby discusses the various ghost sightings, noises and smells and suggests explanations. Teko, the last otter, is buried here. There are plenty of otters about and ducts have been laid to provide otter runs past the bridgeworks.

Over the Sea to Skye took on a new meaning with the construction of the Skye bridge to carry the A87 from next to the golf course at Plock of Kyle via Eilean Bàn to the Skye shore. Stone for the project was taken from a quarry at the Kyle of Lochalsh end. The 2.4km bridge was Scotland's first financed, designed, built and operated bridge, a concept that was badly soured by the highest bridge toll in Europe until rescinded in 2004. It is the world's longest span balanced cantilever concrete box girder bridge. Embellishments are intended to make it appear like a couple of giant seagulls in flight. It is also Scotland's most exposed bridge site with severe weather during the construction resulting in significant delays. An imposing backdrop comes in the form of 775m Glamaig and other peaks in the Cuillin Hills.

Kyle Akin leads out into Inner Sound. Streams start northwards at HW Dover +0100 and southwards at HW Dover −0500, later in the south and earlier in the north, to 2km/h at salient points. Any rafts of fish farms are watched by seals inside Eilean a' Mhal and other islets leading up to the Black Islands in Erbusaig Bay.

After Portnacloich Point there are more islets dotted along the rocky shore, Eilean na Crèadha, Eilean nan Gobhar Mór, 6m high Eilean Dubh Dhurinish and An Dubh-aird, almost an island, 35m high and covered with

steeply rising heath, fronting Plockton Aerodrome as it lies between Camas Dubh-aird and Camas Deannd. Several hamlets include Drumbuie at the head of Port Cam and Port-an-eorna before Bagh an t-Srathaidh. Cormorants, blackbacked gulls and herons frequent the islands.

Streams are weak at the mouth of Loch Carron. Several navigation marks include a disused 13m light tower on Eilean a' Chait in the Cat Islands and also a spar buoy

Island of Dreams

A Personal History of a Remarkable Place

Dan Boothby

Loch Carron with Loch Kishorn beyond, seen from Erbusaig Bay.

The Harbour between the Crowlin Islands.

Ardban is marked out by its dazzling white beach.

by Hawk Rock. The warm climate around Plockton encourages the growth of palm trees and there is farm with rare breeds.

Alexander Smith's party in *A Summer in Skye* hired a boat and rowers in Lochcarron in 1864 but were deserted by them in Plockton after an evening of heavy rain and phosphorescence. The village, a third of the houses with absentee owners, was used by the BBC for filming their *Hamish Macbeth* series.

The view south from Ardban includes Scalpay and the Cuillin.

Weathered rocks at Ardban. Beyond are Camusteel and Meall na Fhuaid above Applecross.

There was an ancient prophesy of a monster coming from Loch Kishorn. It would rise to the surface three times then sink beneath the waves for ever. The Garra Islands stand at the mouth of the loch. Garbh-eilean is forested while Kishorn Island stands 19m high, the largest of the group. Precast bridge units for the Skye bridge were made near the head of the loch. Because of the depth of the loch it was used from 1975 to 1987 by Howard-Doris as their North Sea oil platform construction site. Their biggest project was the Ninian Central Platform. It stood 237m high, had a 136m diameter base and weighed 600,000t. At the time it was the largest moveable object ever made by man and was towed to its present location 177km off the coast of Scotland where it sits on the bottom in 134m of water. It puts an interesting twist on the old prophesy. After being used to prefabricate parts for the Skye bridge the site was abandoned.

The northwest side of Loch Kishorn climbs in a wall to 896m Beinn Bhàn and 776m Sgurr a Ghaorachain and continues with a steep coast of weathered red sandstone all the way to Rubha na h-Uamha where it is overhanging. At the northern end the Allt a' Chumhaing and Allt a' Chois both have waterfalls over 70m high.

There are occasional small stone beaches that are backed by heather, bracken, foxgloves and trefoils among the flotsam. Fulmars sweep low over the water in their distinctive manner.

Streams in Caolas Mòr begin southeast at HW Dover +0145 and northwest at HW Dover −0415 at up to 2km/h.

On the far side, the Crowlin Islands are a volcanic outcrop in three islands, the two longer of which join up at low tide although mostly separated by a narrow cleft, the Harbour. The largest, Eilean Mòr, rises to 114m at Meall a' Chòis. It has a cave and the ruins of a chapel said to be dedicated to St Cormac.

Eilean Meadhonach lies along its west side while at the north end is Eilean Beag with a lighthouse and caves occupied by common and Atlantic seals. To the west there is, again, a dramatic skyline with a truncated cone rising high above the general trend of the mountains on Raasay.

Loch Toscaig with Toscaig at its head has clear water through which the sandy bottom can be seen. Eilean na Bà stands 22m high while An Ruadh-eilean disappears at high tide in an area which may be used for fish farms.

Ardban, a couple of houses on a peninsula, would hardly be noticed but for the glistening white beaches on each side, shell sand but with a texture like coral sand. Otters might also be seen in the area.

Eilean nan Naomh has a wreck on the inside despite a beacon on each end. It was the Holy Island where St Maelrubha landed in 671. It offers some shelter to Poll Creadha which lies between Culduie and Camusterrach.

A couple of aerials have been erected at Camusteel but steel is also found where the road comes between the shore and Loch a' Mhuilinn to the south of Milton where cars have dropped over the cliff and lie rusting at the bottom. Towards the far end, the Bealach na Bà road is the steepest in Scotland with gradients to 20%, a drove road unsurfaced until the 1950s.

Applecross looks out over Applecross Bay. A deep cleft between the peaks of Applecross Forest is a gouge obviously made by something much larger than the River Applecross which currently discharges here. Applecross House is used by the Applecross Trust. Close by is a chapel which has fragments of a stone cross from a monastery built in 672 by St Maelrubha for fugities, one of the oldest seats of Christianity in Scotland, destroyed by the Vikings.

There was a settlement above Rubha na Guailne but the only signs of man's activity are more rusting cars and a motorbike at the foot of the cliffs. The roads around Applecross Bay are extremely dangerous or the locals

Waterfall at Rubha na Guailne... and a less pretty picture of wrecked cars and a motorbike.

have a disappointingly limited level of environmental responsibility.

Sand is the descriptively blunt name for an inlet with a bay of sand and a virtual cliff of sand flowing down to the beach.

Inner Sound has the deepest continental shelf water around the British Isles, possibly a former river course. For this reason it is used as a submarine exercise area and for carrying out torpedo tests. The British Underwater Test & Evaluation Centre with helipad is in a modern building on the low cliffs and its presence prevented Inner Sound being used for oil platform construction. When a red flag or lights are showing it is necessary to pass through the area without stopping. The coast road was opened in 1976 to serve the centre.

The cliffs seem fairly remote for several kilometres. Occasionally there are caves and Callakille has a natural arch. Waders and otters are likely to be the only life close inshore. Across the sound, Raasay gives way to Rona.

Balanced section of rock strata, an interesting shoreline sculpture.

Across Inner Sound Raasay gives way to Rona.

Distance
46km from Kyle of Lochalsh to Rubha Chuaig

OS 1:50,000 Sheets
24 Raasay & Applecross
33 Loch Alsh, Glen Shiel & Loch Hourn

Tidal Constants
Kyle of Lochalsh:
HW Dover −0440,
LW Dover −0420
Plockton:
Dover −0420
Applecross:
HW Dover −0430,
LW Dover −0420
Loch a' Bhràige:
Dover −0420

Sea Area
Hebrides

Submarine Areas
14 Raasay,
13 Rona South

27 Southeast Minch

For softly and surely, as nearer the boat that we gazed from drew,
The face of the precipice opened and bade us as birds pass through,
And the bark shot sheer to the sea through the strait of the sharp steep cleft,
The portal that opens with imminent rampires to right and to left,
Sublime as the sky they darken and strange as a spell-struck dream,
On the world unconfined of the mountains, the reign of the sea supreme,
The kingdom of westward waters, wherein when we swam we knew
The waves that we clove were boundless, the wind on our brows that blew
Had swept no land and no lake, and had warred not on tower or on tree,
But came on us hard out of heaven, and alive with the soul of the sea.

Charles Algernon Swinburne

Rubha Chuaig brings an inlet in the form of Ob Chuaig. It is fed by the Abhainn Chuaig, next to which a track runs up to the road at Cuaig.

Eilean Chuaig occupies the entrance to Ob Chuaig, offering a notably ship shaped silhouette to the bay. Along the cliffs there are caves. Jellyfish and fulmars are present with cormorants and waders in Ob na h-Uamha. Each side of this latter bay are the low Rubha na Fearna and the Rubha na Fearn. This second point brings a turn into Loch Torridon which has steep shores on the northwest side but weak streams. It is one of the wildest and least spoilt stretches of Highland coastline. It would be difficult to match the mountainscape around the head of the loch in Britain. The peaks of Applecross Forest, Glenshieldaig Forest, Ben-Damph Forest, Torridon Forest, Shieldaig Forest and Flowerdale Forest crowd round with an array of peaks not high by world standards but which have dramatic shapes, mountains with character. Here are Beinn Bhàn at 896m, Beinn Damh at 902m, Tom na Grugaich at 922m, Sgurr Mhor at 985m and Baos Damh at 875m to name a few. Rising behind them are the higher peaks of Beinn Eighe. Travelling for an hour while looking at these is an uplifting experience.

The southwest side of the loch is less dramatic. The rocky shoreline is lower although still able to produce the odd arch and there may be fish farms at intervals at Fearnbeg, in Camas an Eilean and in Loch a' Chracaich.

Loch a' Chracaich and Loch Beag shelter behind the Aird peninsula on the southwest side of Loch Torridon. On the other side of Loch Torridon, 142m high Rubha na h-Airde produces a mirror image with Loch Diabeg. Between the two peninsulas is a gap which leads to Loch Shieldag and Upper Loch Torridon. It is a remote area with guillemots and porpoises for company and still that backdrop.

Loch Diabeg may have fish farms. Above the grey cliffs are the whitewashed croft houses of Lower Diabeg.

From here to Red Point, 10km away, the buildings can be counted on the fingers of one hand. One is the fishing station near Red Point where more fish farms may be located.

The 37m high Red Point is where Loch Torridon is left for the Minch. A large sandy bay backed by dunes is found at Redpoint, a village of a dozen crofts scattered around a viewpoint and the B8056. The dunes hold back a steep marshy area with bog cotton and orchids. The

Beinn Eighe, Beinn Alligin, Liathach and other peaks at the head of Loch Torridon, seen beyond Ob na h-Uamha and Rubha na Fearn.

Gairloch and Charlestown at the head of Loch Gairloch.

Cliffs at Port Erradale contain caves.

birdlife is rather more common with blackheaded gulls and oystercatchers.

Low cliffs hide much of South Erradale and Port Henderson. Between them is Sròn na Carra, the entrance to Loch Gairloch. Peaks around the head of the loch rise to 420m Meall an Doirein but in the distance are the much higher peaks of Letterewe Forest, Fisherfield Forest and Strathnasheallag Forest with Slioch at 980m, Mullach Coire Mhic Fhearchair at 1,019m and 1,059m An Teallach.

The low shoreline of the loch is used by black guillemots and otters and there are brown trout, sea trout and salmon in the loch. Badantionail may have a fish farm while there are mackerel in Caolas Bad a' Chrotha where there is a fish curing station.

The 36m high Eilean Horrisdale takes its name from the Norse god Thor and was used by the Vikings to lay up their longships for the winter. More recently it served as a fishing settlement.

A 2m metal light pedestal stands on 7m high Glas Eilean, to the southeast of which lie Loch Shieldaig and Loch Kerry, entrance to which is past a peninsula with An Dùn, a golf course and Flowerdale House.

Formerly a fishing port where the B8021 leaves the A832, **Gairloch**, where gearr meaning short, is now a place for waterskiing, paragliding, canoeing, windsurfing and sailing. It has had Bronze and Iron Age residents, Picts, and Vikings and retained the population when Sir Hector Mackenzie refused to evict during the Clearances. It has the Gairloch Heritage Museum which covers from the prehistory of the area to the present day, including the

Natural arch to the south of Rubha Rèidh.

from each wave. From the top of the sandstone cliffs there are views to the Hebrides.

Streams start northeast at HW Dover +0430 and south at HW Dover −0115 at up to 6km/h at Camas Mór. Camas Mór is a pristine sand beach, inaccessible by land because of the cliffs. It has arches and a prominent red sandstone stack, well covered with greenery at its top end.

The ringed plover frequents Sròn a' Gheodha Dhuibh. A block which resembles a fortification but is completely natural guards the entrance to Caolas an Fhuraidh which runs inside 20m Eilean Furadh Mór. Sgeir Maol Mhoraidh at its far end links up to the shore at low tide.

In the centre of Loch Ewe is the Isle of Ewe. The loch was where north Atlantic convoys were assembled during the Second World War with an anti submarine boom across the mouth of the loch. It is still used for refuelling NATO ships and the remains of gun emplacements and pillboxes can be seen near a hydrographic survey pillar on the west side of the mouth of the loch. The loch floods from HW Dover +0210 and ebbs from HW Dover

The lighthouse at Rubha Rèidh.

The hidden jetty serving the lighthouse at Rubha Rèidh.

Distance
60km from Rubha Chuaig to the Isle of Ewe

OS 1:50,000 Sheets
19 Gairloch
& Ullapool
24 Raasay
& Applecross

Tidal Constants
Loch a' Bhràige:
Dover −0420
Shieldaig:
Dover −0430
Gairloch:
HW Dover −0430
LW Dover −0420

Sea Area
Hebrides

Submarine Areas
13 Rona South, 5 Minch South, 6 Ewe

17th century Loch Maree ironworks, fishing and illicit whisky distilling. The coast is particularly rich in mosses and liverworts.

Beyond Carn Dearg is Caolas Beag, with shags, guillemots, cormorants, blackbacked gulls, fulmars and porpoises. Streams in the loch are ingoing from HW Dover +0200 and outgoing from HW Dover −0420, reaching a maximum of 2km/h in Caolas Beag. At Big Sand the River Sand enters between the dunes and there is another fishing station beyond the dunes.

Longa Island is 1.4km² of grass and heather covered sandstone, reaching a height of 70m at Druim an Eilein. The island is uninhabited, taking its name from the fact that it was also used by the Vikings to lay up their longships for the winter.

Beyond Rubha Bàn are Port Erradale and North Erradale. Between Peterburn and Melvaig are heather moors with peat cutting and a soft cliffline which has been cut into a series of vertical ribs by water runoff. There are two aerials, each at a Maol Breac, in the middle of the moor. The rest of the coast to Rubha Rèidh is harder with a number of natural arches, those around Sròn na Cléite being particularly fine with an accompaniment of seals.

The ridge of land which peaks at 296m An Cuaidh finishes steeply at Rubha Rèidh with its 25m white tower lighthouse of 1912. A small jetty serves an otherwise inaccessible length of coast. The cleft in which the jetty is located also contains a significant cave which is working back towards the sea from the landward end. Assuming it is natural, it must be doing all its erosion on the backwash

−0415 at up to 2km/h. In the open sea, streams begin north–northeast from HW Dover +0430 and south–southwest from HW Dover −0115 at up to 5km/h.

Isle of Ewe

The Isle of Ewe lies in a sheltered position in Loch Ewe, a sea loch which is only open at its northwest end and which is surrounded by mountains, albeit some distance off. The loch leads out into the Minch and Lewis, the most northerly of the Outer Hebrides, lies opposite the entrance but below the horizon.

Tidal currents in the loch are negligible with a peak of 2km/h on springs. Indeed, a freshet from Loch Maree, flowing out via the River Ewe, can have a greater influence.

Although the route into the Sound would appear to be in a southeasterly direction, the deep water channel at Gob na Lice actually runs at right angles to this and close to the island so that little of the ocean's energy has been absorbed as the waves arrive.

Turning the corner at Gob na Lice, the northerly foot of Sitheanan Dubha, brings dramatic and instant shelter from the prevailing wind. The mainland seems mellower, too, with slate roofed white houses dotted about the rolling hillside at Mellon Charles. The Coigach peaks keep their distance. Only the Navy's green roofed Nissen huts with their lines of semi circular yellow ends seeming out of place.

The island's bay, sheltered by Gob na Lice, contains the inevitable fish enclosure. A few fishing boats are moored in the sound, overlooked by a couple of houses, the only ones on the island apart from the farm. Even so, the number of outfalls into the sea exceeds the number of dwelling places.

The overriding mood is one of rural tranquillity in rugged surroundings and that is something even the Navy's presence does not dispel.

The island is nearest to the mainland at Mellon Charles but the pier belongs to RN Aultbea and is not accessible

Mellon Charles seen from Gob na Lice.

Coigach peaks seen from the loch.

The eastern side of the island.

A house with a boat profile by the loch.

Looking south from the island to the NATO fuel jetty.

to the public. Launching by the pier at Aird Point is the most practical proposition.

Two large mooring buoys are located in the middle of the Sound, both on the extension of the navigation guideline through Gob na Lice at the northern end of the island and Sgeir Maol Mhoraidh at the mouth of the loch. The Sound is a popular mooring point and there is sheltered deep water and good holding ground for anchors north of Aird Point. It was used by the Royal Navy in both wars, was an assembly point for ships joining convoys to Murmansk and Archangel in Russia and has been used more recently as a quarantine mooring

The island's old ferry, moored at the jetty.

The southern end of the Isle of Ewe in Loch Ewe.

The peaks of Flowerdale Forest to the south of the loch.

The western side of the island.

area. Three dolphin piles are prominent while the eastern end of the bay has a clapper bridge over the Allt Beithe, the best example of its kind in Scotland with six river openings and one dry channel, the openings being 900mm wide, 1.2m high and 4.6m long, carrying the road to Mellon Charles. Loch Ewe Distillery is housed by Drumchork Lodge Hotel.

The conspicuous pier belongs to NATO. Used for refuelling, it has a battery of pipes at its seaward end and sees warships calling for refuelling most weeks.

The final jetty of note, if somewhat smaller, is that on the eastern side of the island, to which is moored the island's car ferry, a boat with a ramp at one end. From the jetty a track runs up to the island's farm, a farm which grazes sheep and black Aberdeen Angus cattle. Walls and fences dividing the fields descend to the low tide mark, running out into the sea to break up the hidden submarine territory for the rest of the time.

The island is of low undulating sandstone at all except its northwest end. The foreshore is mostly stones and boulders. Rock, where it does form low cliffs, is angled back sufficiently to permit easy exit anywhere at the southern end if necessary.

The climate is mild, as indicated by the subtropical Inverewe Garden beyond Loch Thùrnaig at the head of Loch Ewe, a benefit of the Gulf Stream.

Vegetation on the island is less exotic, mostly grass and bracken. Trees are almost absent but this was not always the case. In 1549 Dean Monro talked of its wooded character. The forests gave important cover to thieves and desperate men so burning the trees was an effective way of flushing them out. The lesson did not go unheeded and robbers used the same process to smoke out innocent victims for plunder.

Forests without trees are the basis of the dramatic panorama which forms a curtain beyond the southeast end of the loch. Strathnasheallag, Fisherfield, Letterewe, Flowerdale and Shieldag forests all rear their dramatic peaks into the sky in a breathtaking display if the clouds permit. Beinn Eighe is hidden but many distant mountain tops are visible above the end of the loch and the summits of An Teallach rise above Aultbea. The view, contrasting sunshine and dark cloud, the clear air and the scent of the sea on the breeze can be intoxicating.

Near high tide a pointed black rock just to the west of the southern tip of the island resembles a sleeping seal.

Moving up the southwest side of the island brings the occasional scene of dereliction, a pile of corrugated iron sheets thrown down a low cliff face or a line of large rusty floats washed up on the rocks but the eye is taken to the far shore of the loch, to the occasional settlements and single houses and to the tops of three aerials on the headland above.

The cliffs begin to rise as the island climbs at its northwest end to its heather clad highest point, 72m above sea level. There is the occasional cleft and birdlife is at home here. Gulls wheel about and shags pass by on their way. Black guillemots swoop in close to look, their white wing patches contrasting with their black bodies and comical red feet projecting at angles to make up for their stubby tails. In winter their plumage becomes mostly white with black edging. Eider ducks are also present and hooded crows appreciate the cliffs.

Sgeir a' Bhuic, attached to the Isle of Ewe at low tide, and the larger (but not visibly so) two islands which make up Sgeir an Araig mark the start of the exposed portion of the Isle of Ewe, the face with its sometimes red cliffs causing clapotis as the waves bounce off them, with clefts and the starts of caves and with gulls and cormorants resting on the rock ledges high above the water.

A fish farm by Sgeir a' Bhuic at the island's eastern corner.

Looking east past Sgeir a' Bhuic.

Distance
The Isle of Ewe is 4km long and lies 700m off Mellon Charles

OS 1:50,000 Sheet
19 Gairloch & Ullapool

Tidal Constants
Gairloch:
HW Dover −0430,
LW Dover −0420

Sea Area
Hebrides

Submarine Area
6 Ewe

29 Northeast Minch

Rain falling down meets
springs gushing up –
they gather and carry down to the Minch
tons of sour soil, making bald
the bony scalp of Cul Mor. And frost
thrusts his hand in cracks and, clenching his fist,
bursts open the sandstone plates,
the armour of Suilven
Norman MacCaig

Leaving Loch Ewe, Slaggan Bay is conspicuous for its golden sandy cliffs, Slaggan village at its head having a nature trail. At Gob a' Gheodha there is a return to rocky cliffs. These are deeply fractured and in one place a block has dropped away to leave what looks like a shadowy doorway in the rock.

Greenstone Point is low and flat, marked with a 3m iron pole. A wreck lies 200m north of the point and other vessels are misled by a magnetic anomaly in the area. Porpoises are to be found all around Rubha Mór. There are couple of arches, the second near Leac Mhór. Beyond Rubha Beag is Mellon Udrigle, near where a kelpie or water spirit was once said to have lived, while to the south of Meall nam Meallan is Loch na Béiste, loch of the beast.

Tidal streams are weak in Gruinard Bay which takes its name from the Norse *grunna fjord*, shallow ford. At its southwest corner is Laide where a line of rocks protect moorings and there are the remains of a chapel next to a caravan site, located where St Columba is said to have founded a church. There is also a salmon fishing station and maybe a fish farm. A cave precedes the hamlets of First Coast and Second Coast. Suddenly several rivers carve deep channels into the bay, the Little Gruinard, the Inverianvie and the Gruinard Rivers, the latter with Gruinard House and its sawmill by the loch.

The cliffs at Gob a' Gheoda offer doorways into the unknown.

Rubha Cadail light is low on the shoreline at Rhue. Beyond is Annat Bay.

Ben Mór Coigach towers above Isle Martin and Loch Kanaird.

The most important feature in the bay is Gruinard Island, over 2km long with a steep gravel spit in the southeast corner and rising to 106m at An Eilid. Formerly inhabited, today it stands as a monument to the follies of biological warfare. In 1942 it was used for an experiment in which sheep were infected with anthrax. Landing was strictly prohibited until 1990 when it was sold back to the previous owners for the £500 they had been paid for it. Rabbits, seals and seabirds are unaffected and sheep are once again grazing on the island but protesters sent soil samples from the island through the post several years ago to the authorities and they were found to contain viable anthrax spores. If such an experiment was necessary why was such a large and accessible island used rather than one which was small and remote?

Little Loch Broom is crossed between Stattic Point and Cailleach Head, a loch subject to heavy squalls. Southwesterly winds bring whirlwinds so anything static is appreciated. Even so, the remote village of Scoraig, which had been abandoned, has been repopulated and there may be fish farms. The flood in the loch begins at HW Dover +0210 and the ebb at HW Dover −0415 at up to 2km/h.

Cnoc Sgoraig, at 147m high, drops as a ridge ending with 45m rock and earth cliffs, topped by the 6m white tower of Cailleach Head light beacon. At the southern edge of the headland the red rock dips steeply at Sròn a' Gheodha Dhuibh while the intervening earth layers support vegetation so that the cliff is coloured in striking red and green diagonal stripes.

Camas na Ruthaig gives shelter to terns and boats from prevailing southwesterly winds while rounding Carn Dearg into the long mountain edged sweep of Annat Bay which provides further shelter as 635m Beinn Ghobhlach towers overhead and even the ruin at Badacrain is a significant landmark.

Loch Broom ebbs away from HW Dover −0415 and floods from HW Dover +0200. The flows are very weak but the loch can be subject to squalls. Vessels passing in and out include the car ferry between Stornoway and Ullapool. A possible collection point for Prince Charlie after Culloden was Loch Broom but no French ship arrived here for him.

Landing may be made on a beach of rounded stones to the east side of the lighthouse at Rhue, from where a track leads up the hillside to the parking area at the end of the road.

The low rocks at Rhue have a series of inlets which collect large numbers of moon jellyfish with a summer westerly wind. Further off, killer whales attempt to catch seals, fulmars sweep past and shags move to safer distances.

The Rubha Cadail light is a 9m white tower down

on the shoreline at Rhue although its position makes it a conspicuous and important navigation mark. Beyond are Carn Dearg and the Summer Isles, not the Summerisle of *The Wicker Man*.

Protecting the mouth of Loch Kanaird is Isle Martin, 1.6km², 120m high and named after St Martin, his remains marked

141

Horse Island and Meall nan Gabhar merge together across Horse Sound.

by a large cross. The island had a monastery. There was a herring curing factory in the late 18th century and there has also been a salmon curing house, 33 people being resident at the start of the 20th century although they had all gone by the start of the Second World War. One of the more spectacular travellers was a cooper who was miraculously transported to South Rona by the fairies to cut brooms and was then transported back again. The west side of the island includes cliffs of red Torridonian sandstone.

These are insignificanct against the mainland coast rising steeply up to 743m Ben Mór Coigach, some of the oldest rocks in the world. To see the mountain full height with a menacing dark blue storm sky behind, just a wisp of white cloud peeling off its pointed peak like cigarette smoke, is a magnificent sight.

Culnacraig is the start of the road again. The Coigach mountains gradually withdraw. Beyond the 25m high cliffs of Rubha Dubh Ard, Horse Sound is sheltered by Horse Island and Meall nan Gabhar, although there is no protection for feeding gulls from the attacks of the great skuas trying to take possession of their food. Blackbacked gulls also search for food items to steal. Other notable birdlife is to be found on 60m high Horse Island which is no longer inhabited but may have a fish farm. There have been wild goats since 1937. Armada gold was said to have been hidden here in 1588.

The wall of a Pictish tower is to be found to the east of the low red sandstone cliffs of Rubha Dùnan. Another tower is round the point near Achiltibuie in Badentarbat Bay. The village has a hydroponicum which grows bananas and other exotic fruit and vegetables, a salmon fishing station and a smokehouse for seafood and meat and even used to have a buffalo farm. A ferry service runs across the bay to Tanera More, the Viking Hawrarymoir, haven islands, and boats also visit the rest of the Summer Isles which were used for summer pasturage and number about twenty in total. These consist of Torridonian sandstone covered in peat, blooming with flowers in the summer, and many are grazed by sheep. Their caves, cliffs and lochans are also home for breeding seabirds, greylag geese, herons, shelducks, fulmars, eider ducks and otters.

Most interest relates to the largest of the islands, Tanera More at 3.3km², rising up to 122m at Meall Mor. The Anchorage or Cabbage Patch is one of the best natural harbours in the northwest, a 15th century anchorage for Dutch herring boats. A fishing station was founded in 1783 at Tigh-an-Quay, thriving on the plentiful herring in the sea with up to 200 ships in the bay at a time and exports going as far as the West Indies. A century later there were 119 people resident, just enough for an illicit whisky distilling business, but the last tenants left in 1931.

From 1934 to 1944 its most important resident lived here, farmer and pioneer ecologist Frank Fraser Darling who wrote his *Natural History in the Highlands and Islands* and *Island Years* here. Human life returned to the island in the 1960s when the schoolhouse and some cottages were restored, there now being permanent residents again and 250 sheep. The Summer Isles Post Office issues legal stamps for carriage to the mainland. There may be marine farms and the rich plant life continues to the thrift and luxuriant lichens on the rocks. Sailing is another local activity.

Streams start north–northeast past the Summer Isles from HW Dover +0500 and south–southwest from HW Dover −0100 at up to 3km/h.

An aerial is located on 203m Meall an Fheadain across Dorney Sound. Caolas Eilean Ristol cuts inside 71m high Isle Ristol and is frequented by cormorants and curlews. There are moorings for fishing boats in the channel while smaller craft can get into the natural harbour at Old Dornie and land at the jetty or moor in the shallows. A drying reef from the island to the mainland allows passage for small craft at most times into Loch an Alltain Duibh. The island's 18th century herring curing factory did not survive but there is a smokehouse at Altandhu on the mainland and maybe a marine farm close by although there is also a less attractive slide of rubbish down into the sea, a car included in the debris.

The road ends at Reiff where Reiff Bay is exposed to the prevailing wind. On a clear day the peaks of Lewis in the Outer Hebrides can be seen 60km to the west.

The coast along to Rubha Coigeach is rugged and broken up by the inlets of Camas Eilean Ghlais and Faochag Bay, frequented by black guillemots, cormorants and oystercatchers. The cliffs are not particularly high, being 18m at the point, but the area is remote. At the point the streams flow north–northeast from HW Dover −0515 and south–southwest from HW Dover at up to 5km/h. Once into Enard Bay, the prevailing wind will produce a swell which may be surfable.

Achnahaird Bay can be a marine farm site despite most of the bay being subject to dune conditions or drying sand. It also has peregrine falcons and shags.

Enard Bay has a backdrop of peaks which few others can approach, not only for the number and height but also for the distinctive shapes. At the southern end is Ben Móre Coigach, other notable peaks including Stac Pollaidh, meaning pool stack, at 613m, 769m Cùl Beag, 849m Cùl Mor, small and big back, 731m Suilven, the pillar, as climbed by 83 year old Sheila Hancock in *Edie*, and 846m Canisp, white hill. These are salient features of the Inverpolly Nature Reserve, Britain's second largest, covering 109km². Many of the summits are of white

Tanera Mor on the far side of Badentarbat Bay.

Looking from Altandhu over Isle Ristol and the Summer Isles with Strathnasheallag, Fisherfield, Letterewe and Flowerdale Forests and the coast to Rubha Rèidh.

quartzite covering red Torridonian sandstone on a base of Lewisian gneiss, the oldest British rock at 1,400,000,000 to 2,800,000,000 years. As well as the summits, cliffs and features of geological interest at a high level, there is woodland, moorland and bog, almost uninhabited and attractive to a range of wildlife including golden eagles. A network of lochs are drained into Garvie Bay by the Abhainn Osgaig and Polly Bay by the River Polly.

Beyond Green Island there is a dun on Rubha Pol-laidh. A calm landing is given where the road meets the shore by Eilean Mór, Fraochlan, Eilean Mòineseach and what is virtually another island, Rubh' a' Bhrocaire, which shelter Loch an Eisg-brachaidh. Stunted birches and pines also derive enough shelter to take a foothold here.

Loch Kirkaig is the mouth of the River Kirkaig which drains another network of lochs and forms the southern boundary of Sutherland. The name sounds odd for the most northerly part of the country but it was the south land for the Vikings.

The entrance to Loch Inver is sheltered by Soyea Island which has a number of islets at its east end. Bo Caolas is the most dangerous to shipping and is marked with a green post and cage structure. Seals use this as a popular area for hauling out.

Loch Roe forms another sheltered inlet before Ach-melvich Bay with its white sand. Much more conspic-uous is the approach to Bay of Clachtoll. A large wedge of red rock has slid some distance down its sloping strata, from the distance seeming to leave an imposing vertical sided doorway. Razorbills swim about.

Between Clachtoll and Stoer on the B869 is a broch overlooking the Bay of Stoer with white sand and caves. Wildlife seen here could be anything from falcons to whales. Rock strata around the bay suggest that a meteor 1–2km across, the largest to hit the British Isles, left a crater some 40km across towards the east side of what is now the Minch, 1,200,000,000 years ago.

The hamlet of Balchladich overlooks Balchladich Bay off which is an area with a local magnetic anomaly of up to 15°.

Snipe might be seen near Cluas Deas. From here to Point of Stoer the flows start north northeast from HW Dover −0515 and south southwest from HW Dover at up to 5km/h.

Stoer Head lighthouse, a 14m white tower of 1870, is set on the cliffs. It is accompanied by the award winning Loo at the Light although its claim to be the country's most remote has been disputed. They are above an assort-ment of rock slabs ditched in the sea. Geodh' nan Uan

The dramatic skyline of peaks to the east of Enard Bay, including Quinag, Suilven, Canisp and Cùl Mor, rising to Ben More Assynt.

Soyea Island and assorted reefs make entry to Loch Inver more hazardous for fishing boats.

143

Stoer Head lighthouse atop wave battered cliffs 3km south of Point of Stoer.

tumbles down from the cliffs between assorted caves, but the primary feature of interest is the Old Man of Stoer, a 70m detached column of sandstone, first climbed in 1966. It takes its name from the Norse staurr, stake. Puffins might be seen on the water and skate below the surface. A race runs off Point of Stoer.

Although the Lewisian gneiss, which forms the shore of Eddrachillis Bay, is some of the oldest rock it has managed to resist the elements remarkably well. Geodha an Leth-roinn is another place where a stream has failed to carve itself a valley in the rock before dropping to the sea.

Rubh'an Dùnain has a cave, a natural arch and a dun but approach needs to be made with care as it also has a

reefbreak where the larger swells rise and break quickly without warning. It may be safer to land behind the jetty in Bay of Culkein and walk along from Culkein.

Eilean Chrona, at 22m high, is a miniature of 100m high Oldany Island. Both may have fish farms and lobster pots set around them. Oldany is used for grazing and is separated from the mainland by a narrow sheltered channel in an archipelago of islets and drying channels. Small fishing boats are pulled up on rocks covered with a thick layer of seaweed like green moss and lobster pots are piled up. Seals and herons wait about and would probably not turn down any reject fish morsels. The only trees around are, inevitably, stunted.

The stark needle of the Old Man of Stoer.

Aird an t-Sionnaich by its 17m height and a larger size though both have clear passages inside and similar layouts, especially at high tide. After Eilean a' Bhuic, passage across the mouth of Scourie Bay, at the back of which the A894 runs, leads into the Sound of Handa. Although sheltered from most winds, there are flows through the sound at up to 6km/h, starting northwards at HW Dover +0400 and southwards at HW Dover −0200. There are heavy overfalls over Bodha Morair and over Bodha Iasg through the Dorus Mór. Flows are a couple of hours earlier than the main coastal flows. It may be possible to find eddies on the downstream side of Handa on the second half of the flow.

A midden of limpet shells left between Port an Eilein and Traigh an Teampaill shows that there has long been human occupation of Handa. The island was used extensively as a graveyard for people on the mainland to prevent corpses being disturbed by wolves. Until the middle of the 19th century there were seven families here with the oldest woman as queen and the men having a daily parliament to discuss the work to be done. They lived on potatoes, fish and birds' eggs until the 1848 potato famine, when they emigrated to America.

In 1962 the 3km^2 island was declared a nature reserve and RSPB seafowl sanctuary with the only inhabitable building being refurbished as an ornithological base with a warden in the summer. The island rises steadily from the sound to 123m high Sithean Mór almost on the far side of the island, the north and west coasts having red and brown Torridonian sandstone cliffs to 110m high on a Lewisian gneiss base. These include Great Stack, three pillars with 12,000 breeding birds, horizontal white lines of guillemots, kittiwakes, gulls, razorbills, fulmars, puffins, shags and other seabirds, especially during the breeding season. Some 141 species have been recorded, 35 breeding. The last whitetailed sea eagles nested here in 1864. Arctic skuas have been resident from 1968, the year after the death of an albino oystercatcher, now in the National Museum of Scotland in Edinburgh. Other species include meadow pipits, wheatears, skylarks and curlews. The rough pasture has been used for grazing sheep and for rabbits and there is plenty of peat bog.

Some 216 species of plant have been recorded including heather, deer grass, purple moor grass, lodgepole pine, alders, heath spotted orchid, bog asphodel, northern marsh orchid, lovage, pale butterwort, pyramidal bugle, eyebright, devils bit, ragged robin, biting stonecrop and over a hundred varieties of moss. There are lobsters offshore. White sand faces the sound. RSPB members may stay in the bothy if booked in advance through the Edinburgh office.

Rebecca Ridgeway opens the prologue to her book, *Something Amazing!* with the description of a capsize off Handa Island. She also notes that no house in Tarbet has failed to lose at least one of its menfolk to the local waters.

Port of Tarbet is relatively sheltered, offering a small jetty and a limited parking area.

Culkein Drumbeg hamlet overlooks Loch Dhrombaig, the first of several inlets along the shore, followed by Loch Nedd, Camas nan Bad and Loch na Droighniche. It is not the shoreline which is impressive, however, but what stands above. This section of coast is dominated by the peaks of Quinag, milk pail, Sàil Garbh, rough heel, being the highest at 808m but 776m Sàil Gorm, blue heel, being closer to the water and only 2km from Loch a' Chàirn Bhàin which runs inland from the southeast corner of Eddrachilis Bay.

The eastern side of Eddrachillis Bay is littered with islands with heather slopes and stunted trees and bushes in places. At 41m high Calbha Beag has grassy slopes and caves at its south end, being overlooked by the slightly larger and higher Calbha Mór.

The Badcall Islands are in two groups. The southwest group comprise Meall Mór and Meall Beag. The larger northeastern group are bunched in the mouth of Badcall Bay. Seals haul out on the northeastern corner of Eilean na Rainich, facing towards Eilean na Bearachd and Ceannamhór, the highest island at 48m. The 31m high Eilean Garbh divides into two at high tide, giving a passage through in suitable conditions.

A hut circle site is found located behind the next bay. The coast is too rugged and rocky to permit landing under most conditions.

Eilean a' Bhuic is distinguished from the islet off Rubh

Distance
126km from the Isle of Ewe to Tarbet

OS 1:50,000 Sheets
9 Cape Wrath
15 Loch Assynt
19 Gairloch
& Ullapool

Tidal Constants
Gairloch:
HW Dover −0430
LW Dover −0420
Tanera Mór:
Dover −0420
Loch Inver:
Dover −0420
Badcall Bay:
Dover −0400
Loch Laxford:
Dover −0400

Sea Area
Hebrides

Submarine Areas
6 Ewe, 3 Stoer

Looking north through the archipelago towards Handa with Oldany Island on the left.

30 Sutherland

The British
mainland's
highest
vertical cliffs
and best
linked caves

Call all, call all! from Reedswair-Path,
To the wild confines of Cape-Wrath;
Wide let the news through Scotland ring,
The Northern Eagle claps his wing!
Sir Walter Scott

On moving north from Tarbet the shelter of Handa Island, Eilean an Aigeich and the Sgeirean Glasa is gradually lost. Fulmars are the commonest of the circling gulls but, to the southwest, the vertical cliffs of Handa will be seen wheeling with flocks of assorted birds.

The red rocks of the low Rubha Ruadh brighten the coast which has darker rugged rocks. Behind, darker and frequently with heads in the clouds are the summits of 721m Ben Stack, 757m Arkle and 908m Ganu Mór, the highest peak of Foinaven. Cutting in towards them is Loch Laxford. The Norse for salmon lax and local accents retain a Norse whirr.

Adjacent is Loch Dùghaill. Cormorants and gannets fish off the mouth of the two lochs.

The coast continues steep and rocky to Lochan nam Meallan with hills up to 120m high, while the offshore area is littered with islets, Eilean na Saille the largest at 36m high. The Dubh Sgeirean include 17m high Whale Islet with the Whale Back drying 4m.

Bàgh Loch an Ròin has a narrow exit at the back from Loch an Ròin while Loch Ceann na Saile is almost as tortuous, located to the south of 17m high Glas Leac and Eilean Dubh. Between these two and the bold red Rubha na Leacaig is the mouth of the rather larger Loch Inch-

ard. This gives access to Loch Bervie, the main fishing harbour for Kinlochbervie. It stands on the isthmus created by Loch Bervie and Loch Clash, the latter less well sheltered but also used by a few fishing boats. The most northerly port on the west coast, Kinlochbervie is important for the white fish it sends to Aberdeen, Hull, Grimsby and Europe. The port has a rescue line throwing apparatus.

The mouth of Loch Clash is protected from the northwest by 52m high Eilean a' Chonnaidh and 5m high Na Cluasnadh.

Oldshoremore is where Hakon began his invasion of Scotland in 1263, providing the first sheltered landing on the west coast. Nevertheless, it produces surf on westerly or northerly swells, best at the higher end of the tide. As ever, it has plenty of midges and fish boxes.

The 37m high Eilean na h-Aiteig has vertical cliffs on its southeast side. These provide a divider from the bay at Oldshore Beg with its dune system. On a larger scale, 63m high Eilean an Ròin Mór and Eilean an Ròin Beag run out from the shore, giving more shelter, a race running through inside the former. Birdlife includes razorbills, guillemots,

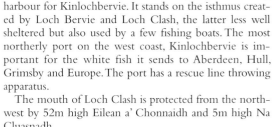

Loch Clash with Eilean a' Chonnaidh beyond. The leading light is for Loch Bervie, across the isthmus to the left of the picture and approached from the opposite direction.

Eilean an Ròin Mór and Eilean na h-Aiteig seen across the dunes from Oldshoremore.

A race forms between Eilean an Ròin Mór and the mainland.

black guillemots, puffins, oystercatchers, eider ducks and blackbacked gulls.

Port Chaligaig has a pier with scant shelter, as evidenced by the mush of rotting weed lying among the rocks. Picnic tables and the hamlet of Droman are little reason for landing but this inlet is important as the last road access point before the Kyle of Durness, a serious and committing section of coast.

There are now continuous cliffs to Rubh' a Bhuachaille. Flows start north to Cape Wrath at HW Dover −0530 and south at HW Dover +0045 at up to 3km/h but an eddy on the southgoing tide means that the flow inshore is almost continuously northwards.

The final offshore rocks here are 10m high Dubh Sgeir and 19m high

Droman is the last road access point on the west coast but there is little protection from westerly winds which drive straight onto the boulders.

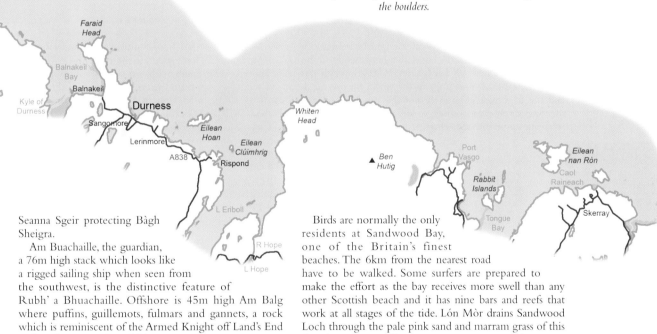

Seanna Sgeir protecting Bàgh Sheigra.

Am Buachaille, the guardian, a 76m high stack which looks like a rigged sailing ship when seen from the southwest, is the distinctive feature of Rubh' a Bhuachaille. Offshore is 45m high Am Balg where puffins, guillemots, fulmars and gannets, a rock which is reminiscent of the Armed Knight off Land's End at the other extremity of this coast.

Birds are normally the only residents at Sandwood Bay, one of the Britain's finest beaches. The 6km from the nearest road have to be walked. Some surfers are prepared to make the effort as the bay receives more swell than any other Scottish beach and it has nine bars and reefs that work at all stages of the tide. Lón Mòr drains Sandwood Loch through the pale pink sand and marram grass of this fine dune system. The currents are strong and the waters

The distinctive shape of Am Buachaille at the suthern end of Sandwood Bay.

Sandwood Bay can be one of the finest beaches and best surf breaks in Britain but it is a long walk to reach it.

chilly. The ghost of a bearded sailor might be seen and it is the haunt of mermaids. Local shepherd Sandy Gunn met a mermaid here on 5th January 1900. Although this is not the most obvious place in the world for mermaids and the beginning of January not the usual season, the meeting surely had nothing to do with this being the sobering up period after Hogmanay. Later in the century the hermit James McRory-Smith was a regular beach-comber who may have added to the rumours.

The coast continues with red vertical sandstone cliffs and rugged coves. Inland from here is one of the largest areas of uninhabited land in Britain. Like tundra, the Parbh is 260km^2 of peat bog, heather, scrub and oak.

Cape Wrath takes its name from the Norse hvarf, turning point, where the west coast of Britain meets the north coast. Nevertheless, the usually assumed meaning of the name is not inappropriate. This is the windiest corner of Britain and catches all winds except the ones between southwest and southeast. It is almost always turbulent and can be dangerously so with strong winds. For the last kilometre to the cape there is a race inshore and usually clapotis from the swells to foil any attempt to go inside

Cape Wrath from the race in calm conditions and at neap tides.

Clò Mór, the highest vertical cliffs in mainland Britain at 281m. The white is mostly guano.

Whitewashed cottages around the small east facing harbour at Rispond.

the race. Any inshore passage should be made in settled conditions with neap tides. The 110m high red headland is topped by the 20m white lighthouse tower built by Robert Stevenson in 1828, from where there are views to the Hebrides and Orkney. Those wishing to experience the view usually have to cross the Kyle of Durness by ferry in the summer and then travel in a minibus for 18km along a section of road which is not connected to the rest of the road system.

From the corner there are arches at the start of a coast which is well endowed with cliffs all the way to Dunnet Head, albeit frequently indented. The easterly stream starts at HW Dover +0415 and the westerly stream at HW Dover −0145 at up to 6km/h, although there are eddies locally and sometimes there are temporary local flows up to 1km/h from northeasterly to southeasterly. Their cause is not known.

The first landing place is a jetty at Clais Chàrnach. The first beach is where the Kearvaig River enters.

Flows begin eastwards from Stack Clò Kearvaig at HW Dover +0545 and westwards at HW Dover −0030. The stack is two pillars with a fallen block wedged between them. They would look more impressive were it not for the cliffs behind them, the highest vertical cliffs in mainland Britain, rising 260m directly from the water. There are interesting plants such as the Scots primrose which has pink or purple flowers and is not found south of here. There are birds of prey. Huge colonies of nesting seabirds which create a deafening din. At some distance there is still a dizzying wheel of fulmars and guillemots with collisions not unknown. Seals keep a much quieter presence.

Off Cléit Dubh, the black cliff, is An Garbh-eilean, 33m high but being reduced in size by bombing. A target buoy is moored off it. Live rounds are fired from ships and from aircraft which fly in from as far away as Germany. The army also fire on the 34km² range. The danger area stretches from Cape Wrath to Faraid Head and the range is the largest of its kind in Europe. When in use there are red flags or vertical pairs of red lights. Navigation is permitted but not cruising. A flag at half mast warns of being in the exercise area. The pattern of use is irregular but usually quiet during the lambing season, April to mid May, although guillemots and razorbills have been deserting nesting sites because of the bombing and have been found with blast concussion.

The coast then becomes white marble with red veins.

The Kyle of Durness drains for 7km, barely perceptible currents flooding from HW Dover +0300 and ebbing from HW Dover −0315. There are weak streams across the entrance. The east side of the entrance opens into Balnakeil Bay, edged with dunes which cross the neck of Faraid Head.

Faraid Head, seen from Leirinmore.

Whiten Head seen across Eilean Hoan from Leirinmore.

Caves and arches don't come much better than at Rubh'Ard an t-Siùil. Eilean Hoan is visible through the centre arch.

Balnakeil church, now ruined, was built in 1619 and the churchyard contains a monument to the Gaelic bard Rob Donn. A skull and crossbones in the church wall form a rather different monument for highwayman Donald MacLeod who was said to have killed at least eighteen

The Stacan Bána add further character to Whiten Head.

people and to have paid at least a thousand pounds for this special position to prevent desecration of his grave.

Only twice this sum was paid for the buildings which form Balnakeil craft village, the country's first of its kind and the only one owned by its residents. It was built as an early warning station but never used as such and since 1984 has housed sixteen businesses with horn work, paintings, jewellery, knitwear, pottery, candles, winemaking, leatherwork, woodwork, bookbinding, metalwork, printing, picture framing, photography, stonework, weaving, sculpting in bronze and aluminium, fish box furniture and driftwood sculptures.

The 100m high Faraid Head has a puffin colony nesting. Strong streams sweep round the head and indented cliffs follow to An t-Aigeach. Puffins and other seabirds occupy the 51m pinnacle of Clach Mhòr na Faraid at the end of a line of rocks which run out from the shore like jagged canine teeth. A less conspicuous second line follows at Aodann Mhór, including the dun site at Seanachaisteal, old castle.

Durness, on the A838, comes from the Norse dyrnes or dyra ness, deer, beast or wolf promontory. The area has crofting and sheep farming these days while a visitor centre has displays on the landscape and people of the northwest. There is a Highland gathering in July, surfers gather when the swells into Sango Bay arrive from the north and John Lennon used to come here for his holidays as a youngster.

Geodha Smoo takes its name from the Norse smjuga, a cleft or creek. The Allt Smoo has cut a straight channel into the narrow band of marble and limestone which stretches to Spar Cave on the south coast of Skye. More importantly, it has produced the three magnificent caverns of Smoo Cave. The first chamber is 60m x 34m where the river drops 24m down a shaft. The second cavern is flooded and may only be explored in a rubber raft. The final 37m chamber is dry again and has a large opening at the high tide mark. The caves are floodlit and have been made accessible to the public. In the past they have been associated with both smugglers and the supernatural. There is a helicopter landing site nearby.

Eilean Hoan, at 24m high, was used as a local burial site to avoid disturbance by wolves. In 1840 four families lived here but now it is only used for grazing. In 1980 it was bought by the RSPB, without whose permission landing is not permitted. There are great northern divers and up to 400 barnacle geese in winter. The reserve is a nesting site for eider ducks, oystercatchers, ringed plovers, lapwings, arctic terns, lesser blackbacked gulls, storm petrels, black guillemots, and many other species.

Currents up to 1km/h begin southeastwards at HW Dover +0420 and northwest at HW Dover −0150. The corresponding times for weak flows into and out of Loch Eriboll at An t-Aigeach are from HW Dover +0300 and −0315, respectively. The two halves of 13m high Eilean Clùimhrig stand off the point at the entrance to the loch.

Despite its sheltered position, Rispond Bay is a surf break. It needs to be approached from the calm waters of the hidden harbour but parking is difficult without causing obstructions for the residents.

Loch Eriboll's name comes from the Norse for a home on a gravelly beach. During the Highland Clearances the population were moved from the fertile east side to the rocky west side, where they remain today. It is one of the deepest sea lochs and sheltered by steep hills. This is where Atlantic convoys gathered in the Second World War, to whose crews it was Loch 'Orrible. At the end of the war it was where the German U boat fleet surrendered. These days it is the gathering point for nothing more disturbing than great northern divers prior to their spring passage to Iceland although that could change with proposals to build the UK's first spaceport to its east in the A' Mhoine area.

Beyond the head of the loch are the peaks of Foinaven, Arkle and Meall Horn while 927m Ben Hope lies due south beyond Loch Hope, from which flows the River Hope.

Geodha an t-Srathain is one of several waterfalls down the pink cliffs. There are caves in 43m high Freisgill Head but they are totally eclipsed by those on Rubh'Ard an t-Siùil which are possibly the best linked caves and arches on the British mainland. A large cave leads into a smaller one which turns a corner and disappears into the darkness. A cloistered exit leads through arches to a deep round cave with three large exits. Seabirds nest on ledges. There is something disturbing about watching a brown shape on a ledge gradually unroll to reveal an alligator shape of head with amber eyes glowing in the darkness as the slapping of waves echoes around, the very stuff of horror stories even if it is only a cormorant.

Flows are weak across the mouth of Loch Eriboll but increase to 6km/h around Whiten Head, flows starting east to Strathy Point at HW Dover +0545 and west at HW Dover −0030.

There are confused seas off the head. Cliffs reach up to 160m high, white crumbled quartz and dark slate coloured with red veins. In reasonable conditions there are passages inside a series of rocks off the coast. The most notable are the white stratified quartz pillars of the Stacan Bána rising 54m and 46m from the sea. Pioneering climber Tom Patey fell to his death here in 1970 while abseiling down from one of the pillars.

Some 6km of cliffs to 240m height follow to Achininver but there are now plenty of lobster pots and small boats out checking them, so the coast is not as deserted as might otherwise be the case. Inland, the ground rises to 408m Ben Hutig.

Achininver Bay is at the mouth of the Strath Melness Burn where the MV *Sealagair* is stranded on the beach.

Port Vasgo provides a sheltered landing point with road access. Inland is an aerial although it is not as conspicuous as the one on Ben Tongue on the east side of the Kyle of Tongue, another Norse name. The kyle itself opens into Tongue Bay at the north end and is littered with islands. Sgeir an Oir rises to 43m with a natural arch in the centre.

The Rabbit Islands were Eilean na Gaeil, the island of strangers, used by the Norsemen. In 1745 a French sloop went aground on them with gold for Prince Charlie. The islands these days are a surf break with a dune system and numerous breeding birds.

The largest island is Eilean nan Ròn or Roan, meaning seal island, red sandstone rising to 75m and extended westward by Eilean Iosal and Meall Thailm. There are several caves and arches and also a secret entrance to an inner sanctuary. Ruins remain from when the island was abandoned in 1938. A century earlier the residents made their living by drying fish in the salty wind. Mackerel are to be found in the local waters now.

Between Eilean nan Ròn and the mainland Caol Raineach flows at up to 4km/h. At HW Dover +0545 the southgoing stream west of Eilean nan Ròn divides to flow east through Coal Raineach and south into the Kyle of Tongue. At HW Dover −0310 this southgoing flow meets the flow that is ebbing from the Kyle of Tongue and produces turbulence between Eilean nan Ròn and the Rabbit Islands. At HW Dover +0030 the ebb stream from the Kyle of Tongue meets the westgoing stream through Caol Raineach to produce dangerous turbulence off Sleiteil Rocks. At HW Dover +0300 the westgoing stream through Caol Raineach divides to flood southwards into the Kyle of Tongue and west northwest to the sea when the turbulence subsides.

The first road access after Tongue Bay is Skerray Bay, sheltered on the west by land and on the northeast by a rock platform.

Distance
77km from Tarbet to Clashbuie

OS 1:50,000 Sheets
9 Cape Wrath
10 Strath Naver

Tidal Constants
Loch Laxford:
Dover −0400
Loch Bervie:
HW Dover −0350
LW Dover −0400
Kyle of Durness:
HW Dover −0340
LW Dover −0320
Portnancon:
Dover −0310

Sea Areas
Hebrides, Fair Isle

Range
Cape Wrath

Submarine Area
3 Stoer

Dramatic coastline to the east of Whiten Head.

151

North Highland

The thistles climb the thatch. Forever
this sharp scale in our poems,
as also the waste music of the sea.

The stars shine over Sutherland
in a cold ceilidh of their own,
as, in the morning, the silver cane

cropped among corn. We will remember this.
Though hate is evil we cannot
but hope your courtier's heels in hell

are burning: that to hear
the thatch sizzling in tanged smoke
your hot ears slowly learn.
Iain Crichton Smith

many of the evictions. Some of the worst atrocities were committed in the Strathnaver clearances of 1814 and 1819, recorded in the Strathnaver museum in Farr's 18th century former church. Another room is dedicated to Clan MacKay and the churchyard contains the Pictish Farr Stone, a fine example of early Christian Celtic art.

Semiprecious stones can be found in Farr Bay where the surf works to produce lefts on the top half of the tide and rights at low tide.

Farr Point is steep with caves, rising to 110m Ard Farr. A natural arch under an isthmus marks the position of the remains of Borve Castle, a medieval stronghold of Clan MacKay.

An aerial on Cnoc Mór faces out over Kirtomy Bay to 140m high Kirtomy Point, the first of several such points.

Port Mór, after Ardmore Point, has some caves and a large flying buttress. It also has fish nets staked out, as has Port a' Chinn. The latter has quite an unusual appearance with an assortment of net drying poles on

Torrisdale Bay seen from Bettyhill.

A gap in the rock shelf on the northeast side of Skerray Bay allows an exit to Caol Beag which runs inside Neave or Coomb Island, a 70m high structure with pink quartz and mica slate in stripes which are nearly vertical. It was the site of the earliest Christian settlement in the area and St Cormaic is said to have been heard preaching by the congregation on the mainland across Caol Beag.

The cliffy coast is indented as far as Strathy Point with weak streams inshore.

The River Borgie and the River Naver with its salmon feed Torrisdale Bay. Between the two rivers is the Invernaver Nature Reserve with fine dunes and many interesting plants. Birdlife includes eider ducks, oystercatchers, fulmars, guillemots, black guillemots and cormorants. In bad weather the sea breaks well out. There is a beachbreak with a good right on rivermouth bars, best on the lower half of the tide although quicksand is a danger.

Between Torrisdale and Bettyhill there are a number of antiquities, a dun, a chambered cairn, a broch and a settlement.

Bettyhill was set up as a fishing and agricultural centre during the Highland Clearances and named after Elizabeth, Countess of Sutherland, wife of the Duke of Sutherland who was responsible for

top of the cliff and an aerial ropeway to get the catch up to Armadale. The bay is studded with rocks and pointed stacks, including one with large holes, one of which can be passed through by a small boat, the structure being more hole than stack.

Round the corner is Armadale Bay with its best surf at high tide when it gives lefts and rights.

Strathy Point projects 4km out from the

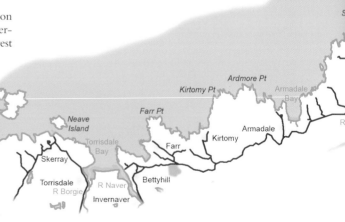

A distinctive stack pierced by a large round hole in Port a' Chinn.

coast. The most conspicuous feature on its west side is Boursa Island, covered with grass like a pitched roof.

Strathy Point is often subject to local windy conditions. The lighthouse on the point, opened in 1958, stands as a 14m white tower on a 35m high headland yet its windows have been hit by waves during gales. During better weather it is possible to see Cape Wrath, Dunnet Head, Orkney, a natural arch and a pile of rubbish tipped down the side of the cliff to fall into the sea. It is on a migratory bird route, best seen in May and September. Gannets and skuas nest on the cliffs and puffins, storm petrels and blackbacked gulls might be seen. In June and July it has rare flowering plants, not to mention specimens eating insects. Whales, dolphins and basking sharks may be seen, especially after August. A sheltered route passes between Garbh-eilean and the point itself but there are flows up to 6km/h off the point and a tide race and overfalls where the nearly continuous northgoing flow, resulting from the eddy on the east side of the promontory, meets the main longshore flow. Out to sea, the eastgoing flow begins at HW Dover −0610 and the westgoing flow at Dover HW at up to 4km/h.

Caves dot the cliffs at intervals down the east side of the point and there is a jetty halfway along although the climb up to the road is long and steep. The sea is sheltered from the prevailing wind and is inhabited by razorbills, rizostoma jellyfish and porpoises, to name a few species.

The River Strathy enters Strathy Bay past sandhills up to 60m high. Although protected from westerly swells, surfers may find good rights off the rocks at the east end. Strathy has some of its buildings thatched, now rare in the Highlands.

The 90m cliffs of Baligill Head are topped by Baligill and a couple of fort sites, one Iron Age, while another is beyond the 80m cliffs of Rubha na Cloiche.

Portskerra was a fishing village

Rubha na Cloiche.

Portskerra at low tide.

created at the time of the Clearances, well sheltered from the prevailing wind by Rubha Bhrá, the red rock, but with boats having to be negotiated through the rocks and pulled up the steep grassy cliff.

The mouth of the Halladale River opens into Melvich Bay. Melvich stands behind orange sandhills up to 35m

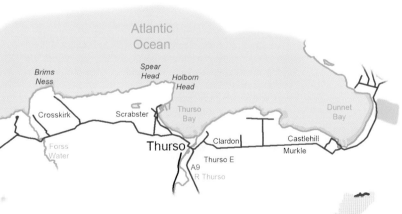

high and has rescue apparatus. The surf gives a good right off the rocks at the east end of the bay but is protected by Strathy Point from westerly swells. Lobsters, crabs and mackerel are found in the bay, together with the inevitable midges. On the southeast side of the bay is Bighouse, the ancestral home of the Clan MacKay, overlooked by 96m Rubha an Tuir. Low hills with coarse grass and

Sandside Head, often surrouded by a foam carpet at its base.

Forss Water empties over the stones into Crosskirk Bay.

heather occupy the coast to Sandside Head where there is a 44m overhanging cliff guarded by the Stags, a pair of offshore rocks. There are holes in the cliff strata and incipient caves. Even when Sandside Bay is turbulent there is usually a calm jetty landing at Fresgoe, the harbour built about 1835 by Bremner, using nearly vertical flagstones capped by massive stones. Slots at the sides of the entrance were for boom gates to be fitted to protect against storms. The bay is the mouth of the Sandside Burn and has a good dune system. It catches surf from northerly or large westerly swells. Because of low tide rocks it is better to surf at the higher end of the tide where there are lefts off a reefbreak and both lefts and rights on bars at the beach.

In 1437 Sandside Chase was the site of a battle where the Mackays slaughtered the locals. Reay was rebuilt in 1740 when the village was inundated by dunes. The buildings from that date include the whitewashed church which has the pulpit facing the raised laird's loft where there is a gallery for the laird's family.

In 1797 Reay schoolmaster William Munro watched a

The successive headlands of Ness of Litter, Spear Head and Holborn Head.

mermaid combing her hair but the report did not appear in the *Times* for another dozen years as it would not have been good for his professional reputation. Two girls had reported seeing mermaids in the area in 1804 and other claimed sightings were not unusual.

There is a lobster fishery in the bay. A point of concern with the water and the beach is the fact that radioactive particles are being washed up and deposited from a leaking 60m shaft at the nuclear power station. The shaft is used for dumping waste radioactive material and resolving the problem was estimated at £500,000,000.

From Isauld to Brims Ness there are low, dark, vertical cliffs. As with so much of Caithness, they have a sloping rock chamfer at the bottom, making landing very difficult. Flows along the coast run at up to 1km/h.

It was on the low cliffs between the castle and chambered cairn at Lower Dounreay that the Dounreay Nuclear Power Development Establishment was set up in 1955, Britain's only prototype and the world's first com- mercial fast reactor power station, closed in 1977 after 18 years of use, having been superseded by a bigger proto- type fast reactor to its west in 1974, closing in 1994. The site was marked by the distinctive 58m diameter reactor sphere on the cliffs. Its purpose was to develop technol- ogy. It has been proposed as a nuclear waste burial site, a strategy which must be enhanced by the fact that it is so remote from protesters, but the area already suffers from a cluster of childhood cancer and leukaemia. A large irreg- ular concrete block on the shore protects a 65m deep shaft containing radioactive waste. In 1995 there was a brief foray into wavepower when Osprey 1, the first commercial sized wavepower generator, was installed off the coast. It broke up and sank a few days later.

The cliffs have only the occasional cairn or broch site until a heavily fenced establishment at Crosskirk with two aerials, one of which is 220m high. Forss Water flows into Crosskirk Bay past another broch site, St Mary's Well and St Mary's chapel. This may be 12th century and has doors which are low and taper at the top in the Irish style. Black guillemots, oystercatchers and seals might be seen in the bay while gannets and possibly the blow of a whale might appear further out to sea. Less attractive is the rubbish being tipped down the side of Ushat Head. The head is 35m high but the cliffs reduce towards Brims Ness.

Brims Ness, Norse for surf point, is aptly named. It offers surf when all other breaks are flat. There is tidal disturbance where the Atlantic flow runs over the Whale's Back at up to 6km/h. Like Thurso East, the break has the strata in a sawtooth formation, rising gently then drop- ping vertically a number of times in an irregular pattern moving shorewards. The Bowl gives fast rights to more than 2m, best towards the top of a tide. The Cove is a slightly slower version. The Left is a left point break with rides to 100m on the lower half of the tide. Fishing boats have sunk in boils welling up. Approach to the breaks is through the yard of a long-suffering farmer. The ruined Brims Castle is adjacent and there is a chapel site by the point.

The cliffs gradually increase in height to become steeper again with a couple of fort sites. Ness of Litter has caves and disused quarries on the side of 115m Brims Hill and there are more caves beyond Spear Head. Blowholes are present in the cliffs. Holborn Head has a viewpoint but needs to be treated with care. In 1842 Commander Michael Slater fell to his death while setting up a survey theodolite station here for the Hydrographic Office.

Streams start east–northeast from Holborn Head from HW Dover –0600 and west–southwest from HW Dover at up to 4km/h although they only reach half this rate across Thurso Bay and Dunnet Bay. Eddy streams start north at HW Dover +0530. Scrabster Road's northern part has an outgoing undertow with easterly weather.

A 17m white light tower stands on what is confusingly called Holbornhead but more clearly understood as Little Head. Scrabster was a 19th century port for exporting flagstones and is now a vehicle ferry terminal at the end of the A9 for Stromness (Orkney) and summer services to Seydisfjörder (Iceland), Thorshavn (Faeroes), Bergen (Norway) and Hanstholm (Denmark). Port facilities range from oil storage tanks and a lifeboat to a fishmarket and icehouse, lobster creels and salmon nets, fish landed including coalfish, cod, conger eels, pollack, skate and halibut to over 100kg. The beach at Scrabster can produce small surf.

The most northerly town on the British mainland is **Thurso**, taking its name from Thorsa, Norse Gaelic for the mouth of Thor's river, the River Thurso entering here. Although dating from Viking times with the remains of Scrabster Castle from 1328 or earlier to the west of the new town, it was not laid out in its grid pattern until the early 19th century by Sir John Sinclair, whose statue stands in Sir John Square. It was then that Thurso became a flagstone exporting town. The town tripled in size in the 1950s with the development of Dounreay. The ruined St Peter's church, used until 1832, was built by 1125 with much rebuilt in the 17th century. Many former aspects of the vicinity, the Ulbster Stone, the Pictish relic with carved symbols, agricultural and domestic life, local trades, crafts and the room of an old Caithness cottage are to be found in the Caithness Horizons Museum. The town boasts the only indoor heated swimming pool on the north coast and Neil Gunn's *Highland River* talks of playing bowls at midnight. There are also glass workshops.

Thurso is a world championships surfing venue. Thurso Reef or Sewer Pipeline gives lefts and rights in small swells but only rights with big swells. Seabirds gather around the outfall pipe to feed. Thurso East, Castle Reef or the Mecca Break is the classic, a flat paddle out then rights with long tubes onto the reef, working at all states but best at the top of the flood. It has been surfed above 4m. It would have been better if the reef had not been dynamited for boat access at the start of the 20th century. Maximum northerly swells cause the two reefbreaks to close out. In this situation a bombora forms in the middle of Thurso Bay but it has never been ridden. The River Thurso brings in a strata of brown peaty water. Only the big waves suck up water from the bottom so there is the novelty of waves colour coded for size, the biggest waves being a suitable brown.

A disused cannon overlooks Thurso East with Thurso East Castle behind, built in the 17th century for the 6th Earl Sinclair and largely rebuilt in 1872, now a substantial ruin. A little further on, Harold's Tower marks the grave of Earl Harold, the 12th century ruler of part of Caithness, Orkney and Shetland. Caithness is said to take its name from the Teutonic Catti settlers.

Caves and clear water are to be found at the foot of Clardon Hill, marked by a range of radio and radar masts and a sphere. Tank traps are placed around Murkle Bay beyond Methow Hillock. The area is difficult to access, of concern to surfers who wish to try the lefts which run at Nothing Left, Silos and the Pole in northerly or westerly swells and off the Spur when there are large swells from those directions.

A wreck remains on the Spur, a boat which didn't pick the right wave, and the cries of curlews set a forlorn mood. A beacon in Murkle Bay marks the launching point of a submarine power cable to Hoy.

The rock platform continues for 3km until Castlehill where there is a small harbour, used for salmon netting and pleasure craft, fish nets being staked out in Dunnet Bay in several places. Castletown was developed on a grid in the 19th century when the now disused quarry was opened. Flagstones were exported south and even to India, Australia and New Zealand. Square flags still edge many of the local fields as walls. There have been few trees on the north coast but the woods here were planted in 1824 by James Traill who founded the quarries. There is a Castlehill Flagstone Industry interpretive trail, including a small conical tower among the local brochs.

Thurso East on a day when no exaggeration of wave size was required.

Distance
60km from Clashbuie to Castlehill

OS 1:50,000 Sheets
10 Strath Naver
11 Thurso
& Dunbeath
12 Thurso & Wick

Tidal Constants
Portnancon:
Dover –0310
Scrabster:
HW Dover –0240,
LW Dover –0230

Sea Area
Fair Isle

32 Caithness

Their mouths are filled with the magic words they learned at the collier's hatch
When they coaled in the foul December dawns and sailed in the forenoon-watch
Or measured the weight of a Pentland tide and the wind off Ronaldshay,
Till the target mastered the breathless tug and the hawser carried away.
Rudyard Kipling

A magnificent 3km sweep of sandy beach runs from Castlehill up the east side of Dunnet Bay, backed by an extensive dune system. The bay catches westerly and northerly swells, giving surf breaks along the bars on the beach with lefts at the south end and rights at the north. There is a disused airfield behind the dunes at the end. The public tend to use the north end with its carpark and natural history displays but there is plenty of room for all. Dunnet has Mary Ann's Cottage which is a traditional Caithness croft house with assorted relics and vintage farm machinery on show. Lake Orcadie included the Moray Firth from Dunnet to Fraserburgh and beyond Orkney 380,000,000 years ago.

In the bay and around to Dunnet Head there are many seabirds, terns, black guillemots, fulmars, cormorants, razorbills, guillemots, skuas, blackbacked gulls and puffins while wildlife in the sea includes rhizostoma jellyfish and seals.

Picnic tables are sited beside a slipway at Point of Ness while Dwarwick Head is the landing point of several disused submarine cables.

From Briga Head to Dunnet Head there is an almost continuous north to northeast going eddy. The cliffs are over 60m high, a warm honeycomb colour but heavily weathered and not infrequently subject to falls. Older sections of cliff are highlighted with ledges of pink thrift.

Large waves may be met at Briga Head. A northwesterly swell produces confused seas off Dunnet Head which is 102m high with vertical cliffs, the 1831 lighthouse on top by Robert Stevenson being a white stone tower a further 20m high, yet its windows have been broken by stones thrown up in winter gales over the cast iron parapet rail with its lion's feet. Dunnet Head may be Penn Blathon in *The Mabinogion*, where *How Culhwch won Olwen* states that Drem, who lived in Cornwall, could see a gnat rising with the morning sun here, presumably high enough to allow for the Earth's curvature.

This is the most northerly point on the British mainland. Just 12km away across the Pentland Firth and joined to the mainland until the last ice age are the unstable cliffs of Orkney, some of the highest cliffs in Britain, changing colour with the light. This is Hoy with the Old Man of Hoy visible at the west end. To the east is Scapa Flow, the Flotta oil terminal flare stack and then South Ronaldsay. On a still day the throb of engines from unseen ships can be heard across the firth. From the visitor centre on top of Dunnet Head there is a view to Cape Wrath. In the middle of summer the sun has still not set at 2230 and is up again before 0330.

Formerly an eastwards flowing river tributary valley to a north flowing river, the Pentland Firth is the fastest, most treacherous and most feared tideway in Europe. On

Dunnet Head, mainland Britain's most northerly point. There is a sleeping seal in the centre of the picture.

The Haven at Scarfskerry with Dunnet Head visible to the left.

Atlantic
Ocean

Island
of Stroma

Pentland
Firth

Dunnet
Head

Men of
Mey   St John's Pt

Boars of
Duncansby

Scarfskerry

Gills
Bay

Duncansby
Head

Brough   Ham

A836   Kirkstyle   Huna

Stacks of
Duncansby

Mey   John o'
Groats

Dunnet   Canisbay

Dunnet
Bay

Skirza
Head

Freswick
Bay

Castlehill

Freswick   Ness
Head

A99

Auchengill

Nybster

Dunbeath
Water

Dunbeath

Dunbeath
Bay

Keiss

Ramscraigs

Borgue

Berriedale
Water

Sinclair's
Bay

▲
Braigh na
h'Eaglaise   Langwell
Water   Berriedale

Noss
Head

Reiss   Ackergill

Staxigoe

Papigoe
Broadhaven

Ord Pt

Wick   Wick
Bay

Old
Wick   S Head

Helmsdale

Helman
Head

Thrumster

L of
Yarrows   Sarclet
Sarclet
Head

Ulbster

Whaligoe

Bruan

Mid
Clyth

Lybster   Moray
Firth

Reisgill
Burn

Forse

Latheron

Latheronwheel

Dunbeath
Water

Dunbeath

Dunbeath

springs it usually runs to 22km/h although 30km/h has been recorded, among the world's fastest. Streams start east at HW Dover +0500 and west from HW Dover −0100 at 6km/h off Dunnet Head but flows begin earlier near the coast. There is heavy turbulence in the races even in calm conditions and it is dangerous when streams are opposed by strong winds or swell. To add interest, patchy fog is common and can arrive with astonishing rapidity.

The east side of Dunnet Head is a nesting site for line after line of seabirds. Various cliff nesting sites between here and Helmsdale must satisfy the nesting requirements of a significant proportion of Britain's guillemots.

A northgoing eddy runs for twelve hours from HW Dover +0500 in Brough Bay. Little Clett stack in the corner of the bay, first climbed in 1970, has a grass top and is white with seabirds. The pier was built in the 19th century to be able to service Dunnet Head and other lighthouses by sea.

By the Stacks of Brough is a souterrain. Skylarks and curlews add their own distinctive contributions to the environment.

The pier at Ham is built of flagstones and served a now derelict watermill above the beach which was used to grind corn shipped with oatmeal to Scottish, English and European ports. A reefbreak gives lefts so the narrow entry to the pier would not have been easy to negotiate with a sailing ship.

Sir John's Castle and a chambered cairn precede further reefbreaks at Kirk o' Tang and the Haven, the latter with a steep slipway up to Scarfskerry. Scarf-

skerry has a reefbreak and another at Tang Head works on the upper half of the tide.

The harbour at Harrow, serving lobster boats, was built in the 19th century to export flagstones. A flagstone cutting factory was built in 1871 and there is an overgrown light railway near the harbour.

Overlooking Cairn of Mey is Castle of Mey which was built between 1566 and 1572 by the 4th Earl of Caithness, a Z plan castle. In 1952 it was restored as the home of the late Queen Elizabeth the Queen Mother.

St John's Point has the distinction of being one of the two most distant points on the British mainland as the crow flies, being 977.2km from Lizard Point in Cornwall at high water, slightly more at low water, although Dunnet Head and Duncansby Head are each only just over 100m short of this distance. Off the point, the Men of Mey rocks stand 11–18m high, always with enough swell causing turbulence to prevent passing between them. On a westgoing flow the Merry Men of Mey stretch out all the way to Hoy, a race which might be treated as a 14km long stopper for practical purposes. The eastgoing stream starts at HW Dover −0545 at up to 10km/h. The most violent part of the race is 6km west of Stroma on a westerly flow. This is just clear of the Swelkie, a 5km eddy which forms on the downstream side of the 4km long island on the westerly flow, that on the easterly flow being a mere 2km long. If all else fails, St John's Point is only 15m high and the portage is not as difficult as some. The cost of getting it wrong can be high and porbeagle sharks can add to the interest. *Hereward the Wake* tells how Hereward and his Viking crew were followed through the

St John's Point in windy conditions with the Merry Men of Mey stretching out towards Hoy.

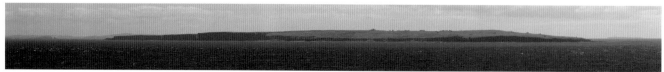
Stroma in the centre of the Pentland Firth.

John o' Groats harbour with Stroma across Inner Sound.

Duncansby Head with its lighthouse.

firth by an ominous witch whale. In *Redgauntlet* Robin Hastie claims Nanty Ewart could steer through the Pentland Firth blind drunk, an obviously wild claim.

A tidal power sub surface array to the south of Stroma is producing 1.5MW per turbine There will eventually be 269, the largest tidal power project in Europe. The 18m blades take some nine seconds to rotate on units fabricated at Nigg Energy Park.

Flows at the edges of Inner Sound start eastwards at HW Dover +0340 and west from HW Dover −0230 at up to 2km/h. However, in midchannel they start at HW Dover −0530 and west from HW Dover +0030 at up to 9km/h with a violent race off Ness of Huna on the eastgoing stream.

On the west side of Gills Bay there is a northgoing eddy for nine hours from HW Dover −0230.

More surfing opportunities at mid tide, lefts at the west end and rights at Ness of Quoys, are possible at Gills Bay, backed by the A836. The water itself is clear and porpoises might be seen in the bay.

Canisbay church with an unusual pitched roof to its tower is at Kirkstyle, seeming more Norman than traditional Scottish. The church dates from the 15th century although there was an earlier one there from 1222.

At Meal Mill the A836 crosses the oldest surviving bridge in Caithness, a 3m stone arch built by Cromwell in the 1650s.

After winning Orkney back from Norway, James IV instructed Jan de Groot to start a ferry service to Orkney in 1496. That most Scottish of names was actually Dutch. The site of the man's house is marked by a mound and flagstaff. In the summer a passenger ferry still operates to Bur Wick on South Ronaldsay. Why John o' Groats should have become such a legendary place is hard to see, apart from being at the end of the A99 and the terminal for a minor ferry. Its sole claim to fame is as the village most distant from the most westerly point on the English mainland. Even Sennen to John o' Groats or Land's End to Duncansby Head would be more logical for walkers, cyclists and the rest who want a long distance route. At least John o' Groats offers a harbour and slipway rather than the high cliffs at Land's End, allowing visits to be made to Caithness Candles, John o' Groats Pottery, a satin craft studio and the Last House in Scotland Museum. Flows here are up to 7km/h.

Ness of Duncansby is an innocuous low grassy point from where the Duncansby Race runs out into the Boars of Duncansby. It is only significant and to be avoided on the southeast going stream which starts at HW Dover −0500, flowing at up to 17km/h. The race extends northwards from the ness at HW Dover −0220 and begins to subside at HW Dover +0040. The northwestgoing stream begins at HW Dover +0115 at up to 15km/h with a temporary cease in the race. From HW Dover +0500 the race forms again until HW Dover −0530 when there is another cease.

In the distance Muckle Skerray presents a silhouette which resembles a submarine.

The 60m vertical cliffs of Duncansby Head are topped by the 11m white lighthouse tower, by David Stevenson in 1924, both building and lantern tower being square. There are superb spring flowers and a cliff packed with extremely noisy and odorous nesting guillemots watching what is happening on the water in front of them. For most boats, Duncansby Head's race is less significant as it is at the foot of the cliffs and, so, easily avoided. Not so the small boat facing turbulence throughout on the southeastgoing stream or a northgoing stream which is usually fast.

On the south southeastgoing stream there may be a northgoing eddy round the corner. The Moray Firth has a weak clockwise circulation and colder water but the problems generally subside once sufficiently clear of the Pentland Firth. The whole Pentland Firth needs to be

Ledges of guillemots at Duncansby Head.

studied thoroughly in advance. Neap tides, calm conditions and slack water all help reduce the difficulties.

South of Duncansby Head the scenery is spectacular with the 60m arch of Thirle Door, the Knee stack, the twin pointed Stacks of Duncansby and numerous caves and clefts in the cliffs which are still 30m high at Skirza Head, along with an assortment of geos. Wife Geo offers two entrances and another has a natural arch across it. There are oystercatchers around the Stacks of Duncansby.

Below the broch at Skirza Head there is a large seabird colony and seals haul out on the rocks. There is a reefbreak with long heavy lefts. The surf drives weed in beside the pier at Skirza where it collects and rots to produce a putrid smell and a polluted white colour to the water, not enhanced by pieces of broken glass lying around. Beaches from here to the Forth may throw up semiprecious stones such as serpentine, jasper, amethyst, smoky quartz and agate.

Behind Freswick Bay the Gill Burn is crossed by the masonry arch Freswick bridge from 1726 or earlier with a prison cell in the abutment. It has the Sinclair coat of arms above its window opening. The mouth of the burn has a sand and boulder reefbreak, backed by a good dune system. In the centre of Freswick Bay is a wreck. The bay

The Knee and Thirle Door. The northgoing race is already running quite strongly through the gaps.

The Stacks of Duncansby, the only major rock features here easily visible from on land

Seals sunbathing on rocks below Skirza Head.

has a northgoing eddy from HW Dover −0545 to HW Dover +0315 and significant surf.

After Ness Head, with its broch site, is Bucholly Castle, just one wall remaining of the 12th century stronghold of the Norse pirate Sweyn Asleifson. The Vikings of the late Norse are featured in the Northlands Viking Centre at Auckengill, together with Picts, chambered cairns and brochs, there being dun and broch sites near the shore at Nybster.

An 18th century Category B baronial mansion is inhabited. Its 16th century Keiss Castle predecessor is now just a tower on the shoreline. Brochs overlook the fierce race around Tang Head but Keiss has a small crab fishing harbour with a warehouse and icehouse from the herring fishing days.

A pillbox and tank traps line the shore at Rough of Stain where there is a reefbreak producing lefts. A 5km sweep of beach backed by dunes and by golf links edges Sinclair's Bay. There is a reef break at Keiss and the best beachbreak is at the mouth of the Burn of Lyth, entering just south of another broch site, although there is beachbreak right down the bay.

Old submarine cables landed at Reiss, near which there are shallow reefbreaks with rights.

The Category A Ackergill Tower, built five storeys high, is one of the oldest inhabited dwellings in the north of Scotland. In 1699 it passed into the hands of the Dunbars and is now a hotel. Ackergill has a small fishing harbour which is backed by Wick Airport. The lifeboat slipway of 1910 is thought to be the first reinforced concrete

Noss Head with the contrasting silhouettes of Castle Sinclair and Castle Girnoe along the southern edge of Sinclair's Bay.

The island at the Brough.

slipway in Britain, built in the style of a timber structure and still in good condition.

Castle Girnoe was built in 1476 to 1486 and neighbouring Castle Sinclair in 1606/7, strongholds of the Sinclairs, the Earls of Caithness. Both were deserted about 1679 and in ruins by the end of the century.

There is a continuous easterly flow around the southern edge of Sinclair's Bay, ending at Noss Head which is vertical and 43m high, a major seabird colony. There is a fierce race around the head, on which is the circular 18m white stone lighthouse tower of 1849 by Alan Stevenson. Streams start south southwest from Noss Head to Wick at HW Dover −0430 and north northeast at HW Dover −0140 at up to 3km/h. The coast is low and rocky but contains caves. A broch site is located between Staxigoe and Broadhaven at Papigoe with another beyond Broadhaven.

Wick Bay has no currents but heavy seas can build up with onshore winds and moon jellyfish collect during calmer conditions. North Head is 14m high with low cliffs and a battlemented memorial tower. There may also be unexploded ordnance on the north side of the bay.

Wick was a Viking anchorage. Vik is Norse and inbhir uige Gaelic for creek or rivermouth. It became a Royal Burgh in 1589 and has 18th century housing on a medieval street plan, much enlarged in the 19th century to a street plan by Telford to the south of his 1811 harbour extension. The outer harbour extension of 1825 built by Bremner uses flagstones set nearly vertically. There was storm damage to various walls, notably to the southern breakwater of 1868, of which a 1,350t section was lost in one storm, soon followed by its 2,600t replacement. The harbour is subject to seiches.

In its heyday the port had 1,000 herring boats and the large fishmarket remains. The Main Harbour brings in lime, coal, cement, fertilizers and road salt, exporting barley, while the River Harbour has six fuel tanks used by the oil and gas industry. Windfarm fabrication work is undertaken here. Caithness Glass was set up in 1960 by Lord Thurso, especially known for its paperweights, and there is a ceramics factory nearby. Wick Heritage Museum covers domestic life, cooperage, a blacksmith's shop,

A refreshing geo at the Brough.

kippering kilns, herring fishing, a fishing boat and a lighthouse.

The south side of the bay to South Head has a white octagonal tower and a 3.7m iron beacon which marks the end of a former breakwater on a spit. Blackbacked gulls watch near a swimming pool set in the rocks.

The coast has dark indented cliffs to Helman Head, often pierced by caves. The square tower ruins of Castle of Old Wick or the Old Man of Wick, one of the oldest castles in Scotland, with 2.1m thick walls, date back to the Norse occupation in the 12th century. These days they come under fire from a rifle range, a flag and lookout seated alongside indicating firing.

A steep island in the Brough deserves closer investigation. A high passage runs through it from end to end and the centre of the roof has fallen in, added to which is all the noise from a seabird colony.

Four aerials follow the A99 and the former Wick–Lybster railway from Wick to Thrumster, the highest 99m tall. From Helman Head with its cairn the cliffs are more

Yet another stack, this time the Stack of Ulbster. The Caithness hills are becoming clearer in the background.

Invershore was once Scotland's third largest fishing station.

The Needle, the air filled with flying guillemots and a quite deafening sound from the tens of thousands lining the ledges.

broken to Sarclet Head, where eider ducks might be seen. Ires Geo has a major seabird colony. The Haven at Sarclet is a fishing harbour with ruined breakwaters on each side.

From Sarclet Head to Clyth Ness the cliffs begin to rise again, up to 46m high with the hills behind reaching to over 160m, the site of a large number of antiquities, stone rows, settlements, standing stones, cairns, chambered cairns, forts and brochs sited between Loch of Yarrows and Bruan.

Beyond Stack of Ulbster there is a major seabird colony at Ulbster. Whaligoe claims to be a fishing village but is a minute beach with two rusty boat mooring chains attached to the overhanging cliff, approached down 365 flagstone steps which are slippery when wet. About 1855 it had 35 boats, sustaining 300 people. Boats had to be pulled up the cliffs above wave height as it was exposed to southeasterly gales until a rock platform was blasted out about 1812. Herring had to be carried up to a curing shed on the cliffs.

Round the corner, Wester Whale Geo was a herring station. A natural bridge across the mouth of a cave is an interesting variation on the cliff scenery. More major seabird colonies are found at Bruan and Halberry Head. Above Stack of Mid Clyth are the monument and stone rows of Mid Clyth. Ousbacky is a notably insignificant point, barely a bend in the coast although marked by the Clythness lighthouse, a 13m tower low down on the cliffs.

Seals rest up near the Stacks.

The **Lybster** lobster and crab fishing port of Invershore at the mouth of the Reisgill Burn is easy to miss, the lighthouse in Lybster Bay being well hidden by the cliff on the east side. In fact, at the height of the herring fishing boom it was the third largest fishing station in Scotland, provision for a hundred boats being made after 94 Caithness fishermen were lost in a gale in 1848. It was where wave hight was first measured accurately, highest waves of 4.1m being met in November to February. Most of the boats have gone but the oystercatchers, gulls and midges remain. The golf course on top of the hill is possibly the shortest in Britain but it makes up for it with its views.

The cliffs increase in height to over 50m at Forse Cove and then drop away again to Latheronwheel. Forse Castle dates from Norse times, retaining some of its walling including a 9m tower.

Latheron has a belltower, two Bronze Age standing stones and the Clan Gunn Heritage Centre in a 1735

Kenn & the Salmon from Highland River *at Dunbeath. Wave defences are tetrapods, unpleasant to negotiate.*

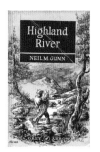

church, charting Scotland's oldest clan from Norse origins. Along the road, Latheronwheel with its broch and two chambered cairns stands above the tiny fishing harbour and stack, arch and caves although ropes leading out to fishing nets in the sea are more important features to notice.

The cliffs are low to Dunbeath, rarely exceeding a height of 20m but with frequent offshore rocks. Knockinnon has the Laidhay Croft Museum, a cruck constructed barn and a stable dwelling and byre in a longhouse of 1842. The Dunbeath Heritage Centre records the natural and social history of the area from the Vikings and early settlers to more recent crofting and fishing. It was an important herring fishing centre but suffers from the activity of Dunbeath Water which regularly brings down boulders, needing to be removed from Dunbeath Bay, the rivermouth frequently changing position. There are wrecks in the centre of the bay and on the west side. Through all the debris a power cable runs out for 18km to the production platforms on the Beatrice oilfield. A picnic table is conveniently placed near the pier and a statue of Kenn & the Salmon recalls Highland writer Neil Gunn, born here in 1891. It was Dunster, the setting for *The Silver Darlings*, his *Morning Tide* was also set here and Dunbeath Water was his *Highland River*.

There is another cave at the end of Dunbeath Bay and then a striking castle. Dunbeath Castle is painted white

and is imposing in its 20m clifftop setting. Built in 1428 or earlier for the Sutherlands, it was enlarged in the 19th century. It has changed hands several times and is still inhabited. The surrounding waters have hundreds of seals and thousands of shags.

Flows start southwestwards to Berriedale at HW Dover −0400 and northeastwards at HW Dover +0200 at up to 2km/h, past cliffs up to nearly 50m high.

Another chambered cairn, broch and standing stone follow at Ramscraigs while, down at Borgue, An Dùn is another major seabird colony.

Berriedale Water joins Langwell Water at Berriedale to discharge at a rivermouth which is frequently choked with boulders. The village has the Kingspark llama farm with rare breeds and guided llama walks. The hamlet also has two towers, Berriedale Castle ruins and a graveyard near the rivermouth, Achastle's 14 to 15th century ruins and Langwell House, the Caithness estate of the Duke of Portland, containing white deer and a windmill.

Flows south begin at HW Dover +0200 and north at HW Dover −0330 at up to 1km/h, setting towards and away from the coast as implied. Cliffs run up to 150m high, red sandstone with white streaks. Over the next 6km the seabird colonies reach their zenith with Inver Hill, Badbea and the 61m Needle. The colonies are huge, including the largest guillemot colony on the mainland with 130,000 birds. As well as the thousands of birds in flight and calling at any time there are countless ledges of birds creating a loud and urgent background buzz which resembles a very large and angry beehive. The whole experience is totally deafening and dazzling, accompanied by regular wafts of stale fish odour.

There are occasional brochs and a monument at Badbea. The high cliffs rise to the Paps of Caithness, 626m, Scaraben with East Scaraben and Sròn Garbh about the same height while Morven rises higher to 706m behind with white quartz at the top which looks like snow.

The Ord of Caithness rises to 230m, from where there are spectacular views of the scenery, possibly including herds of red deer. Braigh na h-Eaglaise rises to 422m and Creag Thoraraidh to 405m with a radio mast. The great fault at Dùn Glas separates Mesozoic from older rocks.

A rather specific piece of folklore warns that it is unlucky for a Sinclair to cross the Ord on a Monday dressed in green. This derives from the fact that William, Earl of Caithness, led 300 troops in green tartan this way to support James IV at the Battle of Flodden, all but one perishing among 10,000 Scotsmen.

Helmsdale has cliffs with granite outcrops, a wide area of reefs forming for a kilometre to the east of the town. In calm conditions it may be possible to weave a route between them but usually it is necessary to remain outside. Landing at the east end of the harbour gives a slipway to parking on the quiet road alongside the harbour.

The harbour at Helmsdale. Entry is in the far corner and exit is easiest in the foreground.

33 Dornoch Firth

Some of the most beautiful sunsets on the east coast

Dunrobin Castle, by the way, I nearly had forgot
And the reckless stanes o' cairn that mairks the hoose 'o John o' Groat
Bert Jansch

Helmsdale is from the Norse Hjalmundalr, Hjalmund's dale. The Timespan visitor centre covers the area from the Picts to North Sea oil and has a riverside garden. The fishing port is at the mouth of the River Helmsdale, from which freshets flow well out to sea and a bar of stones and boulders collect off the harbour. In addition, the breakwater is damaged, convenient for easy departure from the harbour for small boats. The A9 bridge crosses next to the harbour, its construction requiring the ruins of the castle to be cleared and the entrance of the Old Harbour to be blocked. An 18m white war memorial clocktower is located on the west bank, as is a memorial to evicted crofters who emigrated. Pottery is made in the town and gold prospecting takes place in the hills.

Long distance boaters tend to cut the corner here, not least to avoid the Tain bombing range.

The cliffs are very low to Brora and this was a suitable place to land submarine cables, now disused. The A9 is joined by the North Highland railway line between Thurso and Inverness, both now following the coastal strip.

The water is fairly clear with moon jellyfish, cormorants, terns, oystercatchers, fulmars, blackbacked gulls, shelducks and razorbills. This stretch of coast is very mild so palm trees can thrive at Portgower while the hillside behind is a blaze of yellow broom flowers. Skylarks twitter by the shore and many seals lie up on the sandy beach at Kilmote. Dug up at Loth were the bones of a plesiosaur. Caravans behind the beach to Lothbeg Point show how much more benign the conditions are than further north.

Lothbeg, on the river which flows from Glen Loth, has the Long Cairn chambered cairn on one side and, on the other, the Wolf Stone which records the shooting

Dunrobin Castle is one of the most distinctive in Scotland with its spires and gardens based on Versailles. It is the largest house in northern Scotland. The Maritime Quarter features a Mumbles tram, fully working Abbey Woollen Mill, lightship *Helwick*, steam tug *Canning*, 500t oak trawler *Katie Anne* and an old Mumbles lifeboat. It was constructed around a 1275 square keep by Robert, Earl of Sutherland, on a natural rock terrace, as the home of the Countess of Sutherland, making it one of the oldest continuously inhabited houses in Britain despite its appearance. It was captured briefly by the Jacobites in 1746. Most of it dates from 1845–50, based by Sir Charles Barry on Balmoral and French architecture, as the seat of the Dukes and Earls of Sutherland. The interior is mostly by Sir Robert Lorimer following a fire in 1915 and contains French furniture, paintings which include Canaletto views of Venice and family portraits by Reynolds and Landseer, silver Wemyss Ware, ceramics, tapestries, a 10,000 volume library, a horsedrawn steampowered fire engine, a Victorian museum, hunting spoils, local archaeology, Pictish stones, natural history, geology and Clan Sutherland exhibits including robes, uniforms and medals. A private station was built for the 3rd Duke who also had his own carriages and engine. A couple of other buildings close by are circular with conical roofs, mimicking the style. The 394m high Beinn a' Bhragaidh is topped by the massive Ben Bhraggie Statute by Sir Francis Chanter of the 1st Duke of Sutherland, the Leviathan of Wealth. Such a man needs no monument. Between 1810 and 1820 he evicted 15,000 tenants, often violently, to make way for sheep and the damage he did to the Highland population lasts to this day.

Golspie is a Norse farm name. The town is on the

The bar at the mouth of the River Brora.

in about 1700 of the last wild wolf in Scotland. Other than occasional sections of rock platform, the shore is sandy beach all the way to **Brora**. Kintradwell Broch is Iron Age, measuring 9.4m across inside its double walls. Excavation in 1880 unearthed two headless skeletons.

Rhizostoma jellyfish float about on one side of the beach while golfers do likewise on the other.

A bar of gravel and rock can make entry to the estuary of the River Brora difficult.

Flows begin southwest at HW Dover –0600 and begin northeastwards at HW Dover –0100 at up to 1km/h. The coast is low although there is a 15m cliff terrace inland, rising eventually to 521m Ben Horn. It is a good area for wildfowl at sea.

After a memorial the well preserved lower walls of Carn Liath Broch stand near the entrance to the Dornoch Firth.

The distinctive Dunrobin Castle.

Golspie Burn where Golspie Mill is said to be Scotland's only organic waterpowered flourmill. The Orcadian Stone Co have a geological exhibition with natural stone products, cutting, grinding, polishing, tumbling and jewellery sales. The 17th century St Andrew's church has a fine Sutherland loft of 1737.

Off the town is the Bridge bank but there is no tidal stream to cause problems.

Golspie Links offer one of the country's longer bunkers as golfers play shots back off the sandy beach. Beyond the golf course and a caravan site the dunes take on a more natural form.

The River Fleet enters Loch Fleet and then discharges to the sea past Littleferry. Shallow water results in a race out to sea on the ebb. There is a sand bar across the entrance and sand spits on each side at the mouth. The ferry ceased in 1815 when Thomas Telford built the Mound causeway across the head of Loch Fleet to carry what would become the A9. The loch is flanked by pinewoods with rare creeping lady's tresses orchid and twinflower in Ferry Links woods. Ducks (especially eiders), waders and other birds are attracted by the loch and there are seals and migratory salmon. Jackdaws are seen around the 14th century Skelbo Castle.

The coast continues low and sandy along to Dornoch Point. Embo is fairly conspicuous, including the Category A Embo House with its high white front. There is a burial chamber before the caravan site which continues as far as the

Bishop of Caithness. Except for the central tower it was mostly destroyed by fire in 1570, but was restored in the 17th century, 1835–7 and 1924, retaining fine 13th century stonework and outstanding stained glass. There is a craft centre with jewellery, tartan weaving and exhibits in the former jail cells. The Sutherland Show is held in July. Earl's Cross stands to the north of the town while the Witches Stone in Littletown marks the burning at the stake in 1722 of Janet Horn for turning her daughter into a small horse and taking her to the Devil to be shod, the last person in Britain to be executed for witchcraft. There is also a landing strip to the south of the town.

Dornoch Point is a spit which is continually changing shape, 4m high with marram grass on top.

Gizzen Briggs, a bank of drying quicksand with a Norse name, stretches out for 3km into the firth, eventually meeting up with Whiteness Sands to form the Tain

pier. A cairn is sited in front of another less conspicuous caravan site at Embo Street.

Of the two golf courses at the end of the A949 at **Dornoch,** Royal Dornoch is the third oldest golf course known. The town is built of local stone and has a Mercat Cross and 16th century Bishop's Palace, now the Dornoch Castle Hotel. The cathedral was formerly the cathedral of the Bishops of Caithness, founded in 1224 by Gilbert, Archdeacon of Moray and

Bar. The flood tide begins at HW Dover −0530 and the ebb at HW Dover +0120 at up to 1km/h but increasing to 2km/h on the flood and 3km/h on the ebb off Dornoch Point, increasing with snow-melt or after heavy rain, although it can feel faster in the shallow water. The shifting banks of Dornoch Sands are over 1km wide at low

The A9 crosses the Dornoch Bridge. The Cuthill Sands, beyond, are popular with seals for sunbathing.

tide and lead on to Cuthill Sands. Other than a few eider ducks, swans and herons, the area is the preserve of large numbers of seals which rest up out of the water which can be very warm in the summer.

The 780m long Dornoch Bridge carries the rerouted A9 across the end of the Kyle of Sutherland, draining the rivers Oykel and Shin. The flood at the bridge begins at HW Dover –0330 at up to 4km/h and the ebb at HW Dover +0215 at up to 5km/h.

The most conspicuous buildings in Morangie house the Glenmorangie distillery, in which the 16 Men of Tain produce a malt whisky aged for ten years. Distilling has been undertaken here since at least 1703 and the older buildings date from 1843. It is one of the smallest distilleries in Scotland and is unusual in having a coastal location. The kilns are small and lightly peated but have the tallest still columns in Scotland at 5.2m, using hard barley from the Black Isle. The whisky matures in bourbon soaked oak casks from Missouri.

Tain is named after the Viking for thing or council. It is Scotland's oldest Royal Burgh, receiving its charter in 1066. The 900 Roses Garden was planted to celebrate the 900th anniversary. It was the birthplace of St Duthus about 1000. St Duthus' Chapel was built between 1065 and 1256 but destroyed by fire in 1427. The saint is buried in St Duthus Church, built in Decorated style about 1360 by William, Earl and Bishop of Ross, which became a centre of Christian pilgrimage. James IV came every year for twenty years and James V came on foot from Edinburgh. Robert the Bruce's wife was dragged from sanctuary here and taken to England. Highland Clearances were administrated from the town centre. There are a Victorian Gothic town hall, the Category B Tower

St and the Tolbooth, a square tower that overlooks the Mercat Cross. Exhibitions include the Tain & District Museum & Clan Ross Centre. Pottery and Highland Fine Cheese manufacture are among the local industries. St Mary's Well is just below high tide level while the River Tain winds around the town and then flows across Whiteness Sands to Tain Scalps between the various sandbanks.

Sandbanks and shallows make navigation difficult for larger boats. The nearly 100km^2 of the Dornoch Firth and the metre high Morrich More marshes were used as the Tain firing and bombing range. There are lookout towers among marram grass and dunes on Innis Mhór and its neighbouring island. Large herds of seals still lie up on Whiteness Sands off Rubh'na h-Innse Moire.

Inver is a fishing village. Fishing boats are just able to slip out of Inver Bay and up the east coast of the firth. Portmahomack, at the end of the B9165, is one of the few places on Scotland's east coast to enjoy beautiful sunsets, perhaps the reason why caravans are lined up in front of the drying sandbanks and rocks along the shore. There is a golf course above the village. A Reformation church has an unusual domed tower and there is a Victorian iron drinking fountain by the beach. The Oystercatcher Rest-

Sunset seen across the Dornoch Firth from Portmahomack.

Britain's second tallest lighthouse on Tarbat Ness.

Seafront houses at Portmahomack.

aurant and the Castle Hotel are both by the beach. It is a lobster fishing village with a sheltered position and lack of tidal flows.

Portmahomack to Tarbat Ness has pebble ridges edged with rocks through which there are a number of narrow inlets, accessible in calm conditions. Salmon nets arc strung out in the sea at several points.

The lighthouse on Tarbat Ness is 41m high, the second highest in Britain, its white tower striped with red bands.

Ballone Castle on low cliffs.

Near Geanies House, the Moray shore beyond.

The peninsula itself is less than 60m high with relatively gentle slopes up from the water so it is less severe than many such points.

Gentle flows start northeast at HW Dover +0120 and southwest at HW Dover −0450 although the eastgoing flow can pick up close to Tarbat Ness. Strong west to southwesterly winds with heavy rain inland and snow-melt can all make the east northeasterly stream run longer and more strongly. Once round the point, flows start a little earlier and more strongly, heading southwest from HW Dover −0530 and northeast from HW Dover +0100 at up to 1km/h.

The line of red sandstone cliffs start out as gentle slopes of grass and gorse, gradually getting steeper and becoming higher with seabirds. Salmon nets are staked out from mid February to late August.

Wilkhaven is a fishing village with a jetty conveniently close to the point. The cliffs here are only 12m high but they increase to twice that height further south, topped by a framework radio tower at Bindal.

Roofless remains of Ballone Castle, built for the Earl of Ross, later owned by the Mackenzies and abandoned in the 19th century, stand on the cliffs near Rockfield.

Rockfield has a jetty which can be invaluable as the shoreline is mostly studded with rocks which make landing difficult although there is a flat strip of land all the way along the coast between the cliffs and the shoreline, easy to traverse once ashore.

The red sandstone cliffs increase towards 50m high at Cadboll Point with just a token cave. A grassy shore at Cadboll has the remains of Cadboll Castle. Cadboll Mount was said to have been built by the Laird of Cadboll who had a feud with Macleod of Geanies and who wished to look down on his neighbour.

On the other hand, Hilton of Cadboll is on the shore, a former fishing village with the remains of a chapel and an adventure playground.

Balintore was also a fishing village at the end of the B9166, its harbour overlooked by the Commercial Inn.

Shandwick Bay has frequently rollers but the southern end is the landing point for the pipeline from the Beatrice oilfield which is taken between Clach a' Charridh and an airfield for the final land leg to the oil terminal at Nigg Bay. In quiet conditions it can also be a convenient landing point for small boats. A limited amount of parking is available next to the sandy beach.

Higher cliffs approaching Cadboll.

Distance
82km from Helmsdale to Shandwick

OS 1:50,000 Sheets
17 Helmsdale & Strath of Kildonan
21 Dornoch & Alness

Tidal Constants
Helmsdale:
HW Dover +0030, LW Dover +0040
Golspie:
HW Dover +0030, LW Dover +0040
Meikle Ferry:
HW Dover +0100, LW Dover +0110
Portmahomack:
HW Dover +0040, LW Dover +0100
Balintore:
HW Dover +0040, LW Dover +0050

Sea Area
Cromarty

Range
Tain

Connection
Kyle of Sutherland – see RoB p118

34 Moray

Once and again, as the Ice came south
The glaciers ground over Lossiemouth.
Rudyard Kipling

Flows from Shandwick begin southwest at HW Dover −0530 and northeast from HW Dover +0100 at up to 1km/h.

Salmon fishing nets run out from the coast between mid February and late August. Beds of kelp will also be met in the clear water. Blackbacked gulls, guillemots, razorbills, oystercatchers, cormorants and eider ducks all frequent this coast with its steep red cliffs which can usually be climbed, although landing through the rocks on the shoreline cannot be attempted except in the calmest of conditions. Forts and a homestead remain hidden on the top at Port an Righ but there is the occasional clump of trees and gorse spills down the hillside. Several waterfalls also drop down, including the burn fed by Bayfield Loch on Kraken Hill.

The largest of the caves is King's Cave which looks out

Beds of kelp below the cliffs at Port an Righ.

over the Three Kings spoil dumping ground and there are some arches at the approach to the mouth of the Cromarty Firth. There are Sutors Stacks, meaning shoemakers, on the south side of the entrance. The firth is the best deep water harbour in northeast Scotland and one of the largest natural harbours in Europe. In the distance the Invergordon distillery can be seen but this is much less conspicuous than massive oil rigs being refitted in the Nigg Bay fabrication yard and numbers of them anchored in the firth.

Dunskeath Castle and an earthwork are not likely to be noticed on 150m high North Sutor, but the village of **Cromarty** is clear enough beyond the 140m high South Sutor.

The gap can act as a wind funnel. Tides flow in from HW Dover −0400 and out from HW Dover +0115 at up to 3km/h while the flow across the mouth starts west southwest at HW Dover −0600 at up to 1km/h and east northeast from HW Dover +0030 at up to 2km/h.

South of the firth lies the Black Isle, neither an isle nor black although it does remain free of snow when the surrounding hills are covered. Indeed, at the foot of 156m high Gallow Hill, the end of a ridge to Rosemarkie, are Blue Head and Red Nose, the green vegetation gashed by new slips to reveal red rock beneath. A marine farm may be moored off the cliffs.

McFarquhar's Cave and St Bennet's Well near a cliff stream continue the symmetry about the firth.

Eathie fishing station has fossils on the foreshore. These were new to science in the days when stonemason and geologist Hugh Miller learned his craft here.

Caves continue and there are small stacks which mock the TV masts on the ridge above. Occasionally there are beaches which can only be reached from the water or by air, as indicated by curlews which pace sedately across the sand.

Behind Rosemarkie Bay on the A832 is Rosemarkie with its red stone houses and its red sandstone exposed by landslides around the Fairy Glen with two waterfalls.

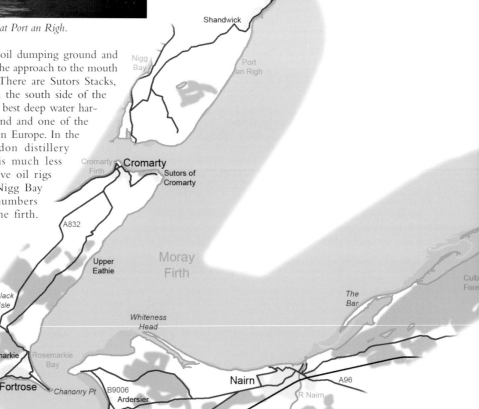

Waterfall down the cliff near King's Cave.

This resort includes the Groam House Museum which has the Rosemarkie Stone, an intricately carved Pictish slab, and other stone carvings from the time of the Picts, together with archaeological displays.

Chanonry Ness is an unexpected spit which runs out into the Moray Firth, ending at Alan Stevenson's 13m white light tower of 1846 at Chanonry Point by the former ferry pier for Fort George. The ness also has a golf course, a cross and a memorial to the 17th century prophet Brahan Seer who made portents of doom for the Mackenzie family. For his pains he was burned in a barrel of tar on the point, presumably an outcome he did not foresee.

After the North and South Channels have merged, crossing the Moray Firth and the line of the Great Glen Fault at this point is simpler in terms of shipping movements but there can be consid-

Inaccessible beach near the Sutors of Cromarty.

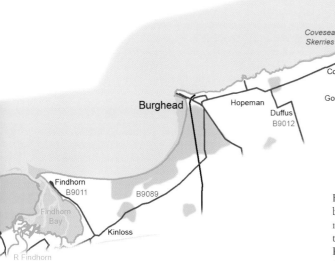

erable turbulence between Chanonry Point and Fort George at peak flows. Streams run southwest from HW Dover −0400 at up to 5km/h with a slack at Dover HW and then northeast from at HW Dover +0115 at up to 6km/h with another slack at HW Dover +0530.

The largest population of dolphins around the coast live in the Moray Firth, probably over a hundred of them. There are white beaked dolphins and common porpoises, too. Some 49,000 waterfowl winter in the inner Moray Firth include 2,800 redshanks, 2,100 bar tailed godwits, 1,400 red breasted mergansers, 1,400 red throated divers and long tailed ducks and common and velvet scoters. The RSPB claimed that they were at risk of permanent damage from pollution and land reclaim.

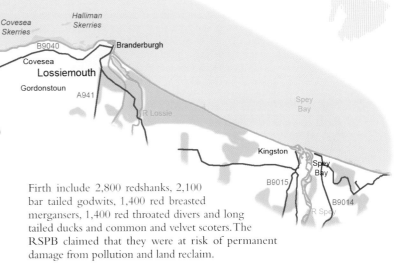

The North Sutor at the entrance to the Cromarty Firth.

Fortifications at the entrance to the Cromarty Firth.

and rough grassland up to 24m high, forming the Carse of Delnies, used for a golf course at the east end.

The Golf View Hotel, Invernairne Hotel, a children's playground, an ornamental iron bandstand and swans on the sea are clues along the front that **Nairn** on the A96 is a refined resort. Indeed, it was the favourite resort of Charlie Chaplin. Granted a charter in the 12th century by Alexander I, it was to become a spa but in *A Journey to the Western Islands of Scotland* Dr Johnson claimed it was in 'miserable decay', the place where he first heard Gaelic and saw a peat fire. It has a mild climate and low rainfall. It also has Highland games in mid August while local features include ornamental gardens, a clocktower with a spire and a swimming pool. The Duke of Cumberland spent his 25th birthday here in 1746. The Jacobites attempted a surprise attack at night but daylight arrived too soon and they retreated to Culloden, where, exhausted and hungry, they lost their final battle the next day, a battle which is featured with other local history in the

The 18th century Fort George was sited to control entry to Inverness and beyond from the Moray Firth.

Aerial activity also results from Inverness Airport 5km to the southeast beyond Ardersier.

Fort George at the end of the B9006 dominates the opposite side of the Moray Firth from Chanonry Point. Built from 1748 to 1769 for 1,600 infantry for George II following the Jacobite rebellion and the Battle of Culloden, it never saw action and remains one of the finest late artillery fortifications in Europe. Land approach is through two tunnels and over a timber bridge across a ditch, all covered by at least two walls of cannons. The 17ha site is protected by 1.6km of ramparts. It contains the Highlanders Museum with the Seaforth Highlanders, the Queen's Own Highlanders and the Cameron Highlanders, medals and uniforms, the Seafield Collection of arms gathered by Sir James Grant in the 18th century for a regiment of foot and militia, an Armstrong gun of 1865 with early rifling and typical barrack rooms of 1868, 1813 and 1780, the oldest featuring Private James Anderson of the 42nd Royal Highlanders. Subsequent visitors included Johnson and Boswell. The fort is still in use as a barracks and military depot, including the chapel of 1763–7. More recent features are a helicopter landing site and a water tower. Firing on the ranges normally stops while boats are passing.

A narrow shingle ridge at Whiteness Head ends alongside a lagoon and saltings, the greater part of which dry. The area was the site of McDermott's massive oil platform construction yard.

The low shingle ridge develops into sand dunes

Nairn Museum which has herring fishing in the steam drifter era, model boats, the Moray Firth and domestic life.

The harbour is off the River Nairn, a pre-Celtic name for penetrating river, the mouth of which is obstructed by a drying sand bar at low tide. Indeed, the river also drains and even a kayak would have difficulty ascending the gravel rapid to gain entry.

To the south stands the Ord, a 214m high summit. Beyond another golf course begins a dune coast with drying sandbanks to Findhorn. Ridges of shingle stand 3–8m high. Some 10km of spits, the Bar and the Old Bar with the Gut inside were islands at high tide until recent years and are are subject to continual change. There is a wreck offshore. The area is a nature reserve with a winter roost for a thousand greylags on the Bar, skylarks in the summer and seabirds and waders all year. Culbin Sands are the largest dune system in Britain following a series of storms which overwhelmed a village and rich farmland in the 17th century. The formerly bare sandhills up to 30m high now support 15km of the Culbin Forest, its conifers forming one of the most thickly wooded coasts in Britain.

It has many rare dune and pinewood plants and wildlife includes roe deer, badgers, red squirrels and crested tits. Capercaillies became extinct in Britain in the mid 18th century but were reintroduced to Scotland in the 1830s. They have been in decline again since the 1970s and are probably below 2,500 in number now

Nairn harbour, looking inland, the entrance on the left.

The Gut at low water divides the Bar from Culbin Forest.

so those who shoot them for pleasure have proposed a voluntary ban on killing them.

After the Bar the Highland region gives way to Moray. The resort of Findhorn, at the end of the B9011 and at the mouth of the River Findhorn and Muckle Burn forming Findhorn Bay, is the third village of this name. The first was buried beneath sand in fierce storms in the 17th century and the second was destroyed by floods in 1701. A spit running out from the entrance to the bay has its sand with razor and mussel shells and dozens of sunbathing seals in settled conditions. With even moderate northerly weather a confused sea breaks over the bar. Huge numbers of longtailed ducks and common scoters winter offshore and ospreys might be seen. This is the main yachting centre for northeastern Scotland. In 1962 the Findhorn Foundation religious retreat was set up 2km to the south with interests in ecology, organic gardening, weaving, pottery and candlemaking. The Findhorn Heritage Centre has the story of the village, a salmon fisherman's bothy and some models.

Two picnic areas are surrounded by tank traps in the dunes. Along the southern shoreline of Burghead Bay are a line of pillboxes in various states of capsize. They were to protect the airfield at Kinloss. An aircraft might be seen through the pines on the 3–15m high sandhills at the back of the beach, as will be aerials and an aerogenerator, but military aircraft will also be seen and heard landing and taking off. The Burma Road got its name from its insects and dense undergrowth during wartime training in 1944.

Formerly Moray's main grain port, the busy fishing harbour of **Burghead** is at the end of the B9089 with a prominent white mark and 300m of quays handling barley and Scandinavian timber. There is a considerable sea off the port in strong winds but it is protected from easterly winds. The 20m high promontory is of heavily weathered honey coloured sandstone strata that is heavily disfigured with spraypaint graffiti. The Category B coastguard station occupies an Iron Age fort from 400 with a high chamber well cut into the rock, possibly an early Christian baptistery. It was the largest promontory fort in Scotland but stone from it was reused for Telford's har-

Pillboxes around Burghead Bay defended RAF Kinloss.

bour. Steps remain down into a stone tank well. Another old ceremony is the burning of the Clavie at the Clavie Stone, the breaking up of a blazing tar barrel which has been carried round the village on the old New Year's Eve, January 11th, possibly a ceremony of Norse origin. Torfness House was an early 19th century granary, its four floors with rare oak beams and 12m wrought iron trusses. The village has a visitor centre and a maltings in a large concrete building. At St Æthans a set of radio masts dominate the skyline behind the B9012 and B9040.

The rocky shoreline with its grassy slopes gradually increases in height to 70m at Hopeman where the freight railway from the south of Burghead formerly ran along the coast to beyond Hopeman.

The 19th century quarrymen's village and fishing harbour of Hopeman mostly dries and entry is impractical in heavy weather. It has a watersports centre which was well known to the Duke of Edinburgh and Prince Charles in their respective years as pupils at Gordonstoun.

After a disordered collection of beach huts, 50m sandstone cliffs continue to Covesea, initially topped by a golf course and later by a quarry with a scree slope of tailings,

A masterpiece of sculpting by the sea, a freestanding arch at Covesea.

Covesea Skerries light faces out towards Halliman Skerries with their daymark.

four radio masts and a 10m white coastguard lookout tower. Reptile footprints predate the dinosaurs. From Clashach Cove there are an assortment of caves, including Sculptor's Cave. Early cave paintings and headless human skeletons were found here. Arches include a superb free-standing arch which looks as if it has been made by balancing sandstone slabs precariously on each other. Neil & Jane are a ridge of drying rocks off the coast.

Covesea was formerly the estuary from Loch Spynie, now 7km away and only 1km long but once occupying a substantial area inland. St Peter's church at Duffus, now a ruin, was built on an island in the loch.

Streams as far as Portknockie start east at HW Dover +0200 and west at HW Dover −0420 at up to 1km/h.

Covesea Skerries lighthouse of 1846 by Alan Stevenson is a 36m white tower standing among the dunes by the beach and follows the loss of 16 vessels in a storm in November 1826. The Covesea Skerries themselves are not marked but there is a 15m iron pyramid framework, based on the Carr Beacon at Fife Ness, on the Halliman Skerries, which are closer to potential shipping routes. The Little Skerries and Ooze Rocks lie off Lossiemouth's west beach, on which there is a charge for landing. Aircraft fly low over the beach and the adjacent golf course to land beyond at RAF Lossiemouth. Tank traps and a pillbox also provided defences for this airfield. Offshore targets were used by 633 Squadron in preparation for their Operation Rhine Maiden. On Christmas day 1806 the entire active male population of 21 were lost to a storm.

Lossiemouth was developed as the port for Elgin on the former port of Spynie silting up. The Spynie Canal drains Loch Spynie into the River Lossie, the river of herbs, which discharges on the east side of the town over a drying bar. The streams run northwest from HW Dover −0300 at up to 3km/h with a south wind, more if heavy rain has put the river in spate. The east facing harbour at

Lossiemouth Fisheries & Community Museum includes a reconstruction of the study of the Labour Party's first Prime Minister, Ramsay MacDonald. Also of note in this resort is the belfry of St James' church.

Maggie Duncan's Corner takes its name from a boat which came to grief near the entrance. Beyond the River Lossie, crossed by a footbridge, the beach of concrete boulders gives way to a long sandy beach backed by sand-hills up to 15m high with forest behind all the way to Spey Bay. There is a beachbreak which works best at high water with a big swell, size increasing on further beach-breaks eastwards. Fulmars fly over the sea but the airfield behind the trees is now disused. Having Leuchars House at the end of the main runway could cause confusion with the former RAF Leuchars in Fife.

An 11km shingle spit up to 9m deep is second only to Dungeness, the largest in Britain. Binn Hill rises to 68m towards the far end of the beach, helping to locate an active rifle range with a danger area extending offshore.

Kingston, at the end of the B9015, is where Charles II landed in 1650 but it was named after Kingston upon Hull, home of timber merchants who began floating logs down the Spey from the Rothiemurchus and Glenmore pine forests to build ships for international use. In 1976 these operations proved the Spey a public navigation in the river access case which Clive Freshwater won in the House of Lords. The shape of the estuary was altered by the 1829 Muckle Spate. The village declined after steel ships began to be made.

Spey Bay has huge numbers of longtailed ducks and common scoters wintering offshore despite the fact that the sea breaks a long way out with northeasterly winds. The spit changes position at the mouth of the river with overfalls and tidal swirls off the end. The head of the bay is silted up by sand and gravel brought down by the Spey, the most rapid river in Scotland.

Near the end of the Speyside Walk footpath in the village of Spey Bay at the northern end of the B9014 is the Tugnet Ice House museum, Scotland's largest ice house, dating from 1830 and restored with an exhibition on the Spey, salmon fishing, ice packing for salmon and a display on wildlife.

The beach has beachbreaks which work best at high water with a big swell. In quieter conditions a landing may be made onto the track where a campsite is located to the east of the hotel which fronts one of the village's two golf courses.

the end of the A941 was hewn from solid rock as a seine net fishing harbour in Branderburgh which was founded in 1830. It suffers considerable scend with easterly winds and has been breached. Its 600m of quays import coal and export oats. There is also a covered fishmarket. The

Distance
88km from Shandwick to Spey Bay

OS 1:50,000 Sheets
*21 Dornoch & Alness
27 Nairn & Forres
28 Elgin & Dufftown*

Tidal Constants
*Balintore:
HW Dover +0040,
LW Dover +0050
Cromarty:
Dover +0020
Fortrose:
Dover +0100
McDermott Base:
Dover +0100
Nairn:
HW Dover +0040,
LW Dover +0050
Findhorn:
HW Dover +0040,
LW Dover +0050
Burghead:
HW Dover +0040,
LW Dover +0050
Lossiemouth:
HW Dover +0040,
LW Dover +0050
Buckie:
HW Dover +0040,
LW Dover +0050*

Sea Area
Cromarty

Ranges
*Fort George,
Binn Hill*

Connections
*Cromarty Firth – see RoB p122
Beauly Firth – see RoB p126*

The mouth of the Lossie with the harbour on the right and dunes backing the surfing beach.

Fishing villages on a rugged coast

The reprieve was coming o'er the brig o' Banff
When they stood on the Galla' Hill to see
They put the clock three-quarters fast
And hanged him tae the tree.
Anon

From Spey Bay the coast continues low, flat and sandy to Portgordon. Once again there is forest hiding a landing strip and there is also the line of a disused railway, which formerly reached the coast at Portgordon where gorse now covers the slopes as the A990 joins the coast. To the south is 264m Whiteash Hill with a 99m aerial on its east side.

Portgordon is a village of Old Red Sandstone houses from the 18th century. The salmon caught with net and line were stored in Gollachy Ice House. One dispute over herring fishing resulted in police being thrown into the harbour. The drying harbour was closed in 1947 and a spoil ground to the north might not be helping its depth. It has been repaired after being much damaged in a 1953 storm.

church in the north of Scotland during a period of persecution. St Ninian's Chapel is the oldest post-Reformation church in Scotland which is still in use. St Peter's is a more recent Roman Catholic church, dating from 1857, while the North church of 1879 has a crowned tower.

In 1814 two Buckie fishermen of integrity were 400m offshore in calm conditions when they saw a merman near them, close enough to see no scales on his tail. He dived and came up some distance away, accompanied by a mermaid while the men rowed for the shore and safety as quickly as they could.

The coastal road is now the A942 passing Portessie, a much simpler fishing village where boats are beached on the gravel.

Craig Head rises to 60m with an obelisk on the summit, the coast now being cliffy to Scar Nose. Behind a golf course is the ruin of a castle built by the Ord family. Thomas Ord also had workmen's cottages built in 1716 in Findochty. A measured mile leads past caves and a former smugglers' route.

Surrounded by reefs and with a drying bar across the

The entrance to Buckie harbour.

Beyond the next golf course Buckpool harbour was filled in the 1970s and converted to a park. However, Cluny harbour remains a fishing port with boat refitting and importing and exporting timber and grain. With 400m of quays, it is one of the largest commercial harbours in the Moray Firth, serving Buckie. It was suggested in 1805 by Telford and endorsed by the Stevensons. It receives a dangerous swell in northerly winds. There is a light tripod on West Muck and the leading lights are to avoid this outcrop rather than to lead into the harbour, the end of which is marked by a lighthouse. By 1913 the town had the largest steam drifter fleet in Scotland and was the major fishing port of the Moray Firth with net makers and fish processors. **Buckie** had a new lifeboat station in 1995. These days the fishing has changed from herrings to scampi, although the guillemots and cormorants find plenty of lobster pots marked by flags off the harbour. The Peter Anson Gallery has exhibits and paintings relating to the coastal fishing communities. The town boasts Inchgower distillery. The 6.4m First World War memorial is one of the finest in Scotland. The twin spires of St Gregory's church of 1788/9 mark the first Roman Catholic church built in Scotland after the Reformation, a church which was the secret headquarters of the Roman Catholic

outer harbour, entry to **Findochty** could be dangerous in a strong northerly. In quieter conditions, eider ducks swim placidly in front of caves and a war memorial. For once the caravans parked in this former fishing and smuggling village are upstaged by the colours of the houses, particularly the stepped window surrounds. Originally painted for weatherproofing, they now present a colourful and cheerful background to the harbour. To the south the bald headed Bin of Cullen rises above the surrounding forest to 320m.

The former fishing and pleasure craft harbour at **Port-knockie** has silted and partly dries but is the best naturally sheltered harbour on the south side of the Moray Firth although it suffers from considerable scend in the harbour with fresh northerly winds. The village is sited on top of the cliffs. It dates from the Iron Age and has a

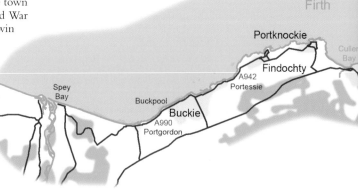

Findochty's reef strewn harbour overlooked by brightly painted houses.

Bow Fiddle Rock is one of the most spectacular formations on this coast.

7th century Pictish fort. It also has a church with a belfry. During the 19th century religious revival the villagers used Preacher's Cave, the largest of three caves in the cliffs, where the rocks are covered with mussels and blackbacked and other gulls, fulmars and dolphins are found offshore.

Scar Nose ends with Bow Fiddle Rock, a flying buttress where granite beds dipping steeply to the southeast have been eroded by the sea.

Streams to Knock Head start at HW Dover +0430 and begin eastwards at HW Dover –0150.

A golf course backs Cullen Bay with its fast breaking lefts and rights but **Cullen**'s most conspicuous feature is the disused 23m high 19th century masonry viaduct with 8 and 13 arches, designed to look like an ancient gateway. It was required because the Countess of Seafield would not allow the Great North of Scotland Railway across her land. Old Cullen, 1km up the Burn of Deskford, has the 17th century Cullen House with the 14th century Auld Kirk of St Mary the Virgin in use in its grounds. With 16th and 17th century additions, it was the burial place of Robert the Bruce's queen. In 1823 the Earl of Seafield and Findlater moved Cullen to its present site in order to give his house greater privacy. The railway structures are complemented by a domed and pillared pavilion. The entrance of the drying

fishing harbour with its entrance mark is dangerous in strong northerly winds. The town is known for Cullen skink, a haddock, onion and potato soup.

At the back of the shore is an extensive pet cemetery. Along the coast are the Three Kings and Boar's Craig rock formations and Black Lady's Cave. The caravans on the cliffs look down onto gulls, shags, kittiwakes, razorbills, guillemots, puffins and the Moray/Aberdeenshire border.

Logie Head has 60m high vertical strata. Somebody singlehandedly built a flight of steps down to the head so that walkers could reach the water but then everyone rallied round to build a monument to record his efforts. Thrift and orange lichen coats rocks that are the haunt of tiny orange butterflies.

A large white dovecote on the hillside precedes the cliffs where the 15th century Findlater Castle ruin is to be found, built as an Ogilvie stronghold.

Sandend Bay surfing is best at low to mid tide. There are the Glenglassaugh distillery and a windmill behind the bay. Much further south the land rises to 430m high Knock Hill.

Entry to **Portsoy** is difficult with a swell. It was declared a Burgh of Barony in 1550 by Mary, Queen of Scots, and a charter was granted to the Ogilvies of Boyne.

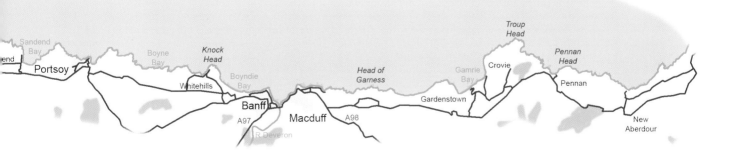

Vertical strata, monument and steps at Logie Head.

Rock strata dominate the landscape at Logie Head.

Looking east from Logie Head past West, East, Knock, More and Troup Heads.

The drying old harbour was built in 1692 with stones laid vertically by Patrick Ogilvie, Lord Boyne, for fishing and for marble export, the latter including cargoes to France, not least two of the chimneys for the Palace de Versailles. The Old Star Inn of 1727 has an arch which led to a previously cobbled courtyard which was a smuggling centre. The new harbour was built in 1825 by Lord Seafield and rebuilt in 1839 after it was breached in a storm. It imported coal, seed grain, iron and salt, exporting grain, herring, salmon and timber, and is still used by crab and lobster boats. In the 1880s the steep railway line serving the harbour was closed. A Saltire Award was received for the restoration work on the 17th and 18th century harbour warehouses and tenement houses refurb-

ished for accommodation, a precursor for subsequent docklands projects elsewhere. A prominent local business is Portsoy Marble and Pottery, based in the late 18th century Category A Corf House, polishing local red and green marble, the green serpentine coming from the Breeks. A 1.2GW electricity cable is being installed across the Moray Firth from Noss Head. A recent development has been the Scottish Traditional Boats Festival which includes a race to Sandend where each boat picks up a creel of smoked fish, returning to Portsoy where it is cooked on the pier. There are 50 traditional sailing boats, models, vintage commercial vehicles, boatbuilding, creel and net, lace, clootie rug, quilt and basket making, coopering, knot tying, fish filleting, knitting, wood turning, weaving, crochet and embroidery, music, dancing, drama, street theatre and jugglers.

Cowhythe Head is composed of crystallized limestone which has been used in nearby limekilns. By Boyne Bay is the ruin of Boyne Castle, an Ogilvie stronghold of about 1580. To the south lies a disused airfield.

Whitehills developed around a sheltered fishing harbour which has 300m of quays and a mark. It is the smallest northeast village to retain its own fishing fleet and daily fishmarket, dealing in cod, haddock, sole, plaice and whiting. Red Well was built by the Romans and in the 19th century it became fashionable to take the waters from the chalybeate spring.

Streams flow east from HW Dover −0130 and west from HW Dover +0430 at up to 1km/h.

Behind the cemetery in the centre, Boyndie Bay has the remains of an ancient church. Reefs at the west end of the bay break in deep water on bigger swells and there is a long right reefbreak at the east end of the bay which works best at mid tides in low to medium surf but through to high water on bigger swells. There are two caravan sites behind the bay and a children's playground at the west end.

Banff at the end of the A97 takes its name from the Gaelic banbha, a sucking pig. In the 12th century it was a Hanseatic trading port but silted up in the 19th century and now dries. It has 500m of quays but is exposed to northeasterly winds, the sea breaking a long way out with a moderate breeze. Banff Bay is shallow and exposed to the north with a groundswell even during an offshore wind. It sets to the east, especially with a northerly wind. The eastgoing stream starts at HW Dover −0130, changing slowly from northeast to east southeast. The westgoing stream starts at HW Dover +0430 at up to 1km/h, changing slowly from southwest to west northwest. The River Deveron results in shifting sands and undercurrents with lefts breaking over a sandy rock reef onto the rivermouth on all tides. The river is crossed by the A98 on a seven arched bridge of 1772–9 by John Smeaton. Beyond are a golf course, woodland walk and Duff House, built in Italianate Georgian baroque style for Lord Braco between 1725 and 1740 by William Adam, later a hotel, a sanitorium then used for Second World War accommodation for captured German merchant naval officers, now part of the National Gallery of Scotland. Following a refit with decorations in period style, it has 17th to 19th century works of art including Baekhuysen's Shipping in a Choppy Sea. The Temple of Venus is a fantastically designed building and there is no shortage of Greek columns, crowstepped gables, Venetian windows and delicate steeples around. Georgian buildings result from when this was a fashionable winter resort. The town's museum, the oldest north of Perth, features Banff silver, arms and armour, local history, natural history, geology and 18th century astronomer James Ferguson. Bowls, tennis and the MacDuff distillery add to the entertainments.

In 1700 noted fiddler and Robin Hood style thief James Macpherson was hanged in Banff when the clock was put forward before his reprieve could be delivered. He is said to have written and played the stirring *Mac-*

pherson's Rant on the gallows and then broken the fiddle to prevent it from being played after his death. The Clan Macpherson Museum in Newtonmore claims to have the instrument.

Across the river is **Macduff**, which is noted for its sunsets. Begun in 1786, the fishing harbour with 400m of quays, fishmarket and 11m white lighthouse is partly protected, even from the west, and is also engaged in some coastal trade. Fishing nets are made for deep sea trawlers and others. The port is the start or finish each year for the North Sea Yacht Race to or from Stavanger. Landmarks include a war memorial and a church with a domed tower. In front of the golf course to the east of the town is a break in the cliffs which leads in to a group of four paddling and swimming pools, a playground and a rock arch in the form of an inverted V.

Thirty metre cliffs of indented slate containing limestone bands are to be found to Head of Garness, after which the cliffs increase in height to More Head, which is 140m high.

At the southern corner of Gamrie Bay, built above a ravine in 1513 to commemorate a victory over the invading Danes in 1004, is St John's church, now ruins. It faces Gardenstown where the drying fishing harbour has 500m of quays, exposed to swell from northeasterly winds but protected from the northwest by the 7m high Craig Dagerty ridge.

Crovie, with its pier and a slip, is beyond a picnic area. Much of the beach is inaccessible from the road as the houses hug the slope, built with ends towards the sea for protection from the weather.

Cliffs 110m high continue to the 112m vertical Troup Head with guillemots, gulls and gannets nesting on the cliffs around Collis Head in their thousands and black guillemots, puffins, kittiwakes, shags and cormorants all present, not to mention sea urchins.

Between Lion's Head and Cullykhan Bay are the Hell's Lum chasm, Fiddes Fort and a cave.

The fishing village of Pennan has some surf and was formerly used for smuggling. Uniquely, the telephone box on the front is a listed historical monument, playing a central role in the film *Local Hero*, much of which was shot here.

Dry arch to the east of Macduff.

More Head with Troup Head in the distance.

Pennan Head is 110m high and is subject to violent downdraughts with offshore winds but with plenty of seabird colonies. The purple cliffs continue 120m high to Strahangles Point, hiding the radio masts on Windyheads Hill. The red sandstone cliffs run on to New Aberdour with holes through the base and a very large arch. At one point there is a bird hide but it would be equally suitable for watching the seals.

There is parking by the beach nearest New Aberdour in an area where there are many spring flowers. The 10th century church of St Drostan was founded at the centre of the original village, one of the oldest in the north of Scotland although the modern village is further inland.

Many of Crovie's houses are built end on to the weather.

Pennan has its houses tucked away at the foot of cliffs.

Distance
54km from Spey Bay to New Aberdour

OS 1:50,000 Sheets
27 Nairn & Forres
28 Elgin & Dufftown
30 Fraserburgh

Tidal Constants
Buckie:
HW Dover +0040,
LW Dover +0050
Cullen:
Dover +0050
Whitehills:
HW Dover +0050,
LW Dover +0100
Banff:
Dover + 0100
Gardenstown:
HW Dover +0100,
LW Dover +0110

Sea Area
Cromarty

Landing fish, gas and oil

I go North to cold, to home, to Kinnaird,
Fit monument for our time.
This is the outermost edge of Buchan.
George Bruce

There are several large caves and arches in New Aberdour's red sandstone with channels into them through the rock shelf as the tide rises. East of here there are blue mica cliffs, decreasing in height towards Rosehearty, with oystercatchers, eider ducks, black guillemots, blackheaded gulls, cormorants, fulmars, gannets, seals and starfish.

Dundarg Castle ruin and a fort are located at the end of the rock shelf. There is a dovecote tower at Quarry Head and a control tower near the picnic tables by **Rosehearty**, looking out towards the former bombing range.

Rosehearty was founded in the 14th century by shipwrecked Danes, is one of the oldest fishing villages in Scotland and is accessed by the B9031. Entry is difficult with onshore winds and there is a shorebreak. Features of the village include a seawater swimming pool, golf course and 19th century Mounthooley Doocot.

To the south of the village are a radio mast, the ruin of Pittulie Castle and, almost between them, the ruin of Pitsligo Castle. This castle was built in 1424 by the Frasers of Philorth, the 4th and last Earl Pitsligo being generous to the poor and successfully evading arrest after the 1745 uprising. It became a stronghold of the Forbes family.

The coast beyond Rosehearty begins low and sandy, backed by dunes, but becomes more rocky towards Sandhaven.

Sandhaven was a fishing village but the harbour is disused, having been badly battered in 1953. Sandhaven Meal Mill survived longer. It worked for two centuries until 1981. Wiseman's barrel surf break is on the west side while Phingask, West Point and Broadsea follow on to Kinnaird Head, Broadsea being particularly testing, surf

Scotland's oldest lighthouse and its smaller replacement.

Fishing boats back at base in Fraserburgh Harbour.

being best in the spring. From Sandhaven to Fraserburgh, at the end of the A90, the coast is rocky and has drying ledges that are frequented by seals and blackheaded gulls and other birds.

Kinnaird Head is 20m high, topped by a 10m white lighthouse tower on top of a 1570 castle by Sir Alexander Fraser, after whom **Fraserburgh** was named in 1592. Scotland's first lighthouse was added in 1787 and attached to it is the Museum of Scottish Lighthouses. Also close by is the three storey Wine Tower which has no floors and the purpose of which is unknown despite the name. The 2°W line of longitude is here, this being the one with which the National Grid is aligned.

A 21m lighthouse is built on Balaclava Pier, part of the major fishing harbour and fishmarket at Fraserburgh, Europe's largest shellfish port. Some 3km of quays service the large fishing fleet, import coal, lime, iron, timber and salt and export oats, potatoes, pickled herrings and preserves. Surfers enjoy a left break at the harbour wall and kitesurfing is popular. Inside, there is a tight turn to port for fishing boats, particularly difficult with a southerly wind.

A room in the library is devoted to the work of Thomas Blake Glover who spent his childhood here, commissioned one of the first warships for the Japanese navy and helped found what became the Mitsubishi corporation. A 17th century Mercat Cross is unique in having pre and post union royal arms of Scotland.

Along the back of Fraserburgh Bay dunes up to 30m high ashelter a golf course and the B9033 while a good beachbreak may be found in front, perhaps with jellyfish for added interest. At the east end of the bay the Water of Philorth enters from the direction of the restored Cairnbulg Castle or, in the distance, Mormond Hill with its array of NATO aerials.

Cairnbulg Briggs is a drying rock ledge, marked by an 8m light on Cairnbulg Point which resembles an oil rig from the distance. Cairnbulg is a fishing village with a harbour built in 1987.

Rock ledges and shoals continue to Inzie Head. **Inverallochy** is a fishing village at the end of the B9107. It still lacks a harbour but has surf.

Whitelinks Bay has a wreck offshore and a golf course and aerial on land. St Combs is another harbourless fishing village with surf and 18th century cottages and the remains of a church dedicated to St Columba, hence the village name. The Tufted Duck hotel has a name to appeal to all of its customers, mostly birdlovers and bird shooters. Inland is Inverallochy Castle ruin.

A ridge runs 2km east from Inzie Head then dunes begin and then continue all the way to Peterhead with a beachbreak as far as Rattray Head. Halfway down the beach a stream discharges from the 2km² Loch of Strathbeg in a 9km² RSPB nature reserve. It is on the migration routes to Iceland and Scandinavia. Hides look onto fresh and saltwater marshes and dune slack pools in one of the most important wildfowl havens in Britain, especially in the spring and autumn. It is a major breeding centre for geese and otters and a roost for large numbers of wildfowl in winter including whooper swans, greylag geese, mallards, wigeon, pochard, tufted ducks, goldeneyes, goosanders and pinkfooted geese. In summer there are great crested grebes, eider ducks and breeding terns. Some 2,000 greylag and pinkfooted geese and 600 whooper swans roost in autumn and birds on passage include green sandpipers, mute swans and marsh harriers. In all there are 40,000 birds present per year. Around

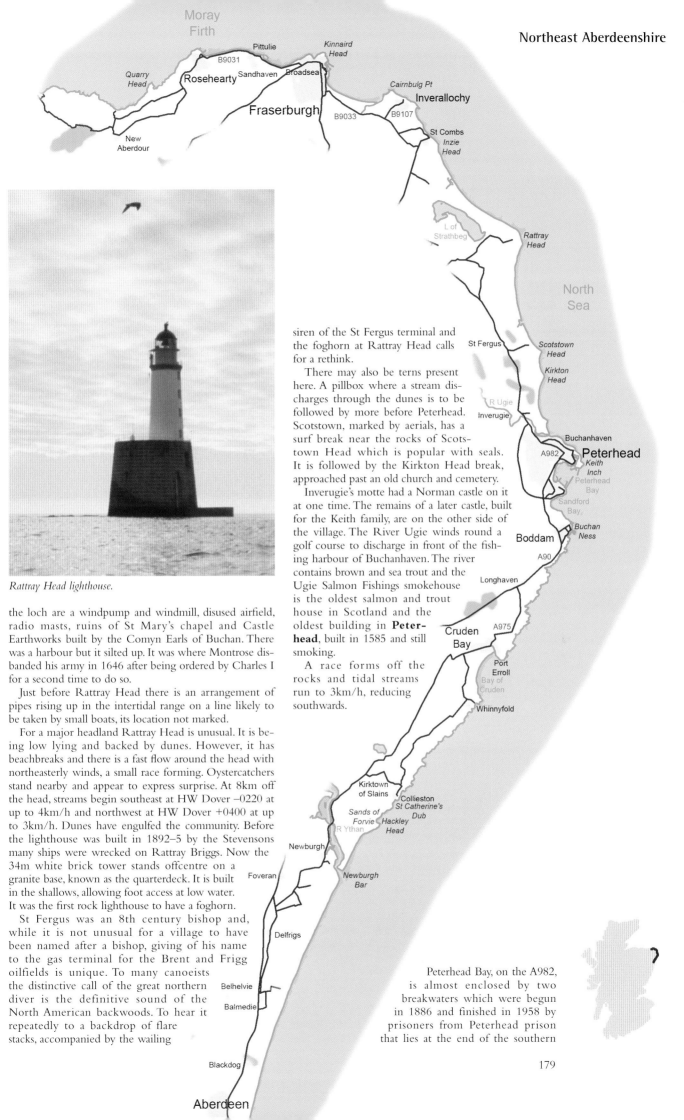

Rattray Head lighthouse.

the loch are a windpump and windmill, disused airfield, radio masts, ruins of St Mary's chapel and Castle Earthworks built by the Comyn Earls of Buchan. There was a harbour but it silted up. It was where Montrose disbanded his army in 1646 after being ordered by Charles I for a second time to do so.

Just before Rattray Head there is an arrangement of pipes rising up in the intertidal range on a line likely to be taken by small boats, its location not marked.

For a major headland Rattray Head is unusual. It is being low lying and backed by dunes. However, it has beachbreaks and there is a fast flow around the head with northeasterly winds, a small race forming. Oystercatchers stand nearby and appear to express surprise. At 8km off the head, streams begin southeast at HW Dover −0220 at up to 4km/h and northwest at HW Dover +0400 at up to 3km/h. Dunes have engulfed the community. Before the lighthouse was built in 1892–5 by the Stevensons many ships were wrecked on Rattray Briggs. Now the 34m white brick tower stands offcentre on a granite base, known as the quarterdeck. It is built in the shallows, allowing foot access at low water. It was the first rock lighthouse to have a foghorn.

St Fergus was an 8th century bishop and, while it is not unusual for a village to have been named after a bishop, giving of his name to the gas terminal for the Brent and Frigg oilfields is unique. To many canoeists the distinctive call of the great northern diver is the definitive sound of the North American backwoods. To hear it repeatedly to a backdrop of flare stacks, accompanied by the wailing

siren of the St Fergus terminal and the foghorn at Rattray Head calls for a rethink.

There may also be terns present here. A pillbox where a stream discharges through the dunes is to be followed by more before Peterhead. Scotstown, marked by aerials, has a surf break near the rocks of Scotstown Head which is popular with seals. It is followed by the Kirkton Head break, approached past an old church and cemetery.

Inverugie's motte had a Norman castle on it at one time. The remains of a later castle, built for the Keith family, are on the other side of the village. The River Ugie winds round a golf course to discharge in front of the fishing harbour of Buchanhaven. The river contains brown and sea trout and the Ugie Salmon Fishings smokehouse is the oldest salmon and trout house in Scotland and the oldest building in **Peterhead**, built in 1585 and still smoking.

A race forms off the rocks and tidal streams run to 3km/h, reducing southwards.

Peterhead Bay, on the A982, is almost enclosed by two breakwaters which were begun in 1886 and finished in 1958 by prisoners from Peterhead prison that lies at the end of the southern

Flare stacks and other columns are part of the St Fergus gas terminal behind the dunes.

The dune shoreline at Scotstown Head.

1.2km² bay seems to be a vast empty area when viewed from outside the breakwaters.

The town itself is built of pink granite from Boddam. The Arbuthnot Museum of the 1890s has a local trader's Arctic wildlife and covers whaling and seal fishing, herring, Arctic and Inuit, local history, photographic and coin displays. The Peterhead Maritime Heritage Museum tells about the region's whalers, fishermen, sailors and navigators. In front of the Town House is a statue of Field Marshal James Keith, a favourite general of Frederick

The large Peterhead Bay with oil industry supply vessels and Europe's largest fish market.

Buchan Ness, together with its lighthouse and bridge over the dry channel.

Sheltered channels among rocky islets at Dundonnie.

breakwater. In 1715 the Jacobite King James had landed here for his uprising.

Britain's principal fishing port is Peterhead Harbour. It has one of Europe's busiest fishmarkets, up to 400 boats and 14,000 boxes of fish per day, and was the principal whaling port. Basking shark fisherman Tex Geddes was born here. Cook Annie in Nevil Shute's *Requiem for a Wren* had worked in the herring industry here before emigrating to Australia. The port also deals in grain, fertilizers, coal and limestone with a total of 2km of quays. Peterhead Bay Harbour is a supply base for the North Sea oilfield and has a tanker jetty to import fuel. The

the Great, the statue being presented by William I of Prussia. Other notable buildings include from the pre-Reformation the Old St Peter's church and Kirkburn Mills which made wool and woollen cloth. Keith Inch is the most easterley point on the Scottish mainland.

Sandford Bay has surf, best at mid tide. It has a large modern power station, its high chimney a prominent landmark but not enough of a landmark to prevent a wreck being deposited on the Skerry directly in front of it.

The pink granite fishing village of **Boddam** is surrounded by rocks on which seals haul out and around which eider ducks swim. The 36m lighthouse on Buchan Ness was built in 1827 by Robert Stevenson and had the fastest revolving reflectors when built. The ness is linked to the mainland by a bridge but at most states of the tide there is solid rock beneath the bridge and no passage for boats.

Red granite cliffs up to 73m high stretch down the coast as far as Bay of Cruden with Cave o' Meakie and other caves, arches, stacks and blowholes. A castle site is just south of Boddam. Seals and moon jellyfish frequent Dundonnie and Long Haven is an important seabird colony, from where the 1.4GW North Connect high voltage DC cables will run for 665km to Sima on Norway's Hardangerfjord. There are innumerable seabirds at the Bullers of Buchan (the name coming from boil), a cauldron hollowed out by the sea to a depth of 60m and entered by boat by Boswell and Dr Johnson during their Scottish tour in 1773.

This pair also visited Slains Castle, built in 1597. In the 17th century it was extended and rebuilt by the 9th Earl of Erroll and became the centre of a tourist boom in Edwardian times when the railway arrived, being partly demolished in 1925 when interest waned. The most important visitor was the Port Erroll holidaymaker Bram Stoker who saw the castle and was inspired to use it as the setting for *Dracula*. In 1862 inky black rain fell in an easterly storm all along this coast, never explained satisfactorily.

Fish nets are staked out at various points on this part of the coast. Bay of Cruden is surrounded by dunes and the inevitable golf course. There is a powerful break which works best in the winter. In 1997 a school of seven sperm whales were washed up. Port Erroll is the harbour for **Cruden Bay** on the A975, located at the mouth of the Water of Cruden and home to lobster fishing boats.

The skerries of the Skares signal the start of another run of rocky cliffs as far as Hackley Head. Whinnyfold has an important seabird colony. It is the landfall point for oil and gas pipelines from the Forties field with 40% of the UK's production for onward overland passage to Grangemouth. Cave Arthur lies to the south of the village.

Off Mains of Slains is Broad Haven (which lies north of North Broad Haven), on the south side of which is the ruin of the old Slains Castle, destroyed by James VI when he discovered the Earl of Erroll was involved in a plot to land Spanish troops. The castle has been further ruined by the construction of a three storey chalet in front of it.

Caves to the north of Colliston were used by smugglers from the fishing village. St Catherine's Dub was named after the Spanish galleon *Santa Catherina* which was wrecked in 1594. This was the holiday destination for TE Lawrence, perhaps attracted by the area to the south, one of the largest dune systems in Britain, undisturbed but shifting, a miniature Arabia. A continuous sweep of 20km of beach runs down to Aberdeen, mostly backed by dunes up to 60m high. The dunes, which have overwhelmed Iron Age and medieval settlements in the last two millennia, now form the 10km^2 Forvie National Nature Reserve. Forvie church ruin is all that remains of the village of Forvie, probably overwhelmed during a nine day gale in 1688. The Forvie Centre near Sand Loch has information on the wide range of fauna and flora. This is an important feeding ground for wildfowl and waders and the 2,000 pairs of eiders form the largest breeding colony in Britain for the species. Common, Arctic, little and Sandwich terns all breed and there are 50 species of bird and 60 species of plant in the area. The beach has many shells and the nets suggest that the sea provides stocks of salmon.

Newburgh is near the mouth of the River Ythan with a harbour, Udney Links golf course, an annual raft race and windsurfing. The channel position constantly changes over the Newburgh Bar but beachbreaks can be found.

Tank traps line Foveran Links to the south of the river and pillboxes are seen at intervals.

A coastal vessel was wrecked off Menie Links and surf breaks continue from here to the River Don, north of Aberdeen. At Delfrigs is the Trump International Golf Links, expected to lose its SSSI status as the formerly dynamic dunes, moving at up to 11m/year, are now static.

Slains Castle, the ruin inspiring Bram Stoker to write Dracula.

Balmedie has a country park with picnic site, barbecue stands and visitor displays on the shipwrecks, wildlife and dunes and their conservation. Behind are Pleistocene hills of water rounded gravel, sand and clay. Beachbreaks are found here and at Blackdog. A range creates a danger area out to sea at Blackdog, marked by yellow buoys 2km off the coast.

Hackley Bay, the last outcrops before the beach to Aberdeen.

In 1871 the Ordnance Survey set out a baseline from Belhelvie to Blue Hill, south of Aberdeen. The length was computed from a baseline at Hounslow. When the 8km line was measured it was found to be in error by about 80mm. By coincidence, the two baselines are near to what have become Britain's two busiest airports, Heathrow and Dyce, the latter being unusual in having mostly helicopter traffic heading for the rigs, as is only too obvious to anyone on this coast.

As the only rock for 20km, Blackdog Rock is small but distinctive. Just to the north is the mouth of the Blackdog Burn, fished by a heron. A track comes down to the shore where submarine cables land and it might also be a place for small boats to land.

Blackdog range and the dunes reaching into the distance.

Distance
76km from New
Aberdour to Blackdog

OS 1:50,000 Sheets
30 Fraserburgh
38 Aberdeen

Tidal Constants
Gardenstown:
HW Dover +0100,
LW Dover +0110
Fraserburgh:
HW Dover +0110,
LW Dover +0100
Peterhead:
Dover +0140
Aberdeen:
Dover +0220

Sea Area
Cromarty

Range
Blackdog

37 Southeast Aberdeenshire

As the waves lash the platform and soak us with spray,
The rig seems to twist in the teeth of the gale.
Our fumbling fingers just get in the way
But the drill never stops as we cling to the rail.
When we flew out this morning with three weeks to go
Even Aberdeen's granite seemed warm to our eyes,
Each thinking how bitter these northern winds blow,
Unwilling recruits only trying to get by.
It's hard working away, working away.
Alistair Russell

The beach crosses over from Aberdeenshire to Aberdeen at Blackdog and continues south past golf courses at Balgownie and **Bridge of Don**, the latter carrying the A956 in front of an exhibition centre. Standing off the beach are 11 wind turbines, including the world's two most powerful at 8.8MW, 204m high with 80m blades.

The River Don or Deen, in dialect, may formerly have entered the sea east of Seaton Park or joined the River Dee near to the harbour. A sharp demarcation line can be seen in the fickle currents at the mouth of the Don where peaty brown river water meets the blue green sea. Just occasionally the surf can be worthwhile here but the rivermouth can be dangerous.

The Donmouth nature reserve has a hide and the waters contain flounders, eels and mackerel. Dolphins, seals, eider ducks, guillemots and cormorants might be seen in the area.

Aberdeen is Scotland's third largest city, its high

rise skyline fronted by a 3km promenade and a beach of groynes, off which there is surfing, especially at the southern end. The Granite City takes its nickname from the by law which has required all buildings to have granite fronts, supporting local quarrying interests. Most buildings are built completely of the grey granite with mica flecks. These include Marischal College, the world's second largest granite building, formerly part of Aberdeen University but now the city's council headquarters on the university's exodus to the Old Aberdeen King's campus. In 1717 Colin Maclaurin was elected professor of mathematics at the age of 19. In John Hadfield's *Love on a Branch Line* Professor Pollux was revealed to have been no more than an Aberdeen University clerk. Dugald Dalgetty of Drumthwacket in *A Legend of Montrose* quoted more than anybody from his student days at Marischal. The quadrangle of 1836–44 buildings includes the newer Mitchell Tower. Despite the size of the building and its 1km distance from the open sea, its tower has been measured to rise and fall 20mm with the tide.

The city is Scotland's largest resort and a frequent winner of the Britain in Bloom competition with roses, crocuses, daffodils and other spring flowers in profusion despite the latitude. A 1994 party to celebrate Union Street's bicentenary attracted 100,000 people. Aberdonians have often been the most generous supporters in Britain of student charity activities despite a reputation for meanness. The city produced annual *Aberdeen Almanacks*, early comprehensive reference manuals. Montrose brought an army in 1644 to sack the town. Along the front are the King's Links golf course and several amusement centres. The Beach Leisure Centre has a sports hall, climbing wall, pool, flumes, Linx ice area, skating, ice hockey, disco and curling. Codona's Amusement Park claims to be Scotland's largest funfair. Times have changed since Lord Byron was resident as a youth. Beach replenishment has used 70,000m³ of sand brought from Montrose. The North Pier was designed by Smeaton and built in 1774–80 to intersect sand drifting south into the mouth of the River Dee and to scour away the sandbar. It was extended by Telford from 1811 and again by Cay later in the century. South Breakwater repeats work by Telford and Cay. Aberdeen harbour, off the estuary of the Dee, is one of the largest fishing ports in Britain with a large fishmarket and is the main base for the North Sea oil industry. A modern marine operations centre overlooks the harbour, which was exporting fish, hides and wood to England and Europe in the 13th century. Fortunately, the city seems to have lost much of its 1970s oil town Americanism. It has also lost the mermaids who were heard singing hymns around the estuary several times in 1688. Perhaps these were seals. There is vehicle ferry traffic to Lerwick, Stromness, the Faeroes and

The world's most powerful wind turbines.

Oil industry vessels mostly anchored off Aberdeen.

An oil industry vessel leaves the mouth of the Dee.

Bergen. Footdee is the fishing village designed in 1808/9 with input from the fisherfolk.

One of the boats built here was the tall ship *Malcolm Miller* in the late 1960s, the city having given its name to the Aberdeen clippers in the 19th century. The Tall Ships Race has since visited the harbour. In Frederick Marryat's *Frank Mildmay; or the Naval Officer* boatswain's mate Thompson was an Aberdonian. This was a centre of activity in *Eye of the Needle*.

Flow in the Dee may reach 11km/h and there can be an outward flow even on a flood tide. Entry between the two breakwaters can be difficult over the bar, especially with easterly winds which can also produce significant clapotis off the southern breakwater, inside of which is a surf break.

The lighthouse on Girdle Ness was built in 1832 by Robert Stevenson as a round tower 40m high that is now visible for 36km. It was the only one in Scotland to have been fitted with two fixed lights, the lower 21m below the upper one. The minaret shape includes cast iron work with birds and animals. There is a race off the point on the southgoing stream. Streams flow southeast from HW Dover −0230 and northwest from HW Dover +0330 at up to 6km/h, staying strong close inshore.

Nigg Bay is the possible former mouth of the River Dee and is being developed as Aberdeen South Harbour. Boulder clay at the northern end of the head of the bay is covered with glacial sands and gravels. Some morainic material further south includes erratics in drift brought from Belhelvie, Boddam, Strathmore, Deeside and Oslo. On the north side of the bay St Fittick's church was granted by William the Lion to the abbey of Arbroath. The bay was used for saltmaking and lay below the gaze of the Torry Battery. Oil rigs have been anchored in the bay and to the southeast of Greg Ness, above which aerials are prominent. Deposited boulders create a reef with impressive surf.

The cliffs are almost continuous from here to Inverbervie with Stonehaven the only major break. To Garron Point they are almost vertical with mica slate over granite. Running along the edge of the cliffs is the Aberdeen to King's Cross railway line as far as Stonehaven, seen several times in the form of viaducts over clefts. Behind the railway the A90 is close for much of the way but remains hidden from the sea.

At Bridge of One Hair there is a layer of red Strathmore boulder clay with quartzite and lava to add to the geographical jumble.

Above Doonies Yawns is Crab's Cairn, a picnic site and a model farm with rare breeds, Clydesdales, cattle, sheep, pigs and Shetland ponies.

Caves are found in the cliffs, on top of which is Altens industrial estate where many of the oil industry support companies have their premises.

Cove Bay has a well sheltered harbour with fishing boats pulled up on the beach and hanks of rope hanging up to dry. There is moraine material to the northwest and more Strathmore drift from the south with signs of glacial polish on the rocks.

There are quarries at Hare Ness and Blowup Nose, the latter name suggesting blasting operations. Between them the coast returns from Aberdeen to Aberdeenshire.

Findon recalls Finnan haddies, haddock lightly smoked over cottage fires until the 19th century when legislation was used to stop the industry and allowed it to be moved to Aberdeen smokehouses while the village nearly died. Portlethen village, separate from the much larger modern community of **Portlethen**, was formerly a fishing village working off the beach.

Stones set on a hillside at **Newtonhill** were from a former breakwater when this was a busy fishing port. The boats sitting on the beach at the mouth of the Burn of Elsick suggest that the steep hillside would have made access to the harbour somewhat inconvenient on a regular basis.

Muchalls castle has some fine 17th century architecture with notable plasterwork in the Great Hall, the Burnett coat of arms and fine fireplaces. There was a tunnel to the Gin Shore that was used by smugglers until it was blocked in the 19th century.

Garron Point is the distinctive end of the Highland Boundary Fault which runs right across Scotland to Bute. Brown dolomitic rock can be seen dividing the Highland Border from the Precambrian rocks. Below the golf course. Craigeven Bay has cut into the older rocks, exposing spilites, red jaspers and black shales with Cambrian fossils, dipping steeply north but leaving the Highland Border rocks at each end. The ruined chapel of St Mary & St Nathalan was built by the shore.

Cowie is a fishing village based around a weathered quartz porphyry dyke through sandstone. The village replaces a previous royal burgh created by David I but burned down in 1645 on the orders of the Duke of Montrose, a Royalist supporter in the Civil War.

Stonehaven Bay has streams to 2km/h where lion's mane and moon jellyfish swim. At the northern end of Stonehaven, Cowie Water descends under Glenury Viaduct as the railway heads away inland.

Stonehaven is where the B979 meets the A957, the name coming from the Old English Stanehythe, stone wharf. Stonehaven's harbour is built at the mouth of the Carron Water although the town occupies the space between the two rivers. Few fishing boats remain in the harbour, unlike the hundred herring boats at the end of the 19th century, but the resort does have some yachts. The Stonehaven Tolbooth Museum is located in a 16th century storehouse that belonged to the Earls Marischal but was later used as a prison. Three Episcopal ministers were incarcerated in 1748 for breaking post Culloden laws which banned them from holding services for more than 5 people but they were still able to baptize babies passed in through the windows to them. The museum also has displays of fishing, local history and archaeology and a set of seven hole stocks.

A notable event is the Fireball, a festival with origins lost in time but undoubtedly relating to the Vikings. As the church clock strikes midnight to announce the New Year, about a score of fireballs are lit. These are wire cages each about the size of a pillow on a wire handle, stuffed with pitch and other inflammable materials. The bearers walk up and down the main street, swinging the fireballs around their heads until they burn out after about 20 minutes. By this time the crowds are melting away and the more sociable have given up trying to share their flasks with supervising policemen.

The cliffs are of coarse conglomerate from Downie

Dunnottar Castle, steeped in history on the cliffs to the south of Stonehaven.

Rocks impersonate a submarine below the village at Catterline.

A lighthouse marks Todhead Point which is quite insignificant on a map.

Point to Craig David. Birds find no problem gripping, this although they leave it in a much more soiled state than would be the case with fine grained rocks.

A war memorial above Strathleven Bay consists of a deliberately unfinished circle of pillars and pediments to represent the unfinished lives.

In the 5th century the site 50m vertically above Castle Haven was fortified for St Ninian. Dunnottar Castle was built in the 14th century and visited by Mary, Queen of Scots, in 1562, when it was like a fortified village. In 1645 the 7th Earl Marischal, a Covenanter, retreated inside at the approach of the Royalists under the Duke of Montrose who could not get in and so burned the earl's lands instead. The Scottish crown jewels were lowered to a fishwife when Cromwell attacked in 1651. She carried them past the Roundheads to safety in Kinneff church. During Monmouth's rebellion of 1685 122 men and 45 women Covenanters were locked in the Whigs Vault, a 5m x 16m room, for several months, during which many of them died. The original ridge of land from the shore was cut through by the defenders for extra security. These days iis in a ruined state but was used by Zeffirelli for his filming of *Hamlet*.

There are aerials on the top of the cliffs. The occasional blackbacked gull gives way to increasing numbers of gulls nesting on the cliffs, cliffs with caves in the conglomerate. A blowhole has diverted the Crawton Burn eastwards to form a fall over the cliff at Trollochy. Fowlsheugh (birds cliff) is an RSPB seabird colony, one of the largest mainland seabird colonies with 30,000 kittiwakes, 30,000 guillemots and hundreds of razorbills, fulmars, herring gulls, shags, puffins and eiders breeding between April and July.

Cliffs change from grey to deep red brown at the village of Crawton, largely abandoned. Three basalt lava fingers containing quartz and agates, the lower central flow with angular columns, run into the sea between Lower Old Red Sandstone and there are eroded conglomerates in the bays, dipping gently west. Rock platforms and stacks add to the geological interest.

Catterline has a pier and is frequented by seals, terns and artists. A maroon outcrop in front of the village has the oversize silhouette of a submarine.

Todhead Point has 15m cliffs topped by a 13m white lighthouse tower with many nesting birds. It seems to be another place which is not significant enough to justify a lighthouse even though the following red cliffs, the Slainges, are quite impressive. Whistleberry Castle remains are close to the cliffs while at Shieldhill the cliffs overhang the sea. The 137m high Bervie Brow, a radio tower on top, brings the cliffs to an end. King's Step is where David II and his wife, Johanna, were driven ashore

Reefs run out into the sea at Milton of Mathers.

in a storm after escaping the English while returning from a nine year exile in France.

Inverbervie is at the back of Bervie Bay where Bervie Water enters and there can be surf. The village has a seafood factory and also a jute mill. Hallgreen Castle is by the shore.

From here to Milton Ness there are grassy slopes to a foreshore which was wide enough to take a railway from Montrose, now dismantled. There is stiff black shelly clay and a fairly continuous rock platform with reefs running out into the sea at right angles with inconvenient regularity.

Gourdon has a fishing harbour which can only be entered in moderate weather but is a village which looks better from the land than the sea, the latter vista being of a rather rundown and industrial community. On the hill behind it has a long cairn and fort.

Mill of Benholm is a working mill that is set on a stream with a waterwheel and a selection of farm animals. The stream leads down to Haughs Bay.

The most notable building when seen from the water is Lathallan School, set in trees at Johnshaven which is a lobster fishing village. The village has a drying harbour and surf over reefs.

Ruined cottages, new chalets and a shoreline caravan park mark Milton of Mathers. A stream flows down to the water through Den Finella, named after a 10th century queen who killed her husband, King Kenneth, and then threw herself down a 12m waterfall.

The rock platform comes to an end at Milton Ness. Tangleha is a small harbour, at low tide reached through a narrow break in a reef, when the route up to the beach is silty at first.

The small harbour approached through the rocks at Tangleha.

Distance
55km from Blackdog
to Tangleha

OS 1:50,000 Sheets
38 Aberdeen
45 Stonehaven
& Banchory

Tidal Constants
Aberdeen:
Dover +0220
Stonehaven:
Dover +0230
Inverbervie:
Dover +0300
Montrose:
HW Dover +0320

Sea Areas
Cromarty, Forth

38 Angus

A surfeit of sand

Beautiful town of Montrose, near by the seaside,
With your fine shops and streets so wide.
'Tis health for the people that in you reside,
Because they do inhale the pure fragrant air,
Emanating from the pure salt wave and shrubberies growing there
William Topaz McGonagall

Tangleha is left past Milton Ness which is the end of the rock platform for the time being. Montrose Bay eats into the hillside with a castle site at the end of the bay, the 70m high cliffs below the Heughs of St Cyrus, the spire of one of St Cyrus' two churches prominent.

The River North Esk acts as the boundary between Aberdeenshire and Angus but first comes a marsh lagoon and the St Cyrus National Nature Reserve with a marine life tank and over 300 plant species including clustered bellflower and wild liquorice. Birdlife ranges from herons, cormorants, oystercatchers and eider ducks to terns, fulmars and gannets at this end of the bay.

An 8km sweep of dunes run to **Montrose** with two golf links, used by the Royal Montrose Golf Club and four others. It is one of the oldest courses but no longer with its original 25 holes, before cranes take over. Montrose is a commercial and fishing port which has become an oilfield supply base and now includes the Montrose Fire & Emergency Training Centre for offshore workers. From the 13th century it was a seaport, exporting skins and hides and importing timber and flax. The Old Pretender departed from here after the failure of the 1715 rebellion. In 1746 the *Hazard* fired her 60 guns and 24 swivel guns on the town for 72 hours before being captured by the Jacobites and renamed *Le Prince Charles*. Montrose Museum covers local maritime and natural history, local art, Pictish stones, Montrose silver and pottery, whaling artefacts and Napoleonic items including a copy of the emperor's death mask. For heads of the Royal Family and sculptures the William Lamb Memorial Studio is the place to go.

The shoreline changes abruptly with the River South Esk which discharges through the large Montrose Basin and out through the dredged channel which can have breakers to the end of the dredged section even when there is calm weather. Streams run in the channel when the Annat Bank is dry but spread out over the bank as the tide floods, weakening at the outer end. The ebb sets south across the harbour entrance from HW Dover −0300 and sets north from HW Dover +0320 at up to 13km/h, heavy rain and snowmelt decreasing the flood and increasing the ebb. The drift direction reversed in 1991, the beach having now scoured back to its 1940 line, exposing antitank blocks and barbed wire.

The lighthouse on Scurdie Ness at the mouth of the River South Esk, Montrose.

The limekiln on Boddin Point.

Red Castle on the right breaks the skyline of dunes above Lunan Bay.

A tall lighthouse is located on Scurdie Ness and daymarks edge the southern side of the channel. The Gaelic monadh ros means moor on the promontory. The rock platform now begins again, the haunt of blackheaded gull and curlew. The lifeboat used to be housed in a tower at Mains of Usan.

Those who suffer pink elephants need to be wary of a red one. Elephant Rock is an extrusion which has been sculpted to give a trunk and legs.

An apparent castle on Boddin Point is a massive lime-kiln which was used to prepare fertilizer for the farmland. These days it is surrounded by drying salmon fishing nets in the midst of waters with cod and lobsters. Agates may be found on the rocks. A real castle is Dunninald Castle, up the hill and hidden beyond the Aberdeen to King's Cross railway which runs along the cliffs for 3km, crossing Black Jack and another chasm on high viaducts.

A fort and monument begin Lunan Bay which is backed by dunes and catches surf but the distinctive feature is the tottering ruin of Red Castle which stands on the bank of Lunan Water at the centre of the bay. It was probably built in the 15th century to replace an earlier fort constructed by Walter de Berkeley for William the Lion and given to Hugh, 6th Earl of Ross, by Robert the Bruce in 1328. The current structure has been a ruin since 1770.

The rocky shoreline recommences at Ethie Haven, continuing to Arbroath, in the form of red sandstone cliffs from 80m high Red Head to Whiting Ness. On top of it are the site of a chapel and a number of forts, including Praile Castle, while guillemots, razorbills, puffins, blackheaded gulls and moon jellyfish frequent the lower levels.

In the 18th century red caves in the cliffs were used for smuggling at Auchmithie, the harbour not being constructed until the 1890s. At the height of its prosperity the harbour had 33 fishing boats but it was damaged by a loose German mine in the Second World War. At one time the men were carried to the boats on the women's backs to avoid getting their feet wet, a wonderful precedent for chauvinists. Arbroath smokies originated at the beach, the local method of preparing haddock.

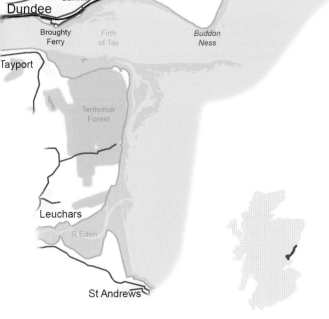

From Lud Castle (with its cave through the head) forts and caves continue to Maiden Castle, an Iron Age earthen promonotory fort. The Deil's Head, Pint Stoup and Poll Stack are assorted names for a vertical finger of rock near the Needle E'e, a block with a suitably shaped hole through it. This section of coast has a nature reserve with a nature trail visiting sea plantain, scurvy grass, red campion and wood vetch.

The cliffs of Red Head.

187

The Needle E'e with the Deil's Head beyond.

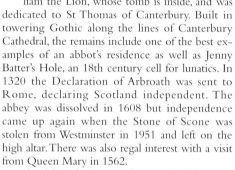

In calm conditions there are routes through the rock platform and past the remains of a walkway to reach the parking area with toilets, an ice cream van and an old well at the approach to **Arbroath**.

The rich Arbroath Abbey, now a set of red sandstone ruins, was founded in 1178 by William the Lion, whose tomb is inside, and was dedicated to St Thomas of Canterbury. Built in towering Gothic along the lines of Canterbury Cathedral, the remains include one of the best examples of an abbot's residence as well as Jenny Batter's Hole, an 18th century cell for lunatics. In 1320 the Declaration of Arbroath was sent to Rome, declaring Scotland independent. The abbey was dissolved in 1608 but independence came up again when the Stone of Scone was stolen from Westminster in 1951 and left on the high altar. There was also regal interest with a visit from Queen Mary in 1562.

Between the fishing harbour at the mouth of the Brothock Burn (from the Gaelic brothaig, little boiler) and the football stadium is the disused signal tower of 1812, designed by Robert Stevenson, used to signal to the Bell Rock 18km offshore. Robert Southey's *Inchcape Rock* tells of a feud between the abbot and the wrecker, Ralph the Rover, who cut the warning bell's rope on the rock. The tower is now a museum for the history of the town, fishing, the sea, the flax industry, Shanks lawnmowers, folk life, wildlife, archaeology and the Arbroath lifeboat. In 1885 a Scottish football cup tie set the world record score of 36–0 against Bon Accord, Aberdeen not being formed until 1903 and doing slightly better than their forebears. The score would have been higher if there had been nets so that time was not wasted recovering the ball. Arbroath Art Gallery features local artists. A red stone battlemented tower of castle proportions on the skyline is a disused Victorian water tower.

The Bell or Inchcape Rock has a lighthouse built by Robert Stevenson with backing from Rennie, the world's oldest still in its place and working.

Dunes replace the rocks, being followed by the A92 for 2km, the Aberdeen to King's Cross railway to Carnoustie and Kerr's Miniature Railway of 1935, a 260mm gauge line with steam and petrol engines that haul passengers. Beyond Elliot Water is a golf course and tank traps remain along the dunes.

The last section of rocky shoreline before St Andrews continues to Carnoustie with a gap at East Haven, with its picnic area, after a disused airfield and a pillbox add to the fortifications.

Sailing, windsurfing, swimming and angling take place at **Carnoustie** on the A930, although it is probably best known for its golf course.

Carnoustie has the longest British golf course at over 6.58km and is an Open venue. Barry Links are a problem area with rifle ranges along the sides firing east and west over the sea and heavy gunnery in the centre. Lookout huts are located along the 6–9m high dunes which back Barry Sands along two sides of the triangular peninsula. In places there are obvious areas of tipped rock to resist where the sea has been on the attack. On the other hand, Gaa Sand runs out from Buddon Ness for a considerable distance and usually has breaking waves over it. It is getting longer and passage over it is dangerous for most boats but large numbers of seals congregate here.

There are two disused lighthouses, the Old Low and the Old High, the latter having a 32m white tower. In addition there are isolated piles left in the sea. The dunes increase to 9–12m high.

Barry Buddon camp and the golf course at **Monifieth** are on an 8m beach, across which the Aberdeen to King's Cross railway runs to follow the shore and across which the Angus/Dundee border also runs. Dunes are covered in marram grass but caravans detract from the shoreline.

Mary Godwin, later to be Mary Shelley, stopped here with friends as a girl and began to formulate ideas on the shoreline which later emerged in *Frankenstein*.

Dighty Water separates Monifieth from Barnhill which merges into Broughty Ferry, the town where the wealthy **Dundee** jute barons built their mansions. The dominant building on the point is the 1547 Broughty Castle with a square tower, formerly levying tolls and controlling the ferry, now a museum on local history, the growth of the town, fishing, the lifeboat, ferries, Dundee whaling industry relics including harpoons, knives and scrimshaw, seashore wildlife, arms, armour and the military history of the castle.

There is turbulence off the point, especially on the ebb with westerly winds. Rain and snowmelt decrease the flood (which has a northwest set) and increase the ebb. There are plenty of yachts while small coasters are restricted to the fairway. Upstream are the Tay road and rail bridges.

The Firth of Tay separates Dundee from Fife. **Tayport** used to be the ferry port to cross to Dundee before the Tay Road Bridge was built. Standing off the drying harbour and Larick Scalp is a disused timber pile lighthouse, threatening to collapse under the weight of guano. The church at Ferry-Port-on-Craig has a 17th century tower with a list but a more substantial building is a spinning mill.

The northeast of Fife has some of the finest weather in Britain with low rainfall and long hours of sunshine,

Arbroath's disused Bell Rock signal tower.

Broughty Castle at the Tay entrance.

especially in the spring and in September and October. The Fife shoreline can throw up an interesting selection of semiprecious stones including agate, smoky quartz and amethyst.

Tentsmuir woods follow the coast for 8km, consisting mostly of pines behind a line of tank traps growing on an 8m beach. Flows are strong north of Lucky Scalp, which does not cover, the flood setting towards Tayport and the ebb towards Green Scalp where a wire fence runs out into the estuary.

Running out into the North Sea is the spit of Abertay Sands, uncovered for 6km at low water and frequented by large numbers of seals. The sands are unstable, increasing in length, the Elbow and Bar moving northeast, and considered dangerous for boats to cross.

The Tentsmuir National Nature Reserve is formed of Tentsmuir Sands consisting of acid dunes with curlews, chaffinches and yellowhammers plus gannets off the coast, a nature trail and a picnic site.

Leuchars Airfield is no longer in use but shortlisted as having potential spaceport involvement.

The estuary of the River Eden almost dries up as far as Guardbridge and is a nature reserve. The extensive mud-flats are good for winter birds. A count put the curlew as the most prolific summer species with 200 birds, ahead of oystercatchers at 187, but the excitement was reserved for the single Chilean flamingo which had lost its way.

Landing can be made at Out Head which has plenty of public carparking beyond a beach littered with razor and other shells.

Larick lighthouse, a derelict timber piled structure off Tayport.

Distance
64km from Tangleha to Out Head

OS 1:50,000 Sheets
45 Stonehaven & Banchory
54 Dundee & Montrose
59 St Andrews

Tidal Constants
Montrose:
HW Dover +0320
Arbroath:
HW Dover +0310
LW Dover +0300
River Tay Bar:
Dover +0320
Monifieth:
Dover +0340

Sea Area
Forth

Range
Barry Buddon

Connection
Firth of Tay – see RoB p131

39 Fife

A coast of saints and kings

St Andrews by the northern sea,
A haunted town it is to me!
A little city, worn and gray,
The gray North Ocean girds it round;
And o'er the rocks, and up the bay,
The long sea-rollers surge and sound;
And still the thin and biting spray
Drives down the melancholy street,
And still endure, and still decay,
Towers that the salt winds vainly beat.
Ghost-like and shadowy they stand
Dim-mirrored in the wet sea-sand.

A broken minster, looking forth
Beyond the bay, above the town!
O winter of the kindly North,
O college of the scarlet gown,
And shining sands beside the sea,
And stretch of links beyond the sand,
Once more I watch you, and to me
It is as if I touched his hand!
Andrew Lang

St Rule's Tower and St Andrews cathedral.

The castle at St Andrews.

West Sands stretch south from Out Head to St Andrews. They are popular as the city's main beach but are best known as one of the settings for the film *Chariots of Fire*. Behind the beach are the Links, including interesting dune plants. **St Andrews** has seven golf courses including the Royal & Ancient, one of four clubs, the home of golf since at least 1547 and a place of pilgrimage for golfers from around the world. The rules were first set down in 1754 and the clubhouse built exactly a century later, acting as the headquarters of the game. The world's first ladies' club was established here in 1887. The name may come from the Dutch kolf, a club, or the Scottish gouf, to strike. The rest of the game's history, including the British Open, together with memorabilia, documents, clubs and balls, appears in the British Golf Museum. There is a Golf Week and, for those who miss it, every second shop in the city seems to be golf related.

St Regulus or St Rule was shipwrecked off the coast in 347 and founded a church here, bringing the bones of St Andrew, attracting pilgrims in the days of the Celtic church. It had become an ecclesiastical establishment by 747 and the country's most important bishopric was founded in 908 with an Augustinian priory following in 1126. St Andrews cathedral was the biggest in Scotland. Founded in 1160, it included the 33m 12th century St Rule's Tower, the cathedral itself being mostly 12th and 13th century Celtic with medieval carved stones including an 8th or 10th century sarcophagus, perhaps built to hold the relics of St Andrew. It was the ecclesiastical capital of Scotland. Here James V married Mary of Guise, the daughter of Mary, Queen of Scots, who visited the cathedral in 1563 and 1564. The foundation above the harbour is that of the ruined Celtic church of St Mary of the Rock. Holy Trinity Church was founded in the 12th century, moved to its present site in 1410 and restored in 1909 with notable stained glass.

The castle was founded in 1200 with a bishop's fortified palace, a fortress and a prison, including a bottle dungeon with no exit, carved out of the rock. Also on show are rare mine and counter mine medieval siege techniques. Cardinal Beaton, who was the scourge of the Protestants, was murdered here in 1546 by Protestant preacher George Wishart and hung from a window. John Knox was condemned to be a French galley slave when he

and other Protestants were besieged in the castle, the start of the Reformation struggle. Stones from the castle were used in the 16th century to repair the harbour.

The university is the oldest in Scotland, founded in 1410. At its heart is St Salvator's Chapel with John Knox's pulpit. The initials in the cobbles are those of Lutheran preacher Patrick Hamilton, burned at the stake in 1528. The face which appears to be etched high on an arch is said to have been his since the time he was martyred. The Old University Library was founded in 1612 and the Scottish Parliament met here in 1645/6. In 1795 Alexander Hill graduated at the age of 10. The Celtic Group was formed to take an interest in folk music. The royal presence has also kept the university in the public eye.

Other notable works in this small city are the Pends, a magnificent vaulted gateway to the Priory Precinct, predicted to collapse when the wisest man in Christendom walks under the arch. So far he has had the sense not to do so. There is also a remarkable 16th century Precinct Wall. The A91 meets the A917 and many of the streets are Victorian and Edwardian. There is the St Andrews Museum with local history and the St Andrews Preservation Trust Museum with fishermen's houses, gro-

cer's shop contents, chemist's, fishing equipment, photographs, weights and measures, furniture and paintings. The Byre Theatre has been set up in an old cowshed, there is a Kate Kennedy Pageant in April and a biannual St Andrews Festival with revue, opera, film, jazz, dance, folk, exhibitions and theatre. The Lammas Market fair in early August is the oldest medieval market. Not forgetting the sea is the Scottish Oceans Institute and St Andrews Aquarium.

The shoreline becomes rocky now with smoky quartz, agate and amethyst sometimes being found. The harbour, rebuilt in the 17th century with stones from the abbey and some not already reused from the castle in the 16th century, is used by fishing and pleasure craft but dries despite being fed by the Kinness Burn. A caravan site overlooks the east end of the city. Surf breaks are found north and south of the city.

Cliffs run 20–30m high. Birdlife includes blackheaded gulls, fulmars, oystercatchers, sanderlings, cormorants, curlews, herons, blackbacked gulls and eider ducks, while both moon and compass jellyfish are found in the water.

The Rock & Spindle is an interesting geological feature, like a rectangular chimney with a large bevel gear wheel leaning against it. A little further along is Buddo Rock, a large rectangular block which has an Islamic arch shape in the centre.

Kenly Water flows down through Boarhills. The popular white beach of Cambo Sands is below Kingsbarns.

Close by are Cambo Gardens with walled gardens, bulbs, lilacs, blossoms, over 200 varieties of rose, a notable Chinese bridge, Cambo Woodland Walk & Nature Trail, 18th century farm, farm machinery display, Living Land display, rare breeds, traditional poultry, Scottish farm animals, pets corner, fossils, adventure playground and BMX track, not to mention more caravans.

The square tower of Balcomie Castle is above a golf course while, offshore, Carr Brigs are marked by the North Carr Beacon, a red column of 1821 by Robert Stevenson, on a stone base, a prototype for many others around the Scottish coast. The base was part of failed attempts by Stevenson over the previous 11 years to build a stone tower, for which the workyard remains can still be seen on Fife Ness. A lightship was used from 1877 to 1975, now replaced by a buoy. The final kilometre to the ness is well littered with rocks which have claimed many ships. Its has 10m high dark cliffs with a 5m white lighthouse building.

There was a Danish settlement here, recalled by Danes Dike (where an aerial is located) and by King Constantine's Cave, named after the Scottish monarch murdered by the Danes in 874.

Low cliffs, grassy banks and a rocky foreshore are typical to Elie Ness, good for birdlife, while further offshore is a submarine and minesweeper exercise area. Flows run at up to 3km/h off points.

The rocky shoreline normally acts as a barrier to the nature reserve at Danes Dike and to the picnic area by the disused airfield above Kilminning Castle.

The Rock & Spindle to the south of St Andrews.

Crail, one of the jewels of the East Neuk coast.

Lobster pots piled up on the quayside at Crail harbour.

A collection of chalets and caravans give a less attractive welcome to the very attractive East Neuk or corner of Fife, a line of villages which grew affluent on trade with France, the Low Countries and Scandinavia in medieval times. They exchanged wool, coal, leather and fish for timber and manufactured goods, also

importing Flemish crowstepped gables. In the 19th century there was a big herring fleet instead and now tourists make a contribution to the local economy. East Neuk can also have overtones of eccentricity.

The first village south of Fife Ness is **Crail**. Its harbour cannot be entered with strong southeasterly winds although stoplogs can be positioned to close off the harbour entrance. Some stone blocks are set vertically and the outer face of the pier has stone blocks held in place with wooden wedges to resist waves. There is a beach of shell sand which adheres tenaciously to everything. Above the red boulder harbour are crowstepped houses with red tiled roofs, some with fishing motif decorations, some with outside staircases so that fishermen can live above their workshops and net storage. There are lobsters, crabs and sea urchins around, a building beside the harbour offering to cook lobsters to order. Toilets are an adjacent service. The village was an important ecclesiastical centre from the 12th century, important enough for the Devil to have thrown the Blue Stane at the church, currently lying in the churchyard, having missed its target. The 13th century collegiate church has fine woodwork and an early Pictish cross. The 16th century Tolbooth was both library and town hall with a 1602 coat of arms and a gilded salmon weathervane on which gulls can comfortably perch and aspire to higher things. The Dutch tower was also a town hall with a Dutch bell of 1520, the oldest in Fife. A Mercat Cross has a unicorn which is now rather worn. Crail Museum and Heritage Centre in an 18th century cottage features local history, people and archaeology, the Isle of May, golf, miniature dolls, lace, HMS *Jackdaw* and fishing. There is a 17th century customs house. Indeed, it was a prosperous town in the 17th century but never recovered from an outbreak of the plague.

Viewed from here, the Isle of May's distinctive profile, rises steadily from the east and ends abruptly with vertical cliffs on the west, magh being Celtic for plain. The 51ha island is of greenstone and basalt. David I founded a chapel, dedicated to St Aidan, murdered by the Danes in 870, and gave it to his sister, Queen Maude of England, for the monks of Reading Abbey to found a priory. The 12th century monastery is built on the grave of St Aidan. There is good sheep grazing. There were 15 fishing families living on the island in the 18th century with an annual party to celebrate the end of the herring fishing season. Fishermen from Crail and Pittenweem used to join in but in 1837 a boat capsized, drowning 13, mostly women, and the festivities were discontinued. There had been a coal fired lighthouse on the island since 1635, the demolition of which Sir Walter Scott managed to prevent in 1815, instead the 12m height being halved, leaving the 7.6m square building with turrets as a fishermen's refuge. From 1815 the island was owned by the Northern Lighthouse Commissioners, when and for whom Robert Stevenson built a square lighthouse on a house, in 1836 fitting the first British dioptric fixed light. A second low light was added in 1844 in transit with the Carr Rocks. The island has been a National Nature Reserve since 1956 with large breeding seabird colonies and a seal rookery. Fife Council permission is needed to land. The bird observatory was furnished from shipwrecks. The island has been the site of naval battles involving the Picts, Norse, Danes, English and pirates and wreckage includes two steam driven submarines.

The A917 follows the coast from Crail to Kirkton of Largo. Located on the rocky shoreline are the ruins of the Pans and, near a cave, the Hermit's Well. More caravans grace the coast at Kilrenny.

Anstruther Easter, at the end of the B9131, allows use to be made of some sheltered waters behind the reefs. There is a small harbour near the Haven Restaurant but the main harbour has two parts and 1.2km of quays. It is a fishing harbour, of which the inner basin dries, and can be rough with strong winds from the south or east. It was developed in the 16th century. The major work was by D&T Stevenson, during which Robert Louis Stevenson worked for the family firm in 1868 but showed more interest in the arts than in engineering. Until the 1940s it was the home of the East Neuk herring trade. The Smugglers Inn had a tunnel used for carrying contraband. The Scottish Fisheries Museum is housed in 16th to 19th century buildings with an aquarium, fishing and ship's gear, a Fifie fishing boat and models, fishermen's home interiors, Anstruther lifeboats and the 1900 herring drifter *Reaper*. A local recordbreaker was a 5.6kg onion.

Anstruther Wester has a golf course behind a small but distinctive tower, the course reaching Billowness with its eiders, shags and turnstones to Pittenweem, Pictish for place of the cave. St Fillan's Cave is a shrine, having been a 6th century missionary hermitage, although later used by smugglers. It is under a yellow sandstone overhang below the priory where witches were put to death, the Great House and prior's lodging being built by Augustinian monks from the Isle of May in the 12th century. The parish church of 1588 is noted for its tower and spire with a Swedish bell of 1663. Also imported was the Flemish architectural style. The small fishing port is busy, the inner basin drying. It is the home of the Fife fishing fleet and has a fishmarket with codlings, flatfish, crabs and lobsters. In *The Heart of Midlothian* Scott describes the robbery here of Kirkcaldy's collector of customs, to lead on to the Porteous riots in Edinburgh.

There is an unusual 8.2m high x 6.1m diameter windmill of 1772–4 on the cliffs at Pans Goat. In good condition, it has a cylindrical body, a flattened conical roof and flimsy looking sails, apparently a disguise for something else. In fact, it was built to pump sea water the 4.9m up to nine salt drying pans located on the cliffs, where it was boiled using local coal brought from a mine at **Pittenweem** harbour by wagonway.

St Monans or St Monance takes its name from the Irish missionary who had a cave or shrine close to the church. St Monans Auld Kirk may have been a Ninianic foundation of about 400. David I was cured of an arrow wound here. In 1265 Alexander III started new building work and David II renovated it in 1362 in thanks for delivery from a storm at sea. About 1460 James III gave it to the Dominicans and it became a parish church in 1646. Inside the transept hangs a fully rigged model of 1804 of a 100 gun sailing ship donated by a local naval officer (who made money out of the Napoleonic wars) as a memorial to 37 fishermen who lost their lives in a storm in 1875.

Although it is only a small fishing port, it was one of the four biggest in Scotland in the 1790s with 14 boats. The harbour dries but is not easily approached in strong southeasterly winds or with a northeasterly swell.

On the rocks is the block of Newark Castle, the 17th century home of the Covenanter General Leslie, defeated at Dunbar by Cromwell. A little further along the coast is

The busy harbour at Pittenweem.

another castle ruin at Ardross, near which is a souterrain. On the other hand, the round stone tower on Saucher Point is Lady's Folly, the private bathing box of 18th century beauty Lady Janet Anstruther who used to bathe unrobed after a bellringer had been sent through the streets of Elie to warn away onlookers.

Elie Ness, topped by an 11m white light tower, has flows to 2km/h and is at the outer end of the Firth of Forth. At the head of Wood Haven or Ruby Bay are toilets and parking, together with banks of thrift and other flowers. The royal burgh of Elie & Earlsferry has a larger bay with windsurfing and a golf course. Lucy Sansom had a cottage at Elie which she offered to lend to Logan Mountstuart for writing in William Boyd's *Any Human Heart*.

Chapel Ness at **Earlsferry** is named after a chapel that was built in 1093 by the Earl of Fife for pilgrims visiting St Andrews. Off the ness is East Vows, marked by a 12m pyramidal cage, while the West Vows are more likely to have singing seals on top and be surrounded by diving gannets and terns.

The 63m Grangehill ridge climbs steeply in what is otherwise rather flat terrain, topped by a radio mast. Kincraig is a volcanic plug, hollowed out and undercut by the sea. One cave is said to have sheltered Macduff from Macbeth. Some strata run vertically and there is a lookout point on the hillside.

After Shell Bay and the low Ruddons Point comes the sandy sweep of Largo Bay, the Scottish Riviera, backed by a former railway line and a four arched viaduct and with fish nets on the beach. The 290m Largo Law is a distinctive volcanic peak against the generally higher ground of the Lomond Hills. There are reefs and mussel banks along the beach near Lower Largo. Up the hill is Scotland's Larder, a restaurant in an old farm barn offering high

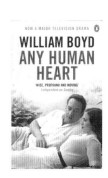

The rivermouth at Lower Largo.

class local produce. Down from it is the Temple area of Lower Largo, named from its association with the Knights Templar, now with parking and toilets and very crowded when used for sailing regattas. The village was a haddock fishing hamlet and still lands lobsters and crabs although it is subject to scend with southerly winds. Guillemots and little gulls live in the bay. It was the birthplace in 1676 of Alexander Selkirk who spent over 4 years on Juan Fernandez off the Chile coast after asking to be put ashore from a Spanish ship which had captured him and which was shipwrecked subsequently with most of the crew killed. He inspired Daniel Defoe's *Robinson Crusoe*, of whom there is a statue outside Selkirk's former house. The book has been described as the first true English novel.

The unique Largo & Newburn parish church with its 16th century spire supported only on the chancel roof is in Kirkton of Largo or Upper Largo. It has a Pictish stone in the churchyard with designs including a hunting scene. Graves include that of Sir Andrew Wood who was Scotland's greatest admiral, whose *Yellow Caravel* led the Scottish fleet to victory against the English in the Forth in 1489. Only one tower remains of Sir Andrew's Largo House which had been designed by Robert Adam for the Durhams, the lairds of Largo. When Sir Andrew became too ill to travel to church he had a 200–300m canal dug to it, the first in Scotland, so that he could be rowed to services by English prisoners of war.

Wemyss Castle, less well-fortified than many.

Interesting architecture at West Wemyss.

Grass covered spoil from Blair colliery is black on the beach.

There are golf courses on both sides of the A915 at Lundin Links, two of them 18th century, leading to a caravan park. On one of them are the Standing Stones of Lundin, sandstone blocks which may have been memorials to the Druids or to a battle with the Danes. There is a tower near them. This is considered to be the gateway to the East Neuk and from here there is some industry and deep water moorings to Burntisland.

The entry point for the Scottish court when travelling to Falkland Palace was **Leven**. It later became a coal port although it is no longer commercial, having become blocked by shifting sands and being subject to a considerable sea with a southwesterly wind. In winter, scaup collect around the sewage outfall near the River Leven. The A955 crosses the river and follows the coast to Kirkcaldy.

Off **Methil** there is a wreck. The docks, which were begun in 1860, have 840m of quays remaining after some infilling, trading with Copenhagen, Hamburg and Spain. It is a town of tower blocks. A 1930s post office contains smaller items of the town's history in the Methil Heritage Centre.

Methil and **Buckhaven** run together on the B931 and were made a single burgh in 1891. Buckhaven harbour is silted up and disused but a museum features the region's fisherfolk in better days. The church hall was the Church of St Andrew, a Gothic pre-Reformation church which had stood in St Andrews for four centuries before being rebuilt here. Wise Eppie was the best informed person in Buckhaven, the ale seller, midwife and nurse.

Macduff's Castle at **East Wemyss** is a ruin of two towers and a red block sited in a cemetery, the stronghold of the Macduff thanes of Fife, perhaps. Close by are two caves or weems, after which the village is named, with Bronze Age to medieval inscriptions and with the risk of rockfalls. Court Cave is where James V is believed to have received gypsies and contains a Viking picture of Thor with his hammer and earlier Pictish designs. Doocot cave has square niches which may have been for dove nesting boxes or for funeral urns.

Coaltown of Wemyss is not what it was. The Michael Mine was closed in 1967 but estate houses are well kept. Wemyss Castle stands at the top of wooded cliffs. Wemyss ware pottery was made here from 1880 until moved to Bovey Tracey in 1930.

Housing around the harbour at West Wemyss includes a marvellous selection in a style which would not look out of place on a Mediterranean coast.

Black spoil spills down onto the beach from Blair colliery, to contrast with the whitewashed, crowstepped gabled houses at Dysart, grouped in front of ruined St Serf's church tower which was built as a refuge against pirates. It was the home port of the brig *Covenant* in *Kidnapped* and where Victor de Montaiglon landed from France in Neil Munro's *Doom Castle*. Visiting boaters to the harbour these days mostly come in yachts. The John McDouall Stuart Museum is in a 17th century building which was the birthplace of the first explorer to cross the heart of Australia from south to north in 1861. The Tolbooth was used as a powder magazine in the Civil War until a drunken Cromwellian soldier wandered in with a lit torch. The roof has since been put back. An ornithologists' hide stands by the beach.

The Aberdeen to King's Cross railway now follows the coast, as does a nature trail running through the woods to **Kirkcaldy,** the Lang Toun, Fife's largest town. A hovercraft service was proposed across to Leith.

Ravenscraig or Ravensheugh Castle, now with a surreal backdrop of three tower blocks, was to be one of the first constructed to withstand artillery. It was built in 1460–3 by James II in octagonal shape, later passing to the Sinclair Earls of Orkney. On a promontory, it has two D shaped towers for cannon, a four storey one serving as a keep and an artillery platform added to a raised curtain wall in the early 16th century. Kirkcaldy has a small commercial port handling cut timber. The town's prosperity was built on linoleum from 1847, of which it was the world's leading producer, and this is featured in the Kirkcaldy Galleries, together with linen, mining, industrial heritage, local history, craft and art including Scottish paintings, notably Scottish Colourists, especially Samuel Peploe. The Adam Smith Theatre recalls the economist and author of *The Wealth of Nations*, born here in 1723. Georgian architects Robert and James Adam were also born here, as was Michael Scott, the medieval wizard and astrologer to the Holy Roman Empire. Historian Thomas Carlyle taught here as a schoolmaster from 1816 to 1819.

Fine 17th century houses in Sailor's Walk are now occupied by HM Customs, while coal dust on the beach remains from the past and the Links Market on the Esplanade is one of the oldest fairs in Britain. The A921 runs along the Esplanade past a large stadium and follows the coast.

Part of the sea wall collapsed near Seafield Colliery, which was the deepest mine in Scotland and one of the largest undersea mines in Europe. The Seafield Tower remains to look out over the Vows and their seals, the East Vows actually being west of the West Vows.

Kinghorn, with its grey sandstone buildings, has been a royal burgh since the 12th century. A monument records how Alexander III met his death here in 1286 when his horse stumbled in the dark and threw him over the cliff. Noted fiddler Patie Burnie was from Kinghorn. The village has a railway station high above the beach.

Pettycur harbour on Kinghorn Ness dries. The hillside behind is steep but not too steep for a golf course and hundreds of chalets, although the A921 is squeezed in next to the railway.

Inchkeith in the middle of the firth is a 55m high island of igneous rock on which landing is forbidden without Fife Council permission. It was given to Robert de Keith of Keithness (Caithness), chief of the warlike German clan Catti, together with the hereditary title Grand

St Serf's church tower and houses at Dysart.

The view from St Colm's Abbey tower.

St Colme's Abbey.

Marischal of Scotland, for his help in resisting the Danish invasion of 1010. It was later used as a plague island with an asylum built in 1497. A castle was added for Mary, Queen of Scots, in 1564 and the island garrisoned by French soldiers, a 19m stone tower subsequently being built on the site of the castle and acting as a battlemented lighthouse.

The island was fortified in the Napoleonic and both world wars with triple fortifications and batteries in 1881 able to cover the whole of the firth at this point. James IV carried out the experiment of leaving two babies on the island with a deaf and dumb nurse to see what language they would speak, the result being passable Hebrew. Dr Samuel Johnson visited in 1773 although the commonest visitors these days are birds, this being an RSPB reserve.

A prominent landmark for this part of the coast is the radio mast on the Binn, a high ridge behind Burntisland. The sandy shore, used for staking out salmon nets, dries for a kilometre.

Entertainment in **Burntisland** includes a museum and an Edwardian fairground, a summer regatta, Highland games in July and a prominent waterslide next to the bay. The octagonal towered church was the first post-Reformation church in Scotland and here the James I Assembly of the Church of Scotland suggested the Authorized Version of the Bible. Somerville Street and Square were referred to as Quality Street because of the nature of the residents and the fine 17th century town houses. Lammerlaws Point has former fortifications. The military involvement goes back a long way, Agricola having landed his legions here at Portus Gratiae, the best natural harbour in the estuary, in the 1st century and Second World War convoys having been mustered here. James V built bulwarks and piers, to which Cromwell added. In 1850 it was the terminal for the world's first train ferry, landing wagons from Granton. Shipbuilding, herrings, whales, coal and bauxite have been its trade but it now looks to the oil industry. To the east are Royal Navy degaussing ranges, marked by four yellow buoys, and no approach should be made when Navy vessels are there. The firth is now controlled by the Dockyard Port of Rosyth. Beyond Ross Point is another aerial.

Silversands Bay has children's playgrounds, trampolines, putting green and toilets. Aberdour with its small harbour used for sailing and water skiing is beyond Hawkcraig Point. The castle ruin is part 14th century, built by the Douglas family with a walled garden started in the 16th century and a fine circular doocot. St Fillan's parish is one of Scotland's best Norman buildings, part 16th century with fine stained glass.

A series of stepping stones cross the firth, those to the north of the Oxcars Lighthouse being part of Fife while those to the south are part of Edinburgh. Between them are two deep water channels for large vessels. The first is Mortimer's Deep with tidal streams up to 5km/h, running north of Car Craig, a fairly narrow channel marked by red and green lateral buoys. It primarily caters for tankers up to $60,000m^3$ serving the Braefoot terminal for Mossmorran petrochemical complex which exports natural gasoline, ethylene, propane and butane. An amber flashing light on the jetty shows from two hours before a tanker movement is due until the movement is completed.

The largest of the islands is Inchcolm, 27m high and mostly greensand, named after St Colme or Columba who was resident in the 6th century. St Colme's Abbey was founded in 1192 by Alexander I after being saved from shipwreck by the resident hermit who shared his own meagre supply of milk and shellfish. It has a square tower with a grey spire, 13th century octagonal chapter house and monastic buildings which are the best preserved early medieval architecture in Scotland. Known as the Iona of the East, it was the place to be buried to be

Oxcars lighthouse with Edinburgh beyond.

close to heaven. It was abandoned in 1560 after the Reformation and was mentioned in *Macbeth*. More recent buildings are fortifications from the two world wars. There used to be many stones with the arms of Norsemen but only one remains. Wildlife includes grey seals and puffins. Fife Council permission is needed to land and there is a charge but responsible groups of canoeists are sometimes allowed to camp here. The *Maid of the Forth* trip boat operates from Queensferry with several loads of tourists per day.

Between Inchcolm and the Oxcars Lighthouse is the Forth Deep Water Channel, which is the main route down the firth. It ebbs to 2km/h and floods to 1km/h, the flow reversing rapidly and being affected by melting snow and rainfall. Traffic includes tankers and vessels of the Royal Navy from Rosyth. Some 7km upstream are the Forth Bridge, Forth Road Bridge and Queensferry Bridge, the former with probably the world's most distinctive bridge silhouette.

Oxcars lighthouse is a 22m white tower with a red band, built on rocks which cover and was the site of a 1915 hydrophone to listen for submarines. A spoil dumping ground separates it from the Cow & Calves which all but cover and yet still need council permission before landing.

RSPB permission is needed to land on Inchmickery, which is a bird sanctuary with a roseate ternery and other breeding birds, for which the grass is kept cut short. It covers only 1ha and rises to 15m. The name means isle of the vicar and it may have been the dwelling place of the priest from Inchcolm. It is nearly covered with Second World War fortification designs in battleship profile but the Mickery Stone, a standing stone, survives. The Forth has 72,000 winter wildfowl including 8,900 knots, 2,800 bartailed godwits, 4,100 redshanks and 8,900 pinkfooted geese, which the RSPB claimed were at risk from marina development and land reclaim. It was used in filming Iain Banks' *Complicity*.

Cramond Island is uninhabited and needs council permission to land. The 8ha island is connected to the mainland by a causeway running across Drum Sands. Cramond has evidence of occupation from about 8500 BC, the oldest known mainland site in Scotland. The name is a corruption of caer Almond, the Romans having built a fort at the mouth of the River Almond which housed the 2nd and 10th legions under Lollius Urbicus as a supply base for the Antonine Wall. These days the rivermouth forms a pleasant harbour area with parking but sewage pollution discourages swimming and the local mussels are no longer safe to eat.

Cramond at the mouth of the River Almond.

Distance
80km from Out
Head to Cramond

OS 1:50,000 Sheets
59 St Andrews
66 Edinburgh

Tidal Constants
Monifieth:
Dover +0340
Crail:
Dover +0340
Anstruther Easter:
Dover +0320
St Monance:
Dover +0330
Lower Largo:
HW Dover +0330
LW Dover +0340
Methil:
Dover +0340
Dysart:
Dover +0340
Burntisland:
Dover +0340
Aberdour:
HW Dover +0350
LW Dover +0340
Granton:
Dover +0340

Sea Area
Forth

Connection
River Forth – see
RoB p141

40 East Lothian

A capital coast for stories

And now, when close at hand they saw
North Berwick's town, and lofty Law,
Fitz-Eustace bade them pause a while,
Before a venerable pile,
Whose turrets view'd, afar,
The lofty Bass, the Lambie Isle,
The ocean's peace or war.
Sir Walter Scott

The main flight path into Edinburgh Airport at Turnhouse crosses the coast between the tower on the shore at Cramond and the turreted tower house of Lauriston Castle, built in 1590 by Sir Archibald Napier, whose son invented logarithms. John Law, the founder of the Bank of France and of the Mississippi Scheme, spent his early years here. The castle houses fine paintings, furniture and Blue John ware and has spy and listening holes for watching guests. In front of the castle are Silverknowes golf links and a rugby pitch while beyond are Bruntsfield links, expanded from their original six holes.

The estuary moves out of the control of the Dockyard Port of Rosyth and restrictions ease slightly.

The Category B Granton gasholder of 1898–1903 is Scotland's most notable. At 77m in diameter and 11m high, it formerly held 200,000m³ of gas and has distinctive external framing. Beyond the gasholder and an aerial is the Category A Caroline Park, a 17th century mansion built by Sir George McKenzie, Viscount Tarbat, the chief minister for Scotland. The house was renamed after Queen Caroline in 1740 and is now offices.

Granton Harbour has been chosen to house Edinburgh Marina. It draws some of its prestige from the presence of the headquarters of the Royal Forth and Forth Corinthian yacht clubs.

The A901 follows the coast to Newhaven, a fishing harbour which dries but is still used by shellfishing and recreational craft. Among its larger neighbours it would hardly be noticed but for the smartly painted disused white lighthouse and the equally smartly painted buildings in a deep plum colour around it. With a name like Newhaven, it isn't, inevitably, having been founded in 1500 by James IV. George IV said the fishwives were the most handsome women he had ever seen.

Leith has become a trendy port town and, until the 1980s, was where Crabbie's green ginger wine was produced. Much has been improved since the description of it in Irvine Welsh's *Trainspotting*. The dominant harbour here is the Port of Leith at the mouth of the Water of Leith, one of the oldest ports in Britain, in existence by 1329. It contains the Royal Yacht *Britannia*, in service from 1953 to 1997. It is where the French landed 6,000 troops plus artillery in 1549 to support the Scots against the English and so the port was blockaded three years later to prevent the arrival of further French. Queen Mary landed here on her return from France in 1561. There was much trade with the Low Countries, thus the influence on the architectural designs by Rennie. A 9.1m high sea wall 1.3km long has protected it since 1896. A 260 x 34m entrance lock has allowed entry of 11m draught ships since 1969. Victoria Swing Bridge of 1871–4 with a

clear span of 37m was the largest in the UK until Kincardine Bridge was opened in 1937. Some 4.8km of quays serve commercial traffic and form an oilfield and pipeline construction base. The deep water approach channel has been dredged northwest from the entrance, across which tidal streams flow east–west at up to 3km/h with an eddy off Leith Breakwater during the flood. There is a ternery on a caisson and a substantial roost of eider ducks, cormorants and blackheaded gulls on the east side of the port entrance where there are stone blocks at first until the coastline deteriorates to broken concrete and twisted reinforcing steel. The base of a Martello tower sits surrounded by stacks of pipes until oil tanks take over. A freight railway passes a sewage works but the end of the industrial area is indicated by a metal framework off the coast. Jellyfish gather in the waters next to the port. Leith Links were in use by 1744 by what would become the Honourable Company of Edinburgh Golfers, Charles I playing here when informed about the Irish rebellion. *Frank Mildmay; or the Naval Officer* refers to soldiers who had been brought up in Leith as glassblowers. *The Raiders* notes Yawkins was hanged and tarred here for piracy.

Now come residential areas, a golf course at Craigentinny and views across **Edinburgh**, notably 251am high Arthur's Seat, Meadowbank stadium, Nelson Monument, Edinburgh Castle and the Pentland Hills beyond. Built on the volcanic rock of Din Eidyn, Edinburgh Castle, including the 12th century St Margaret's Chapel, is the oldest building in Edinburgh. It includes the Great Hall of James IV, the Old Palace with the Regalia of Scotland, the honours or crown jewels, the Scottish National War Memorial of 1927, Mons Meg (a 500 year old siege cannon) and the National War Museum. It is where Queen Mary gave birth to James VI of Scotland and I of England in 1566. The Scottish capital uses an Old English form of a name derived from the Old Welsh, Eidyn Gaer, Eidyn's fort. Edinburgh received its present name when the Angles took Din Eidyn in 638 but it has often been referred to as Auld Reekie, old smokey.

Portobello is a district founded in 1739, the year Puerto Bello in Panama was captured. The name was given by George Hamilton, who fought there with Admiral Vernon. Music Hall's Harry Lauder was born here in 1870. Effie Deans eloped on a boat from here in *The Heart of Midlothian*. A sandy beach with groynes reaches almost to Joppa where there is another daymark.

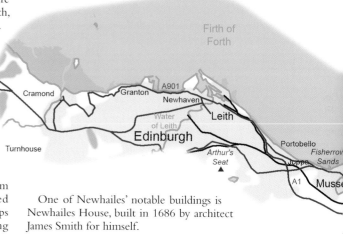

One of Newhailes' notable buildings is Newhailes House, built in 1686 by architect James Smith for himself.

Fisherrow Harbour from at least 1592 dries and it is

mostly used by yachts. Water skiers have no such needs and cross Fisherrow Sands to operate in Musselburgh Road. The River Esk forms the boundary between Edinburgh and East Lothian. **Musselburgh** was a mussel and herring fishing centre, named in the 11th century, although, sadly, the mussels which form banks off the rivermouth are now too polluted to eat. A third of British wintering scaup gather around the Seafield sewer outfall to feed on grain waste and the area is noted for winter wildfowl and waders. Birds range from oystercatchers and curlews to goldeneyes, eiders and swans. In 1332 this important Roman seaport became known as the Honest Town when the citizens cared for the dying Earl of Moray, the Regent of Scotland, and then declined a reward from his successor, the Earl of Mar. The town has a sporting tradition. In 1504 James IV played on Musselburgh Links, the world's oldest golf course was established in 1672, initally with five holes, and there has been a club since 1774, hosting the Open until 1889. The horse racecourse was established in 1816, the oldest in Scotland, and there has been a shoot on the links in late May by the Royal Company of Archers since the 17th century for the Silver Arrow. There were more serious arrows in 1547 when the Scots were defeated here in battle.

The Tolbooth was built with stones from the Chapel of Loretto of 1590. Loretto School is a public school for boys, Scotland's oldest boarding school, part of which is located in Pinkie House with its painted gallery of about 1630 and its plaster ceilings, the seat of the Abbots of Dunfermline.

To the east of the rivermouth are 1.2km^2 of lagoons to take waste pumped 4km as a slurry from the former Cockenzie power station. The lagoons were intended to take 5,600,000t of ash during the lifetime of the power station. Coal has been mined here for 800 years, the first mine in Scotland, as shown in the Prestongrange Industrial Heritage Museum which has a history of coal mining, a Cornish beam engine installed in 1874 and features on the production of pottery, soap and glycerine together with brewing and weaving.

The B1348 becomes the coastal road to Longniddry. It passes **Prestonpans**, its name from the 12th century salt

the Jacobites achieved a significant victory when Prince Charles Edward defeated General Cope in the first battle of 1745 after the Jacobites were shown a route at night through a morass which Government troops thought impassable, a monument cairn marking this historic event. Herman Melville makes reference to the weapons in his *Benito Cereno*. Cockenzie broke new ground for a power station in that the sandstone bedrock was able to be accurately excavated by motor scrapers during construction. Half the site was reclaimed from the sea and ash has been filled to adjacent lagoons.

In days gone by, the fishermen of Prestonpans and Cockenzie would not put to sea if their paths were crossed by pigs, lame men or strangers. A good many fine fishing days must have been lost. Cockenzie & Port Seton is now one village with two fishing harbours. Cockenzie Harbour is a small port begun in 1630 to export salt and coal. The Earl of Winton forfeited his estate after the 1715 uprising but developed the harbour, including the building of a 3km wooden wagonway, one of Scotland's first, to bring coal from Tranent's coal pits. Ironically, it was this route which led to the 1745 Jacobite battle success. The wagonway was used for 160 years. Port Seton dries.

Seton House was built in 1790 on the ruins of Seton Palace. Close by is a chapel which was formerly the Collegiate Church, a late 15th century building with a fine vaulted chancel and apse, buttressed walls of red and grey stone, tracery windows and a stump tower.

Seton Sands are protected by Long Craigs, a line of rocks largely unbroken across the bay. Elsewhere, tank traps are located along the shore. Unsheltered in Cockenzie Road are deep water moorings to Gullane Point.

The golf course in front of **Longniddry** belies the fact that it has been a coal mining village for 500 years until the coal ran out in the 1920s.

From Ferny Ness the A198 generally follows the coast to the A1, initially past bays which drain to leave great expanses of sand. Gosford Bay is overlooked by the ostentatious gatehouses of Gosford House, set in a red wall. The house itself, its dome showing above the trees, was the seat of the Earl of Wemyss and was designed in the late

18th century by Robert Adam. Some 6km inland the Hopetoun Monument and an aerial are placed on top of the Garleton Hills which rise to 186m.

Peffer Burn discharges into Aberlady Bay which completely empties at low tide to leave the Gullane Sands, a nature reserve, the burn following the southern edge of the bay to continue past Craigielaw Point and cross Gosford Sands. Low dunes separate the nature reserve from Gullane Links with three golf courses, one of which has

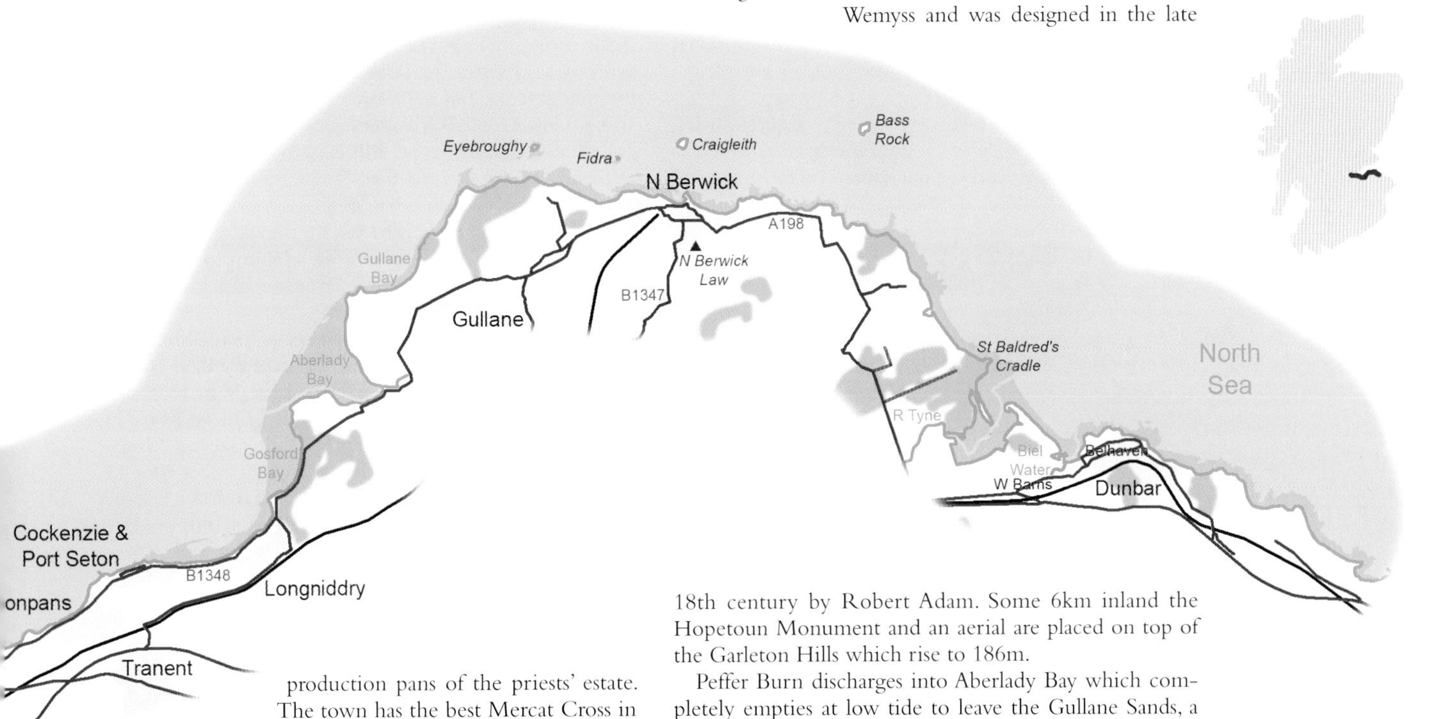

production pans of the priests' estate. The town has the best Mercat Cross in the country, the ruined Preston Tower (which is a medieval fortification with a huge dovecote) and Hamilton and Northfield Houses, 17th century lairds' houses. Most important, though, is the battlefield where

Map labels: Eyebroughy, Fidra, Craigleith, Bass Rock, N Berwick, A198, Gullane Bay, N Berwick Law, B1347, Gullane, Aberlady Bay, St Baldred's Cradle, North Sea, Gosford Bay, R Tyne, Biel Water, Belhaven, W Barns, Dunbar, Cockenzie & Port Seton, B1348, Longniddry, onpans, Tranent

Coastal Scotland

Fidra, inspiration for Robert Louis Stevenson's classic adventure book, Treasure Island. *Beyond is the Fife shore.*

hosted the British Ladies' Championship, and the odd seal keeping watch. There is also saltmarsh at the back of the bay, mussels and winkles which are unsafe to eat and no less than five wrecks.

The roofless church of St Andrew at **Gullane** dates from the 12th century, the last vicar being dismissed by James VI for smoking. At the other end of Gullane Bay are the remains of a chapel and between the two is Muirfield golf course, founded in 1891 by the Honourable Company of Edinburgh Golfers. It has been used for the

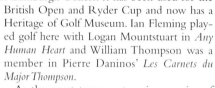

British Open and Ryder Cup and now has a Heritage of Golf Museum. Ian Fleming played golf here with Logan Mountstuart in *Any Human Heart* and William Thompson was a member in Pierre Daninos' *Les Carnets du Major Thompson.*

As the coast turns east again, a series of isolated islands run parallel with the coast, beginning with the small Eyebroughy, a bird sanctuary.

After caves behind Weaklaw Rocks, the Briggs of Fidra separate the mainland from Fidra, a 30m high island with a 17m white brick towered lighthouse, David Stevenson's first in 1885, the remains of a church dedicated to St Nicholas, a burial ground and the White Lady of Fidra, a natural bridge shaped like a veiled female figure. This is the island which inspired Robert Louis Stevenson's *Treasure Island* and which he described in *Catriona* although it has also been claimed that the geography fits Monterey's Point Lobos after he lived there. It is a bird sanctuary with puffins and requires RSPB permission to land.

This is considered to be the end of the Firth of Forth. Flows run up to 2km/h along the North Sea coast, low and sandy to North Berwick. Behind Longskelly Point a nature trail follows. In *The Annals of Imperial Rome* Tacitus describes the North Sea as the roughest in the world. It may have been the case as far as the Roman knowledge of oceans went.

The Lamb is a 24m high cormorantry, again requiring RSPB permission to land, as does Craigleith, which is also known as the Lamb. Craigleith is 51m high with steep sides. Much more conspicuous over most of the estuary, however, is North Berwick Law, a 187m high grassy

North Berwick Law behind North Berwick.

200

volcanic pyramid with a Napoleonic watchtower on top and a whale jawbone arch visible from the sea, a Second World War lookout and trees planted on its side in 1707 to celebrate the Union.

North Berwick harbour, a notable example of a small harbour, has 120m of quays used by crab and lobster fishing boats and recreational craft. It was built to its current shape after Robert Stevenson reported on storm damage in 1811. **North Berwick**, at the end of the B1347, was made a royal burgh by Robert II. In 1590 200 witches were addressed in the church of St Andrew Blackadder by the Devil in the form of a black goat, possibly the Earl of Bothwell, the heir to the throne, who called for the death of James VI by sorcery. He escaped but many of the women were condemned to the stake. In the 19th century the town became a fashionable resort and has been reported to have the highest coastal house prices in Scotland. A museum features the local history, fishing, golfing, archaeology, wildlife and the Bass Rock.

Beyond the Sisters rocks off the harbour there is waterskiing in Milsey Bay and a golf course between Rugged Knowes and Leckmoram Ness.

Bass Rock is a 107m high phonolite plug, pyramidal in shape with precipitous sides and a tunnel through which it is possible to pass, the cliffs white from guano. It is the world's third largest gannetry with 7% of the world population hatched here, hence the scientific name of *Sula bassana*. In addition to 21,000 pairs of gannets there are breeding fulmars, cormorants, razorbills, guillemots and puffins. Albert Ross, a blackbrowed albatross, appeared in 1967 and was seen around Scotland for at least another four decades. There are seals in the caves and rare plants include Bass mallow. This bird sanctuary needs East Lothian Council permission to land but the birds were not always so well protected. Until the end of the 18th century gannets were harvested for food, peaking at 2,000 per year in 1850, also providing eggs, feathers for bedding and fat for medicine and waterproofing of boots.

St Baldred, a disciple of St Kentigern, sought refuge here in a hermitage in 600. A dry stone chapel was built to the saint's memory in 1400. The island was owned by the Lauders from 1056, always remaining loyal to the Stuarts. A fort was held for James II after his abdication until it surrendered in 1689. Jacobite prisoners seized the island from their guards in 1691 and held it for three years as a garrison for James II against William II. The fort was destroyed in 1701 in case of another Scottish uprising. Covenanter Richard Blackadder had been a prisoner and mainland people still occasionally hear chanting of psalms by the Sweet Singers, the Covenanter prisoners, on dark nights. A 20m white lighthouse tower and buildings of 1900–2 were constructed on the old gun platform by David Stevenson. There was an addition to the rock's folklore when Robert Louis Stevenson had David Balfour imprisoned here in *Catriona*.

After Gin Head the red stone ruin of Tantallon Castle stands on a 30m promontory. A 14th century Red Douglas stronghold, it resisted the siege of James V in 1528 until stormed after three weeks and hosted Queen Mary in 1566. It was partly destroyed in 1651 by General Monk, whose siege guns dropped the wall into the moat after 12 days of bombardment, allowing it to be taken for Cromwell. It was built with earthwork defences, a 14th century 15m curtain wall and round corner towers and a four storey gatehouse across the promontory rock. It contains a display of replica guns and was used by Scott in *Marmion* and briefly in *The Fair Maid of Perth*.

The Gegan is a surf break at Seacliff. Some 2km of red sandstone platform running along the coast reaches out towards the Bass Rock, ending at St Baldred's Boat, a column topped with a cross marking it. A substantial stone wall runs across the fields and ends right at the top of the vertical cliffs.

Once the low sandy coast begins, Ravensheugh Sands

produce surf from low to mid tide and St Baldred's Cradle can produce lefts.

The River Tyne discharges past Tyninghame House, its 18th century walled, secret and terraced gardens, wilderness and church. A substantial beech wood was planted in 1707 by the 6th Earl of Haddington but it was cut down for the war effort and not replanted until 1945. It is the only place in Scotland where hawfinches breed. The estuary has a heronry and plenty of wildfowl and waders.

The 6.7km^2 John Muir Country Park is named after the founder of America's national parks and Sierra Club, born in Dunbar in 1838. It includes a natural history trail. Along its southern edge is Biel Water which flows past West Barns and discharges into Belhaven Bay. The bay is a surf break with long rides from mid to high water but strong currents. Belhaven Brewery is now owned by Greene King. It is the golf course which is prominent.

There are two harbours at Dunbar, the west one, the Victoria Harbour, being approached via a narrow inlet past arches and ruined stonework. It can be difficult to enter when the wind is between west northwest and east. Indeed, it can be difficult even finding the entrance in rough conditions. Victoria Harbour with 180m of quays is used by recreational craft and for landing fish and lobsters. The exit at the far end leads to the Old Cromwell Harbour, partly paid for by him after beating the Scottish army of David Leslie in the 1650 Battle of Dunbar. There was a direct route from the sea but concrete blocks have been tipped in the Meikle Spiker entrance. Twenty years before construction began in 1555 it was called Lamerhaven.

Dunbar is from the Gaelic for hilltop fort. Edward II fled from Dunbar after being beaten at Bannockburn. Queen Mary took refuge in the castle three times. After the murder of Darnley (allegedly organized by Bothwell) in 1567 she was taken there by Bothwell (willingly or

The Bass Rock seen from Seacliff.

otherwise), allegedly raped by him and agreed to marry him. It belonged to the Earl of March in *The Fair Maid of Perth*. The ruin is now the home of kittiwakes.

Scotland's oldest Methodist church, from 1764, has stained glass and an oak pulpit from St Giles' Cathedral in Edinburgh.

In the 17th century the harbour was Scotland's top fishing centre with 20,000 workers but it declined in the 1920s, apparently as a retribution for fishing on Sundays. Notable architecture includes Lauderdale House by Robert Adams while the 17th century Town House is now a museum featuring local history and archaeology. Dunbar is said to be the sunniest place in Scotland and the leisure pool and glass roof and sides above the harbour makes best use of the weather.

A conspicuous small tower on the low shore beyond a golf course, contrasts with a monument to a battle of 1650 which is well hidden.

White Sands bay has parking and picnic tables surrounded by birdsfoot trefoil, rockpools teeming with wildlife and beautifully clear water with codling, mackerel, wrasse, dabs, plaice and flounders. It is a surf break.

The striking red clifftop remains of Tantallon Castle.

Dunbar with the inconspicuous entrance to the Victoria Harbour.

Distance
61km from Cramond to White Sands

OS 1:50,000 Sheets
66 Edinburgh
67 Duns, Dunbar & Eyemouth

Tidal Constants
Granton:
Dover +0340
Leith:
Dover +0340
Cockenzie:
HW Dover +0330,
LW Dover +0340
Fidra:
Dover +0340
Dunbar:
HW Dover +0340,
LW Dover +0400

Sea Area
Forth

*The first time that I gaed to Coudingham Fair
I there fell in with a jolly beggare*
Anon

Perhaps the White Sands get their name from the white dust from the large Dunbar cement works behind the bay but it is more likely that the restored limekilns at Catcraig, formerly producing for fertilizer, bleaching agent and iron foundry flux, were relevant. There are fossils in the limestone and there is a geology trail along the shore which is in the vicinity of the Southern Uplands fault here. The hills force the A1 and the East Coast Main Line against the coast as far as Cove.

David Stevenson's 37m white towered lighthouse of 1899–1901 stands on the low Barns Ness, as do a host of caravans. The rock shelf has resulted in dangerous wreckage but the surf break is appreciated by those in more manoeuvrable craft.

A monument on Chapel Point indicates the position of Skateraw Harbour, now unusable. Much more conspicuous is Torness nuclear power station with two advanced gas cooled reactors, operational in 1987 and due to close in 2023 although it is one of two power stations generating over half of Scotland's electricity, surrounded by tetrapods which would make landing very difficult in an emergency. In 2005 a retired Concorde was landed on the jetty from a barge during its journey from the River Thames to the National Museum of Flight at East Fortune. More caravans are parked at Thorntonloch and cormorants and gannets are indifferent to these unnatural neighbours.

At the Dunglass Burn, which passes Dunglass church, East Lothian gives way to the Borders region. There are three bridges across the lower end of the burn, one 40m high which was said to have been the highest in the world when built in 1786.

Reed Point with its oystercatchers is a fairly inaccessible surf break and Cove's surf break is hardly more approachable, reached via a 500m track with a locked gate at the top so that it may only be used by an approved vehicle. Part of the track is unstable and threatening to disappear down the cliff face. At the bottom a long rock tunnel of about 1752 takes a footpath through to the small drying harbour of which the current edition dates from 1831, used by fishing vessels and formerly used by smugglers who appreciated the caves in the cliffs. The 2.5m x 3.2m high tunnel was cut 56m long and drops 6m over its length, one of the earliest non mining tunnels in Britain. A sandstone block by the harbour has been weathered to look like the inside of a human throat. Cove is at the end of the Southern Uplands Way

Barns Ness lighthouse and Torness nuclear power station.

Cove harbour at low tide.

Cove's sandstone sculpting.

long distance path from Portpatrick. On a quiet day with no surf the cliffs seem to absorb all sounds except those of birds and the occasional sheep.

Further up the hill, Cockburnspath church dates partly from the 14th century and the Mercat Cross has a thistle and a rose of 1502 to celebrate the marriage of James IV to Princess Margaret, the daughter of Henry VI.

Pease Bay has a four arched viaduct somewhere behind the sea of caravans. If there is surf anywhere it will be found here but it is frequently blown out and the road down is private. Siccar Point, with its caves, was studied by pioneering 18th century geologist James Hutton to learn about rock ageing and is also a surf break, again without easy access.

For the next few kilometres there are high inaccessible cliffs with small offshore rocks, somewhat reminiscent of the cliffs to the north of Helmsdale. The waters are clear with moon and compass jellyfish among the kelp, seals, urchins on the rocks, eider ducks, blackbacked gulls and fulmars. Sometimes there are rock pillars and vertical strata, caves,settlements and forts on the clifftops and waterfalls, even a measured distance for ship speed gauging although it can be difficult todetermine exact landmarks. Fast Castle on Telegraph Hill was a Home stronghold above the Wheat Stack surf break. One of the caves is said to contain a fortune in 16th century gold collected to free Mary, Queen of Scots. Contorted grey mudstone cliffs lead to Pettico Wick where the St Abb's Head Fault introduces steeper pink and purple volcanic lavas.

St Abb's Head has 90m nearly vertical red sandstone pillars with clefts between them which can be entered in calm conditions. The head appears like an island from the distance. Tidal streams run strongly around the head with turbulence, especially with opposing winds. The southeasterly stream sets towards the head yet there is a surf break for the determined. On top is the St Abb's Head light of 1862, a 9m white tower and buildings by D&T Stevenson, Scotland's first foghorn following in 1876 but now disused. The St Abb's Head national nature reserve was established in 1983, 78ha including the most important location for cliff nesting birds in southeast Scotland with 50,000 seabirds including guillemots, kittiwakes, razorbills, fulmars, shags, puffins, herring gulls and eiders. Wheatears, meadow pipits, skylarks and stonechats nest on the headland where there is purple milk vetch and Kirn Hill has rock rose, on which feeds the northern brown argus butterfly. Grey seals, herrings, crabs, lobsters and prawns are to be found offshore

A fisherman checking lobster pots in the mist near St Abb's Head. Gulls on the gunwale check the fisherman and his catch.

is visible but there have been several attempts at improvement since 1660. With winds from the north and east the bay is a mass of broken water. The Eyemouth Museum features the Great East Coast Fishing Disaster of October 1881 when 129 men and 23 boats from the port were lost. It has the 4.6m Eyemouth tapestry showing Black Friday and displays on the fishing and farming history of

Gulls surround a cave near St Abb's Head.

in the first Marine Nature Reserve in Scotland, relevant because diving is popular here.

At the end of the B6438, St Abbs was named after Aebbe, the daughter of Edilfred, King of Northumbria. She went to sea to avoid the attentions of the King of Mercia and was washed up here where she founded an unusual combined convent and monastery on Kirn Hill, not to be confused with the Nunnery Point ruin which is only medieval. St Cuthbert visited in 661 and Aebba ruled as abbess until her death in 683, the buildings being destroyed by raiders, possibly Vikings, in the late 9th century.

Each July a Herring Queen Festival takes place, the Queen being carried from St Abbs along the rugged coast to Eyemouth on the B6355.

The inner harbour dries. Beach huts face out into Coldingham Bay where the surf funnels in but a notice bans launching.

An aerial on Hallydown is located above fort sites of 1547 and a more recent caravan site on Hairy Ness.

Following one of the earliest investigations by the Hydraulics Research Station, a new harbour was built into the golf course at **Eyemouth**, a port known as the Hope of the Town as it was nearest to the best of the white fishing grounds. The old port at the mouth of Eye Water was fortified by the French against the English. Some sloping masonry from Smeaton's work in 1769–73

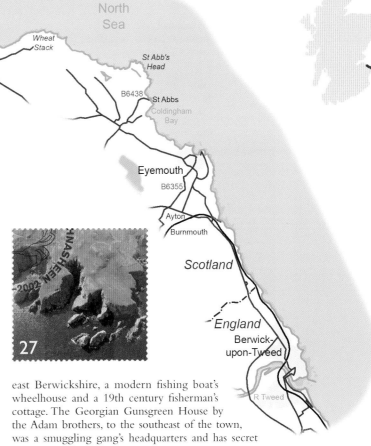

east Berwickshire, a modern fishing boat's wheelhouse and a 19th century fisherman's cottage. The Georgian Gunsgreen House by the Adam brothers, to the southeast of the town, was a smuggling gang's headquarters and has secret

203

Eyemouth is sheltered from all directions except the north.

Another rock sculpture to the south of Eyemouth.

The position of the border between England and Scotland has fluctuated over the centuries. Currently, it is not at its most obvious, being some 6km north of the Tweed on a section of coast with a rocky shoreline and no road access. A notable lack of any distinctive geographical features separates the Borders region from Northumberland. The cliffs and the rocky shoreline continue unbroken with not even a stream to mark the national boundary. Caravans on the cliff above Marshall Meadows Bay are the first positive fix on English territory.

The Needles Eye has a large hole through at sea level and is extensively used by nesting kittiwakes, despite the jets streaking across to head for the hills. The holes improve and Brotherston's Hole is a series of caves and passages in the cliffs. Golfers pace about above and waders do the same on occasional pieces of beach. Another caravan site occupies the land between Sharper's Head and Ladies Skerrs but there are also some publicly reachable beaches.

Parking behind Ladies Skerrs by the Magdalene Fields Golf Club at the northern end of **Berwick-upon-Tweed** is the first time the shore can be reached with any ease although walkers are kept back from the edge of the crumbling cliffs. A sea water bathing pond is sited at the high water mark.

Needles Eye, home to countless kittiwakes.

Distance
41km from White Sands to Berwick-on-Tweed

OS 1:50,000 Sheets
67 Duns, Dunbar & Eyemouth
75 Berwick-upon-Tweed

Tidal Constants
Dunbar:
HW Dover +0340,
LW Dover +0400
Cove Harbour:
HW Dover +0330,
LW Dover +0350
Eyemouth:
HW Dover +0320,
LW Dover +0340
Berwick:
HW Dover +0340,
LW Dover +0320

Sea Area
Forth

Connection
Cheviots — see CBEW p6

passages. The village also has the first house to be powered by hydrogen fuel cell.

In another of those coastal anomalies, East Carr lies west of West Carr. Cliffs are up to 93m high to Burnmouth, a small lobster fishing harbour which dries, but thereafter they are only 18m high and decrease towards Berwick-upon-Tweed, once again followed by the A1, the railway and lines of rock teeth. On 199m high Ayton Hill are two aerials.

Brotherston's Hole, last stop before the crowded beaches.

Index

Abbey Head – 8, 9
Aberdeen – 139, 146, 181, 182, 183, 185, 187, 188, 195
Aberlady Bay – 199
Abhainn a' Ghlinne Bhig – 89
Am Balg – 147
An Ceannaich – 100
An Dubh-aird – 131
Annan – 6, 9
Annat Bay – 140, 141
Anstruther Easter – 192, 197
Anstruther Wester – 193
Applecross, River – 132
Applecross Bay – 132
Arbroath – 183, 187, 188, 189
Ard Beag – 104
Ardlamont Point – 35, 36, 38
Ardmeanach – 76
Ardmore Bay – 73, 104
Ardmore Point (Armadale Bay) – 152
Ardmore Point (Mull) – 73
Ardmore Point (Waternish) – 104
Ardmucknish Bay – 66
Ardnacross Bay – 39
Ardnamurchan – 80–83
Ardnish – 116
Ardpatrick Point – 44, 45
Ardrossan – 22, 23
Ardscalpsie Point – 33, 34
Ardtornish Point – 71
Ardwell Point – 15
Ardyne Point – 31
Armadale Bay (Caithness) – 152
Armadale Bay (Skye) – 92
Aros – 72
Arran, Isle of – 20, 22, 23, 25, 28, 30, 32, 33, 35, 36, 38, 39, 40, 45
Ascrib Islands – 104
Asgog Bay – 36
Atlantic Ocean – 29, 43, 47, 51, 58, 59, 61, 136, 151, 154
Auchencairn Bay – 8
Auliston Point – 73, 80
Ayr – 20, 21, 23

Bach Island – 64
Badcall Bay – 145
Badentarbat Bay – 142
Balcary Point – 8
Baldoon Sands – 10
Balgowan Point –
Balintore – 167, 173
Banff – 174, 176, 177
Bar, The – 170, 171
Barmore Island – 37
Barns Ness – 202
Barr Water – 44
Barry Links – 188
Barsalloch Point – 12
Bass Rock – 200, 201
Bay of Cruden – 180, 181
Bay of Stoer – 143
Bearreraig Bay – 111
Bennane Head – 17
Bernera Island – 68
Berriedale Water – 163
Bervie Bay – 185
Berwick – 204
Biel Water – 201
Black Head – 16
Black Isle – 166, 168
Bloody Bay – 73
Boddam – 180, 183
Boddin Point – 186, 187
Borness Point – 9
Boyndie Bay – 176
Boyne Bay – 176
Brest Rocks – 19
Bridge of Don – 182
Brims Ness – 154
Broadford Bay – 4, 115, 117, 119, 130

Brora – 164
Brunerican Bay – 42
Buchan Ness – 180
Buckhaven – 196
Buckie – 173, 174, 177
Buddon Ness – 188
Burghead – 171, 173
Burntisland – 195, 196, 197
Burrow Head – 11
Bute, Island of – 24, 25, 28, 30, 31, 32–35, 184

Cailiness Point – 13
Cailleach Head – 141
Cairnbulg Point – 178
Calbha Beag – 145
Calbha Mór – 145
Calgary Bay – 74
Calve Island – 72
Camas Eilean Ghlais – 142
Camas Mór – 136
Campbeltown – 39, 42, 45, 93
Campbeltown Loch – 40
Cairn Head – 11, 12
Caliach Point – 74
Caolas Beag – 136
Caolas Mòr – 132
Caolas Scalpay – 115, 128, 130
Caol Mòr – 115, 127, 129, 130
Caol Raineach – 151
Caol Rona – 125, 126
Cape Wrath – 74, 107, 118, 145, 147, 148, 149, 151, 153, 156
Cara Island – 44
Carnoustie – 188
Carradale Point – 39
Carr Brigs – 191
Carsaig Bay (Kintyre) – 46, 47
Carsaig Bay (Mull) – 45, 47, 78, 79
Castle Haven – 185
Castlehill Point – 7
Chanonry Point – 169, 170
Chapel Ness – 193
Clachaig Water – 44
Clanyard Bay – 13
Cloch Point – 28, 29
Cockenzie & Port Seton – 199, 201
Coigach – 137, 142
Corrie Glen –
Cove Bay – 183
Cove Point – 40
Covesea Skerries – 172
Cowie Water – 184
Craigleith – 200
Craignish Point – 47
Craignure Bay – 71
Crail – 192, 197
Crammag Head – 13
Cramond Island – 197
Crinan Canal – 37, 39, 47
Cromarty – 163, 167, 168, 169, 173, 177, 181, 185
Cromarty Firth – 168, 169, 170, 173
Crowlin Islands – 130, 132
Cruden Bay – 181
Cuillin Hills – 92, 93, 95, 96, 98, 99, 101, 102, 103, 105, 112, 117, 119, 121, 123, 127, 128, 129, 130. 131, 132
Culbin Forest – 170
Cullen – 175, 177
Cullen Bay – 175

Danna, Island of – 45
Deil's Head, The – 187, 188
Dornoch Firth – 164–167
Drum Sands – 197
Duart Bay – 70
Duart Point – 70
Dunbar – 193, 201, 202
Dunbeath Bay – 163

Dunbeath Water – 163
Dunnet Bay – 155, 156
Dunnet Head – 149, 153, 156, 158
Dunoon – 28, 29, 30, 31
Duncansby Head – 158, 159, 163
Dunvegan Head – 100, 101, 107
Durness – 150

Earadale Point – 43
Earlsferry – 193
Easdale Island – 51, 56
East Loch Tarbert – 37, 39, 105
East Wemyss – 195
Eddrachilis Bay – 145
Edinburgh – 15, 97, 104, 145, 193, 196, 197, 198, 200, 201
Eggerness Point – 10
Eilean a' Chalmain – 78
Eilean an Ròin Mór – 146, 147
Eilean Chrona – 144
Eilean Fladday – 111, 125
Eilean Flodigarry – 108, 112, 113, 115
Eilean Furadh Mór – 136
Eilean Hoan – 149, 150
Eilean Ighe – 87
Eilean Mòr (Ardmucknish Bay) – 66
Eilean Mòr (Corryvreckan) – 53, 54
Eilean Mòr (Crowlins) – 132
Eilean Mòr (Enard Bay) – 143
Eilean Mòr (Kintyre) – 44, 45
Eilean Mòr (Kyles of Bute) – 35
Eilean Mòr (Loch Fyne) – 37
Eilean Mòr (Loch Snizort) – 110
Eilean Mòr (Mull) – 78
Eilean Musdile – 3, 64, 68, 79
Eilean na Bà – 132
Eilean na h-Airde – 94, 95
Eilean nan Gobhar – 86
Eilean nan Ròn – 151
Eilean Shona – 83, 84–85, 90
Eilean Tigh – 125
Eilean Trodday – 107, 112, 119
Enard Bay – 142, 143
Eorsa – 75
Erraid – 76, 77, 78
Ettrick Bay – 32, 34
Eyebroughy – 200
Eyemouth – 201, 203
Eyre Point – 127, 129, 130

Fairlie – 28
Fairlie Roads – 22, 23
Faraid Head – 149, 150
Farland Head – 22
Farr Point – 152
Fidra – 200, 201
Fife Ness – 172, 191, 192
Findhorn Bay – 171
Findochty – 174
Firth of Clyde – 10, 17, 18, 19–23, 24, 25, 27, 28–31, 32, 33, 35, 39, 42, 77
Firth of Forth – 159, 185, 189, 193, 194, 197, 198, 200, 201
Firth of Lorn – 51, 52, 60, 64, 68, 78, 80
Firth of Tay – 188, 189
Fisherrow Sands – 199
Fishnish Bay – 71
Forss Water – 154
Frank Lockwood's Island – 78
Fraserburgh – 156, 178, 177, 181
Freswick Bay – 159

Gairloch – 134, 135, 136, 139, 145
Gamrie Bay – 177
Gare Loch – 20
Garroch Head – 33
Garron Point – 183, 184
Gigha Island – 44
Gills Bay – 159
Girdle Ness – 183
Girvan – 18, 23

Glenan Bay – 36
Glen App – 17
Glen Brittle – 96
Glenelg Bay – 90, 119
Glen Loth – 164
Glenlussa Water – 39
Glenuig Bay – 86
Golspie – 164, 167
Golspie Burn – 165
Gometra – 74
Gosford Bay – 199
Gourock – 16, 29, 30
Grass Point – 79
Great Cumbrae Island – 24–27
Greenstone Point – 140
Greg Ness – 183
Greshornish Point – 104, 110
Gruinard Bay – 140
Gruinard Island – 141
Gruinard River – 140
Guillamon Island – 130
Gulf of Corryvreckan – 46, 47, 52, 54, 55
Gullane – 200
Gullane Bay – 200

Hackley Head – 181
Halladale River – 153
Halliman Skerries – 172
Handa Island – 145, 146
Hare Ness – 183
Head of Garness – 177
Heads of Ayr – 20
Helman Head – 161
Helmsdale – 158, 163, 164, 167, 202
Hestan Island – 8
Hoe Point – 100
Hoe Rape – 100, 106
Holborn Head – 154, 155
Holm Island – 111
Holoman Bay – 125
Holy Loch – 30
Horse Island – 142
Horse Isle – 22
Horse Sound – 142
Idrigill Point – 98, 104
Inchcolm – 196, 197
Inchkeith – 195
Inch Kenneth – 75
Inchmarnock – 33, 34
Inchmickery – 197
Inner Sound (Raasay) – 108, 115, 125, 126, 127, 129, 130, 130–133
Inner Sound (Stroma) – 158, 159
Inverbervie – 185
Inverie Bay – 90
Inzie Head – 178
Iona – 23, 39, 45, 51, 71, 72, 75, 76, 77, 78, 79, 120, 196
Irvine – 22, 23
Irvine Bay – 22
Isay – 103, 108
Island Davaar – 39, 40, 45
Islands of Fleet – 9
Isle of Ewe – 136, 137–139, 145
Isle Martin – 140, 141
Isle Ristol – 142, 143

Kames Bay – 32
Kennedy's Pass – 18
Keith Inch – 180
Kentra Bay – 83
Kerrera – 51, 57, 60–64, 68, 78
Kilberry Head – 45
Kilbrannan Sound – 38
Kilbride Bay – 36
Kilcreggan – 28, 29, 30
Kilchattan Bay – 33
Kilfinan Bay – 37
Kilmory Bay – 45
Kilt Rock – 109, 114
Kingairloch – 61, 62, 66, 68
Kinghorn – 195
Kinnaird Head – 178
Kintyre – 35, 36–45
Kirkcaldy – 193, 195

Kirkcudbright Bay – 8
Kirkton Head – 179
Kirtomy Point – 152
Kishorn Island – 132
Knock Bay (Rhins) – 16
Knock Bay (Skye) – 91
Knock Head – 175
Knoydart – 89
Kyle of Durness – 147, 149, 151
Kyle of Lochalsh – 5, 87, 90, 91, 117, 119, 131, 133
Kyle of Sutherland – 166, 167
Kyle Rhea – 89, 90, 91, 118, 119
Kyles of Bute – 5, 31, 32, 33, 35, 36

Lady Isle – 22
Laggan Deer Forest – 78, 79
Langwell Water – 163
Largo Bay – 193
Largs – 25, 27, 28, 32, 97
Largs Bay – 28
Leuchars – 173, 189
Leven – 195
Lismore – 62, 63, 64, 66, 67–69, 70, 79, 106
Little Cumbrae Island – 23, 25, 26, 29, 33
Little Loch Broom – 141
Little Minch – 101, 104
Little Ross – 8
Loch Ailort – 86
Loch Ainort – 115, 129
Loch Aline – 71
Loch Alsh – 90, 118, 119, 133
Loch Arnish – 125
Lochar Water – 6, 9
Loch Bay – 103
Loch Bharcasaig – 97
Loch Bracadale – 96, 97
Loch Brittle – 96, 101
Loch Broom – 141
Loch Buie – 78, 79
Loch Carron – 130, 131
Loch Clash – 146
Loch Coruisk – 95, 96, 99
Loch Craignish – 47
Loch Crinan – 47
Loch Don – 79
Loch Dunvegan – 101, 103, 108
Loch Eishort – 92, 93, 97
Loch Eriboll – 151
Loch Etive – 65, 66
Loch Ewe – 136, 137, 138, 139, 140
Loch Fad – 32
Loch Feochan – 61, 64
Loch Fleet – 165
Loch Fyne – 36, 37, 38, 39
Loch Gairloch – 134, 135
Loch Gilp – 37, 38
Loch Harport – 97, 119
Loch Hope – 151
Loch Hourn – 88, 89, 90, 94, 119, 133
Loch Inver – 143, 145
Loch Kanaird – 140, 141
Loch Kirkaig – 143
Loch Kishorn – 131, 132
Loch Laxford – 145, 146, 151
Loch Linnhe – 64, 66, 68, 69, 79
Loch Leathan – 111
Loch Long – 23, 29, 30, 31
Loch Melfort – 47, 48, 49, 51, 59
Loch Moidart – 83, 84, 85, 86, 90
Loch Morar – 87
Loch na Cille – 45
Loch na Dal – 91
Loch na Keal – 72, 75
Loch nan Ceall – 87, 88
Loch nan Uamh – 86
Loch Nedd – 145
Loch Nevis – 88, 89, 92, 95
Loch of Yarrows – 162
Loch Poolteil – 100, 107
Loch Quien – 32

Loch Riddon – 35, 36
Loch Ryan – 13, 16, 17
Loch Scavaig – 95, 96, 99, 120
Loch Scridain – 75, 76
Loch Shieldaig – 135
Loch Slapin – 93, 94, 98
Loch Sligachan – 112, 117, 124, 127, 129
Loch Snizort – 104, 109, 110, 119
Loch Snizort Beag – 104
Loch Spelve – 78
Loch Striven – 30, 31
Loch Sunart – 80
Loch Sween – 45, 70
Loch Torridon – 134
Loch Tuath – 74
Logie Head – 175, 176
Longa Island – 136
Longay – 4, 117, 130
Longniddry – 199
Lossiemouth – 168, 172, 173
Lothbeg Point – 164
Lub Score – 107, 111
Luce Bay – 8, 11, 12, 13, 15
Luce Sands – 13, 15
Luing – 46, 47, 48, 49, 50–51, 52, 55, 56, 61, 62, 78
Luinga Mhor – 87
Lunan Bay – 186, 187
Lunan Water – 187
Lunderston Bay – 29
Lunga – 51, 52, 78
Lybster – 162, 163
Lyndale Point – 104
Lynn of Lorn – 65–66, 68, 69

Macduff – 176, 177, 193
Machrihanish Bay – 43
Maidenhead Bay – 19
Malcolm's Point – 78, 79
Mallaig – 83, 85, 87, 88, 90, 92, 95
Manish Point – 125
Melvich Bay – 153
Men of Mey – 158
Mersehead Sands – 7
Methil – 195, 197
Milleur Point – 16
Millport – 5, 23, 24, 25, 26, 27, 28, 31, 65
Milton Ness – 185, 186
Minch, The – 87, 107, 109, 134–136, 137, 140–146
Mingay – 104, 108
Moidart – 82, 83, 84, 85, 86
Money Head – 15
Monifieth – 188, 189, 197
Monkton – 22
Monreith Bay – 12, 13
Montrose – 81, 182, 185, 186, 189
Montrose Basin – 186
Moonen Bay – 98, 100
Moray Firth – 156, 159, 169, 170, 174, 176
Morvern – 63, 64, 68, 70, 71, 72, 80, 83
Mull, Island of – 46, 47, 49, 50, 51, 52, 55, 56, 58, 59, 60, 61, 62, 63, 64, 65, 66, 67, 68, 69, 70–79, 82, 83, 123
Mull of Galloway – 13, 14
Mull of Kintyre – 42, 43
Mull of Logan – 15
Musselburgh – 199

Nairn – 170, 173, 177
Narrows of Raasay – 111, 124, 125, 129
Neave Island – 152
Neist Point – 100
Ness Head – 160
Newburgh Bar – 181
Newtonhill – 183
Nigg Bay (Aberdeen) – 183
Nigg Bay (Cromarty) – 167, 168
Noddsdale Water – 28
North Berwick – 198, 200
North Channel (Arisaig) – 87
North Channel (Loch Modart) – 84, 85, 86

North Channel (Ulster) – 13, 15, 16–18, 40, 43, 80
North Sea – 132, 164, 177, 180, 182, 189, 200
Noss Head – 160, 161, 176

Oban – 5, 56, 57, 59, 60, 62, 63, 64, 66, 68, 69, 71, 72, 73, 79
Ockle Point – 83
Oisgill Bay – 100
Oldany Island – 144, 145
Ornsay – 91, 94
Oronsay (Loch Bracadale) – 97, 104
Oronsay (Loch Sunart) – 80

Pabay – 116, 130
Pennan Head – 177
Pentland Firth – 156, 158, 159
Peterhead – 178, 179, 180, 181
Peterhead Bay – 179, 180
Pittenweem – 192, 193
Point of Ardnamurchan – 81, 82
Point of Knap – 45
Point of Sleat – 92, 96
Point of Stoer – 143, 144
Polliwilline Bay – 40
Port an Righ – 168
Port Bannatyne – 31, 32
Port Cam – 131
Port Castle Bay – 11
Port Erradale – 135, 136
Portlethen – 183
Port Kemin – 13
Portknockie – 172
Port Logan Bay – 15
Port Mary – 8
Port of Spittal Bay – 15
Portree – 100, 103, 105, 111, 112, 119, 124, 127
Port Righ (Kintyre) – 13
Portsoy – 175, 176
Port Vasgo – 151
Portyerrock Bay – 11
Prestonpans – 32, 199
Prestwick – 21, 22

Quarry Head – 178

Raasay, Island of – 104, 111, 112, 115, 117, 119, 124–127, 129, 130, 132, 133, 136
Rabbit Islands – 151
Rascarrel Bay – 8
Rattray Head – 178, 179
Ravenshall Point – 9
Red Head – 187
Reed Point – 202
Reisgill Burn – 162
River Almond – 197
River Annan – 6, 9
River Ayr – 21, 22
River Bladnoch – 10
River Borgie – 152
River Brora – 164
River Conon – 106
River Cree – 10
River Dee (Aberdeen) – 182, 183
River Dee (Kirkcudbright) – 8
River Deveron – 176
River Don – 181, 182
River Doon – 20
River Eden – 189
River Findhorn – 171
River Garnock – 22
River Helmsdale – 164
River Hope – 151
River Irvine – 22
River Kirkaig – 143
River Lossie – 172, 173
River Naver – 152
River Nith – 6, 7
River North Esk – 186
River Polly – 143
River Spey – 173
River Strathy – 153

River Thurso – 156
River Tweed – 204
River Tyne – 201
River Ugie – 179
River Ythan – 181
Rona, Island of – 109, 111, 124, 125, 126, 127, 133, 136
Rosemarkie Bay – 168
Ross of Mull – 75, 76, 79, 82
Rothesay – 28, 31, 32
Rothesay Bay – 31, 32, 35
Rubha an Ridire – 71, 79
Rubha Ard Slisneach – 89
Rubha Bàn (Bute) – 35, 36
Rubha Bàn (Loch Gairloch) – 136
Rubha Beag (Gruinard Bay) – 140
Rubha Beag (Loch Fyne) – 37
Rubha Charn nan Cearc – 92, 97
Rubha Dubh (Bute) – 35
Rubha Dubh (Loch Buie) – 78
Rubha Dubh (Loch Scridain) – 76
Rubha Dubh (SE Soay) – 121, 123
Rubha Dubh (SW Soay) – 123
Rubha Hunish – 107
Rubh' a' Mharaiche – 43
Rubha na h-Àirde Glaise – 111
Rubha na h-Aiseig – 107
Rubha na h-Easgainne – 94
Rubha Mòr – 72
Rubha na' Leac – 127
Rubha nam Brathairean – 109
Rubha na Fearn – 134
Rubha nan Cearc – 77
Rubha nan Clach – 97
Rubh' an Dùnain – 96, 101
Rubha Raonuill – 88, 89
Rubha Rèidh – 136, 143
Rubha Ruadh – 146
Rubha Suisnish – 93
Ruddons Point – 193

Saddell Bay – 39
Saddell Glen – 39
St Abb's Head – 203
St Andrews – 188, 189, 190, 191, 192, 193, 195, 197
St Baldred's Cradle – 201
St Catherine's Dub – 181
St John's Point – 158
St Monans – 193
Saltcoats – 22
Samalaman Island – 86
Sandaig Bay – 88
Sandaig Islands – 89, 90, 91, 94
Sanda Island – 40, 42, 45
Sandend Bay – 175
Sandford Bay – 180
Sandhead Bay – 13
Sandside Bay – 154
Sandside Burn – 154
Sandwood Loch – 147
Sanna Bay – 83
Sanna Point – 83
Sarclet Head – 162
Scallastle Bay – 71
Scalpay (Harris) – 109, 128
Scalpay (Skye) – 4, 115, 117, 127, 128–130, 132
Scalpsie Bay – 32, 33
Scarba – 46, 47, 48, 51, 52–55, 61, 78
Scotstown Head – 180
Scourie Bay – 145
Scurdie Ness – 186, 187
Sea of the Hebrides – 98, 120
Seil – 48, 50, 51, 56–59, 61, 78
Seil Sound – 48, 50, 51, 59, 64, 79
Sheep Island – 40, 42
Shuna – 48–49, 52
Shuna Point – 48
Shuna Sound – 48, 49, 50, 51, 52
Siccar Point – 202
Sinclair's Bay – 160, 161
Skelmorlie – 28, 32
Skipness Point – 38
Skirza Head – 159, 160

Skye, Island of – 5, 82, 89, 90, 91–119, 120, 121, 122, 123, 124, 125, 127, 128, 130, 131, 132, 150
Sleat – 88, 90, 91, 92, 93, 105, 106, 119
Soay – 96, 99, 120–123
Soay Sound – 96, 99, 100, 123
Solway Firth – 6–9
Sound of Arisaig – 85, 86
Sound of Bute – 33, 38
Sound of Gigha – 44, 45
Sound of Handa – 145
Sound of Insh – 56
Sound of Iona – 76, 77
Sound of Jura – 45, 46–47, 52
Sound of Kerrera – 56, 60, 61
Sound of Luing – 50, 51, 52, 54, 55
Sound of Mull – 5, 64, 71, 72, 75, 80, 81
Sound of Raasay – 111, 124, 129
Sound of Sleat – 86–90, 92, 94, 95, 96, 119
Sound of Ulva – 74
Southerness Point – 6, 7, 9
South Head – 161
Soyea Island – 143
Spear Head – 154, 155
Spey Bay – 173, 174, 177
Sròn a' Gheodha Dhuibh – 136, 141
Stacks of Duncansby – 159, 160
Staffin Bay – 108, 113, 114
Staffin Island – 108, 113, 114
Stattic Point – 141
Stevenston – 22
Stonehaven – 183, 184, 185, 189
Strathaird – 94
Strathy Point – 151, 152, 153
Stravanan Bay – 33
Stroma, Island of – 158, 159, 163
Strone Point – 29, 30, 31
Summer Isles – 141, 142, 132

Tan, The – 23, 25, 26
Tanera More – 142
Tarbat Ness – 166, 167
Tarbert – 5, 35, 36, 37, 38, 39, 45
Tarskavaig Point – 92, 97
Thurso – 155, 163, 164
Thurso Bay – 155
Tianavaig Bay – 111
Tobermory – 5, 72, 73, 79, 80, 83
Todhead Point – 184, 185
Tongue Bay – 151
Torrisdale Bay – 152
Torrs Warren – 13
Torsa – 48, 50, 51, 59
Toward Point – 30, 31
Tranent – 199
Treshnish Isles – 70, 74
Treshnish Point – 74
Troon – 22, 23
Trotternish – 104, 106, 108, 110
Troup Head – 176, 177
Turnberry Bay – 19

Uig – 103, 105, 111
Uig Bay – 105, 111, 119
Ulva – 74, 75

Water of Girvan – 18
Water of Leith – 198
Waternish – 101, 104, 109, 110
Waternish Point – 104
Wemyss Bay – 28, 31, 32
West Kilbride – 22
West Loch Tarbert – 44, 45
Wheat Stack – 203
Whiten Head – 149, 150, 151
Whiteness Head – 170
Whithorn – 11, 12
Wiay – 97
Wick – 155, 161, 163
Wick Bay – 161
Wig, The – 16
Wigtown – 10
Wigtown Bay – 8, 9, 11
Wigtown Sands – 10

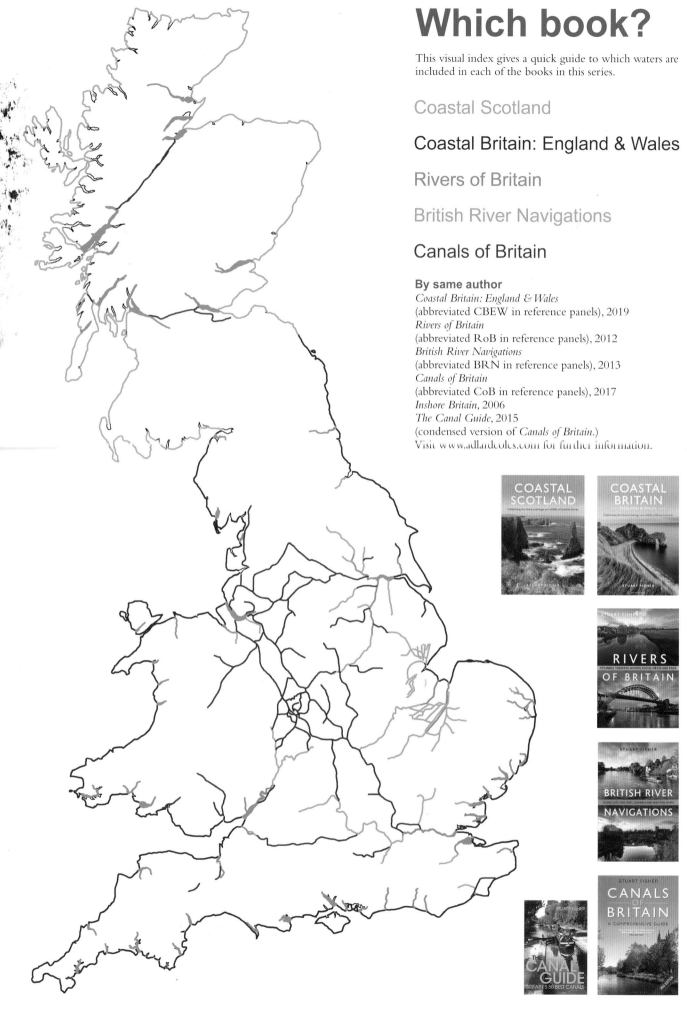

Which book?

This visual index gives a quick guide to which waters are included in each of the books in this series.

Coastal Scotland

Coastal Britain: England & Wales

Rivers of Britain

British River Navigations

Canals of Britain

By same author

Coastal Britain: England & Wales
(abbreviated CBEW in reference panels), 2019
Rivers of Britain
(abbreviated RoB in reference panels), 2012
British River Navigations
(abbreviated BRN in reference panels), 2013
Canals of Britain
(abbreviated CoB in reference panels), 2017
Inshore Britain, 2006
The Canal Guide, 2015
(condensed version of *Canals of Britain*.)
Visit www.adlardcoles.com for further information.